COLONIALISM BY PROXY

COLONIALISM BY PROXY

Hausa Imperial Agents and
Middle Belt Consciousness in Nigeria

Moses E. Ochonu

Indiana University Press

Bloomington and Indianapolis

This book is a publication of

Indiana University Press
Office of Scholarly Publishing
Herman B Wells Library 350
1320 East 10th Street
Bloomington, Indiana 47405 USA

iupress.indiana.edu

Telephone   800-842-6796
Fax   812-855-7931

Manufactured in the United States of America

Library of Congress Cataloging-in-Publication Data

Ochonu, Moses E., author.
  Colonialism by proxy : Hausa imperial agents and Middle Belt consciousness in Nigeria / Moses E. Ochonu.
    pages cm
  Includes bibliographical references and index.
  ISBN 978-0-253-01160-2 (cloth : alk. paper) — ISBN 978-0-253-01161-9 (pbk. : alk. paper) — ISBN 978-0-253-01165-7 (e-book) 1. Middle Belt (Nigeria)—Colonial influence. 2. Middle Belt (Nigeria)—Ethnic relations. 3. Middle Belt (Nigeria)—Politics and government. 4. Great Britain—Colonies—Africa—Administration. 5. Muslims—Political activity—Nigeria—Middle Belt. 6. Hausa (African people)—Politics and government. 7. Fula (African people)—Politics and government. I. Title.
  DT515.9.M49O25 2014
  966.903—dc23

                          2013032679

1 2 3 4 5 19 18 17 16 15 14

for my Mother

Contents

Preface

W<small>HEN</small> I <small>BEGAN</small> this book project in 2007, my aim was to explain why the colonial form practiced in the Nigerian Middle Belt deviated so drastically from the familiar, fetishized British system of indirect rule. I wanted to engage in a simple corrective scholarly endeavor to highlight the limitations of the indirect rule paradigm and point scholars in the direction of less familiar but equally consequential forms of colonial rule.

One question in particular framed my initial inquiries and reflections: how is it that Northern Nigeria is seen in the Africanist colonial studies literature as a bastion of indirect rule when, all over the vast Middle Belt region, a system of colonization that violated the foundational rationale of indirect rule held sway? What began as a modest effort to supply evidence that mitigates the status of Northern Nigeria as an elaborate theater of indirect rule morphed into a huge scholarly undertaking. This required the collection and dissection of several genres of evidence, multiple research trips to Nigeria and Britain, oral interviews, informal discussions, archival adventures, immersion in relevant secondary literature, and many zigzags and detours that took me into several comparative geographical fields.

Another question that inspired my early quests is whether one could conceptually and empirically posit African groups as colonizers even in a circumscribed sense, given the overbearing influence of nationalist historiography, which frowns upon conceptual constructions that are outside the European colonizer/ African colonized binary. Or whether one could demonstrate that subalternity was not always a bar to colonial, and in this case subcolonial, initiatives.

I recognize that I was not only going against the established, if problematic, premise of nationalist African history but also against a conceptual architecture of empire studies in which the notion of subalterns as subcolonizers and self-interested drivers of the colonial enterprise often gets a hostile reception. I pressed on only because I was convinced that the Middle Belt story, which advances a conceptual and empirical counterpoint to these scholarly consensuses, was worth telling on its own narrative merit as an exploration of an unorthodox colonial form. The main arguments and conceptual interventions in this volume then took shape around this important story, an unfamiliar story that compels one to rethink colonization in this and several other parts of Africa.

Once I actually began to collect and read archival materials and to conduct and examine oral interviews, the stories told in this volume emerged with clarity and coherence. The book also took a turn in a direction that I had not anticipated. My initial impulse was to engage in a straightforward political historical analysis, but increasingly the project became as much about intellectual history as about political events. I became captivated by the constellation of ideas and ideologies, British and caliphate in origin, which converged to produce and sustain the colonial manual of "alien African" rule, or subcolonialism.

In my early reflections and subsequently during the writing stage, I became engrossed in the complex genealogies and etymologies that underpin and produced subcolonialism as a form of colonial practice. I also became interested in how Hausa subcolonial rule was intellectually packaged, rationalized, and justified against the suffocating backdrop of British obsessions with the tenets of indirect rule, especially the cardinal idea of indigenous mediation. I came to see that the excavation of these instrumental ideas and rationales and their mutations over several decades are as important as the story of how subcolonialism unfolded in remote colonial districts in the Middle Belt.

As readers will notice then, the chapters of this volume have long stretches of intellectual historical explorations. These intellectual histories help ground the stories in prior processes of thought and claim making. They also reveal the intermeshing of caliphate and British ideas about the Middle Belt and its peoples and cultures, and about precolonial caliphate–Middle Belt relations and the necessity and legitimacy of Hausa subcolonial rule among non-Muslim Middle Belt communities.

Working on this volume reeducated me profoundly on the illuminating interplay between political and intellectual histories. Understanding the origins and evolution of usable ideas about caliphate superiority and Middle Belt inferiority and subordination became crucial to my analysis of how and why subcolonialism endured despite official acknowledgement that it fell short of and in fact contradicted the professed ideals of indirect rule.

This is an insight that will incubate in me and continue to inform my craft as a historian, for it is now obvious to me that the history of political ideas can clarify the contours of political events and practices that emanate from those ideas. Political history and intellectual history may have divergent protocols of understanding and analysis, but there is a vast field of play between them. Historians, especially historians of Africa, will enrich their stories about politics, chieftaincy, colonial rule, political traditions, honor, warfare, statecraft, and postcolonial political unravelings if they examine politically consequential ideas and formulations in the same analytic frame as starkly physical or institutional political phenomena.

It is particularly important that scholars who work on empire and imperial matters pay close attention to the dynamic histories of ideas that undergird imperial practice, since colonial acts occur not in ideological vacuums but within shifting grids of policy-relevant ideational consensus.

Learning about unorthodox imperial repertoires and habits and the intellectual histories that produced them has been one of the rewards of writing this book. Telling the story of a neglected form of colonial rule with consequences for contemporary politics in Nigeria is another satisfaction. Readers of this volume, specialists or not, can share in the allure of this untold, unfamiliar story of colonization.

Acknowledgments

THIS BOOK HAS been at least six years in the making. It has mutated along the way to respond to shifting research and epistemological priorities and to the robust input of many individuals and institutions. I am indebted to them all.

Major research for the book was funded by a grant from the Harry Frank Guggenheim Foundation. A yearlong fellowship of the American Council of Learned Societies (ACLS) enabled me to conduct supplementary research and complete the writing. Supplementary funding came from Vanderbilt University's Scholars Research Grant.

He may not realize it, but it was Richard Fardon who got me started on the path of writing this work. On reading an initial exploratory article on the broad topic explored here, he encouraged me to consider expanding it, quipping perceptively that my article was crying out to be a book. His advice did not register immediately, but it lit a fire of curiosity under me a few months later. That began the long process of inquiry and reflection that produced this volume.

I thank Fardon for planting the motivational seed in me. As catalytic as that moment was, however, the initial idea of writing a book on a subject as contentious as subcolonialism and its legacies would have atrophied without the support, advice, and input of many: colleagues, friends, and family. Steven Pierce read several little pieces of various aspects, offering advice and nudging me in ever more ambitious directions. His motivational imprint is on the book. John Edward Philips read a smaller written version, in the form of an article, and offered encouragement. I am grateful for the intellectual stimulation that my friend and brother, Farooq Kperogi, consistently offered on a range of topics related to the subject of this book. Over the years, he has become my go-to sounding board, a trusted intellectual confidant with whom I tested ideas and contentions as they occurred to me.

I appreciate the constant and, I might add, passionate support of my doctoral dissertation advisers and present mentors, Mamadou Diouf and Frederick Cooper. Both of them helped me through bouts of intellectual anxiety and graciously read portions of this work as recommenders and interested mentors. David Cohen, Elisha Renne, and Kevin Gaines were productively involved in the long process of creation. I am grateful to Ricardo Larémont, who offered encouragement and support.

Emmanuel Taqwai was a tireless research assistant who, over several months, helped arrange many interviews and less structured conversations with informants. Professor Okpeh Ochayi Okpeh of Benue State University, Makurdi,

Nigeria, provided me with valued research advice, logistical assistance, and on-ground support. His assistance helped push the project to the finish line. Professor Yakubu Ochefu, vice chancellor of Kwararafa University, Wukari, Nigeria, was a silent research support; his collection of oral data and transcribed interviews from Idomaland proved invaluable for reconstructing some of the stories I include here. Faculty members of Nasarawa State University, Keffi, Nigeria, were exceptionally helpful, granting me generous access to student dissertations and to their own works. Professor Mailafiya Aruwa Filaba, the head of the department of history in 2008–2009, showed me remarkable scholarly hospitality. Dr. Jonathan Ayuba Mamu gave me a copy of his book, which in turn opened new, promising research vistas to me in the Keffi-Eggon area. When I returned to Keffi in 2012, Mamu facilitated my connection to a network of informants and villages. Also in Keffi, Tanimu Yusuf of the English Department, a friend of mine from our undergraduate days at Bayero University, Kano, provided logistical support and guidance. Moses Anduwa was a resourceful research assistant and informant in the Gudi/Nasarawa Eggon area. Professor Sati Fwatshak of the University of Jos gave me research support in the Jos-Plateau axis. Also in Jos, Abdullahi Samuel Sani and Larab Ayuba helped in chasing down documents. Okoh Emmanuel Adikwu and Albert Teryima Anloho assisted with research in the Benue area.

The late Philip Shea, my undergraduate adviser, sensitized me to many of the questions that inform this book. My academic debt to him is immense, and I hope that my trajectory as a historian and the completion of this work have met some of the expectations he had for me. Through several conversations, Murray Last clarified and critiqued some of my initial contentions and assumptions. This book benefited immensely from those productive exchanges. Jean Herskovits engaged me in conversations that sparked new insights and gave me new areas to explore. My colleagues in the history department at Vanderbilt were, as usual, pillars of collegiality throughout the process of researching and writing this book. Their company and the intellectual atmosphere they maintain have nurtured my academic fecundity over the years.

The following people provided intellectual and personal friendship that, however intangible, was crucial in sustaining my enthusiasm for this project: Ann Rall, Afshin Jadidnouri, Michael Hathaway, Leslie William, Susan O'Brien, Rudolf Gaudio, Shobana Shankar, Mohammed Bashir Salau, Sean Stilwell, Vukile Khumalo, William Sutton, Mawasi Keita Jahi, and Lisandro Trevino. Adebayo Oyebade and Clifton Crais are inspirational colleagues whose informal mentoring has been edifying. Professor Toyin Falola's guidance and words of encouragement proved crucial during challenging moments. Ibrahim Hamza was a valuable human reference. During the long creative life of this book, I crosschecked many historical details about our common subject area, Northern Nigeria, with him. He helped confirm the accuracy and deepen my understanding of several familiar facts.

The anonymous readers of the manuscript provided comments that were both substantive and constructive. My revisions, following their suggestions, strengthened key aspects of the book. William Paine proofread the manuscript, and Jonathan Hanson helped with formatting, citations, and other technical issues. Duane Stephenson created the maps. Staffers of the Jean Heard Library at Vanderbilt University were extremely helpful with interlibrary loan requests. They frequently put their expertise at my disposal, helping me locate obscure and out-of-print editions of texts. In Nigeria, the staff members of the Ahmadu Bello University Northern History Research Scheme archive were very helpful, as were those of Arewa House archive and the National Archive, Kaduna.

My interviewees generously gave their time and knowledge, sitting down with me to tell their stories and to respond to my inquiries. Bishop Matthew Hassan Kukah was particularly kind. He found time in his tight schedule to talk with me extensively on salient aspects of Northern Nigerian and Nigerian politics.

My wife, Margaret, and our daughters, Ene and Agbenu, are the true heroes behind the completion of this book. Without their patience and sacrifice, the project would have been stuck in limbo. They deserve the credit for any new insight this volume brings to the questions it addresses.

COLONIALISM BY PROXY

Introduction

Understanding "Native Alien" Subcolonialism and Its Legacies

On February 24, 2004, ethno-religious violence erupted in the small town of Yelwa, Plateau State, in the Nigerian Middle Belt. A multiethnic coalition of self-identified Hausa and Fulani Muslims attacked non-Muslim ethnic communities within the town, maiming, killing, and looting. On May 2 and 3, non-Muslim refugees, former residents of the town who had fled the February violence, embarked on revenge attacks with the support of neighboring non-Muslim ethnicities. They injured, killed, and rendered homeless hundreds of Hausa-Fulani Muslims and their allies.

Non-Muslim "Middle Belters" blamed Hausa-Fulani Muslims for the violence, describing them as "nonindigenes," "settlers," and "migrants" from the territories of the defunct Sokoto Caliphate. Their grievances rested on reconstructed memories of precolonial and colonial-era hegemonic practices of Hausa-Fulani imperial agents. Over time, grievances morphed into allegations of Hausa-Fulani Muslim domination and complaints about Hausa-Fulani competition for resources and political offices they regarded as the exclusive assets of their autochthonous communities. The Muslim residents of Yelwa responded to these accusations by both claiming to be the descendants of the nineteenth-century founders of the troubled town and embracing the glorious Islamic and political heritage of the Sokoto Caliphate. They thus placed themselves within the same historical master narrative as their ethno-religious kinsmen in northwestern and parts of northeastern Nigeria, the core of the defunct caliphate. Since then, at least six major episodes of conflict between autochthonous non-Muslim groups and Hausa-Fulani Muslim groups have occurred, the most recent being the 2009 clash over local elections, which resulted in intermittent fighting and reprisal killings that persisted for months.

These claims about autochthony versus foreignness, indigene versus settler, and non-Muslim ethnic victimhood versus Hausa-Fulani Muslim domination—and the violent conflicts that they have inspired—are not unique to Yelwa. The same claims and counterclaims thrive in the narratives of many recent conflicts in the Nigerian Middle Belt, the vast territory on the southern frontier of the dissolved Sokoto Caliphate. These clashes have brought into sharp focus the construction of a non-Muslim "indigenous" minority consciousness, and its antipode: a "settler" identity embodied by the supposedly intrusive hegemony of Hausa Islamic presence in the Middle Belt.

The conflicts repoliticize earlier confrontations between the Hausa-Fulani and Middle Belt peoples during colonial times and have inspired debates on the indigene/settler question. These discussions, however, have failed to explore how the indigene/settler dichotomy developed historically. The enduring influence of colonial administrative arrangements implicated in current conflicts can be better understood by probing the complexities of those arrangements and by explaining the afterlives of colonial struggles. Hausa assertions of political rights and privileges in the Middle Belt have long, complicated histories that go back to the Sokoto Caliphate's quasi-imperial practices in the predominantly non-Muslim region. Similarly, non-Muslim peoples' fear of Hausa domination and their violent resistance to perceived Hausa Muslim control in the Nigerian Middle Belt have deep and complex roots.

Among other themes, *Colonialism by Proxy* probes some of the historical processes and struggles that underpin today's dueling understandings and claims around the concepts of "indigene" and "settler," and hegemony and noble victimhood. The book attempts to understand one of the historical roots of the violently policed ethno-religious dichotomies present today in Nigeria's Middle Belt: the articulation, bureaucratization, and consequences of a caliphate-centered colonial administrative imaginary. This was a colonial governing ideology founded on a belief in the superiority and administrative utility of significations, practices, symbols, systems of rule, and methods of socioeconomic and political organization associated with Hausa-Fulani Muslim identity, an identity derived from the modes of belonging forged by the Sokoto Caliphate. My analysis, however, does not assume a smug teleology of causality and logical consequence. Instead I argue that debates, memories, and conditions negotiated into existence during the tumultuous process of caliphate-centered colonization have found a reworked and shifting resonance in today's tensions.

Although its power stretched beyond the logic of political utility, the Hausa-caliphate construct in colonial Northern Nigeria was primarily an ideology of governance and social classification. As a philosophy of authority and control, it was a type of manifest destiny the Sokoto Caliphate had first deployed in its relations with the non-Muslim, decentralized peoples on the empire's southern frontier. The British colonials adopted this system, modifying it to serve as a fulcrum of colonial rule in the Middle Belt by mandating Islamized institutions and personnel of the caliphate to perform a civilizing role among the non-Muslim peoples of the Middle Belt on their behalf. This resulted in a subcolonial bureaucracy driven at the grass roots by thousands of Hausa chiefs, scribes, tax agents, and their own Hausa-Fulani agents, who initiated much of the colonial agenda in these Middle Belt districts.

The outline of Hausa subcolonial rule was fairly clear. The British would appoint Hausa chiefs and policemen. The chiefs would in turn appoint lesser chiefs, aides, tax collectors, scribes, judicial officers, and enforcers. Through this process, Hausa agents and chiefs built their own colonial bureaucracies, populated their realms, and swelled the number of Hausa colonial officials. Hausa rule was thus self-replicating, constantly increasing and reaching deeper into the lives of Middle Belt peoples.

Framing the Subject

Scholars of colonialism and empire across many disciplines are familiar with the role of indigenous agents in the domestication of the policies of imperial powers located at a physical and figurative distance. Indeed, this system of imperial rule, which the British called "indirect rule," has found expression in different guises from ancient and medieval empires to modern ones around the world.[1] We know considerably less about a system of preparatory colonial rule that sometimes preceded full-blown indirect rule and in fact violated its foundational tenet: the idea of ruling colonized communities through their own institutions and personnel.

This book explores this fairly unfamiliar imperial system, which had a surprising resonance across colonial Africa in the form of the use of nonindigenous, presumably "progressive" Africans from proximate "civilized" ethno-religious communities as drivers of surrogate colonial rule. These "socially advanced" African outsiders administered "backward" Africans while European overlords stood aside as authoritative observers. African subcolonials—so-called native aliens—used political and cultural gestures derived from their own societies' precolonial hegemonic practices to prepare "backward" peoples farmed out to them by European colonizers to prepare for indirect rule. These nonindigenous, nonmetropolitan colonizers were neither intermediaries nor indigenous colonial agents as understood in the interdisciplinary literature on empire. Their initiatives were far-reaching, and the legacies of their rule deserve to be understood as a counterpoint to the more familiar system of indirect rule and as part of our growing knowledge of the repertoires of colonial governance. This is the task that this book takes up.

Inherent in the logic of indirect rule is the notion that indigenous go-betweens, already socialized into the mores and political culture of a colonized community, would make good administrative allies and offer assistance rooted in indigenous knowledge and customs. African indigenous go-betweens were valued for their status as knowledgeable and embedded insiders, whose commitments to the colonizer's priorities were offset by their deep connections to traditional kin networks. Under a subcolonial system, however, outsiders were valued precisely for their status as detached nonindigenes who would display absolute loyalty to British demands and carry out colonial tasks unencumbered by the pressures of kinship. These "alien" African colonial agents lacked the status of culturally privileged insiders. They brought the baggage of "foreignness" to their roles as the hands, eyes, and feet of the colonizers, a burden that in turn catalyzed colonial interactions that were at times radically different from the familiar colonial relations of indirect rule.

In this book, I analyze the mechanics and consequences of this brand of colonial rule in the Nigerian Middle Belt, where ethnic and religious pluralism and loose or absent political centralization stood in sharp contrast to the political and social systems of the Sokoto Caliphate zone. The chapters of this book explore how and why the system emerged, how it functioned at the grass roots, and the reactions of those who came under its quotidian administrative sway. I trace the imperial activities of the defunct Sokoto Caliphate's Hausa-Fulani Muslim agents in the Nigerian Middle Belt as they morphed from conducting slave raids and exacting tribute in the mid-nineteenth century to exercising a stalemated imperial control in the late nineteenth century and, of primary concern here, to enforcing subcolonial preparatory rule under the British in the twentieth century. I then analyze the reactions of Middle Belt peoples in the face of subcolonial Hausa-Fulani rule, a constellation of responses that, in conjunction with other factors, led to an anti-caliphate Middle Belt sociopolitical consciousness.

Arguments, Correctives, and Caveats

At this point, a set of broad conceptual contexts for Hausa subcolonial rule needs to be established. The outsourced system of colonial rule profiled in this study granted remarkable autonomy of action to Hausa subcolonials in the backwoods of the Nigerian Middle Belt. Along with parallel administrative systems in a few other African contexts, the system illustrates the occasional symbiosis of African hegemonic initiatives and European imperial ambitions. The desire of caliphate-originated colonial agents for the adoption of caliphate political and religious values in the Middle Belt fused with a similar British preference for a Middle Belt colonial domain that closely mirrored the emirate sociopolitical attributes valorized in British colonial discourse.

Whereas standard narratives of colonial rule in Africa often take for granted the value of ethnic difference as a foundation for indirect rule, in Northern Nigeria a bewildering ethno-religious difference between the caliphate zone and the Middle Belt threatened the emergence of a uniform, effective colonial administrative system. Hausa-Fulani subcolonial rule was a British improvisation designed to overcome this threat. Hausa-Fulani subcolonials were thus not mere human tools in the hands of British officials; instead they were essential to the functioning of the colonial enterprise as colonial business essentially devolved to them in most areas of the Middle Belt. Their status as nonindigenes of the Middle Belt and their power to take discretionary actions, almost unchecked, unleashed unique sociopolitical tensions that in turn generated numerous conflicts..

Colonialism by Proxy takes off from the premise that the subcolonial rule of "native aliens" or "foreign Africans," the ways in which it upended the principles of indirect rule, resistances to it by autochthonous groups, and its legacies deserve as much scholarly attention as the more familiar indirect rule system. It tells the story of this approach to the colonial civilizing mission within the broader context of that mission. It is the story of a finite, transitional, yet profound form of colonial rule.

Beyond Colonial Mediation

Studies of colonization in Africa tend to cast African colonial actors as mere intermediaries in the colonial administrative process. In that narrative, African colonial agents lacked the independence to invent or deploy an administrative agenda shorn of colonial authorship. African chiefs and scribes, co-opted by European colonial authorities, were simply middlemen who did the bidding of European supervisors, who in turn consistently vetted the actions of their African subordinates. This perspective rests on a problematic assumption: that European authorities considered indirect rule, along with its elaborate hierarchies and systems of supervision, the foundational administrative template suitable for all African societies. This is not entirely accurate. European authorities regarded some African communities as unready for indirect rule and in need of preparation for the colonial civilizing mission—for indirect rule. Such preparatory rule was often allocated to presumably more socially advanced African groups, who were expected to civilize these communities, preparing them for indirect rule through administrative tutelage.[2]

In spite of this countervailing reality, the indirect rule paradigm has hardened into an explanation of complex and at times contradictory colonial administrative practices as mere variants of the indirect rule analytic frame. Mahmood Mamdani's *Citizen and Subject: Contemporary Africa and the Legacy of Late Colonialism* is emblematic of this approach, arguing that indirect rule was the generic colonial form in Africa and that all colonial administrative systems, including apartheid, were variations on the paradigm.[3] Although my analysis complements the contention that indirect rule was the gold standard of colonial rule in Africa because it was cheap and pragmatic and released Europeans from quotidian responsibilities, the subcolonial system on which I focus demonstrates that indirect rule was not always the instinctive administrative preference of European colonizers.[4] The ways in which colonizers culturally classified an ethnic community sometimes determined whether some other administrative arrangement was implemented in place of the indirect rule ideal.

Colonial addiction to the ideals of indigenous mediation is understandable, for "the concept of empire presumes that different peoples within the polity be governed differently"[5] according to their institutions. In practice, however, this was sometimes unrealistic. This was especially so in situations where the constitutive ethnic units of a colonial state were considered too many, making indigenous customary rule for each community potentially chaotic, and, more importantly, where the requisite political institutions for indigenous rule were deemed absent. The reality of colonial rule, even the most ardent theorist of the constancy of indirect rule would concede, is that colonial regimes sometimes broke the habit of ruling through indigenous elites in the interest of governing ease.

Imperialists, as Burbank and Cooper posit, might prefer to recruit administrative allies from among a conquered population, but for pragmatic reasons might also be drawn to detached outsiders—metropolitan officials, ambitious slaves with little loyalty to their communities, and "civilized" agents trained to inflict civilization on a colonized community.[6] In fact, flexible and improvised colonial practices were more common than one might discern from the guidepost of the colonial archive. For the African colonial state, the range of flexibility in colonial practices was nearly infinite, even if they theoretically began from a baseline of respect for tradition, self-rule, and the preeminence of indigenous customs. This flexibility constantly overlay the narrative of indirect rule and fertilized a great deal of improvisation that, according to Achille Mbembe, subordinated processes to ends in colonial Africa.[7] Thriving on rational disorder and an infinite capacity for authoritarian invention, unorthodox colonial state forms, some scholars argue, triumphed over the formulaic orderliness of indirect rule and subsequently informed the poorly understood logics of postcolonial statecraft.[8]

Administrative arbitrariness and malleability were not incidental to colonial rule. In fact, one could argue that flexibility over time and geography was the most abiding logic of colonial rule. Seen against the backdrop of *actual* colonial practice, the notion that indirect rule was "the order of things" ignores the implication of differential British perceptions of African sociopolitical institutions and British ideas about the civilizational status of African peoples. The British constructed a hierarchy of African peoples based on how "civilized" they appeared to be and documented this in anthropological reports that often formed the basis of colonial policy. The most influential of these colonial knowledge manuals for Northern Nigeria was perhaps Charles L. Temple's *Native Races and Their Rulers*.[9] Temple's work constructed an elaborate spectrum of civilization, social evolution, and racial difference among the peoples of Northern Nigeria. Under this hierarchy, which a long line of colonial writers expanded upon, Muslim societies and societies with centralized political systems and a market-oriented system of production found favor as zones with the personnel and precedents for indirect rule.[10]

Difference and the Logic of Proxy Rule

At the heart of Hausa subcolonial rule in the Middle Belt is a notion of difference that departs from the traditional binaries of colonialism, one that admits the reproduction of multiple kinds of difference along the hierarchies of colonial interactions. It is a view of difference that acknowledges how the power of foundational racial dichotomies authorizes what Catherine Hall, following Jacques Derrida and Gayatri Spivak, has called the "multiple constructions of difference" as opposed to the European-Other template of differentiation.[11] Colonial power, whether exercised discursively or by brute force, wittingly and unwittingly produced multiple narratives of difference, which acquired gradations of value and served to undergird colonial relations at the grass roots.

In African studies, connections between colonial rule and ethno-religious differences among Africa's colonized peoples have focused largely on the emergence of politically charged, socially consequential ethnicities and on the ideologies of ethnic differentiation among subject populations.[12] Colonial policies on ethnic classification and identification, it is argued, coalesced in an indirect rule system founded on the notion of bounded "tribal" customs, ruptured preexisting social affinities, and left a legacy of ethnic expressions that have threatened the cohesion of postcolonial states.[13]

This standard argument identifies key sites of struggle over ethnicity: the bureaucratization of "created" or codified ethnic difference, the imputation of privilege and marginality into these categories, and the colonial and postcolonial appropriation of difference as a device through which Africans make claims to power and resources. The legacies of colonial differentiation have been tragic for postcolonial states, inspiring the construction of oppositional, irreconcilable, and, at times, violently policed ethnic identities.[14] Rwanda dramatizes this colonial desire for bounded ethnic communities; there, observed differences between the Hutu and the Tutsi were not only amplified and codified; they were racialized.[15] Indirect rule, in other words, sparked the evolution of politicized ethnic identities in postcolonial African states.

James Coleman argued as early as 1958 that in Nigeria the divide-and-rule ethos of indirect rule compartmentalized the "diverse elements" of an emerging Nigerian nation, making national unity difficult.[16] Emmy Irobi audaciously contends that indirect rule "reinforced ethnic divisions."[17] Echoing the same thesis, Thomas Davis and Azubike Kalu-Nwiwu remind us that "the structure of British colonial administration" and the drawing of arbitrary boundaries delineating ethnic "territor[ies] restricted the development of a national consciousness within the broad expanse of Nigeria's borders."[18] Ethno-religious differences were thus valued as raw materials for the compartmentalization of culture and custom crucial to indirect rule.

This perspective, insightful as it is in going behind the appearance of primordial ethnicity to locate colonial experiments with ethnic differentiation, fails to account for colonial situations, like that in Northern Nigeria, where real ethnolinguistic, cultural, and religious differences needed not to be reinforced but to be overcome in the interest of effective, uniform administration. Here, the pursuit of sameness in the crucible of preparatory proxy rule, not the creation of "tribal" difference, was assessed as a necessary purgatory on the way to indirect rule.

Efforts by other European colonial bureaucrats and policymakers to create "tribes" were not so drastic as those exercised by the Belgians in Rwanda, but those others, too, moved to render ethnic difference more permanent and consequential while also codifying it in official mediums of documentation and statistical discourse. Throughout much of colonial Africa, difference was a valuable asset to be created, preserved, and reinforced as needed. This underlying reality underscores the uniqueness of subcolonial contexts in which difference, or properly speaking, deviation from a preferred and privileged cultural form, was understood to be the bane of colonial administrative efficiency. The status and (dys)function of difference in these admittedly few contexts deserve careful scholarly attention.

In Uganda, like Northern Nigeria, ethno-cultural lines of differentiation were *already* marked, with Buganda on one side and Bunyoro, Busoga, and other ethnic groups on the other. Here, in a radical departure from indirect rule that mirrored aspects of Hausa proxy rule, the British used Ganda personnel to govern districts in Bunyoro, Busoga, and other areas. As Lloyd Fallers and A. D. Roberts have posited, this was full-blown "native alien" subcolonialism with a system of subordination that corresponded to preexisting ethnic and political fissures.[19] Unlike the Muslim Hausa-Fulani, however, Ganda subcolonial officials were a multireligious group and deployed no discernible religiously inspired symbols and gestures of hegemony.

In Northern Nigeria, an actually existing cultural and religious divide sustained a narrative of difference and deviation and enabled British colonizers to insinuate Muslim Hausa-Fulani officials as "natural" overlords over non-Muslim Middle Belt communities. A calculus of cultural assumptions and ambitions shaped the colonial social hierarchy. The British sat atop their pyramid of sociopolitical sophistication and authority. The Hausa-Fulani inheritors of the caliphate's heritage sat below them and were expected to adopt the ways of the British as much as their so-called native character allowed. The non-Muslim peoples of the Middle Belt, described in both caliphate and British discourse as benighted tribesmen, sat on the lowest rung. They, in turn, were expected to learn the ways of their presumed Hausa-Fulani Muslim superiors through the instrumental pedagogy of Hausa subcolonial agents, caliphate-derived institutions, and the cultural contagion of resident Hausa chiefs and scribes.

Despite being steeped in the general architecture of colonial differentiation then, Hausa subcolonial rule in the Middle Belt stood apart in one key respect: the existence of actual markers of difference prejudiced colonial administrative policy making, actuating a departure from the familiar pattern of differentiation and difference-inspired administrative partitioning. In the familiar case of Rwanda, little actual difference separated the Tutsi from the Hutu. To the Belgians, sameness and homogeneity were obstacles to colonial rule, a reality they had to alter to establish a firm foundation for indirect rule through the creation of ethnic difference and the empowerment of a favored Tutsi elite. In Northern Nigeria, the British faced an actual difference of religion and ethnicity between the caliphate zone and the Middle Belt. Because they considered indirect rule politically inexpedient in this circumstance, their solution was to bring the peoples and cultures of the Middle Belt closer to the cultures and institutions of the presumably more civilized caliphate zone. Subcolonialism, or caliphate-centered rule, was an alluring proposition in this universe of administrative thinking.

Colonial differentiation and the creation of political institutions reflecting perceived ethno-religious identities devolved to what Mamdani calls "decentralized despotism," for the creation of a "monarchical, patriarchal, and authoritarian" customary chieftaincy required the existence of bounded communities of difference.[20] This perspective enriches our understanding of what drove colonizers to, in many instances, fundamentally reorganize African societies. It also posits the generic endpoint of most colonial political experiments: ethnic-specific authoritarian rule. The ubiquity of this rudimentary quest indicates that, for all their elaborate justification of Hausa subcolonial rule and its reliance on the idiom of difference and deviation, a greater British motive for empowering Hausa rulers over Middle Belt communities may have been the simple desire to achieve this colonial ideal of authoritarian rule by whatever means.

The Colonial Case for "Native Alien" Rule

If the accentuation of ethno-cultural difference was as indispensable to indirect rule as scholars of colonialism in Africa and South Asia posit, how then did this practice serve the apparently contradictory goal of promoting a functional cultural homogeneity in Northern Nigeria? The answer entails exploration into the homogenizing ends for which difference was mobilized. To tease out this paradox is not to suggest that the British consciously understood their practice in those terms; that would concede more deliberate intent to British colonialists than they actually exhibited. Rather, it is to assert that British colonial officials needed to constantly reinforce difference, actually existing difference to be sure, to strengthen the case for its erasure. This was the British rationale for sticking with the homogenizing utility of Hausa-Fulani subcolonials. Indeed the British emphasized difference and Middle Belt divergence obsessively. Colonial texts labored to accentuate this difference and sometimes enunciated it, in juxtaposition with the paradigmatic caliphate cultural model, as congenital deviance. But British colonialists in Northern Nigeria sensationalized difference not because it was a prized asset of intrinsic colonial value but because it was a means of legitimizing Hausa rule.

Hausa-Fulani elites also found the British narrative of difference as deficit useful and put their own accents on its outlines. Like other African colonial agents with origins in precolonial proto-imperialist maneuvers, Hausa subcolonial operatives authored their own quasi-hegemonic claims about identity, social exclusivity, origin, and ethnic hierarchy and used these as a blueprint to govern ethnic communities subjected to their rule. In the process they helped give life to the designated Other in the Middle Belt. Nor were narratives of Hausa-Fulani manifest destiny inspired exclusively by caliphal or European modes of social classification; instead, they evolved from multiple, convoluted processes of thought and action.

While African colonials contributed to the rationalization of so-called alien rule, they did not self-consciously set out to do so. Nonetheless, their roles in creating indigenous scripts of ethnic and religious exclusivity call for a systematic and delicate analysis. The ways in which African elites in the orbit of European colonialism worked to engineer new claims to identity and exclusivity have traditionally been ascribed to European influences. But groups of Western-educated Africans with investments in the colonial system created, through their own actions and texts, complementary discourses that normalized the intricacies of colonial rule and their roles in it. As Simon Gikandi argues, influential African figures in colonization displayed a remarkable capacity for constructing new ecologies of social value and then deploying these resources in ways that complicate our understanding of the power-culture dynamic of colonial rule.[21] Gikandi's *athomi,* mission-educated Gikuyu people, were self-assured and powerful shapers of colonial culture.

The generic administrative colonial chief, Mahmood Mamdani argues, was a figure of immense power not simply because he was appointed by the colonial overlord but because his colonial benefactors freed him from the constraints of traditional rule and from the ability of subjects to curtail his power.[22] The result was infinite authoritarian innovation on his part. British-appointed chiefs were powerful figures who approached colonial rule with gusto. The British-appointed Hausa ruler in the Nigerian Middle Belt was much more than a generic colonial chief under a formulaic British indirect rule system because he was an imposed outsider. His power was immense, and the consequences of that power were far reaching. Fully cognizant of their powerful roles, Hausa chiefs and their appointees authored texts and actions that reinforced, by design and effect, their power and the Otherness of Middle Belt peoples.

The initiatives of Hausa colonial agents need to be fully written into the colonial histories of Middle Belt communities, since the intellectual and administrative business of colonization rested almost exclusively in their hands. This revision has not occurred in part because the paradigm of indirect rule hovers conceptually over every analysis of African colonial experiences and in part because Northern Nigeria is viewed as an undifferentiated sociopolitical unit uniformly absorbed into indirect rule. The analyses in this book aim to address this lacuna.

Colonial Mediation versus Subcolonial Rule

My book does not stand alone; it builds on a developing body of literature. Scholars of Africa are increasingly giving voice to the roles played by African intermediaries in colonization—the chiefs, clerks, scribes, tax collectors, trade middlemen, messengers, and other "middle figures" who "bridged the linguistic and cultural gaps that separated European colonial officials from subject populations," and were the "hidden lynchpins of colonial rule."[23] This growing literature provides a counterweight to a historiography that assigns overriding agency to European actors and conceptualizes African colonial operatives as helpless appendages or heroic resisters. But even as African colonial agents emerge as more rational and instrumental actors in this revisionist narrative, they are still portrayed as lacking the initiative and the autonomy necessary to invent and deploy their own administrative symbols, rhetoric, and gestures. They continue to function as auxiliaries of European colonial officials or as rebels and cunning tricksters out to circumvent colonial processes. As a result of this scholarship, coupled with colonial texts that idealize African mediation rather than African colonial agency, African direct participation in the process of colonization has been treated as largely incidental, and colonial agency of any consequence continues to be vested largely in European actors.

This failure to recognize African agency seems to be partly a legacy of historiographical anxieties about whether it is proper to analyze African colonial actors, subalterns to be sure, as self-conscious contributors to colonial oppression.[24] While some recent studies have begun to recognize African colonial agency,[25] the "intermediary" narrative continues to preclude a more nuanced inquiry. A taxonomy that characterizes African colonial actors as "clients" of European colonial "patrons" and as "brokers" of imperial encounters has defined several recent studies. John Philips's analysis of how Hausa-speaking interpreters and middlemen helped shape the linguistic order of colonial officialdom in Northern Nigeria does push beyond the clientage and brokerage model.[26] This important work, however, fails to consider how these interpreters shaped the terms of the colonial encounter, or how control over language may have conferred upon them the power to determine consequential details of colonial rule.

Notably, Michael Twaddle's *Kakungulu* does ascribe full, far-reaching agency to Semei Kakungulu, a foremost Ganda subcolonial chief who at various times ruled in Bukedi and Busoga with British support. Twaddle argues that the administrative changes Kakungulu initiated resulted in a profound political transformation among the Soga and in Bukedi,[27] thus demonstrating how the actions of colonially minted subcolonial chiefs, especially in regions where single-man rule was unfamiliar, disrupted traditional ways people related with each other and with authority.

Depending on their mandate and the discursive underpinnings of their colonial mission, some powerful groups of African conscripts in colonization conceived of themselves as civilizers enacting elaborate political schemes that were largely a product of their own initiatives. Kaguru colonial subjects living in remote corners of Tanganyika had to confront "[nonindigenous] black . . . governmental officials tasked with bringing [the] rural people into the mainstream of colonial African life," a colonial mandate fraught with problems that persisted beyond the colonial era.[28] In many parts of Africa, the "rule of experts," as Timothy Mitchell calls it, was also the rule of African expats—those "foreign" Africans deemed political experts because of a mythologized history of conquest and imperial control.[29] The point of "administrative chieftaincy," after all, was to equip certain individuals with the mandate to administer domains placed under them. From this perspective, subcolonial rule made as much sense as indigenous mediation under indirect rule.

Another bold exploration of the independent ideas of privileged African colonials is Jonathon Glassman's analysis of how Zanzibari Arab elites developed autonomous racial discourses as a basis for their claims to a distinctive civilization. They used this body of ideas about identity and racial superiority to prop up a civilizing ethos that justified their privileged role and the subordinate positions of non-Arabs in colonial society.[30] Whether "British colonialism in Zanzibar rested politically on Arab sub-imperialism,"[31] as Anthony Clayton argues, or merely co-opted the personnel, idioms, and symbols of a prior Omani Arab imperialism, British colonial empowerment of Arab Zanzibaris and their deft deployment of that power among the Swahili and other autochthonous groups deserve to be explored beyond the restrictive frame of mediation.[32] Moreover, demonstrating that caliphate ideas about Middle Belt peoples' Otherness was not an aberration in precolonial Africa, and setting aside the question of how ideas about quasi-racial Othering were deployed in the contest for colonial and postcolonial political and economic positions, new work is now being done to uncover the intellectual histories of racial ideas and their socioeconomic and political correlates in precolonial Africa.[33]

The current literature has succeeded in repositioning African agents as bona fide participants in the colonization process. *Colonialism by Proxy* extends this analysis to African colonial "civilizers" who were not Western-educated, owed their privileged positions to traditional and historical claims, and worked outside their ancestral, religious, and sociolinguistic milieu, and whose initiatives had a profound effect and left a more enduring legacy than those of indigenous colonial mediators. If exercising a civilizing mandate, whether self-defined or bestowed by an outsider, qualified one as a colonizer, Hausa-Fulani rulers in the Middle Belt need to be situated more independently in the framing of African colonial experiences. For they, like nineteenth-century European imperialists who advanced the idea of the "white man's burden" and its claims of European manifest destiny, felt a sense of providential responsibility toward the humanity of the Middle Belt. The scanty texts of Hausa-Fulani colonials point to a keen awareness that they were bearers of a caliphate civilizing burden as much as they were participants in the administrative dimensions of "the white man's burden."

That some African groups exercised a subcolonial administrative agency that went beyond the familiar templates of mediation and brokerage should not supplant the rich body of work on colonial intermediaries. Rather, it should complement it and compel scholars of empire to be more receptive to modes of colonial administration in which a broader set of dynamics were at play than in indigenous mediation. To be sure, some roles played by certain categories of Hausa-Fulani colonial agents fit the intermediary model. Even so, their activities cannot be described simply as extreme versions of colonial brokerage. Some of these rulers put their imprint on colonial rule and clearly became, by design or circumstance, colonials in their own limited rights, taking advantage of a minimal British presence to act in ways that went far beyond mediation. Others transcended their colonial mandates in ways that insinuated them powerfully into colonial business.

To posit African subcolonial agency is also not to diminish the role of European colonial authorities in setting the overarching agenda or to contend that subcolonial agents were in charge of the ideological or programmatic infrastructure of colonial rule. Hausa colonial officials filled spaces created by British superiors and by British ideas about civilization, intra-African social and racial distinctions, and the need for preliminary administrative tutelage in certain regions. In many of the encounters analyzed in the following chapters, the hands of European officials can be seen, whether they were physically present or not. Often, British officials stood ready to intervene to prevent egregious departures from colonial priorities, and the threat of British reprimand often hung in the air, sporadically constraining what Hausa officials could do. There was thus no doubt about who held ultimate power. Yet, the outlines of Hausa-Fulani delegated colonial power were discernible throughout the Middle Belt. British calculation did not preclude the inventive self-assertion of Hausa agents. Hausa colonial officials often settled well into their positions and began to leverage them for their own purposes. They also insinuated themselves into new arenas of colonial relations outside the roles that British colonizers imagined for them.

For the British, subcolonial rule held a clear benefit. It helped them avoid the outrage of non-Muslim communities, as critiques and other forms of anti-colonial expression ricocheted off Hausa-Fulani agents. As a result, in some of the encounters analyzed below, the British were able to position themselves as disinterested arbiters and empathetic moderators of the excesses of Hausa-Fulani agents.

In light of the foregoing, arguments about a deeper-than-assumed African participation in colonial rule should not be seen as a radical departure from the existing perspectives on Africans' roles in colonization but rather as a complementary addition to them. The idea of subcolonialism is not entirely new, since some scholars long ago recognized the reality and consequence of delegated "native alien" colonial rule. Indeed, the conceptual precursor to the idea of sub-colonialism was sketched by A. D. Roberts, who coined the term "Ganda sub-imperialism" to describe the profound Ganda imprint on British colonization in Bukedi, Bunyoro, and Busoga.[34]

Of Martial Races and Civilizing Agents

Hausa-Fulani subcolonial rule was ideologically indebted to etymologies of thought and archives of recorded colonial practice in India and other African sites. The histories of these prior colonial engagements with groups of privileged colonial allies and the discourses that resulted from them are crucial to understanding the meanings that the category of Hausa assumed in British colonization in Northern Nigeria. In India, British assumptions about martial ability and their valuation of princely traditions, hierarchies, and rituals converged in administrative systems that in several of the princely states saw Hindu princes ruling over Muslim communities and Muslim kings, some of them with rich Mughal political heritage, ruling over Hindu peasants.[35] In a few other states the British recruited Sikh and Buddhist princes to rule over states with majority Hindu or Muslim populations. The constant idiom at work here was a belief that the possession of a set of mythologized qualities would translate to administrative efficiency in service of British colonialism. As in Northern Nigeria, assumptions about martial capacity overlapped into British valorization of political traditions or neotraditions—a British colonial order of political valuation that Thomas Metcalf calls traditionalization.[36] Subsequently, the British elevated these two presumably symbiotic criteria—political tradition and martial dexterity—above all others, including notions of indigeneity and legitimacy, in recruiting existing or newly recognized princes as allies.

British obsession with the administrative utility of "martial races" and centralized political cultures was replicated across its empire. In Africa, it pivoted on several considerations, from the starkly utilitarian to the grandly ideological. Sometimes the idea of a martial race and its place in British colonization was a literal belief in the ability of certain colonized peoples to wage successful wars or to display the masculine attributes deemed necessary for success in warfare. Examples abound of how the British came to understand certain ethnic communities as predisposed by natural endowment, sociological evolution, and political sophistication, to effective warring. In Kenya, the British sometimes turned to the Maasai as "natural" martial allies. In the counterinsurgency against the Mau Mau uprising, the British prized the special war skills of the Kamba, whom they deemed a "martial race."[37] The legend of Hausa martial expertise intrigued British colonial officials to the extent that pioneer British colonialists relied on a regiment of so-called Hausa soldiers to "pacify" territories from Yorubaland in southwestern Nigeria to Northern Nigeria and to the Northern Territories and Akan-speaking areas of the Gold Coast colony.[38]

These assumptions then became powerful determinants of colonial administrative policies. Martial capacity was thought to beget managerial, organizational, and administrative skills as well as a disposition to the coveted precondition of indirect rule: political centralization. These ideas endured not just by force of colonial repetition but also by their self-interested deployment by African groups so designated.[39] Once established as a basis for allocating colonial privileges, these designations became coveted categories, and "becoming Hausa" or "becoming Kamba" became a frequent, calculated enterprise.[40]

The trope of the "Hausa force" as a byword for the African soldiers that aided British conquests in many African regions is familiar to historians of West Africa and was well documented by colonial authorities.[41] It also has a complex origin that prefigured British investments in the administrative utility of Hausa subcolonials. Narratives that grew around the military exploits of the transregional empire of the Sokoto Caliphate seem to have circulated widely in West Africa, influencing accounts of early European travelers, who expressed patronizing awe about the political prowess of the caliphate and its emirates. The result was a mobile myth of Hausa martial distinction. By the mid to late nineteenth century, when European "pacification" intensified, the mythic Hausa lay at the center of British colonial military strategy in West Africa. Subsequently, as David Killingray, Sam Ukpabi, and Marion Johnson have shown, this "imagined martial community," as Killingray calls it, influenced British recruiting for the colonial military and police.[42] Hausa became a stand-in for valor and martial ability. Other attributes were then mapped onto this descriptive sketch, producing a usable social myth of wide provenance.

In colonial Uganda, the Ganda elite's Protestantism and the Ganda's monarchical, hierarchical, and centralized forms of social and political organization predisposed them, in the mind of the British, to the role of proxy colonialists. Even though some Ganda operatives in colonial Busoga and Bukedi were Muslim,[43] the political dominance of Protestantism in Buganda was key to British cultivation of Ganda ideas, personnel, and institutions in the administration of Uganda's other peoples. The extension of Luganda as the administrative language of Ganda subcolonial rule completed the ensemble.

In British West Africa, colonial knowledge turned on two markers of superiority: chieftaincy (and its inferior opposite, the non-chiefly societies) and Islamic piety. The quasi-ethnographic writings of early colonial officials, including Ronald Rattray in the Gold Coast and Frederick Lugard in Northern Nigeria, British travel accounts, and the formulaic British Colonial Annual Reports all demonstrate the gradual convergence of colonial discourse on the idea that Muslim chieftaincies were the prototypes of indirect rule preparedness, followed by centralized non-Muslim societies. In both the Gold Coast and Nigeria, this early consensus morphed into a canon that clearly justified the empowerment of personnel and ideas from centralized Islamic and non-Islamic polities over those from decentralized communities.[44] Of particular resonance in the toolkit of British imperial control in West Africa was what Tony Kaye calls "the myth of a Muslim North," which could be enlisted to rule "tribal," "backward," and non-Muslim hinterlands on behalf of the British.[45]

These examples demonstrate a fairly consistent British commitment to administrative improvisations of the subcolonial type. As experiments, some more permanent or less volatile than others, they followed the contours of observed and constructed sociological singularities in a particular site. But the trope of Hausa colonial privilege circulated with constancy in Northern Nigeria even if the ways that it manifested itself varied according to location. What emerges more generally is that the Hausa-Fulani colonials profiled here enjoyed their privileged position not solely because they were Hausa or Muslim. What also seemed to be at work in Northern Nigeria and at other sites where indirect rule was deemed unsuitable were notions, honed in self-reproducing colonial ethnology, that conflated "native" administrative capacity and ethnic political histories. This belief in turn forged pragmatic decisions in the backwoods of empire, dissolving familiar colonial habits like indirect rule and replacing them with alternative arrangements that left tumultuous legacies in the postcolonial period.

A Note on the Caliphate

The foregoing reflections and the analyses in the chapters below may appear to reify a caliphate political system that was more diffuse and fluid than popular understandings might suggest. Assessing the weight of caliphate ideas in the practical unfolding of subcolonial rule by those who claimed a caliphate heritage requires a certain caution. The "native alien" colonial agents discussed here drew upon a range of political and cultural referents in their relations with Middle Belt peoples. Not all were traceable to the defunct caliphate, although for strategic purposes the Anglo-Hausa-Fulani alliance highlighted caliphate ideological origins rather than more quotidian, less glamorous ones. In fact, Hausa-Fulani colonial personnel were often separated from each other by geography and circumstance and by the constraints of dissimilar colonial priorities in different parts of the Middle Belt. Thus, any insinuation that a coordinated, caliphate-inspired agenda tied the Hausa agents to a common, primordial purpose would be problematic. Moreover, these colonial personnel had varying claims to caliphate heritage, ranging from direct ancestry, to convoluted migratory trajectories from caliphate zones, to a more tenuous affiliation resting on adherence to caliphate Islamic orthodoxy and, in some instances, on the superficial fact of fluency in Hausa or Fulfulde. In fact, as demonstrated in chapter 4, some of the powerful "Hausa" colonial officials were neither ethnic Hausa nor Fulani, the only basis for their claim of caliphate-Hausa pedigree being their Muslim faith and their proficient facility with the Hausa language.

It is also important to point out that whatever was left of the caliphate in the aftermath of the colonial conquest retained many of the frictions that plagued it in its heyday. The caliphate was never a coherent entity, troubled as it was by rivalries, intrigues, divisive politics of patronage, and the disruptive ambitions of self-seeking mavericks. What internal cohesion remained on the eve of the colonial conquest hardly survived the divide-and-rule manipulations of British colonizers. Thus, each group of Hausa-Fulani colonizers negotiated its own path in colonization, and its ruling strategies derived as much from localized interests as from caliphate cultures. Further complicating matters was the fact that many Hausa-Fulani Muslim officials were sometimes driven by personal ambitions, merely deploying the idioms and symbols of caliphate power to compel awe and obedience among non-Muslim subalterns. Within the Hausa-Fulani subcolonial hierarchy, there was intense rivalry and occasional sabotage, as careers clashed and as an already brittle caliphate solidarity gave way to ruthless personal maneuvering.

Chapter Breakdown

The book is divided into seven chapters. With the exception of the first and last, each chapter focuses on a geographic region of the Middle Belt, exploring the evolution of Hausa-Fulani subcolonial rule in that region, the British deployment of emirate-centered ideas and institutions in non-Muslim communities, and the region-specific problems that plagued the system as Middle Belt peoples rejected their subordination to Hausa colonial agency.

Chapter 1 traces the multiple precolonial processes by which a coherent Hausa-Fulani identity developed, the emergence of Islamic piety as the supreme arbiter of that identity, and the merging of caliphate and early British colonial narratives and priorities, resulting in a set of associations and assumptions that constituted the ideological touchstone of Hausa-Fulani subcolonial rule.

Chapter 2 discusses the convoluted emergence of Zazzau subcolonial rule in the Southern Kaduna sector. It analyzes the development of Hausa-Fulani colonial agency, the administrative initiatives of Zazzau rulers in the region's non-Muslim communities, and Zazzau rulers' effort to consolidate and normalize their subcolonial control, most notably through the quasi-ceremonial art of touring, which created opportunities for the expression of emirate paternalism through speech and gestures. The chapter also explores the complications of subcolonial rule in this volatile frontier, including the polyvalent reactions and protests of non-Muslim communities and the repositioning of British officials as accidental arbiters in the troubled interactions between the Hausa-Fulani colonial agents and the region's ethnic communities.

Chapter 3 examines emirate subcolonial agency in the Plateau and Nasarawa-Lafia axis. It analyzes how a lack of colonial supervision allowed British-appointed emirate chiefs and their own appointees in charge of non-Muslim communities to gradually insinuate themselves into the colonial enterprise in a way that departed sharply from their mandate to prepare their subjects for self-administration. From their initial roles as guardians and colonial mediators among the Afizere, Alago, Mada, and other peoples, caliphate-originated emirate officials, especially those based in Lafia, transformed into more involved and assertive colonial agents, coming to own certain quotidian aspects of the colonial project in this region and becoming, at least in the eyes of their non-Muslim subjects, the face of British colonialism. This transition took British supervisors aback and riled the Alago people, triggering a series of grassroots uprisings against emirate subcolonial rule. The chapter also considers how the anxieties of late colonialism in the post–World War II period raised the stakes in the struggle against emirate control and stoked a series of ethno-religious crises that departing British colonialists struggled to contain.

Chapter 4 examines the role of a diverse crew of Hausa agents—chiefs, tax scribes, policemen, commercial agents, hunters, rubber tappers, and guards—in the colonial administration of the Benue Valley. It analyzes how the province's position as the southernmost political unit in the Middle Belt limited precolonial contacts with the caliphate, making the importation of Hausa colonial agents, institutions, practices, and symbols particularly jarring.

The Hausa subcolonial presence in Idoma and Tiv Divisions was more diverse than in other regions. As a result, the depth and scope of Hausa colonial agency was more extensive, and the interaction of Hausa officials and institutions with the Idoma, Tiv, Igedde and other non-Muslim groups more fraught. To further complicate this volatile brew, colonial communication was more problematic here because the limited Hausa-Fulani precolonial presence resulted in few if any people speaking Hausa. Because British officials spoke only Hausa, they had to rely on Hausa interpreters who spoke some Idoma, Tiv, or Igedde.

Colonial mediation thus simmered with political misunderstanding. Hausa colonial agents could determine, through linguistic manipulations and other acts of subterfuge, the trajectory of colonial relations and use their positions to further their own interests at the expense of the indigenous peoples without the British knowing about it.

The chapter also considers non-Muslim protests against Hausa subcolonial rule, marked most starkly by violent attacks on Hausa colonial agents, which led the British to reinforce Hausa rule. When the Idoma and the Tiv sought revenge against the unchecked intrusions of an unusually large contingent of Hausa colonial operatives, they only reinforced the notion that the people of the Benue Valley were quintessentially anti-caliphate, a backward people who deserved more, not less, tutelage at the hands of Hausa colonial agents. The intensity of Hausa-subcolonial activities in the Benue Valley was exacerbated by the relative paucity of British personnel there. Benue Province had a reputation in the colonial bureaucracy as a savage backwater in which only incompetent and disfavored officials served. This meant that very few British officials were present there. As a result colonial business was essentially fobbed off to Hausa officials, who improvised from day to day to maintain a fragile colonial order.

Chapter 5 documents the particularities of Fulani subcolonial rule in Adamawa Province. It begins by outlining the way Fulani migrants had embedded themselves in and around non-Muslim communities in precolonial times, cultivating symbiotic if sometimes volatile relations with non-Muslim ethnic groups. Additionally, the Fulani jihad here had not produced coherent Fulani zones with discernible and enforceable frontiers. As a result, fragmented Fulani communities were interspersed among majority non-Muslim communities, producing fluid relations between the two groups, with little or no subordination or hegemony. This was unlike other zones, in which fairly clear demarcations between the caliphate zone and its non-Muslim frontier had made caliphate proto-imperial practice possible.

The chapter examines how these prior conditions exacerbated the disruptions resulting from the British investing Fulani elites with colonial political privileges and administrative mandates over their non-Muslim neighbors. Fulani subcolonial rule here struggled to take off: agents used their newfound power to oppress non-Muslim groups, whose complaints in turn awakened British officials to the drawbacks of Fulani preparatory rule. Talks of phasing out Fulani rule to promote non-Muslim self-administration—essentially a movement toward indirect rule—gained steam, only to be extinguished by the practical utility of Fulani rule. The British preserved the system, instituting only inconsequential reforms that sustained and in some cases reinforced the infrastructure of proxy colonization. Both the British and the Fulani ultimately saw no incentive for change, and the failure of reform efforts in 1937 and 1938 set the stage for more trouble.

Chapter 6 continues from the chronological break point of chapter 5, exploring the gradual unraveling of Fulani subcolonial rule in Adamawa Province even as the on-the-ground roles of Fulani officials remained intact. Understandably, the failure of the British to move toward non-Muslim self-rule and a concomitant reluctance to whittle down Fulani privileges stoked non-Muslim resentment.

The chapter analyzes the tactical versatility of young, mission-educated non-Muslim activists, and a colonial response that at once exhibited sympathy toward what British officials described as the need for non-Muslim "self-determination" and a practical commitment to the Anglo-Fulani alliance. These dueling impulses produced an uncoordinated British response that often focused on silencing the voices of protest through intimidation. At the same time, non-Muslim protest caused officials to recognize the merit of their cause. Still, even as they resurrected the discourse of indigenous self-rule, British officials remained wary of alienating Fulani rulers and hundreds of their appointed colonial agents, who by this time had consolidated their positions and were the mainstays of the colonial system.

British officials consulted the *lamido* of Adamawa, the supreme Fulani subcolonial authority in the province, over planned reforms. In an illustration of how deeply dependent the British were on the system of proxy rule, and of how powerful the Fulani colonial agents had become, the lamido and his officials were able to effectively veto a movement toward non-Muslim self-determination by forcing British officials to suspend plans for administrative reforms. The chapter ends by describing how non-Muslim protests escalated as national independence neared, raising anxieties about the possibility that Fulani officials might convert their subcolonial hegemony to postcolonial political domination. The intersection of new fears actuated by the high-stakes political calculation of late colonialism and the stealthy consolidation of Fulani rule in turn produced continuing challenges to Fulani rule.

Chapter 7 brings together the stories of the previous five chapters by discussing how the disparate and fragmented struggles of Middle Belt peoples across the vast region converged, however imperfectly, in a coherent narrative of Hausa-Fulani political domination and a movement for Middle Belt self-determination in the late colonial and early independence periods. The major catalysts for this development were the novel anxieties of the 1950s and early 1960s, as elites with caliphate pedigree parlayed their colonial privileges into political preeminence in both the regional politics of Northern Nigeria and the struggles of specific Middle Belt areas such as Jos and Makurdi. This new struggle birthed the United Middle Belt Congress (UMBC) as a platform for the expression of Middle Belt grievances and aspirations. Founded on a seemingly implacable anti-caliphate angst inspired by a new Middle Belt consciousness, the new struggle crystallized in a slew of rhetorical innovations that both drew backlash from the dominant

Hausa-Fulani political establishment represented by the Northern Peoples Congress (NPC) and divided the UMBC into hard-line and moderate factions.

This concluding chapter analyzes the flashpoints of Middle Belt–caliphate confrontation in specific local disputes, the violence that sometimes characterized them, and the stakes that dueling elites fought over. I raise for further consideration the contradictions, failures, and successes of the Middle Belt movement in post-independence Nigerian politics and interrogate the dilemmas it threw up in the early independence period. The dilemmas of separatism and of strategic participation in the caliphate-oriented Northern Nigerian political mainstream were factors in the unraveling of the Middle Belt movement in the early postcolonial period, as was the NPC's massive patronage machine, which it deployed alongside ruthless tactics of coercion and punishment to undermine the UMBC and promote the myth of its own inevitable political omnipotence.

Taken together, these chapters have the potential to illuminate a fairly unfamiliar colonial system whose procedures and struggles have had and continue to have consequences for the politics of political representation, ethnicity, entitlement, resource allocation, and nation building in contemporary Nigeria.

1 The Hausa-Caliphate Imaginary and Ideological Foundations of Proxy Colonialism

Bᴏᴏᴋᴛɪsʜ-sᴜᴘᴇʀᴠɪsᴇᴅ Hausa-Fulani colonization in the Middle Belt has a long, scattered, but recoverable ideological history. The reconstruction of this history entails two interrelated quests. One is a search for the origin and development of a Hausa-caliphate colonial administrative imaginary in the osmotic interplay between caliphate and British narratives. The other is the sometimes subtle, sometimes declared entry of the set of ideas that rationalized proxy caliphate rule into official British colonial policy in Northern Nigeria.[1]

The search for colonial administrative coherence and uniformity prompted British officials to craft an administrative policy envisioned to normalize and spread a Hausa-caliphate sociocultural and political model to the non-Muslim areas of the Middle Belt.[2] The process by which this policy emerged in the realm of ideas and debate, evolved, and became a manual of colonial rule in the Middle Belt was long and complex and requires a systematic analysis to unpack. Scrutinizing subcolonialism to reveal its properties is necessary to provide a discursive backdrop for narrative case studies that flesh out the operational vagaries of an unusual infrastructure of colonization.

Hausa-Fulani subcolonialism was a colonial template of Anglo-caliphate rule. It took shape against the backdrop of a canon of colonial and caliphate knowledge that viewed the cultures, religions, and political traditions of the Middle Belt as obstacles to be overcome in the interest of cheap, uniform colonial rule in Northern Nigeria. The idea of supplanting Middle Belt cultures and institutions as a way of preparing the non-Muslim peoples of the region for indirect rule through the instrumentality of Hausa-caliphate ideas, institutions, cultures, and personnel was a logical outgrowth of this prior ideological ferment. A key enabler of this project was the auspicious meshing of British and caliphate ideas.

British rule in the Middle Belt, although encased in a belief that "backward" Middle Belt peoples should embrace the political and cultural attributes associated with the caliphate zone, was not aimed at achieving sociopolitical uniformity for its own sake. Rather, this was a pragmatic administrative project informed by the practical and fiscal impossibility of implementing multiple colonial administrative systems in Northern Nigeria. But if pragmatism dictated Hausa-Fulani subcolonial rule, the system needed quasi-intellectual justification. It also needed an invented narrative of Hausa-Fulani supremacy and Middle Belt inferiority, for only such a narrative could indemnify British colonial supervisors for violating indirect rule by empowering "foreign" mediators over indigenous ones. In this ideological enterprise, preexisting British and caliphate theories about the precolonial sociology and politics of Northern Nigeria and about prior indicators of Middle Belt submission and resistance to caliphate "civilization" proved particularly useful. These theories contributed to the formulation of subcolonialism as an ideology of colonial rule and provided cultural alibis to justify its implementation.

The two fundamental prerequisites of indirect rule—ethnic difference and a preexisting, centralized system of rule—necessitated the creation of both difference and politico-cultural sameness across Northern Nigeria, using the colonially favored Hausa-caliphate model as a reference. This exercise was carried out through the coalescing, over a long period, of caliphate narratives and claims about itself and its "others" on the one hand and British imperial sociological and historical writings on the other. British colonial articulations of sociological assumptions about subject peoples often preceded and guided their administrative ideas. It is what Sean Hawkins, following David Olson, calls "the world on paper," a colonial representational world "divorced from reality" but possessing the capacity to determine colonial administrative and economic policy.[3]

British ideas about racial and civilizational hierarchies and caliphate images of itself and of the non-Muslim peoples on its vast frontier bled into each other in complex ways and solidified into a colonial governing imaginary dependent on the conscription of caliphate ideas and personnel. The most contested site of this colonial administrative policy was the Middle Belt. Colonial and caliphate discourses highlighted the absence of the key raw material for indirect rule, political centralization, in most Middle Belt communities and contrasted this with the centralized political traditions of the caliphate zone. This was a problem that had to be solved. The caliphate, influential colonial ideologues like Frederick Lugard and Charles Temple believed, modeled the institutions and forms of social organization considered the foundations of indirect rule. The mobilization of caliphate ideas, administrative traditions, and personnel to uplift and prepare the peoples of the Middle Belt for indirect rule should thus be viewed as a pragmatic project, although British colonial writers and amateur anthropologists in Northern Nigeria also referenced a set of self-reflexive racial ideologies in formulating their administrative policies for the Middle Belt.

The analysis that follows maps the historical processes through which Hausa-Fulani identity and its associative connotations emerged. The emergence of the Sokoto Islamic Caliphate inaugurated an ideational revolution that transformed Hausa identity and conflated it with a notion of Islamic piety, imperial citizenship, and privilege. After the colonial conquest, a new set of ideas about what Hausa-caliphate identity meant fused with new subcolonial administrative doctrines that affirmed the same claims and created a homogenized Middle Belt Other, fossilizing into concrete colonial administrative policy. This policy then acquired a separate, elaborate life of its own, feeding on both conformity and resistance to it among Middle Belt peoples.

Hausa: More Than a Language

Hausa is not just a language; it is a category synonymous with certain ways of acting, making a living, and worshipping God. As a descriptor and signifier, Hausa correlates with a vast system of meanings and connotations. Hausa now carries with it a variety of clear cultural, economic, and political associations. As a language of trade and social contact in West Africa, and as the language of an ethnic group known as Hausa, it approaches what Ali Mazrui calls a cosmopolitan language.[4] The presence throughout much of West Africa of people who speak Hausa as a second language, and the role of the Hausa language as a lingua franca in much of Northern Nigeria, speaks to the utilitarian importance of a language whose intertwinement with trade and itinerant Islamic practices dates back to a remote Nigerian antiquity.[5]

The Hausa people inhabited the savannah grasslands of West Africa, hemmed between the Songhai and Bornu empires. A receptacle of influences from both empires since perhaps the fifteenth century, Hausaland, then politically constituted into several Hausa city-states, remained largely defined by the linguistic primacy of various dialects of the Hausa language. After the Fulani jihad of 1804–1808, the variegated existence of the Hausa people was subsumed by the Sokoto Caliphate, which was largely constituted by the territories of the old Hausa city-states.

The terms "Hausa," "Hausawa," and "Kasar Hausa," denoting the language, people, and land of the Hausa respectively are actually fairly recent coinages. These terms in their modern usage probably originated from the writings of Othman bin Fodio, leader of the Fulani jihad who, before and during the jihad, homogenized the Hausa-speaking but autonomous peoples of the different Hausa states in what he defined as a collective of bad Muslim rulers and syncretistic Muslim masses.[6] The peoples of these states, and ordinary Fulani migrants who lived among them, were more likely to refer to the Hausa states' citizens by their state of origin: "Katsinawa" for those from Katsina, "Kanawa" for those from Kano, "Gobirawa" for those from Gobir, and others. Following bin Fodio, his brother, Mohammed Bello, discursively formalized "Hausa" as a term of reference for the inhabitants of the former Hausa states.[7]

The Fulani Islamic reform movement, or Fulani jihad, superimposed a central political and religious authority on the fragmented Hausa states of present-

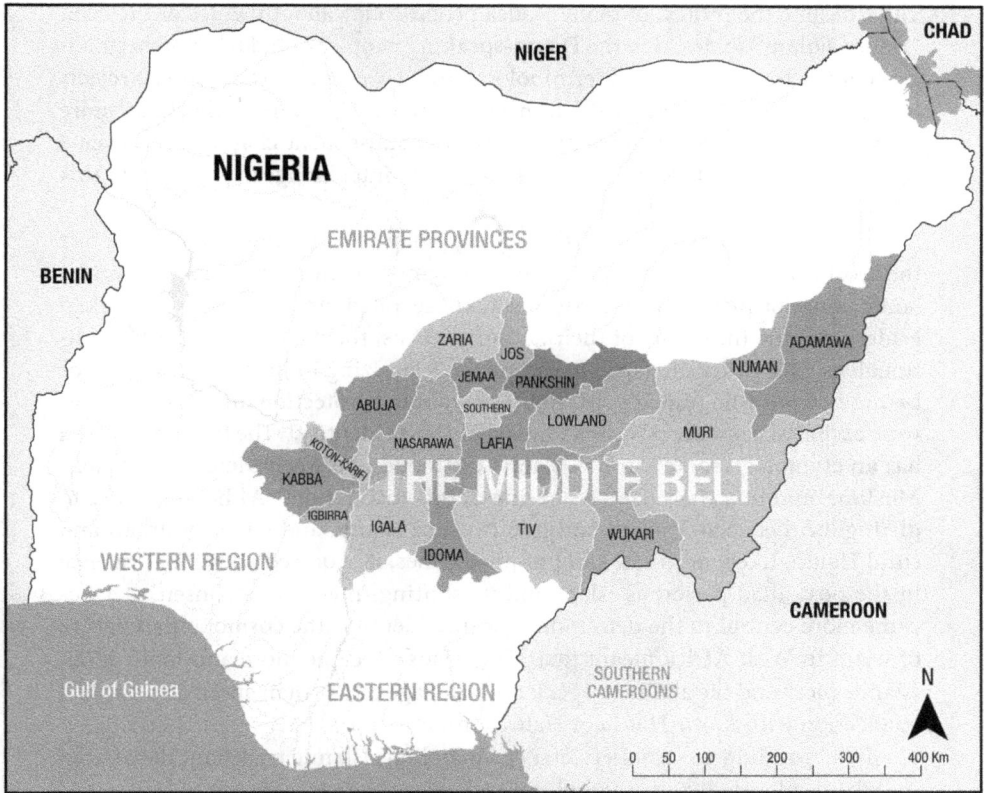

day Northwestern Nigeria and, through conquest and discourse, disciplined them into one politico-linguistic unit. More importantly, the jihad inscribed Islamic piety as one of the most important markers of Hausa identity. Thus, as John Philips argues, to be Hausa gradually came to mean that one was a Muslim, even though not all Muslims in the caliphate were Hausa and not all Hausa were Muslims.[8] The jihad initiated the process of homogenization and the construction of a politically useful concept of Hausa identity, a narrative that was underwritten by religious and cultural associations.

The religious content of the "Hausaization" process was coterminous with the new fortune of Islam as the defining ideal of citizenship within the Sokoto Caliphate, whose core was Hausaland. The new Fulani rulers and their agents adopted the language and culture of their Hausa subjects as well as the administrative infrastructure of the conquered Hausa (Habe) kings. By this process, most of the urbanized Fulani *became* Hausa in linguistic and cultural terms, although a quiet commingling of the two peoples had been taking place before the jihad.[9]

Thus, despite the protest of many Hausa people today about the use of the term "Hausa-Fulani" to describe the Hausa-speaking peoples of today's Northern Nigeria, it is a historically valid terminology, and it seems that their protest rejects the recent appropriations of the term by Southern Nigerian intellectuals more than it does the term's historicity. In this and subsequent chapters, however, I will use the terms "Hausa" and "Hausa-Fulani" interchangeably to denote this compound ethnic category.

The Islamization of Hausa identity is perhaps best underscored by the fact that post-jihad Hausa identity became synonymous with assimilation into an Islamic consciousness that was packaged, consecrated, and policed by the jihad leaders and the inheritors of their authority. Thus, the *maguzawa*, Hausa traditionalists who either managed to escape the Islamizing influence of the jihad or became *dhimis* who traded *jizya* tribute for caliphal protection under Islamic law, were excluded from the post-jihad model of Hausa identity.[10] The term maguzawa has an etymology rooted in the Islamic distinction between Muslims and non-Muslims, and in a Hausaized rendering of this distinction.[11] Although its use to distinguish between Muslim and non-Muslim Hausa, and between urban and rural Hausa, likely originated in pre-jihad times, it acquired additional valence in the post-jihad period as Islam and its shifting interpretive consensuses became more central to the definition of Hausa identity. The cosmopolitan nature of Islam in West Africa meant that *being* Hausa became more and more about Islamic piety and the ability to speak the language rather than about any original connection with *Kasar Hausa* or Hausa ethnic ancestry.[12]

By expanding the frontiers of a cosmopolitan Islamic tradition, the Sokoto Caliphate enhanced the cosmopolitan and incorporative character of Hausa, enabling non-Hausa members of the caliphal Islamic community to become Hausa in geographical contexts that lacked Hausa ethnic heritage.[13] Indeed, because Hausa identity was vested with sociopolitical importance by the jihad, it became, at least within the Sokoto Caliphate, a political identity denoting belonging and privilege. Islamic piety, an acceptance of the religious orthodoxy of the caliphate founders, and an ability to speak Hausa even as a second language granted one entry into Hausahood. It thus became an appealing identity from a purely pragmatic perspective. Affiliation with the paradigmatic ethnic category of a regional hegemony like Sokoto conferred a social currency with polyvalent profitability. The title of "Hausa" had purchase in multiple contexts. Geographic proximity to the Hausa heartland in today's northwestern Nigeria as well as Islamic piety facilitated social and political access to an increasingly coveted Hausa identity.

A plethora of cultural, attitudinal, and performative indicators sprang up to reinforce the linguistic and religious indicators of Hausa identity. It is this constellation of cultural, religious, economic, and political significations that I call Hausa-caliphate imaginary. Steven Pierce argues that this amplification of Hausa identity as a total worldview and way of life is underwritten by the belief among the inheritors of the Sokoto Caliphate Islamic tradition that "Hausa identity . . . also encompassed particular ways of making a living . . . notably Hausa people's fame as traders . . . and a particular approach to agriculture: certain technologies, certain modes of labor mobilization."[14] As a result of these associative reification of Hausa, *being* Hausa or *becoming* Hausa gradually came to denote possessing certain qualities. Islamic conversion or reaffirmation was only the beginning point, as well as the fundamental action, on the path to *becoming* Hausa.[15]

The cumulative outcome of the transformation and elaboration of Hausa as a category of identification was that Hausa became even more fluid and context-determined than it had been prior to the jihad. This fluidity that came to characterize Hausa identity was crucial because proficiency in the Hausa language and in the vocabulary of Islam displaced autochthony as a criterion for belonging. The spread of Hausa linguistic and religious influence made Hausa a category of power, since anyone whose claim to Hausa identity was consecrated by the invocation of these attributes could potentially enjoy the privileges and status that came with being regarded as Hausa in non-Hausa contexts like the Middle Belt. Because Islam was the seminal social marker of the caliphate, and Hausa was its functional lingua franca, anyone possessing these traits was immediately associated with the might and privileges of the caliphate. In the Middle Belt, these attributes functioned as a metaphor for the Sokoto Caliphate and its emirate system, or as Alvin Magid calls it, the Fulani system of political administration.[16]

Jihad, Social Change, Relational Flux in the Middle Belt

As ambitious agents seeking to extend the sway of the caliphate to the non-Muslim areas of Northern Nigeria attacked the sovereignty of states in the Middle Belt, the category of Hausa came to simultaneously assume the status of a feared and awe-inspiring political presence. The various peoples of the Middle Belt devised numerous strategies to either keep Hausa-Fulani caliphate slave raiders and state-builders at bay or selectively bend to their sway in the interest of peace. For instance, the Chamber-speaking peoples of the Upper Benue lowlands and highlands alternated between several strategies to both accommodate and contain Fulani influence. These inhabitants of the Middle Benue hills and plains managed to coexist, albeit uneasily, with pockets of militant Fulani settlers and proto-states through the careful deployment of strategies ranging from half-hearted submission to quiet self-assertion to outright resistance.[17]

The Tiv people kept Hausa-Fulani caliphate agents in check by carefully monitoring their activities on the frontiers of Tivland, attacking their isolated outposts and trade caravans, strategically interacting with them, and building a feared warring infrastructure founded on the infamous Tiv poisoned arrow.[18] The Doma, a branch of the Agatu Idoma, adopted an ambivalent survival strategy against the raids of Hausa-Fulani caliphate agents from Keffi.[19] They, like the Chamba, willfully succumbed to some measure of Hausa-Fulani influence as a gesture of political self-preservation.

What occurred in the precolonial period in terms of the Middle Belt's engagement with caliphal expansion was thus a series of complex stalemates, fluid accommodations, and tense, frequently violated treaties of coexistence that John Nengel calls the *amana* system.[20] These stalemates and negotiated tribute arrangements were desirable not only to the Middle Belt polities but also to raiding emirates, as both groups sought to minimize the possibility of costly long-term conflict. Wars were difficult and expensive to execute because armies were difficult to recruit and maintain; repeated raids resulted in diminished booty, and endless war detracted from other matters of statecraft.[21] As such, the emirates, especially those on the caliphate's frontiers, had a vested interest in some form of negotiated coexistence that ensured the supply of slaves and economic goods to them as tribute. Nonetheless, outright military rebellion on the part of tribute-paying semiautonomous communities often attracted fierce military retribution.

These precolonial tensions and the steady if checkered expansion of the slave raid frontier created resentment and fear-inspired accommodations among Middle Belt peoples. Matthew Kukah sums it up this way: "Around the Middle Belt, the [Hausa-Fulani] Jihadists seemed more preoccupied with slavery, economic and political expansionism than the spread of the [Islam]. As a result, all forms of alliances came into being, but economic considerations were paramount."[22] Although, as Kukah argues, the winning of converts to Islam in the Middle Belt gradually receded in importance, the spread of Islamic and Hausa-Fulani cultural influence did not. Although this was truer for the frontier non-Muslim communities of the Southern Kaduna, Bauchi, and Adamawa corridors than it was for the Benue Valley, the fate of Doma in the southernmost part of the Middle Belt indicates that jihadist aggression and caliphate influence spread to all of the Middle Belt in various degrees. Doma, an Agatu Idoma state, one of the southernmost polities in Northern Nigeria, would become, at different intermittent junctures, a semiautonomous satellite vassal of Zazzau in the mid-nineteenth century through a combination of military defeats and strategic self-preservation through the acceptance of caliphate influence and quasi-control. Caliphate slave raiding and the spread of caliphate culture was assured in the Middle Belt because of the influence and military might of the southern Fulani sub-emirates, and because of the presence of numerous other enclaves of garrisoned Hausa-Fulani settlements in the Middle Belt.[23]

Caliphal and British Origins of the Hausa Imaginary

Although much of the early British ethnological taxonomy was inspired by similar British classifications in India, two important factors reinforced the British preoccupation with the hierarchy of sociological and anthropological categories in Northern Nigeria.[24] The first factor was caliphate imperial writings that represented the caliphate as a benign hegemony and the Middle Belt as its subordinate Other. The second was the elaboration of these ideas by British travelers and, subsequently, by colonial ethnographers, a process that was not teleological but is nonetheless discernible.

The first major effort to delineate the Sokoto Caliphate as an exclusive religious and political community and to define its Other was the *Infakul Maisuri* of Mohammed Bello. This important piece of caliphate writing is best known for its exposition of what one might call the caliphate mind. The document explored the theological and political vision of the caliphate, the case for and the course of the jihad, and the epistolary efforts to place the caliphate above Bornu in the hierarchy of state Islamic piety. Much less known is the fact that Mohammed Bello's *Infakul Maisuri* was the first treatise to articulate a Sokoto imperial hegemony over some areas of the Middle Belt.

In the section of the text dealing with states, kingdoms, and peoples, Mohammed Bello brings within caliphate administrative jurisdiction several areas of the Middle Belt that lay outside caliphate control. This was a discursive annexation that foreshadowed the caliphate's expansion into frontier Middle Belt areas. For instance Bello defines the emirate of Zazzau as encompassing "many places inhabited by barbarians."[25] The use of the term "barbarians" here constitutes an imperial euphemism for the non-Muslim peoples of the Middle Belt located on Zazzau's frontier. He projects Zazzau's sway all the way to the entire Gbagyi country, the Bassa plains in the Lower Benue, and as far south as Attagara (Idah) in Igala country.[26] The oral traditions of the Bassa and the Igala do not attest to these claims, nor do any written non-caliphate sources.[27] Mohammed Bello imagined his imperial sway to include the Niger-Benue confluence zone of the Middle Belt, telling British explorer Hugh Clapperton, "I will give the King of England a place on the coast to build a town. . . . God has given me all the land of the Infidels."[28]

This imperial vision may not have been an accidental occurrence. There appears to be a contradictory assertion of the caliphate's benign hegemony over the Middle Belt and an affirmation of the Middle Belt's alterity in the *Infakul Maisuri*. The travel journal of Hugh Clapperton, the first British traveler to visit the caliph in Sokoto, corroborates Mohammed Bello's imperial vision.[29] It also shows that Bello's claims, later repeated to Clapperton by other caliphate interlocutors, might not have been an idle imperial fantasy but part of a strategic cartographic discursive exercise by Clapperton's aristocratic caliphate informants. Clapperton journeyed through the Sokoto Caliphate in the 1820s, reaching Sokoto in 1825 and befriending Sultan Bello, who had succeeded to the throne at the death of Othman bin Fodio in 1817. It was Clapperton who brought excerpts from the

Infakul Maisuri back to England in 1825.[30] Mohammed Bello was Clapperton's biggest source in his discussion of the non-caliphate world of the Middle Belt.[31] More importantly, most of Clapperton's maps of the caliphate and its Niger-Benue frontier, the first to be published in Britain, were either drawn for him by Mohammed Bello or given to him from Mohammed Bello's collection by a member of the sultan's household. Clapperton made the rest of the maps on the instructions of Mohammed Bello himself.[32]

The maps and their accompanying narratives reveal a strategic but ahistorical inclusion of the entire Niger-Benue zone in the sphere of influence and jurisdiction of the Sokoto Caliphate, and a simultaneous "othering" of the communities in that zone. The Niger River, for instance, is presented as the "largest river in all of the territories of the Houssa [Hausa]."[33] At the time of this declaration, several non-Hausa polities inhabited the banks of the Niger, and most of them had not yet encountered the caliphate. Beyond its reinforcement of the caliphate's self-constructed Hausa image, this narrative, and the cartographic imagination that it may have sought to establish, amounted to a textual annexation of vast, non-Muslim territories in the Niger-Benue region to the Sokoto Caliphate realm. How much of this cartographic annexation comes from Clapperton and how much from Mohammed Bello and his other caliphate informants is not clear, but they were both invested in the text, and its cooperative production illustrates the intersection of caliphate and early British texts in advancing the myth of prior caliphate imperial rule in the Middle Belt—in formulating the narrative of caliphate precolonial omnipotence and civilizational intervention and Middle Belt helplessness and inferiority.

The trajectory of knowledge transfer from the caliphate to the British in the early-nineteenth century seems fairly clear thus far as the caliphate's representation of both its values and those of the peoples in and around its frontiers became part of a growing corpus of British knowledge regarding Northern Nigeria. It is unlikely that the British view of the Middle Belt as a land of barbarians was shaped solely by Bello's characterization of non-Muslim peoples since the British had their own elaborate distinctions between the centralized Islamic caliphate and its non-Muslim, politically fragmented Others. What is clear is that there was a coincidental and instrumental convergence of Mohammed Bello's and British travelers' characterizations of the caliphate/Middle Belt dichotomy. The two narratives reinforced each other and sustained British and caliphal imperial imaginings of the Middle Belt and its peoples.

Much of Clapperton's materials made it to London after his death in 1827, delivered by Richard and John Lander, the next British travelers to travel to Sokoto to meet the caliph. Clapperton had left instructions before his death that Richard Lander, who was his servant, take possession of all his materials and deliver them to the Colonial Office, which sponsored the Sokoto expedition. The

Lander brothers would later depend on Clapperton's connections to the caliphate leadership for sustenance, logistical help, information, and investigative and cartographic guidance.[34]

By constructing the first known British map of the Sokoto Caliphate based on information provided to him by Mohammed Bello, Clapperton initiated the tradition of equating the Sokoto Caliphate and its frontiers with what he called "Houssa [Hausa] Territory."[35] This cartographic and descriptive convention seems to have impacted subsequent British travel writing on the caliphate as travelers relied on the pioneering work of Clapperton and the Lander brothers. The British were subtly investing the Middle Belt with a Hausa-emirate imaginary, connecting the Middle Belt to the caliphate as its culturally inferior subordinate. This comparative conflation carried immense political import. The reification of a growing notion of precolonial Hausa-Caliphate hegemony was important for the subsequent prevalence of Hausa as a viable sociolinguistic category of colonial rule in Northern Nigeria.

Future British travelers relied on earlier depictions and accounts of the Sokoto Caliphate's symbolic and physical relationships with the Middle Belt to reinforce impressions of Hausa-caliphate primacy. An accumulated body of British-produced knowledge emerged from a succession of European explorers who traversed the Benue Valley, the Jos Plateau, the hills of Southern Kaduna, and the Adamawa hinterland. The pronouncements of these explorer-travelers reinforced initial British insights into the sociological makeup of Northern Nigeria. The travelers either submitted their findings to the Colonial Office or published them in Britain, sometimes doing both.

The most well known of these explorers was Dr. William Baikie, whose observations about the people of the Middle Belt often bordered on racist contempt. In 1854, he described the Tiv ethnic group who, along with the Idoma, Bassa, Jukun, Igala, and other groups, occupied the lower Benue Valley, as an "unfortunate tribe [whose] being against everyone, and everyone against it, has rendered it extremely suspicious of any visitors, their crude minds being unable to comprehend anything beyond war and raping. . . . The Mitshis as far as we could judge, are wilder and less intelligent than any of the African races with whom we had intercourse except Baibai and Djukuns."[36] Baikie's words represent the articulation, however crudely, of a certain negative perception of the peoples of the Benue Valley and Niger-Benue confluence region in general, with a particular focus on the Tiv. The evolutionary insinuations in Baikie's description of the Tiv, the Middle Belt's largest ethnic group and the largest non-Hausa ethnic group in Northern Nigeria, are symptomatic of a larger perception in which people outside the Hausa zone were labeled as definitive "Others." Baikie's representational universe and his allusions must be understood as part of a subtle process of inscribing the Sokoto Caliphate's geographical and sociological space as the administrative core of Northern Nigeria. This characterization could emerge convincingly only through the simultaneous and contrapuntal characterization of its assumed periphery—the Middle Belt.

Baikie's use of the derogatory Hausa epithet *mitshis* to describe the Tiv as a people conveys his immersion in the Hausa world of the caliphate and his fondness for the caliphate's narratives on the peoples of the Middle Belt. It is possible that in the mid-nineteenth century, when most ethnic groups were named by their more powerful neighbors or by regional hegemons, Baikie was using mitshis, a corruption of the Hausa epithet *munci,* as a purely descriptive term. It is therefore possible that his use of the term is not implicated in the demeaning associations inherent in the Hausa term "munci" or "munchi." Baikie's affirmative amplification of the meanings associated with the Hausa/Fulani name for the Tiv, however, reads like a conscious effort to flesh out and give evidentiary credence to what was essentially a nomenclature connoting aggression, cattle-snatching, and xenophobia.[37] Baikie's detailed description of the Tiv as a "wild," uncivilized, and unintelligent people definitively rules out the possibility that he was a neutral repeater of an existing cliché. The uncanny congruence between his descriptions and the anecdotal associations surrounding the Hausa word "munchi" is too carefully constructed to be a mere rhetorical coincidence.

The preoccupation of Dr. Baikie's narrative with comparison and deviation should inform any critical understanding of his and other British explorers' thinking. This cultural narrative served to erect a hierarchy of evolutionary maturity (or lack thereof) and operated on two levels; it utilized both absence and presence. First, by casting the Tiv as the wildest and least intelligent of the peoples of Northern Nigeria, Baikie's observations indict the entire non-caliphate sector of the region for a supposed racial and cultural inferiority, for the Tiv were the most populous of the Middle Belt peoples, a demographic representative sample, if you will. The fact that he singles out the Tiv perhaps indicates his desire to find a representative community for his idea of the non-caliphate as his itinerary took him through Middle Belt communities on the Benue River. His specific reference to the Tiv does little to diminish the larger indictment handed to the Middle Belt. Second, Dr. Baikie's absent referent in this elaborate collage of cultural backwardness is clearly the Sokoto Caliphate, described by most nineteenth-century British explorers as the exemplary cultural and political metropole of Northern Nigeria.

In its multiple connotations, the caliphate represented the unspoken paradigmatic cultural formation in the evolutionary hierarchy that was slowly emerging through British pronouncements and writings about the Northern Nigerian area. These ideas presented civilization, as far as its possibility in Northern Nigeria was concerned, as being synonymous with Hausa acculturation. The Sokoto Caliphate occupied the upper perch of an emerging sociopolitical evolutionary ladder, with the Tiv and other non-Muslim groups in the Middle at the bottom.

Baikie would go on, years later, to prove himself a fanatical believer in the Hausa-Fulani as potential colonizing allies of the British, issuing a high-profile recommendation to British explorers and colonialists in Northern Nigeria. Testifying before the House of Commons in 1863 after he returned from his expedition to the Benue and Niger Rivers and after the publication of his narrative of the expedition, Baikie constructed a set of sixteen "rules for dealing with the Natives along the River Niger," among which was this poignant advice: "Never give any countenance to any form of heathen worship. The African is not like the Hindu. . . . If obliged, always give preference to a Mohammedan, as the worshipper of God, to an idolater."[38] Baikie's submissions continued to influence and shape British attitudes toward the caliphate and the Middle Belt zones of Northern Nigeria for decades. Once the attitudinal template was established, subsequent British explorers, traders, soldiers, and colonialists recycled it uncritically as a compass for honing their own attitudes and policies toward the "pagan" peoples of the Middle Belt.

The British cherished the monotheistic civilizational affinity they shared with the caliphate zone and its Hausa-Fulani (and Hausaized Nupe) peoples. They also treasured the political tradition of the caliphate, seeing in it an administrative asset. Again, Baikie set the tone for this paradigmatic British thinking on the utility of an Anglo-caliphate alliance: "I believe that for the promotion of commerce and of civilization . . . it is essential to cultivate the friendship of the Pulo [Fulani] nation as being exceedingly powerful and influential, and therefore likely, under good management, to be useful [to us]."[39] Baikie went on to recommend the signing of a commercial treaty between Britain and the Sultan of Sokoto, arguing that, "such a step gained would be of infinite importance, and would greatly facilitate future progress."[40] The devaluation of the Middle Belt and the concomitant revaluation of the caliphate persisted through the nineteenth century, acquiring an administratively utilitarian character as the colonial project began to evolve in the first decade of the twentieth century. The discursive origins of these registers of colonial knowledge lay in narratives and texts produced in the context of several events and interactions.

There is no evidence that there was an ideological or programmatic conspiracy on the part of the nineteenth-century European explorers of Northern Nigeria with the expressed purpose of subordinating the Middle Belt to the caliphate. However, since explorers often organized their materials and their subjects within the context of the findings of preceding travelers, Baikie's ethnic and cultural categories, and the ways in which they foreground a preexisting European perception of Northern Nigerian historical sociology, are instructive guides to the subsequent development of ideas about caliphal cultural and political preeminence and Middle Belt inferiority.

Before Baikie, both Hugh Clapperton and Heinrich Barth crisscrossed the Sokoto Caliphate, in the early- and mid-nineteenth century respectively. The former visited both Kano and Sokoto, the headquarters of the caliphate.[41] The latter traversed Bornu, Kano, Zaria, Katsina, and parts of Bauchi.[42] Richard and John Lander also undertook a quest to "find" the "mouth of the Niger River" in 1828–29, a mission designed to fulfill the dreams of Richard Lander's mentor, Hugh Clapperton, who died near Sokoto in 1827 on his way to "discover" the source of the Niger.[43] Other European explorers and sponsored adventurers traversed the Sokoto Caliphate in the early- to mid-nineteenth century. The journals of these European travelers are valued as much for what they do not reveal as for what they do. The marginal presence of, and the devaluation of the non-caliphate world of, *dar-al-harb* (the abode of war) in the narrative of these travelers constitute the genealogical foundation of the discourses of Baikie and other explorers of the precolonial Middle Belt region. In these narratives the "pagan" communities of the Middle Belt only make occasional appearances as centers for slave raiding by powerful Muslim emirates presiding over the *dar-al-Islam* (abode of Islam).

A notion of the Middle Belt's peoples' inferiority vis-à-vis the caliphate began to take shape under the weight of these representations, which were influential in Britain as anthropological references on Nigeria. Over time, and along with new administrative exigencies, they helped to produce the doctrine of Middle Belt cultural and political backwardness. This doctrine then crystallized into a foundational creed of British commentary on Northern Nigeria. As E. P. T. Crampton puts it, "there was a general belief [in colonial circles] that pagans [Middle Belters] were of inferior stock."[44] Such is the subordination of the Middle Belt to the Hausa-Fulani caliphate cultural zone in colonial discourse that some scholars believe that British colonialism and indirect rule helped "institutionalize" a belief in the structural inferiority of non-Muslim peoples of the Middle Belt.[45]

By the time of the British conquest (1900–1905), multiple social, political, and cultural patterns were either in the process of coalescing or were in inchoate formation, and resistance to caliphate incursions was intensifying in some corridors even while it abated in others because an uneasy but acceptable stalemate had taken shape. These conditions, complicated as they were, challenged the body of neat assumptions and beliefs developed in British travelers' writings about the caliphate and the Middle Belt. It is not clear if the British understood the troubled precolonial status and semiotic resonances of Hausa as a sociopolitical category in the non-Muslim sector of Northern Nigeria. If they did, it did not stop them from crafting a colonial policy that elevated the emirate system of administration and social organization and encouraged its spread to a suspicious and resistant Middle Belt.

When Frederick Lugard declared the Protectorate of Northern Nigeria on New Year's Day 1900, the associational qualities of Hausa had been fairly settled and widely disseminated throughout the caliphate.[46] In the caliphate, Hausa functioned as an idiom of unity for a multilingual religious community. Outside the caliphate in the Middle Belt, the Hausa language was welcomed and adopted by many for its communicative utility and for the commercial access it facilitated to a vast transregional world of exchange.[47] The religious associations of Hausa identity were, however, widely rejected in the Middle Belt, as the debate over the adoption of the Hausa language as bureaucratic lingua franca in colonial Northern Nigeria illustrates.[48]

The adoption of the Hausa language as a colonial administrative lingua franca in Northern Nigeria produced only limited and short-lived backlash among Middle Belt peoples. This was because, except in the non-Hausa-speaking Benue Valley, Igalaland, Ebiraland, and the Okun Yoruba and Ilorin regions, Hausa was already fairly defused in the Middle Belt through the activities of Hausa traders and through caliphate raids, expansion, and outpost garrisoning. Still, the records of the debate on adopting Hausa as the language of colonial administration reveal colonial attitudes and assumptions that subtly referenced the nonlinguistic connotations of the Hausa category and its assumed Other: Middle Belt identity. These factors were refracted through existing and evolving conceptions of the Middle Belt and the caliphate in the British colonial imagination.

Colonial Doctrine and Hausa-Fulani Subcolonialism

Frederick Lugard's *The Dual Mandate in British Tropical Africa* is regarded as the canonical manual of British colonial administrative practice in Africa. Because of his two terms of service in Northern Nigeria, the empirical examples and references that inform the text are drawn directly from the protectorate. For these reasons, *The Dual Mandate* represents the clearest articulation of how the British imagined and understood the political traditions of the Middle Belt as well as the Fulani oligarchy of the caliphate zone. A critical reading of this text can illuminate some of the conceptual foundations of Hausa-Fulani subcolonial rule in the Middle Belt.

The linchpins of British indirect colonial rule, as outlined by Lugard, were "continuity" and "decentralization." Lugard argued that these were the cardinal principles that guided administrative policy in Northern Nigeria and that these remained constant even though the "customs, traditions, and prejudices of each unit" necessitated different modes of applying the core principles. For the zone of the "conservative Moslem[s]" and the "primitive pagan[s]" as Lugard delineated them, the goal was theoretically the same: to instill British-borne civilization in Africans by meshing their preexisting institutions and ways of life with the markers and benefits of British colonial modernity.[49] Lugard invoked British experiences in India to anchor a critique of administrative practices that privileged "the narrowest of oligarchies" that were "unrepresentative of" those they presided over on behalf of British colonialism. The colonial virtue of a "native ruler," argued Lugard, was that, unlike an "alien usurper," he was inured from xenophobic demagoguery that may result from a "crisis of legitimacy."[50] Lugard's critique lacked self-reflexivity, however, as it could just as easily have been directed at his own emerging administrative policy in the Middle Belt, which was also plagued by "a crisis of legitimacy" and the dangers of "alien usurpation."

The main problem with Lugard's seemingly progressive but hypocritical conception of British rule in the Middle Belt was its theoretical simplicity and its idealistic dislocation from actual British administrative practice. British administrative practice in the Middle Belt belied the principles espoused in Lugard's framework partly because his conception was fraught with internal contradictions. Lugard harped on the instrumental utility of legitimacy and colonially circumscribed self-determination for ethnic groups, but, beginning in the early days of colonial rule, actual administrative practices in the Nigerian Middle Belt undermined these principles. Lugard failed to consult his own prescribed principles in carrying out administrative reforms or made elastic exceptions to his own administrative recommendations.

Lugard wrestled with the problematic simplicity of his pronounced ideals and came to recognize the pragmatic necessity of utilizing "alien usurpers" and nonindigenous African subcolonial agents, in this case, the Hausa-Fulani. He admitted that empowering the Hausa-Fulani over the peoples of the Middle Belt amounted to "supporting an alien caste—albeit closer and more akin to the native races than a European can be," and that it would "deny self-government to the people [of the Middle Belt districts] over whom they rule."[51] But in the same breath, Lugard argued that the Fulani, whom "we consider . . . an alien race," were "more capable of rule than the indigenous [Middle Belt] races." The dilemma that Lugard unwittingly broached here continued to plague British colonial policymakers and administrators in Northern Nigeria for the next few decades.

The problem was that the British began their administrative adventure on a premise derived from a functionalist version of the so-called Hamitic Hypothesis, in which the Hausaized Fulani oligarchy of Northern Nigeria was understood as an alien racial category and as the prior vanguard of a civilizing Islamic modernity among the non-Muslim groups of the region.[52] Properly speaking, the Fulani were mostly a hybrid group, not only in Hausaland but also elsewhere in West Africa, where ethnic mixing and linguistic and cultural exchanges resulted in what Jean-Loup Amselle calls "originary syncretism."[53] Elsewhere, in Zanzibar, British narratives cast the hybrid Swahili derogatorily as a mongrel category of difference that threatened to blur the cultural distinctions at the heart of colonial rule.[54] Although the Zanzibari Swahili's hybrid identity attracted British scorn and offended colonial obsessions with the fixity of racial and cultural boundaries, Swahili personnel came to be valued as partners and trusted go-betweens in the colonization of the communities of the Zanzibari littoral. In Northern Nigeria, British officials rarely acknowledged, let alone characterized, the hybridity of the Fulani. Instead British colonial discourse represented them as a pure, clearly demarcated ethno-racial community, separate from and dominant over the Hausa, and the non-Muslim groups. The Fulani, according to this colonial narrative, conquered and civilized the Hausa and, together with their new Hausa kinsmen, conquered and dominated the non-Muslim Middle Belt peoples.

The Fulani were the architects of the valorized caliphate. Acknowledging the transformation of Fulani identity into a hybrid Hausa-Fulani formation, and admitting the role of genetic mixture and intermarriage in the constitution of Northern Nigerian Fulani identity, would have stood in the way of lionizing the Fulani as a martial "alien" race socialized to rule and civilize less-endowed autochthons. British officials understood the Fulani to be of North African and Middle Eastern descent. In the popular mythology of British travelers and colonial ethnographers, the Fulani were racial superiors of negroid autochthons, an "alien race of conquerors" that possessed an enlightened governing instinct and was thus deserving of high British patronage.[55]

Much as Lugard developed the ideals of indirect rule, he could not throw off the yoke of learned prejudice and approach Northern Nigeria with an open mind. The weight of inherited racialization of differences among non-Western peoples constrained his administrative prescriptions. In this racial-evolutionary system, exposure to Islam and Middle Eastern civilization ranked one closer to the paradigmatic European racial ideal of social Darwinist postulations. The narratives of European travelers and British colonial officials bear out this entrenched bias for colonized peoples with monotheistic traditions (like the Fulani) and their concomitant disdain for peoples without them (like the peoples of the Middle Belt). Colonial practice in the Middle Belt was constrained by these existing standards of colonial thinking and by the prior experiences of British administrative use of "martial races" in India.

For Lugard and his peers in the Northern Nigerian British bureaucracy, Hausa-Fulani Muslim culture was inherently superior to the cultures of the peoples of the Middle Belt, the supreme mediator of this difference being Islam. Lugard contended that the non-Muslim polities "have not produced so definitive a code of law, or such advanced methods of dispensing justice, as the Koran has introduced, and they lack the indigenous educational advantages which the use of Arabic and religious schools have conferred on the Moslem."[56] The policy-relevant gist of Lugard's contention was that the Muslim emirates were more prepared for indirect rule than the non-Muslim groups. Speaking strictly in bureaucratic terms, this was perhaps true for the Middle Belt, since the region was home to many ethnic groups whose political traditions led to decentralized, fragmented leadership.

The problem with Lugard's claim, however, is twofold. First, there were several kingdoms and political systems in the non-Muslim Middle Belt with centralized bureaucracies in the mold of the caliphate, but the British considered their bureaucracies inferior to the emirates'. Second, Lugard himself attributes the possession of political traditions compatible with indirect rule to the influence of Islam: "Comparatively little difficulty, it may be said, would be experienced in the application of such a system [indirect rule] to Moslem states."[57] For Lugard, "profess[ing] the standards of Islam" was the difference between polities that deserved colonial self-determination or colonial self-rule and those that did not and were thus unready for indirect rule. These texts of description and labeling produced the usable myth of the "foreign Fulani" and the "natives," which in turn became a staple of British colonial practice in Northern Nigeria.

For Lugard, the Hausa-Fulani's exposure to Islam and its principles constituted a civilizational substitute for British modernity, a tolerable alternative instrument for conveying the blessings of British rule and enlightenment to Northern Nigeria's benighted "natives." The political and social utility of the caliphate's Islamic tradition within the context of British colonialism was inherent in the religion itself because, like European Christianity, it espoused the superiority of monotheism over what the British understood as pagan pantheism. When British critics, mostly Christian missionaries such as Walter Miller, charged that Lugard's privileging of the Sokoto Caliphate in the colonial engagement with the Middle Belt amounted to a contradictory embrace of an inferior Islamic civilization and a failure to advance European-borne Christianity and its social benefits, Lugard's response was as honest as it was revealing. He stated in essence that the risk of "promoting" the spread of Islam to non-Muslim regions in Northern Nigeria paled in comparison to its pedagogical virtue of bestowing on "pagans" a developed, albeit inferior, tradition of monotheism.[58]

The British-aided advance of the caliphate's Islamic institutions and worldview was preferable, Lugard argued, to the danger of "pagan" backwardness, a state of being incompatible with indirect rule. Lugard affirmed that the institutions and governmental practices of British colonialism were "suitable to the Moslem communities," but he also argued that to impose such methods of colonial statecraft on "the conditions of primitive tribes would be to foist upon them a system foreign to their conceptions."[59] The trope of "pagan" Middle Belt unpreparedness for indirect rule became the overriding rationale for Hausa-Fulani subcolonialism. The logic of subcolonialism was that the more advanced, more indirect rule–ready Hausa-caliphate zone could help prepare the "primitive" institutions and societies of the Middle Belt for a full-fledged implementation of indirect rule.

Lugard's seemingly pragmatic administrative vision, along with his preference for the utilitarian elements of caliphate culture, was grounded in the brotherhood of monotheistic superiority. Understood by the British as a polytheistic and pantheistic tradition, Middle Belt traditionalism ("paganism" in British colonial taxonomy), along with the egalitarian political traditions that flowed from it, was a far greater threat to British colonial administrative visions than were the imperfections of caliphate political culture. This was the core of Lugard's justification for adopting caliphate traditions throughout Northern Nigeria. The Anglo-Hausa-Fulani partnership in the colonial administration of the Middle Belt was, for Lugard, a strategic alliance of two monotheistic cultures cooperating to bring civilization to the backward, "animist" peoples of the Middle Belt.

Muslim oligarchies, like the caliphate-affiliated Hausa-Fulani elites of the emirate system, were "aliens," in the racialized vocabulary of British colonial architects, but Lugard argued that "such races form an invaluable medium between the British and the native [Middle Belt] peasantry." He acknowledged the risk of Hausa-Fulani delegated colonial rule among non-Muslim peoples, conceding that, even though caliphate rule was administratively necessary, "by supporting [Fulani] rule we unavoidably encourage the spread of Islam." Even so, he argued that Fulani rule in the Middle Belt was not as novel as critics like Miller might assume. Fulani subcolonial rule was grounded in the principle of continuity, Lugard claimed, because it respected and formalized the Fulani's precolonial hegemony over the people of the Middle Belt.

Lugard agreed that such "alien" subcolonial rule violated the principle of legitimacy and self-determination at the heart of indirect rule, and counseled that only non-Muslim polities subjected to the caliphate's precolonial hegemony be subjected to their rule now. The power of the Hausa-Fulani oligarchs should "not be reestablished over tribes which had made good their independence, or imposed upon those who had successfully resisted [caliphate] domination," suggested Lugard.[60] This mitigating caveat struggled to find expression in practice as British colonial officials prioritized administrative expedience over doctrinal finesse in their extension of the infrastructure of Hausa-Fulani rule to the Middle Belt.

If actual administrative decisions in the Middle Belt grass roots reduced the mantra of legitimacy and self-determination to empty proclamations, the Lugardian foundational concept of decentralization was given only a geographically relative relevance. In the Muslim provinces of colonial Northern Nigeria, decentralization was an imperative of British colonial administrative reform. The template for achieving this was already present in the form of caliphal titular arrangements and their correspondence to administrative hierarchies and divisions of political labor. In the Middle Belt, British administrative policy departed sharply from decentralization, moving instead in the direction of centralization. In the provinces and divisions of the Middle Belt, the centralizing impulse of British policy wrought violence not just on the preexisting decentralized political arrangements that were considered unsuitable to indirect rule but also on the ideals of self-determination, continuity, and legitimacy that Lugard's canonical

text advanced. Once embraced, British-caliphate colonial administrative partnership in the Middle Belt acquired its own functional logic, trumping earlier
articulated logics of education, preparation, and tutelage.

Centralizing political reforms in the Middle Belt found legitimacy in a widely held notion that it was almost impossible to construct indirect rule around the
decentralized political institutions of Middle Belt peoples. Lugard had made the
case for many colonial officials when he argued that imposing indirect rule on
Middle Belt communities would amount to saddling them with a "foreign" system for which they were not prepared.[61] In the colonial districts and provinces of
the Middle Belt, supervising colonial officials tended to interpret this in absolute
terms, in ways that foreclosed on the possibility of customizing indirect rule to
the political peculiarities of Middle Belt communities. In the end, the Middle
Belt colonial landscape became one huge theater of administrative improvisations with a consistent overlay of emirate-inspired thinking, emirate personnel,
and emirate institutions. Although Lugard stated that embryonic colonial administrative institutions in the Middle Belt need not "follow the model adopted
for the Moslem communities," the point of reference and the ideological subtext
of colonial administrative reform in the Middle Belt remained the supposed inherent superiority of caliphate culture and institutions.[62]

Lugards's framework for dealing with the peoples of the Middle Belt was
fraught with imprecision and confusion. He posited that "it is of the first importance that the chiefs should be elected by the community from among themselves,"
and should neither be "middlemen traders selected for their wealth nor [Hausa-
Fulani] Moslems."[63] This was categorical in its denunciation of the imposition of
Hausa-Fulani chiefs on Middle Belt peoples. Yet he endorsed the subordination of
"pagan" chiefs to the civilizing administrative sagacity of Muslim Hausa-Fulani
chiefs. In justifying this contradictory prescription, Lugard highlighted the lamido
of Adamawa's attitude toward his non-Muslim colonial sphere of delegated influence as a model of what he envisioned as a layered hierarchy of colonial rule in the
Middle Belt, where the British ruled through Hausa-Fulani colonial agents who in
turn relied on chiefs they appointed among the non-Muslim people. The lamido's
framework for the subcolonial rule of caliphate agents is clearly expressed in the
following words: "If they think you are trying to make them Fulani or Moslems
they resent it. I would not put a Fulani headman to live in their country, but he
should constantly tour amongst them, and advise the pagan chief, and tell all the
people that they may appeal to him, but he should not go behind his back."[64]

The sophistication of the lamido's subcolonial vision and the way in which
it mirrored British colonial doctrines registered on Lugard. He recognized the
outlines of British colonial ideals in the lamido's words, but the obvious ways in
which the emir's articulation embodied a parallel, if subordinate, colonial system within the overarching apparatus of British colonialism and the irony of

this revealing set of statements did not seem to have troubled Lugard. What is clear from the way that Lugard venerated this template of subcolonialism is that the British were comfortable, in spite of Lugard's occasional disapproval, with the delegated subcolonial hegemony of Hausa-Fulani chiefs and colonial agents among Middle Belt peoples and saw them as invaluable quotidian civilizers. The lamido put it succinctly in the following words: "as the British govern us through ourselves, so we must govern the pagans through their own chiefs."[65] The British and their caliphate partners understood the partnership and the complementary roles they played in "civilizing" the peoples of the Middle Belt. The lamido's articulation of how caliphate subcolonialism should function among the Middle Belt peoples held a particular allure for Lugard, particularly the condescending paternalism in that articulation.

The Convoluted Trajectory of a Governing Ideology

In the immediate aftermath of the colonial conquest several British officials simply defaulted to the established views bequeathed by earlier European groups about the superior cultural and political disposition of the Hausa-Fulani members and descendants of the caliphate. But the process of formally broaching Hausa-Fulani subcolonial rule as a possibility for how the British would control the diverse population of the Middle Belt was not so straightforward and defied the logic of received pro-caliphate wisdom. This is partly because the generic British obsession with finding and deploying "ruling races" caused some officials to occasionally flirt with possibilities outside the Hausa-Fulani system.

It is worth noting that the Hausa-caliphate sociopolitical tradition was not the only system that the British admired in Northern Nigeria. There was for a time what one could call a Jukun imaginary in the colonial officialdom. It was founded on the ancient Jukun (Kwararafa) kingdom, which, in its heyday in the sixteenth and seventeenth centuries conquered territory as far as Kano on the edge of the Sahel. The British fascination with the Jukun imperial system lasted into the 1930s and spawned several quasi-ethnological and historical writings by British colonial officials and their underlings, the most notable of which is *A Sudanese Kingdom,* written by Charles K. Meek, the official anthropologist of colonial Northern Nigeria.[66] In the final analysis, however, as Margery Perham, a major actor in the Northern Nigerian colonial scene, noted, the attitude of the British toward Jukun was largely one of "mournful fascination in studying this relic of an empire."[67] Although the Northern Nigerian colonial bureaucracy toyed with the idea of reviving the "imperial technique" of the Jukun, "the hope was not fulfilled" because the Jukun system did not offer an administrative model "except that of decay."[68]

While the Jukun imperial tradition fell out of consideration quickly, Hausa was not selected for a functional role in British colonialism a priori or automatically. The British embrace of the Hausa-caliphate system was the product of a convenient confluence of administrative expediency and prior selective knowledge of the caliphate's sociopolitical system. Simply put, at the time of the British conquest, the caliphate, unlike other political formations, had discernible, living traditions that could be mobilized for use in colonial administration.

Broaching Subcolonialism

In 1902, before the conquest of Sokoto, the caliphate's headquarters, Commander Frederick Lugard of the British conquering force and the future governor of Northern Nigeria and governor-general of Nigeria, signaled that the British regarded the Hausa-Fulani Islamic political institutions of the caliphate as the administrative model for all of Northern Nigeria:

> The future of . . . this Protectorate lies largely in the regeneration of the Fulani. Their ceremonial, their coloured skins, their mode of life, and habits of thought appeal more to the native population than the prosaic business-like habits of the Anglo-Saxon can ever do . . . nor have we the means at present to administer so vast a country. This then is the policy to which in my view the administration of Northern Nigeria should give effect: viz to regenerate this capable race . . . so that . . . they become worthy instruments of rule.[69]

Lugard was enunciating the standard British justification for the British adoption of the Hausa-caliphate model of colonial administration, which rested on the logic of cultural superiority and logistical expediency.

Flora Shaw, Lugard's wife and a major contributor to early colonial policy, saw the Fulani as an "aristocratic," race. They were "European in form," had Arab blood, which "penetrated as far as climate could allow," and were of "races . . . higher than the negroid type." Most importantly, they were a conquering and ruling race that occupied their present location in the Central Sudan by "driv[ing the original inhabitants] Southwards". into areas that the "higher type could not live."[70] This fundamental misunderstanding of precolonial political realities in the Northern Nigerian area continued to thrive and in part constituted the early assumption that Fulani migrants and conquerors, by whatever means, had defeated and colonized the peoples of the Middle Belt and had established an undisputed regional political hegemony. This would come to influence future British administrative policies in Northern Nigeria. These policies understandably treated the disparate communities of the Middle Belt uniformly as precolonial vassals of the caliphate. Lady Lugard believed that the Fulani were destined to rule over the peoples of the Middle Belt. She said of the Fulani: "The ruling classes [of the Fulani] are deserving in every way of the name of cultivated Gentlemen, We seem to be in the presence of one of the fundamental facts of history, that there are races which are born to conquer and others to persist under conquest."[71]

Once the concept of Fulani-caliphate political primacy was established, the formulation of colonial policies around it took its course, and the new policy subjected the Middle Belt to the ensuing administrative paradigm. The Middle Belt's status as a periphery had to be formulated with clarity, so that "civilizing" and preparing its peoples for indirect rule through the infusion of caliphate-emirate symbols and agents would be possible and appear legitimate. Colonial ideologues were not simply obsessed with establishing a hierarchy of superior and inferior Africans. Colonial writers such as Lugard and C. L. Temple, whose *Native Races and Their Rulers* was an influential intellectual foundation for the notion of Hausa-Fulani superiority, explored ethnic and "racial" differences among Northern Nigerian colonial subjects. They further enunciated existing Hamitic theories of origin and social evolution to distinguish preferred "martial races," a process mediated by the racial taxonomies of British society.[72]

Colonial ideologues were also concerned with "discovering the nature of the 'native races' so that the most appropriate long-term colonial administration could be constructed for them."[73] The formulation of a Hausa-caliphate imaginary in the Northern Nigerian colonial officialdom thus had a utilitarian end to it—what Zachernuk calls a "balance of interests."[74] It was, properly speaking, the formulation of a governing ideology of colonial rule.

In the convoluted emergence of Hausa-Fulani identity as a generic expression of caliphate ideals and culture, the supreme operative idiom was religious change. Although the sociological sketches of Hausa-Fulani identity already existed, facilitated by intermarriage and increased cultural fusion between the Hausa of Northwestern Nigeria and immigrant Fulani communities, religious transformation via the Fulani jihad of 1804–1808 catalyzed the emergence of that identity as one marked primarily by adherence to Islam. An analysis of the emergence of Hausa-Fulani identity as a repository of a corpus of religious, social, and economic values is crucial to any understanding of the variety of ideas, mannerisms, occupations, cultural expressions, and forms of religious piety that came to gradually define what it means to be Hausa and the recipient of caliphate Hausa-Fulani identity.

The caliphate institutions, identities, ideas, and claims that the British encountered and enlisted in ruling the peoples of the Middle Belt were a culmination of a long process of identity formation. British narratives on the caliphate and its usable political attributes elided the ways in which, even at the time of the conquest, Hausa-Fulani identity was far from settled, being made and remade as the Islamic realm expanded and as Fulani and Hausa migrants flocked to areas outside the ethnic Hausa zone. Even though the jihadist introduction of orthodox Islam as the supreme mediator of Hausa identity clarified the lines between those who were Hausa-Fulani and those who were not, the identity remained porous and negotiable as long as the primary criterion of Islamic piety was met. In a sense then, the British development of a Hausa-caliphate colonial governing imaginary helped to further crystallize an emergent but unsettled system of inclusion and exclusion—to consolidate and politicize an emerging identity. The British helped to construct a new set of associations and connotations around Hausa-Fulani identity. Some of these new constructions were based, however loosely, on preexisting idioms of Hausaness, but others emerged in a new confluence of strategic British and caliphate claims.

Of vital importance are the ways in which the ethnographic and exploratory texts of early colonial administrations, Frederick Lugard's canonical *Dual Mandate,* and caliphate texts meshed in philosophy and purpose to create the mutually reinforcing myths of caliphal civilizational superiority and Middle Belt political and cultural backwardness. The gradual coming together of British and caliphal narratives supplied the intellectual justification for Hausa-Fulani subcolonial rule. Colonial and caliphate texts called into being a caliphate possessing the political and social institutions the British deemed prerequisites for indirect rule and foreshadowed a preliminary colonial administrative project entrusted to Hausa-Fulani subcolonial officials, who would prepare the peoples and institutions of the Middle Belt for emirate-type indirect rule.

2 Zazzau and Southern Kaduna in Precolonial and Colonial Times

COLONIAL REMODELING OF the Southern Kaduna geopolitical area along caliphate emirate lines was authorized by the logic of uniform, cheap, and expedient administration. The legitimacy of this project relied on two other interrelated phenomena. One was a pattern of precolonial caliphate imperial practice that incorporated the non-Muslim peoples and polities of Southern Kaduna into varying levels of proto-imperial subordination. The second was the expanded and administratively instrumental interpretation of that precolonial relationship by the British to produce an elaborate system of proxy colonial rule that empowered Hausa-Fulani agents over non-Muslim autochthonous subalterns.

Through a long, convoluted process, Zazzau emirate, a strategic frontier caliphate state, came to extend a loose political influence to the non-Muslim Southern Kaduna polities. In the early-twentieth century, the British accelerated this historical process. They vested authority in Zazzau, its satellite emirates, and its officials and brought the Southern Kaduna peoples under their sway. British imposition of Zazzau subcolonial rule on the Southern Kaduna peoples culminated in a complicated and volatile subcolonial administrative system comprised of Hausa-Fulani colonial chiefs, scribes, administrators, tax collectors, and other colonial operatives working for the British. The unfolding of this subcolonial system, with its shifting contours, generated backlash and conflicts, but the discernible outlines of Zazzau's precolonial imperial adventures in the Southern Kaduna area and their enduring legacies signposted these later colonial troubles and made the contentions more rancorous. Zazzau's precolonial imperialism in the Southern Kaduna area was always precarious, but in the late nineteenth century it began to unravel visibly. This unraveling needs to be accounted for as a backdrop to the volatile subcolonial system that followed after the British conquest.

Precolonial slave raiding and warfare were expensive, and repeated raids yielded diminished returns. The familiarity and predictability of Zazzau-caliphate aggression toughened resistance among the Southern Kaduna communities and caused many of them to adopt creative strategies that effectively repelled the invaders. These realities compelled Zazzau imperial agents and mavericks to seek pragmatic accommodations with Southern Kaduna communities, producing a confusing and fragile political stalemate that lasted until the British conquest in the first decade of the twentieth century.

This fluid caliphate hegemony found its way into the heart of British colonial administrative practice in Southern Kaduna, and authorized multiple layers of Hausa-Fulani colonials to exercise authority over the peoples of Southern Kaduna. With British support, the subcolonial rule of Zazzau's appointees in the Southern Kaduna heartland was as elaborate as it was effective in extracting the material and symbolic obligations that British colonizers desired from the many non-Muslim ethnic communities of Southern Kaduna. This subcolonial rule went through several phases and was challenged at many junctures, but it endured and became fairly well entrenched as Hausa-Fulani officials consolidated their powers and ingratiated themselves with their British supervisors. The protests and anti-caliphate agitation of Southern Kaduna communities intensified in correspondence to the expansion and consolidation of emirate subcolonial rule. This escalating oppositional agitation in response to the expanding subcolonial rule of Zazzau political operatives culminated in a series of violent confrontations.

Zazzau and Southern Kaduna before the Caliphate

Precolonial caliphate imperialism was real both in its physicality and in its discourses of imperial control. But it relied on pre-caliphate relations that placed the Islamic Hausa zone in a loose superintendent role over non-Hausa, non-Muslim Southern Kaduna polities. The case of the Katab people bears out these foundational pre-jihad political relations. In the eighteenth century, the Katab clans came under the loose suzerainty of the Kauru imperial garrison system. Kauru was ethnically and geographically an appendage of the mother kingdom of Zazzau, performing tribute and operating trade and military networks in the name of Zazzau's rulers. Kauru's control over the Katab in matters of trade and politics was thus technically sustained on behalf of Zazzau. Kauru proto-imperial activity, however, rarely depended on Zazzau's military or administrative infrastructure. Kauru's quasi-imperial projects preceded the state's formal integration into the Zazzau and caliphate systems in the first decade of the nineteenth century.[1]

Pre-caliphate Kauru imperialism fed on its own status as a commercial city-state that developed political muscle largely because the protection and expansion of its trading tentacles necessitated occasional use of force and political threats. The establishment of Zangon Katab, a Hausa trading settlement in the heart of Katab country, by the rulers of Kauru was a strong expression of the commercial character of the Kauru imperial system. From Zangon Katab (or Zangon Fatake) the Kauru rulers imposed and enforced tributes on the surrounding Katab clans. The enforcement of economic discipline and fiscal obligations required an administrative control that evolved over the course of the eighteenth century into a fairly centralized, formalized system of Kauru political supervision.[2] The logic of Kauru control in the Katab area, however, remained essentially commercial, an effort to ensure the safety of its commercial entanglements in the trans-Saharan

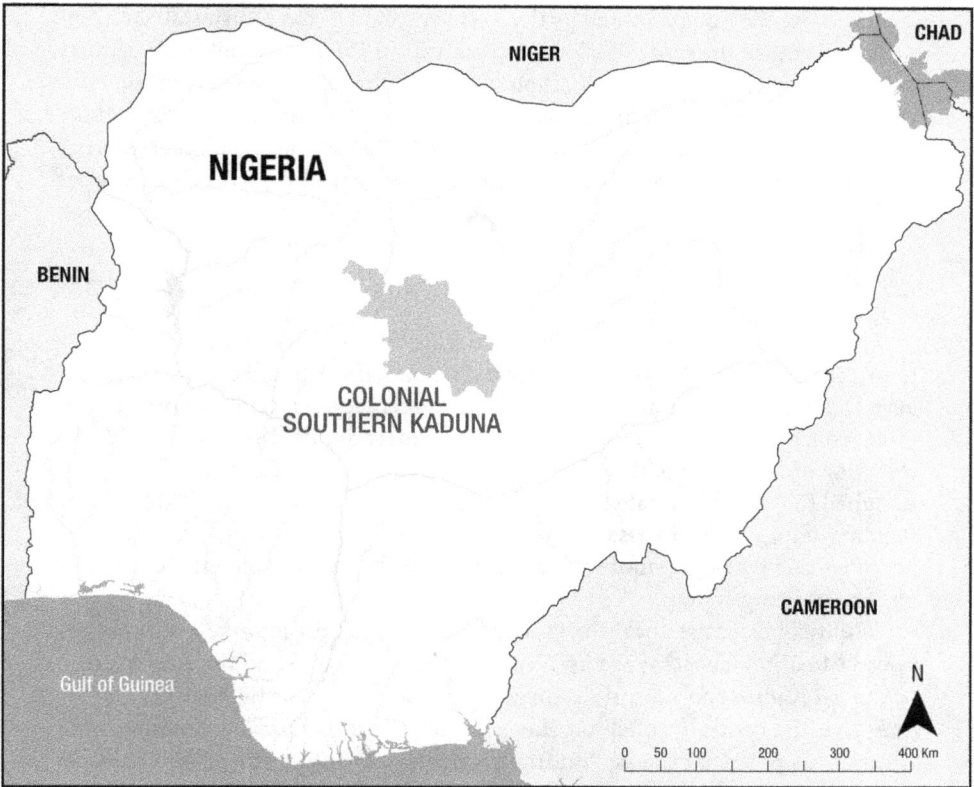

caravan trade, one route of which traversed Katab country.[3] Zangon Katab was part of an uncoordinated complex of many traveling Hausa traders, or *fatake,* settlements scattered across pre-jihad Northern Nigeria. Some of them were no more than campgrounds.[4] Others were larger, more developed settlements that transformed into permanent garrison towns over time. Late-nineteenth-century German traveler Paul Staudinger frames the socioeconomic scene of the fatake settlements of "traveling traders" thus: "Wherever. . . . [Hausa] peoples find a friendly reception and good quarters . . . there they remain for years and perhaps never return to their native city."[5]

The Kauru trading colony of Zangon Katab transitioned steadily to a political enterprise, with the Kauru rulers appointing Hausa village heads for the administrative villages that they "created" out of Katab clans. On the next tier down, Katab headmen were appointed to lead subclans. In this proto-imperial system, the logic of centralization, fiscal order, and political control struggled for supremacy over the preexisting modes of deregulated political and socioeconomic life among the Katab. Backed by the military might of the Kauru state, the outlines of a future imperial relationship emerged in the late-seventeenth century and early-eighteenth century. Without the official religious impetus of a caliphate mandate, however, Kauru imperialism remained localized, and relied more on cultivating Katab goodwill than on imposing a clear agenda. Since Kauru's investment in Zangon Katab was driven by commercial priorities, other areas of Southern Kaduna, outside the Kano-Ghonja trade route that passed through Zangon Katab, held no political appeal. Paramount to Kauru's imperial control was the commercial mastery of the route connecting northward to Kano and southward to Ghonja.

Kauru rulers did not explicitly require the Katab to assimilate into a Hausa political and economic system and were content with the policed normalcy that gave them commercial and quasi-political supremacy. The extension of Kauru sway over the Katab caused no profound socioeconomic distortion in the latter's way of life. The political reforms carried out by the Kauru overlords were designed to merely facilitate tribute, mediation, dispute resolution, and the rudimentary obligations of vassalage. The yoke of pre-jihad vassalage was relatively bearable, and was made more so by the mutually beneficial outcomes of a transnational trading system.

Political scientist Ibrahim James contends that precolonial relations between Muslim Hausa Zazzau and Kauru on the one hand and the non-Muslim Southern Kaduna communities on the other were marked by hostility. He argues that the centralized Hausa states treated the non-Hausa peoples on their frontiers as potential slaves, "raiding them at will."[6] The relationship between pre-jihad Zazzau and the multiple decentralized ethnic communities outside its southern borders involved slave raids and other disruptive attempts to impose Zazzau's will. Much of this, however, took the form of the familiar generic tussles between the domineering impulses of centralized states and the vulnerable but fanatically independent mindset of unprotected, "ungoverned" neighbors.[7] Moreover, the systematized oppression implied in James's postulation has little fidelity to the sporadically enforced military dominance of Zazzau-backed Kauru over the Katab. The emergence of the caliphate and of Zazzau as a frontier enforcer and expander of caliphate authority was the turning point in relations between the Muslim Hausa zone and the Southern Kaduna polities.

The success of the jihad in Zazzau and its environs changed the precolonial imperial landscape in Southern Kaduna. The new Islamo-imperial priorities of the jihad's leaders coursed through the relationship between the new caliphate zone and frontier non-Muslim communities like Southern Kaduna. The imperial discourses and practices that came out of the prescriptive canons of Othman bin Fodio, Mohammed Bello, and Abdullahi bin Fodio were mapped unto preexisting power relations between Hausa kingdoms such as Kauru and Zazzau and neighboring non-Muslim peoples.

Fulani Rule and Zazzau-Caliphate Imperialism

Zazzau was a major target of the Fulani jihad leadership. It was the gateway to the South, where many non-Muslim peoples resided. The jihad's declared central aim was the purification and deepening of institutional Islamic practice. But there was also a proselytizing impulse on its margins. Bin Fodio himself underscored this complementary goal of expanding the borders of the imagined and emerging dar-al-Islam (the land of Islam):

> The waging of Holy war (al-jihad) is obligatory by assent . . . and to make war upon the heathen king who will not say "There is no God but Allah" is obligatory by assent and that to take the government from him is obligatory by assent; and to make war upon the heathen king who does not say "There is no God but Allah" on account of the custom of his town (bi-Sababi 'urfi 'L-baladi) and who makes no profession of Islam is (also) obligatory by assent; and that to take the government from him is obligatory by assent.[8]

Bin Fodio was not speaking here to the immediate task of wresting political control from the Muslim Hausa dynasties of Hausaland, the heartland of the reform movement. He was instead advancing a religio-political mission that targeted the non-Muslim polities of Southern Kaduna and the larger Middle Belt and their political leaderships. To the immediate south of Zazzau, there was a cluster of non-Muslim, non-Hausa communities that, in the new caliphate political imperial discourse, needed to be integrated into the emerging caliphate system as converted Muslim members, tribute-paying vassals, or slave reservoirs. The Southern Kaduna ethnic polities were some of the first, geographically convenient targets of Zazzau's new mandate of caliphate control. They were on the frontlines of the expanding physical and ideological frontiers of the caliphate. They also represented a fertile mission field for Islamic proselytization as envisaged and outlined by bin Fodio's command.[9] More importantly, they held significant numbers of potential slaves.

The extension of the caliphate realm to Southern Kaduna wrought a paradigm shift on existing patterns of proto-imperial relations between the Hausa zone represented by Kauru and Zazzau and the Southern Kaduna communities. Even before the success of Malam Musa, the jihad flag bearer in the Zazzau sector, had been consolidated, Southern Kaduna peoples experienced the change that had occurred and felt the fangs of a new imperial system. Even as the new Fulani dynasty of Zazzau faced probing raids from the ousted Hausa ruler of Zazzau, who was operating from his new base of Abuja in non-Muslim Gbagyi country, the emirate began exerting its authority over the non-Muslim polities to its south.[10] Emirate infiltration in the Southern Kaduna country was swift. Slave raids became more frequent as Zazzau sought to build up its glories with slave labor and to participate in a new caliphate culture of patronage that was lubricated by slave transfers and tribute.

With the defeat of the Hausa dynasty of Zazzau by Malam Musa, the jihad's commander in that sector, the rulers of Kauru pledged their loyalty to the emirate's new Fulani rulers, and their state became a formal vassal. It acquired an official status as an outpost of caliphate power in an area teeming with peoples who were not yet familiar with the Islamic imperial ecumenism evolving around them—peoples who had been subordinated to the more inchoate, irreligious imperial control of Kauru. In the aftermath of the jihad, the Kauru imperial system, along with its vassals, such as Zangon Katab, Chawai, Dingi, Kuzamani, Rumaya, and Ruruma, were subsumed to varying degrees under Zazzau.[11] Zazzau became the most important political power in the immediate vicinity of the Southern Kaduna polities. In addition to perfecting and consolidating this position, Zazzau had more ambitious imperial calculations regarding its southern, non-Muslim neighbors. The consolidation of emirate outposts located in the lands of the non-Muslim peoples and the establishment and empowerment of new ones figured conspicuously in these calculations.

In addition to Kauru, the pre-jihad trading activities of Hausa commercial travelers/preachers and Fulani herders, martial mercenaries, and scholars had birthed a network of garrison settlements and trade towns in Southern Kaduna. These settlements and towns ringed the region in a pattern of immigrant settlements that constituted distinct socioeconomic and religious communities. Kauru itself had started life as such a settlement. Fulani Muslims and Hausa traders established settlements among the Southern Kaduna peoples from as early as the early-seventeenth century.[12] The Jama'a system, as some scholars have termed this pattern of Hausa-Fulani (and some Kanuri) immigrant settlement among the non-Muslim peoples of Southern Kaduna, was a layer of Hausa-Fulani cultural, economic presence in the Southern Kaduna. Kajuru, Kachia, Jema'an Dororo, Jere, Kagarko, Lere, and Zangon Katab were some of the prominent demographic and political strongholds of this presence.[13]

The enclosed settlements were self-contained towns tucked between surrounding hill and plain settlements of Southern Kaduna groups. Boosted by the jihad, the settlements grew throughout the first few decades of the nineteenth century. Since they were usually located along major or minor trade routes and thoroughfares, the lives of these settlements were animated by trade and by the political negotiations and actions required by high-stakes commerce. The outposts engaged in trade and strategic sociopolitical communion with their non-Muslim hosts. The cattle-herding Bororo Fulani exchanged cattle and dairy for the products of agriculture from the host communities.

The Hausa traders exchanged exotic products from Hausaland and beyond and from forest regions to the south for grains and other foodstuffs of the Southern Kaduna peoples. As caliphate military garrisons, the settlements also policed trade caravans and enforced the will of Zazzau and its vassals such as Kauru and Lere. These Hausa-Fulani immigrant enclaves were on the front lines of emirate relations with non-Muslim peoples on the caliphate's southern frontier. In pre-jihad times, the absence of a clearly articulated imperial vision minimized conflicts between the reclusive immigrants and their hosts, although the settlements were garrisoned for protection from raids by resentful locals and for the purpose of launching counterraids and engaging in proactive military action against perceived threats.

During the jihad, the Fulani Jama'a in particular had played the important role of incubators of reformist Islamic agitation; enthusiasts with knowledge of the terrain and peoples led minor jihads in their areas of abode. Relations between the indigenous peoples and the migrants alternated in the post-jihad period between sporadic conflicts and cattle raids and prolonged periods of mutual goodwill. On the whole, the jihad emboldened the Jama'a settlements and transformed some of them into competitors for local power, de facto vassals of Zazzau, and outright claimants to imperial legitimacy over the indigenous peoples of Southern Kaduna. It should be noted that not all Hausa settlers craved membership in the caliphate or subscribed to its notion of imperial Islamic citizenship, but recalcitrant Hausa settlements, the most prominent being Kajuru, which vehemently opposed the jihad, were defeated by Malam Musa's forces. Other Muslim mavericks, seeing what befell Kajuru, pledged allegiance to the new caliphate order.

Different arrangements of vassalage were worked out with several Jama'a towns, and they were in turn authorized to carry on diplomatic, military, and trading outreaches to the non-Muslim ethnicities of the Southern Kaduna area on behalf of Zazzau. Many of the Southern Kaduna groups subsequently came under the de facto influence of the caliphate system through these outposts of emirate political control. Actual on-ground political and economic relations varied from place to place and depended on the character and ambitions of each of Zazzau's sub-emirate outposts. But each walled immigrant town was a fortified stronghold that projected awe and diplomatic strength, while supporting, as needed, passive and active displays of power.

By the time the hostile negotiations and skirmishes of the minor jihads abated in about 1816, Southern Kaduna was enveloped by a new sociopolitical order of Zazzau's influence.[14] To survive, many Southern Kaduna peoples made peace—to different degrees of acquiescence and strategic engagement—with the reality of emirate-caliphate power. John Nengel's conceptualization of these variegated agreements as amana truces characterized by paternal, protective obligations by Zazzau and its vassals and by tribute-paying gestures of loyalty and nonviolence by non-Muslim polities may exaggerate the post-jihad rapprochement between Zazzau and its non-Muslim vassals, since conflicts and resistance marked the actual unfolding of these relations on the ground.[15] Nonetheless it points to the variety of strategies—outside the familiar military template—that the emirates and their non-Muslim interlocutors deployed to establish the political primacy of the emirate system without alienating those who were reluctant to assimilate into it.

Emirate military success brought immediate spoils from subdued and intimidated Southern Kaduna peoples. From the subdued, tribute flowed to Zaria. From the cowed but unconquered, slaves were extracted through raids.[16] Zazzau appointed or confirmed the position of *kofa* (intermediary) for each of the vassals. Zazzau intermediaries in Kauru and Lere directed slave raids and collected tributes from the Southern Kaduna polities in their vicinities on behalf of the emir of Zazzau. Certain flanks of Southern Kaduna came under the indirect control and influence of the southerly Zazzau vassal of Keffi. Particularly, the emirs of Keffi asserted the right of informal control over the Koro of Kagarko and began appointing both indigenous Muslim and Hausa-Fulani chiefs over them from the 1840s.[17] Founded by immigrants as a frontier trade town, Kajuru had a strategic location on the northern edge of the Southern Kaduna area that gave it a prominent role in the effort of Zazzau to police and politically supervise the Gbagyi, Adara, Ada, Bakulu, Angan, Bajju, Ham, and Koro peoples.[18]

In the Kauru-Katab axis, the Zazzau rulers appeared to have asserted a more direct control, delegating imperial authority over the non-Muslim peoples of that axis to one of its most senior titleholders, the *makama*. This prioritization of the Zangon Katab frontier seems to underscore its commercial and strategic importance to the emirate. The makama's representative personally accompanied the chief of Kauru "on his annual visits to Zangon Katab when tribute in the form of slaves was collected town by town."[19] Kauru also had the emirate's juridical mandate over the non-Muslim peoples of the southeastern axis: the Amap, Agbiri, Abisi, Atsam, and others. The frontier Fulani garrison settlement of Jema'an Dororo, for its part, received Zazzau's nod to establish a recognizable emirate imprint on the Fatsuam, Ninkyap, Bajju, Gwong, and others. The farming out of subimperial supervisory responsibilities aimed to achieve a neat territorial delineation. But there were overlaps between territorial spheres of authority, and some Southern Kaduna peoples found themselves struggling and negotiating terms with multiple claimants to Zazzau's subimperial supervisory jurisdiction. The Bajju, for instance, contended with multiple supervisions from the two prominent Zazzau surrogates of Kajuru and Jema'a, and it was not until 1870 that its imperial status was clarified when Jema'a sent a *jekada* (superintending political envoy) to watch over its affairs.[20]

Important as the commercial imperative was, Zazzau's precolonial imperial adventures were not solely dictated by the calculations of commerce. They were also propelled by a remarkably sophisticated political vision. This vision underpinned subimperial military pacification campaigns that resulted in incomplete conquests, partial "pacifications," and stalemates, which nonetheless conferred benefits on Zazzau in the form of tributes and extortions. The political institutions that had taken shape under pre-jihad Hausa dynasties were perfected and expanded by the legitimizing authority of the Maliki School of Islamic exegesis and jurisprudence adopted by Othman bin Fodio and other jihad leaders. The methodical political ordering embedded in the Islamic ideology of the caliphate system and the centralizing and governmental rationalities integral to the Zazzau system contrasted sharply with the free-spirited, unencumbered, and politically ad hoc life of Southern Kaduna peoples.

Zazzau's identity as a representative unit of the Sokoto Islamic Caliphate depended on both the preservation and transformation of its visible Other—the Southern Kaduna peoples spread along its vast frontier. Their minimal exposure to the political cultures of Islam—a product of their preferred insularity and the checkered fate of Islam in the pre-jihad Zazzau—made the Southern Kaduna peoples the target of centralizing political practices emanating from Zazzau. On the flipside, imperial control had to preserve their status as tribute-paying outsiders and not encourage their wholesale assimilation and conversion to the world of the caliphate. After the extension of Zazzau's power or the negotiation of truces that acknowledged it, the emirate's imperial practice shifted quickly from impulsive, punitive, and slave-generating raids to a deliberate project of political reengineering that sought to implant the political culture of centralized accountability and hierarchy in the clan-based, largely acephalous communities of the Southern Kaduna area.

Zazzau's Imperial Strategies

The architecture of Zazzau's imperial activities in the Southern Kaduna area consisted of new and altered political institutions. This framework of control was supported by symbolic and judicial arrangements designed to reinforce the sense of Zazzau's political control while fulfilling the material obligations of subordination. An example of such arrangement was the tradition of exporting Katab criminal offenders into slavery in Kauru and Zazzau.[21] Criminals were forcefully dispatched to Kauru to be enslaved in Zazzau's vast network of domestic and agricultural slavery. Since slave raids could be conducted only on "stubborn" ethnic groups who had refused to capitulate to emirate imperial demands—with understandably limited and progressively dwindling success—the punishment of serious crimes with enslavement achieved the dual goals of reinforcing a sense of imperial discipline and satisfying Zazzau's demands for slaves.[22]

Slave raids intensified in the first three decades of emirate overlordship on the Southern Kaduna plateau. The raids had two effects. First, they wore out the resistance of some of the Southern Kaduna groups, driving them into a nominal acknowledgment of Zazzau's authority and obligating them to pay the annual tributes of slaves, mats, and locust beans.[23] Second, for those determined to cling to their independence, the slave raids provided an impetus to migrate to higher grounds, to hill fortresses that were inaccessible to Zazzau's cavalry.[24] The Gwandara fled from the raids of Zazzau surrogate Jema'an Dororo into the Yeskwa Hills, intermarrying with the Yeskwa and the Koro and birthing a new hybrid ethnic category known in its different geographical locations as Gede, Gede-Chamcha, or Apoyi.[25] Some of the more determined holdouts like the Pitti went beyond natural fortifications, acquiring horses and building up their own cavalry of trained warriors to confront Zazzau raiders.[26] So fierce was the Pitti's independent streak and so paranoid were they of Zazzau aggression that as late as 1913, a whole decade after the imposition of British rule, they refused to be persuaded by the emir of Zazzau or the British colonial resident (highest British supervisory official) of Zaria Province to descend from their hill fortresses.[27]

The cultural economy of slavery in the Sokoto Caliphate was very well developed as early as the first two decades after the end of the jihad.[28] Slaves formed the bulk of tributes to the sultan from the emirs of the various provincial powers like Zazzau, who kept their offices by the grace of the supreme leader.[29] The political and economic centrality of slavery to the caliphate trickled down to its various emirates, including Zazzau. The Zazzau slave market in Zaria city was "held daily, but there were never very large numbers on view as this commodity was mostly dispatched further afield in large numbers, because slaves form the wealth of the province of Zaria and larger payments can only be made in this currency."[30] Because of the number of sub-emirates and anointed Islamic vassals under it, and because of its location on the caliphate's most recognizable non-Muslim frontier, Zazzau's slave economy was one of the most elaborate in the caliphate system.

The most important slave institution in Zazzau was the *rumada* (slave farm) at Taban Sani, which held an estimated labor force of three thousand slaves plucked from the Southern Kaduna plateau as tribute or through raids.[31] It is said that when Mamman Sani, the emir of Zazzau, died in 1846, an audit of his estate showed that he owned ten thousand slaves who worked the emirate's agricultural plantations.[32] Many slaves were taken away from the ancestral lands in Southern Kaduna and exported to Zazzau to build city walls and to participate in other grand emirate projects. The Adara, who were hemmed in between and policed by two Zazzau surrogates, Kajuru and Kachia, appear to have been particularly devastated demographically, resulting in their remarkable geographical dispersal.[33]

An Evolving Relationship

In the late-nineteenth century, the peoples of Southern Kaduna were, to varying degrees, part of the sphere of political influence of the emirate of Zazzau. Several Hausa-Fulani garrison settlements deep in Southern Kaduna country enforced Zazzau and caliphate quasi-imperialism, and protected the Kano-Gonja trade route. Kachia and Jema'a were two of the most established of such garrisons. Jema'a in particular was a thriving Hausa-Fulani outpost of Zazzau, with its own Zazzau-appointed overseer. Under Sarki Sambo (1881–1891), Zazzau appointed the Sarkin Yamma, or commander/overseer of the southern frontier, to secure that axis of the vast Southern Kaduna frontier, especially the strategic Adara town of Kachia.[34]

Rebellions, of which there were many, incurred brutal reprisals that escalated into slave raids. The emir of Zazzau himself led many military expeditions that attempted to subdue and raid the treasures of persistently resistant Southern Kaduna groups. So routine were these high-profile military campaigns that while touring the Southern Kaduna areas in 1913 as a British-empowered colonial chief, the emir, now stripped of his war-making and slave-raiding power, reminded the Southern Kaduna people of Rukuba village how the emirs of Zazzau, his predecessors, used to come to them in war. Portraying himself as a father figure to the non-Muslim people of the town, he discouraged fear, urging the inhabitants instead to trust him as a protector, a man of peace who was operating under a different system than did his predecessors:

"Are children who drink at the breast afraid of their parents? All is now peace. Have you ever seen the emir of Zazzau . . . come to your country in peace before? Did I not formerly come here to make war? Now there is no war, you must not fear."[35]

As more areas of the Southern Kaduna area were brought into the emirate tribute system, slave raids proved less fruitful and more costly in this important imperial gateway. Keeping the Southern Kaduna frontier quiescent in the face of such disruption strained the emirate's military and economic resources. This was compounded by the frequency of rebellions and uprisings even among the groups who had accepted emirate authority. All of these factors made the production of slaves through military means increasingly less appealing as the nineteenth century wore on.[36] Embracing less disruptive methods of extracting slaves from the Southern Kaduna area proved a more promising alternative. One such method was the transfer of serious criminal offenders to Kauru and on to Zaria, discussed earlier.

Another method was discretionary slave removal with the constrained acquiescence of the clan heads of the various Southern Kaduna peoples. Over the course of the nineteenth century, the Hausa-Fulani garrisons of Kajuru and

Kachia invaded the surrounding Southern Kaduna communities and removed thousands of Adara people from their homes.[37] So great was this forced migration that today there are whole neighborhoods within Zaria's walled city that are identified with the descendants of these slaves. As recently as thirty years ago, some Adara relatives of the captives visited their Hausaized and Islamized slave relatives and their descendants in Zaria.[38]

The late-nineteenth-century militarization of the southern frontier of Zazzau led to intensified slave raids. These end-of-the-century raids were so devastating that in 1919, British colonial officials claimed that certain affected districts were "still suffering from the effects of the slave raids of bygone days."[39] The raids seemed to have triggered a fresh wave of Southern Kaduna migrations to hill fortresses. These late hill refugees from Zazzau-directed slave raids seemed to have been the most reluctant of the so-called hill peoples to descend to the plains when the British conquest abated the threat of slave raids a few years later.[40] The threats of slave raids and the manner in which Southern Kaduna clan heads reacted to them may have also enabled the enforcers of emirate authority to reshape some Southern Kaduna political institutions in ways that were profoundly amenable to Zazzau's imperial objectives.

Although the incorporation of new Southern Kaduna peoples into Zazzau's loose imperial network continued throughout the nineteenth century, the task of normalizing and entrenching emirate administrative control formed the bulk of Zazzau's precolonial political interactions with the non-Muslim communities. The delegated supervision of the *wakilai* and *jakadu* was Zazzau's imperial paradigm. The emirs would, however, sometimes tour a representative collection of villages and towns of the Southern Kaduna peoples.[41] This was intended to bring the awesome grandeur of the caliphate to the Southern Kaduna people, resulting in renewed allegiance through fear or respect. Since the actual supervisory interventions of surrogate Muslim officials were sporadic, the emirs' tours were calibrated to bolster their authority.

Reforms and Problems in Zazzau Imperialism

As a precondition for implementing Zazzau's imperial programs in Southern Kaduna, existing political institutions of the Southern Kaduna peoples became the targets of emirate-caliphate reform. The specifics of Zazzau's political transformation of Southern Kaduna political institutions await a more intense exploration, but the outlines are fairly clear. Zazzau sought to engineer more centralization and establish a self-sustaining hierarchy of political accountability. The lack of centralized, secular political authority and the prevalence of participatory, fluid power arrangements among the Southern Kaduna peoples presented an obstacle to this need for accountability, close supervision, and centralized political communication.

In the mid- and late-nineteenth century, superintending Zazzau officials created new secular administrative authorities at the clan and village levels for each of the Southern Kaduna peoples. This new system supplanted the influence of the priest-chiefs who for most of the peoples of Southern Kaduna embodied spiritual and political sovereignty. The period of emirate overlordship on the Southern Kaduna plateau, which ended only with the British conquest in 1903, "was characterized by the gradual separation of secular powers from ritual religious . . . power."[42] The appointed secular heads were subjected to the supervision of the *katukai* and *wakilai,* who oversaw the affairs of each ethnic group on behalf of Zazzau.

The hallmark of this reform was the appointment of Hausa, Fulani, or indigenous Muslim converts as village heads with limited executive power over the indigenous non-Muslim subclan heads. The subclan heads were no more than symbolic members of this administrative hierarchy. The functional political and fiscal obligations that constituted the mainstays of the emirate imperial system were reserved for appointed officials who subscribed to the same Islamic ideology as the rulers of Zazzau and were therefore trusted to pursue emirate objectives with loyalty. Relying on Southern Kaduna oral sources, C. K. Meek, the Northern Nigerian colonial government's official ethnologist, sums up the marginality of the indigenous subclan head to the new administrative hierarchy: "The sub-clan head had not a great deal of authority, being simply an intermediary between the sub-clan and the foreign [emirate] rulers. He had nothing to do with the assignment of or collection of taxes as the Kauru [surrogate] rulers dealt direct with the villages in such matters."[43] Excluded from the consequential administrative processes of the clan, the indigenous subclan head was a personification of the Southern Kaduna peoples' subtle political surrender to institutions that arranged their loose system into a fairly rigid structure of control and discipline. Understandably, the new administrative invention produced a bifurcated allegiance among Southern Kaduna peoples. The period of emirate administrative consolidation on the Southern Kaduna plateau can thus be seen as one in which "voluntary allegiance to the traditional Priest-Chief institution" persisted alongside "involuntary allegiance to the newly introduced political institution of the Village Head."[44]

This political transformation generated backlash among the peoples of Southern Kaduna. They resisted the reforms, which venerated the secular over the ritualistic and brought them further into the symbolic realm of the caliphate. Beyond symbols, the new political configurations represented a bold effort by Zazzau to extract resources from the Southern Kaduna area in a structured format. These factors stood in opposition to the economic freedoms and flexibilities of Southern Kaduna life, which intensified resentment of the emirate-caliphate system. Over time, many Southern Kaduna communities weaned themselves practically, but not symbolically, from Zazzau's control. As a result, although the Katab, Ikulu, Bajju, and other peoples of the Southern Kaduna plateau were still being controlled from Zaria through resident supervisory katukai, or headmen, responsible to Zazzau, the system as a whole had come under considerable internal strain.[45]

Resistance and Challenges to Zazzau's Imperial Maneuvers

As the nineteenth century progressed, emirate control became more tenuous, less rewarding, and more compromised. Southern Kaduna challenges to Zazzau dominance took many forms. As early as the 1840s, a Koro chief displaced by a Zazzau-appointed Keffi Fulani petitioned the emir of Keffi to restore him to the office he inherited from his ancestors.[46] Unwilling to make the sacrifices required to meet the tribute demands of Zazzau appointees, many Southern Kaduna clans sporadically revolted against Zazzau exactions. The Katab were noted for frequently mobilizing to oust the Kauru-Zazzau officials responsible for supervising their affairs.[47] They were also famed for resisting the intrusive disciplinary routine of tribute payment by attacking proximate representatives of emirate power. Such violence was occasionally inflicted on the subclan heads, their own ethnic kinsmen.[48] To reestablish its power and prevent a coordinated assault on its influence, Zazzau adopted counterinsurgency measures that brutally put down violent uprisings, using frontier troops from their surrogate outposts.

Ultimately, though, repression was counterproductive as a mechanism for securing emirate hegemony in the Southern Kaduna area. Each panicky response to resistance wrought a symbolic blow on emirate power and encouraged more resistance. Every Zazzau punitive military expedition against resisting Southern Kaduna groups made the next counterinsurgent campaign smaller and less effective. The countermeasures strained both the military supplies and the food stocks of the Zazzau vassal conducting the operation. Establishing and militarizing the emirate frontier on the southern border of the caliphate proved much easier than maintaining it. Defending Zazzau's political hegemony in Southern Kaduna was more successful and stable as a symbolic proposition than it was on the ground.

It is common and politically profitable in Northern Nigeria's contemporary political debates for some Southern Kaduna intellectuals and politicians to claim that Zazzau's post-jihad imperialist military subdued and oppressed their areas for decades. The convoluted history of Zazzau's control of Southern Kaduna suggests a less certain, less stable imperial trajectory and a less passive imperial victimhood. The Southern Kaduna peoples were as much vigorous and independence-loving resisters as the Zazzau imperial system was a wobbly system of indirect internal colonialism. Zazzau's hegemony was shaky from inception and required constant military reinforcement, which in turn curtailed perceived legitimacy and inspired protest. The proactive resistance of many Southern Kaduna peoples and flawed imperial military maneuvers meant that danger was never far from the seemingly orderly surface. The examples of groups, such as the Pitti and the Gwandara, who took matters into their own hands and fled to secure hill territories were constant indicators of the possibilities of rebellion and the limits of Zazzau's power.

Rebellion, refugee hill communities, and the restraint of Zazzau's surrogates combined to undermine and, in some areas, cripple the emirate imperial project. Take the case of Kajuru. For all its vaunted military effectiveness, the Kajuru surrogate military machine did not appear to have subdued the Southern Kaduna ethnicities within its broad vicinity. For practical reasons, its imperial practices were restricted to areas on its small frontier. Even within those areas, only Southern Kaduna groups living in exposed settlements experienced Zazzau's power in a sustained, intrusive way.[49] The traditions of many of the Southern Kaduna ethnic groups in the vicinity of Kauru, Lere, and Zazzau itself claim that those groups were never subjected to Zazzau's rule—only to its indirect, constantly evolving control.[50]

The enforcement of tribute payment by Zazzau's vassals in the Southern Kaduna area frequently required military mobilization. Military resources were not always available, making tribute payment irregular. Even slave raids preceded by elaborate preparation and directed from Zaria occasionally ran into trouble in Southern Kaduna, failing to yield slaves or tributes.[51] As Zazzau's list of unsuccessful raids and full-fledged expeditions swelled, so too did the desire of many Southern Kaduna groups to "reassert their independence."[52]

Jema'a was the smallest and most vulnerable of Zazzau's outposts in the Southern Kaduna area. It struggled to impose its will on the Ham, Aninka, Bajju, Ninkyap, and Agworok, who lived in settlement clusters within just a few miles of its walls. The challenges to Jema'a's authority, and by extension Zazzau and the caliphate, were often brazen, marked not only by rebellion but also by determined attempts to remove the caliphate presence altogether. Raids by the Kagoro people on Jema'a persisted until the vassal's surrender to the British in 1903.[53] On several occasions over the course of the nineteenth century coordinated attacks nearly toppled the outpost.

Jema'a's weak hegemony was marked by its uniquely pragmatic approach to the survival of its Zazzau identity. Its rulers sometimes turned to some of the Southern Kaduna groups for military support and cooperation to fend off the insurgency of others.[54] They even befriended Kagoma clan-chiefs, entering into an informal alliance of mutual respect and assistance.[55] The expedient recruitment of local groups as allies may have assured Jema'a's survival as an outpost of Zazzau's hegemony. This is perhaps an indicator of the deftness and depth of Zazzau's imperial practice. It calls attention, however, to Jema'a's sense of insecurity and its inability to unilaterally impose an emirate sociopolitical order on its Southern Kaduna neighbors. The necessary incompleteness of its impe-rial mission preserved a measure of independence, self-determination, and re-bellious initiative among Jema'a's Southern Kaduna neighbors. This meant that the delicate caliphate hegemony in that zone became even more fragile through the nineteenth century, constantly being breached by increasingly self-assertive indigenous non-Muslim groups.

So tenuous was Jema'a's hold on the Southern Kaduna communities sur-rounding it that early European accounts reinforce the brittleness of its imperial position: "It appears the Emir's hold over the tribes was very weak and that sub-jugation was nothing more than periodic slave-raids or the acceptance of bribe to buy off threatened raids. No attempt was made to administer the tribes."[56] While Jema'a's subimperial challenges were somewhat unique, its predicament mirrored that of Kajuru, Lere, and Kauru, Zazzau's other enforcers in Southern Kaduna. Throughout the nineteenth century, Zazzau's power, exercised through these sur-rogate states, waned, and Southern Kaduna peoples increasingly tested the resolve and persistence of emirate authority with remarkable success. As the hold of the emirate loosened, many Southern Kaduna peoples were encouraged to seek socio-political and economic freedom from the emirate system. Zazzau's vassals increas-ingly compromised their enforcement by ignoring infractions and open rebellion.

The imperative of survival in a hostile, non-Hausa, non-Muslim milieu made compromises a feature of Zazzau's surrogate hegemonic practices. The surrogate city-states were living socioeconomic organisms requiring trade, sociopolitical relationships, and the cooperation of Southern Kaduna neighbors. In addition to being military outposts, they were population centers and magnets for Hausa and Fulani migrants who, uninterested in Zazzau's imperial agenda, were more concerned with agricultural prosperity and other pragmatic aspirational pur-suits. The Kachia Hausa-Fulani settlement, for instance, was a "thriving farming community" with a vibrant herding sector worked by Fulani herdsmen, in addi-tion to possessing a vaunted garrison infrastructure.[57]

Investments by apolitical residents in subjugating the non-Muslim peoples were minimal, curtailed by the pragmatic need to learn innovative agricultural techniques from the more experienced indigenous peasants and by the economic necessity of the mutual exchange of goods. The garrison settlements generated their own demographic momentum, combining with environmental factors to give rise to a wave of Hausa-Fulani migrations to the Southern Kaduna valley. Many of the migrations resulted in independent Hausa farming settlements, which were sometimes outside the garrisons' protective military shield and were geographically closer to and friendly with the Southern Kaduna ethnic groups that surrounded them.[58]

Zazzau's imperial mission was undercut through the second half of the nine-teenth century, and the appeal of nonmilitary, less-intrusive strategies for profiting from the Southern Kaduna plateau became more popular. The factors responsible for this ideological shift included the ways in which the rapidly changing Hausa settlements diverged from the garrison model and the nature of their relationships with the Southern Kaduna peasants. Seclusion and military enforcement had their psychological cost, as residents of the walled garrison town living in constant fear of a Southern Kaduna uprising had to maintain a geographical and ideological space between themselves and their non-Muslim neighbors. When German traveler Paul Staudinger visited Kachia in 1884, the residents prevented him from exploring "the fairly high hills" that lay to the northeast of the town because "'bad people' *hadna* [*arna*—infidels] lived there."[59] This conscious segregation of the Muslim and non-Muslim realms in a region in which the latter commanded an overwhelming numerical superiority was a fragile recipe for domination. Thus, in most cases, domination, if it can be called that, was tenuous and necessarily conceded considerable autonomy to Southern Kaduna groups.

The Zazzau imperial system was not a model of cohesion. Zazzau's surrogate sub-emirate enforcers jostled to boost their own interests, sometimes at the expense of Zazzau control. Rivalries proliferated and undermined Zazzau's agenda. The supervisory officials (*kofofi;* sing. *kofa*) were often too embedded in the politics and socioeconomic life of their assigned vassal to report deviance from established imperial conduct. Such transgressions often led to the breakdown of imperial control, boosting Southern Kaduna freedoms and self-assertion. Sometimes, the vassals revolted against Zazzau overtly, as was the case of Keffi. The sub-emirate provoked Zazzau into repeatedly raiding it over the course of the nineteenth century, undermining the ability of the Keffi rulers to expand in that sector or to effectively enforce their will over non-Muslim groups there.[60]

As a result of these circumstances, Zazzau's imperial system on the Southern Kaduna frontier was on a steep decline through the second half of the nineteenth century, relying more and more on crude military might, which, in addition to betraying desperation, proved increasingly ineffective as an instrument of control. Consequently, on the eve of the British colonial conquest, a complex set of stalemates and laxly enforced emirate hegemonies had developed on the Southern Kaduna plateau. British colonial authority arrived in the Southern Kaduna areas to confront this substantially weakened and, in some areas, lapsed Zazzau hegemony.

Anglo-Caliphate Colonialism in the Southern Kaduna Area

In 1902, one year before the conquest of Sokoto, the headquarters of the caliphate, the British established themselves in Zaria as the putative colonial overlords of the Zazzau emirate zone. Relying on a fearsome military arsenal and the tentative cooperation of Zazzau's rulers, British troops, doubling as makeshift administrators, declared Zaria a British province on behalf of the British Crown.

The commander of the troops, Captain Abedie, was appointed the first British resident of the province. Between 1902 and 1904, a convoluted military "pacification" resulted in the effective British occupation of the areas on both banks of the Kaduna River up to the emirate of Abuja, including all of the Southern Kaduna plateau. The Fulani rulers of Jema'an Dororo were one of the first groups of Zazzau-affiliated rulers to pledge allegiance to the British in 1903.[61] Subsequent military operations lasting up to 1904 consolidated British colonial presence in the Southern Kaduna area.

From the outset, British colonial perception was deeply affected by a fascination with the vanquished Zazzau emirate system. The decentralized political culture of the Southern Kaduna peoples contradicted the British desire for a centralized administrative hierarchy. Frederick Lugard, the first governor of Northern Nigeria, articulated this contrast and its accompanying vision of political change clearly when he wrote that "among these tribes [the non-Muslim groups], it is my policy to centralize authority as far as may be, in a recognized chief and to introduce the civilizing agency of trade."[62] In the Southern Kaduna area, where political decentralization was the norm and where neither the resources nor the will to create and administer indigenous chieftaincies existed, the easy course of action was, from the British perspective, to continue with slightly modified Zazzau hegemonic strategies from the previous century.

As indicated in Lugard's proclamation, it was not just the political life of the non-Muslim peoples that was to be subjected to the centralization of Fulani administrative surrogates. The Fulani supervisors of British colonialism were expected to also help tutor the Southern Kaduna peoples on how to develop a market-oriented economy and cultivate in them the "the civilizing agency of trade," as Lugard articulated it. Fulani agents of British colonialism were to help "civilize" the peoples of the Southern Kaduna plateau. As architects of the toppled Sokoto Islamic Empire, the Fulani held a special appeal to the British as potential administrative allies. Lugard expressed this vision forcefully while arguing for the continuation of the emirate imperial model over the expensive alternatives of direct British rule or the cultivation of indirect rule through the invention of indigenous centralized authority among the non-Muslim peoples:

> I believe myself that the future of the virile race of this Protectorate lies largely in the regeneration of the Fulani. Their ceremonial, their coloured skins, their mode of life and habits of thought appeal more to the native population than the prosaic business-like habits of the Anglo-Saxon can ever do. This then is the policy to which in my view the administration of Northern Nigeria should give effect, viz: to regenerate this capable and mould them to ideas of justice and mercy, so that in future generations, if not this, they become worthy instruments of rule.[63]

The defunct caliphate and its lower-level administrative hierarchies appealed to the British hunger for a cheap, efficient colonial administration. In Zaria Province, the religious and cultural division between Zazzau's northern, Islamic sector, and its southern, non-Muslim frontier informed the establishment of British administrative units—"divisions" in British colonial parlance. The province was divided into a Northern Division headquartered in Zaria city and a Southern Division headquartered alternately at Kajuru, Kachia, and Zangon Katab.[64]

British colonial administrative thinking was steeped in a Fulani-emirate philosophy that equated Zaria Province with the precolonial Zazzau emirate and that mapped the entire Southern Kaduna area onto Zazzau's political reach. Shunning the complexity of precolonial Southern Kaduna relationships with Zazzau, British officials believed that "Zaria [Zazzau] Emirate is coterminous with the Province. The Pagan Districts paid tribute to the Emirs of Zaria and formed an integral part of the Zaria Emirate prior to the advent of the British Administration."[65] This belief in the totality and stability of emirate precolonial imperial authority was abandoned early in the colonial period when officials realized through their ground-level administration and "touring" activities that many Southern Kaduna communities had managed to escape the reach of Zazzau's power and that many others "were subject to none of the levies that were once customary."[66] This, however, did little to distract the British from espousing the utility of the Hausa-Fulani subcolonial system.

The administrative reforms that ensued confirmed the British investment in a Fulani-administered colonial estate. It had two paradigmatic effects on the Southern Kaduna polities. It gave administrative jurisdiction to Hausa-Fulani leaders from Zazzau and its vassals like Kachia, Kauru, and Jema'an Dororo in areas previously outside the reach of their control, and it expanded the executive power of Hausa-Fulani district and village heads in areas in which there was a prior tradition of Zazzau-appointed administrators.

E. J. Arnett, the assistant resident of Zaria Province, carried out these reforms between 1902 and 1914, formally codifying Zazzau, Jema'a, and Kachia's right to make appointments into the positions of district and village headship among the Southern Kaduna peoples, with Zazzau having the final approving authority. The British began by recognizing the political legitimacy of the heads appointed by Zazzau over its vassals in Kachia, Jema'a, and Kauru, empowering them administratively and militarily to be figureheads of British colonialism in Southern Kaduna. The arrangement preserved Zazzau's control over the Southern Kaduna peoples. Throughout the colonial period, district heads were appointed directly from Zaria in succession to the non-Muslim districts in the Kachia and Jema'a areas.[67] More significantly, communities in Zangon Katab, which used to have a nominal supervisory role overseeing indigenous subclan heads, were centralized and placed under a Zazzau-appointed district head, subject only to British oversight.

The early British administrators placed one half of the Bajju under the jurisdiction of both Zazzau and Jema'a, and the appointment of a district head for the Bajju was vested in Jema'a's rulers. The Kagoma and the northern Yeskwa, along with the Kaningkon, Kafanchan, Ninzam, and Ayu peoples, were also placed under the Fulani rulers of Jema'a. The British believed that Jema'a had previously ruled them by right of conquest. This British assumption was especially problematic since Jema'a had, as stated earlier, been more concerned with its own survival in a hostile non-Muslim frontier than with conquest. Nonetheless, the British proceeded with the empowerment of Jema'a over the Southern Kaduna groups in its neighborhood, committed to a colonial interpretation that theorized Fulani precolonial hegemony as total and stable. In the present circumstances, this romantic vision morphed into a belief, widely shared by British officials, that "the Hausa have a civilizing and educational effect on the [Southern Kaduna] pagans."[68]

The British recognized many non-Muslim clan heads, transforming them into village heads and placing them under Zazzau-appointed district heads.[69] In the late 1920s and early 1930s, as non-Muslim clan-villages proliferated along with recognized village heads, Zaria Province decided to grant Muslim district heads the power to make decisions regarding the recognition or denial of Southern Kaduna clans' claims to villagehood.[70] This new layer of power enabled emirate colonial agent-chiefs to shape and control the emerging political architecture of the Southern Kaduna area, determining which groups gained recognition as colonial administrative units and which ones did not.

The desire of Southern Kaduna peoples to have their clans recognized by the colonial bureaucracy gave Zazzau a new mechanism of control and compelled Southern Kaduna village hopefuls to perform gestures of allegiance and subservience to Zazzau. The only exceptions to this new instrument of Zazzau subcolonialism were the districts of Kagoro, Jaba, and Moroa, which had autonomy under direct British supervision, having been recognized as independent chieftaincies in 1904. Although located on the southern frontier of the precolonial Zazzau emirate in the Southern Kaduna plateau, these three chiefdoms were granted administrative autonomy ostensibly on account of their verified claims of not having been subdued by Zazzau in precolonial times.

Jema'a unsuccessfully challenged Kagoro's claim of precolonial independence. Administrative autonomy was largely symbolic and nominal as the British subsumed the three districts under Muslim polities. Initially placed under the Zazzau vassal of Keffi in Nasarawa Province, the three self-governing chiefdoms were transferred to Zaria Province and placed under the symbolic authority of the emir of Zazzau in 1934, fully consolidating Zazzau's primacy in the colonial system of the Southern Kaduna area.[71]

While British colonial officials recognized the inherent tensions of emirate subcolonial rule among the Southern Kaduna peoples, they welcomed the assertion of emirate authority. Their attitude was one of ambivalence and pragmatism. They expected the Hausa district heads to assert their British-delegated authority in order to extract the resources required from non-Muslim peoples they considered resentful of governmental discipline. As outsiders, Zazzau-appointed officials were perfect for this role, for they lacked the capacity for empathy and the affinity of brotherhood that might compromise their work as colonial agents.

The British expected the Hausa-Fulani officials, however, to adopt a paternalistic, pedagogical style in doing their work. They did not want productive professional detachment to lead to aloofness. British officials celebrated the fact that the "District Heads to an increasing degree regard themselves . . . as 'in loco parentis' [surrogate parents] to their pagan peoples," but they would not tolerate an emirate chieftaincy that completely effaced the political traditions of the Southern Kaduna peoples. Reporting on Chawai District in 1931, the resident of Zaria Province captured this ambivalence poignantly.[72] He claimed that the "present [Fulani] District Head has now definitely established himself in the headship" and that the "district is [now] better administered than it has [been] for years." The resident was satisfied that the district head's "firm control" was balanced by his tolerance for the "customs and traditions of the [non-Muslim] Atsam who formed the bulk of the population of the District."[73] This was a model for what the British desired and recommended to emirate officials: firm emirate control mitigated by respect for indigenous non-Muslim culture.

The pitfalls of ruling the Southern Kaduna peoples through Hausa-Fulani district heads—the *jekadu* and katukai—occasionally registered on British officials. In 1937, dan Madami, the son of the recently deceased Emir Ibrahim (1924–36), was appointed as the district head of Zangon Katab. His approach to administering the Katab people was so high-handed that British officials concluded that he was unsuitable and that "he lacked the necessary tact and patience for administering a District in which pagan elements predominated."[74] His replacement was Dalhatu, who had previously served as district head in the non-Muslim Chikun District and who the British assumed possessed the skills required to administer the Katab without alienating them from the colonial system.

In addition to benefiting economically and politically from the work of colonial district heads, Zazzau initiated several independent administrative reforms among the Southern Kaduna peoples by simply invoking the authority of the British colonial presence. Being the proxies of the British enabled the rulers of Zazzau to subtly shape the Southern Kaduna districts in the image of the emirate. They did so partly by creating a slew of titles and offices that replicated those found in Zazzau and other emirates.[75] These titular innovations represent one of the most profoundly novel elements of emirate subcolonial rule in the Southern Kaduna area.[76]

The British preference for a modified version of the preexisting Fulani imperial administrative system coexisted uncomfortably with the cultures of the people they referred to derisively as "pagans." Subjected to the authority of the emir of Zazzau by British administrative fiat, most of the ethnic communities of Southern Kaduna were "ruled indirectly through their own chiefs and councils by Hausa or Fulani District Chiefs" appointed from Zaria.[77] This was an administrative configuration in which, as M. G. Smith asserts, the "Mohammedans [Hausa-Fulani Muslims] were dominant."[78] The system gave Zazzau clear administrative initiative in the Southern Kaduna area, or Southern Zaria Division, a term that the British coined for it, beneath the supervisory role of British officials. So important was the Zazzau emirate's British-supervised authority in Southern Kaduna that the district headship of some of the non-Muslim districts became coveted royal assignments for Zazzau's princes, training grounds for higher office in the prestigious traditional Muslim bureaucracy of the emirate. One prominent example of this mode of princely ascent is Emir Ja'afaru, who, prior to succeeding to the emirship of Zazzau in 1936, had served as the district head of Zangon Katab for eighteen years.

Under precolonial Zazzau control, the difference of Southern Kaduna peoples was a perverse asset to be preserved, for only people who were non-Muslim and steeped in "pagan" practices could be attacked and enslaved. Under British colonization, an opposite logic was at work in determining how officials perceived Southern Kaduna peoples. Their political and cultural difference was seen as a liability and a threat to the goal of establishing a uniform, cheap colonial administration. Thus, unlike their Zazzau imperial predecessors, British colonial architects sought to profoundly reshape the Southern Kaduna polities along emirate lines, utilizing politically centralized administrative hierarchies and regulated, structured trade as tools.

British colonial efforts to reorient the peoples of Southern Kaduna toward an emirate sociopolitical model and to make them more suitable for indirect rule hit early snags as they were not informed by a recognition of Zazzau's prior difficulties in influencing the ways of life of the Southern Kaduna polities. The British also failed to consider the claims of Southern Kaduna groups that had successfully escaped the reach of Zazzau's power, had successfully revolted against it, or had by shrewd maneuvers and deft brinkmanship effectively won back their full independence by the time of the British conquest. As early as 1920, the subcolonial rule of Zazzau-appointed chiefs had proven barely successful, and the "alien" chiefs commanded neither the peoples' loyalty nor their respect. Like other Middle Belt peoples who were subjected to the mechanics of emirate rule, the Southern Kaduna peoples struggled to reconcile their competing loyalties to indigenous political institutions, Hausa chiefs, and supervising British officials. Often, they preferred to stick to familiar rituals and roles in their communities, shunning imposed Hausa-Fulani chiefs.

Southern Kaduna peoples were so opposed to the subcolonial rule of the Hausa chiefs that they effectively altered what was intended to be a modified indirect rule system into a direct rule system in which only the authority of British officials could sway them into fulfilling their obligations to the colonial state. In reality, this enabled the British to emerge as empathetic and compassionate arbiters in the relationship between Southern Kaduna peoples and Zazzau-appointed colonial officials. But it also evoked the specter of a discredited model of direct European rule. This obvious drawback of the emirate model in practice, especially the ways in which it paradoxically occasionally conduced to direct European rule, forced Governor Hugh Clifford to question the workability of the system. In 1920, he argued that the British colonial officialdom "should abandon once and for all the expectation of ever converting primitive tribal systems (such as they are) into any sort of semblance to the Mohammedan Emirates."[79] Clifford recommended radically scaling back the use of Hausa and Fulani district chiefs in non-Muslim districts, where their presence might cause resentment. British colonial policy, he argued, should use the preexisting emirate system in a manner so limited as to render their administrative presence invisible to non-Muslim subjects. This system should, he further argued, operate in a way that "caus[es] the [non-Muslim] people to feel individually and collectively that the [British] district officer is the real 'de facto' ruler of their country and their secure court of Appeal and Refuge when in trouble."[80]

This remarkable, if implied, recommendation of increased British involvement in colonial administration was something of a rhetorical turnaround. While it did not lead to a policy shift, it highlighted the artificiality and idealism of emirate subcolonial rule. It also alerted British colonial officials to the dangers of subordinating Southern Kaduna and other non-Muslim areas to emirate-appointed agents in ways that recalled precolonial ideological and physical confrontations between the caliphate zone and the peoples of its non-Muslim frontiers.

In the 1930s, Governor Donald Cameron decried the imperial racial idealism that seemed to have informed the commitment to a Hausa-administered colonial bureaucracy in non-Muslim areas. He critiqued "the unhallowed policy insidiously introduced during the latter half of the last decade of thinking of the Moslem Emirates in terms of the Indian States."[81] This statement conceded that the British had not simply envisaged "civilized" and centralized non-Muslim polities; they had also, in farming out colonization to emirate agents, hoped that the emirates would play the role of subimperial autocrats in the mold of more settled empires that predated European colonization in other parts of the world.

The British commitment to the emirate model was aspirational: it embodied the hope that the Northern Nigerian administrative landscape would mirror outcomes produced by the British reactivation of prior Muslim and Hindu imperial systems in India.

Emirate Subcolonialism and Its Discontents

Emirate subcolonial rule was unpopular from its infancy, needing to be periodically normalized and reinforced among Southern Kaduna communities. The British sought to legitimize the system by introducing and ingratiating Zazzau emirs to their non-Muslim subjects in carefully planned, elaborate familiarization tours. The tours were designed to render emirate subcolonial authority legitimate, visible, and familiar to Southern Kaduna districts that were more likely to resist the emirs' authority.

The first of these southern districts tours, as they were called, occurred in 1913, the second and third in 1924 and 1927 respectively. Each one lasted for more than a month and entailed a district-by-district "inspection of the Southern Districts of the province" by the emir.[82] The resident of Zaria Province and the district officer in charge of the province's southern districts chaperoned the emir and his large entourage on each tour. The tours represented an effort by the British colonialists to naturalize Zazzau emirate subcolonial rule in a section of the province still holding bitter memories of their prior interactions with Zazzau. Because there was no precolonial tradition of such demonstration of caliphate power and sartorial splendor among the peoples of Southern Kaduna, the tours also harbored the potential to inflame as much as they awed.

The tours provided the emir a chance to establish the paternal image that British colonial officials wanted him to project, to act as a surrogate parent in line with British expectation. The performance of this emirate paternalism was a mechanism for communicating power in a visual and demonstrative medium. As he toured districts, the emir gave speeches urging peaceful coexistence between Southern Kaduna peoples and Hausa-Fulani settlements in their midst. He commended hill-dwelling non-Muslim groups who "have descended from their hills and now dwell with the Hausawa [Hausa settlers] on the plain in friendship and confidence." He encouraged the non-Muslim groups to "bring in their complaints" if "any [Hausa-Fulani] do them wrong."[83] Emirate subcolonial paternalism was an ideological mainstay of British colonialism in the Southern Kaduna area. The emir of Zazzau was expected to mitigate the hostility with which he was perceived by the Southern Kaduna peoples by displaying a compassionate administrative temperament.

In his account of the 1913 tour, for instance, the resident of the province "admired the Emir's handling of the [Southern Kaduna peoples]." In accompanying the emir, the British resident often set the tone of the political conversation between emir and non-Muslim subjects, ensuring that the former maintained the paternal theme of the tours. Generally, successive emirs obliged and adopted a paternal disposition in the tours. Presenting a new Hausa district head to the people in Rukuba, the emir had this to say: "This [District Head] is your father. He is my son. Am I not your grandfather? You are young children; you have not yet gone out into the world. I and my son will protect you. Shall we not teach you?"[84]

The didactic paternalism that underpinned British investments in the emirate administrative system is on full display in the emir's speech. Yet the emir's own learned and practiced subcolonial paternal disposition toward the subalterns of Southern Kaduna also comes through in the speech. British accounts of the tours raved about how "pagan and Hausa" lived together in peace, how the Kadara, who "formerly . . . would have nothing to do with the Hausa" now commune with them "as one," and how the Adara and Gbagyi peoples had "left their hills and come into the plains" in response to colonial order and the paternal assurances of Zazzau's emirs.[85] The tours, however, revealed the saliently uncomfortable underbellies of the emirate subcolonial system.

Southern Kaduna peoples used the tours to verbalize their grievances, to critique the conducts of their emirate overlords or, as one British official put it, to "complain about Zazzau oppression."[86] The "pagans," British officials realized through the tours, "[would] no longer endure extortion or oppression without complaining."[87] One component of the emir's paternal facade was to reinforce his colonially sanctioned image as a compassionate dispenser of British-borne justice. During the 1913 tour, the emir made a flamboyant show in Chawai of imprisoning a Hausa district head whom a Southern Kaduna man had accused of wrongfully dispossessing him of his goat.[88]

Gestures of justice and compassion were designed to win the trust and confidence of edgy Southern Kaduna peoples. They did little, however, to prevent the Hausa district heads from seeing themselves simply as Zazzau's agents, reminiscent of the kofa (Zazzau's intermediary) of old.[89] The symbolic enunciation of British-emirate compassion did little to erase the tensions of sub-emirate colonial suzerainty among the Southern Kaduna peoples. Protests and aggressive dissent often troubled proclamations about the relational harmony engineered by emirate subcolonial paternalism.

Familiar complaints about the injustice of emirate subcolonial administration filtered through the bureaucracy to British officials' ears. Some concrete allegations were corrected or at least investigated, but the underlying lack of faith in the emirate on the part of Southern Kaduna peoples persisted. This was compounded by the lingering legitimacy deficit of British rule itself, and it was only a matter of time before complaints morphed into conflicts. The spread of Christian missionary education among the Southern Kaduna peoples enabled their emerging elite to imagine a political future outside of emirate, subcolonial domination. This in turn catalyzed organized anti-emirate protest.

In 1944, a number of mission-educated Katab and Bajju men demanded to have their own chief and to be freed from Hausa, Muslim subcolonial rule. They envisioned a chieftaincy "independent of the Emir of Zaria."[90] Throughout that year, the agitators launched a multifaceted campaign of civil disobedience that involved what officials termed "breaches of the law."[91] They openly defied the authority of the Katab Native Authority, which was superintended by the Zazzau-appointed brother of the emir. They also declined to be counted in the annual tax assessment census, and refused summonses from the native courts. They would not participate in or patronize administrative institutions associated with emirate demands and personnel.

The protest movement was large enough to reinvigorate colonial bureaucratic conversations on the need to reform the administrative system and grant more administrative responsibility to the Southern Kaduna peoples, in line with the principle of indirect rule. Very little concrete action followed, however. Instead officials blamed missionaries for convincing new Christian converts to wean themselves off their Hausa Muslim subcolonial overlords.[92] The leaders of the protest movement were arrested and transported to Zaria to face justice in courts staffed by emirate officials. The failure to grant the Katab and Bajju peoples their desired independence from delegated emirate rule stoked the Southern Kaduna peoples' opposition to the emirate colonial system.

In 1946, a new wave of violent protests organized by mission-educated Katab and Bajju youth erupted. Once again, officials adopted a law-and-order approach while reiterating the "urgent need to recall the young Mission adherents to a sense of their allegiance to traditional chiefs."[93] British officials blamed Katab and Bajju clan heads for not "controlling elements of the population susceptible to outside [Christian missionary] influences." Finally, officials acknowledged that the Fulani district head, the emir of Zazzau's brother, had neglected the "necessity for keeping in closer touch with the pagan tribes under him."[94] He was, officials admitted, a distant, out-of-touch subcolonial ruler who had, by his administrative indifference, undermined the Southern Kaduna peoples' faith in the entire structure of subcolonial rule.

The failure to take seriously the demand for Southern Kaduna self-rule ran deep in the colonial bureaucracy. It prompted officials to acknowledge the instability of emirate subcolonial rule, but to take little action in the direction of yielding to Southern Kaduna demands. The report on the crisis spoke vaguely of "concrete plans" that might allow "these tribes [to] at some future date assume greater responsibility for administration of the District in which they form more than 80% of the population."[95] The promise of indirect rule at a future date portended but postponed the completion of the mission of Hausa-Fulani civilizing agents. Barring the total independence of Southern Kaduna peoples from the emirate system, the report's emphasis on "greater responsibility" merely sought to expand the participation of Southern Kaduna communities in the emirate subcolonial system. Even this modest concession was put off, to be implemented in the future—when "the staff position permits."[96]

The problem of emirate subcolonialism among the non-Muslim peoples of Southern Kaduna was not new. It manifested violently in the 1940s, but its roots lay in earlier times. In the 1930s subcolonial arrangements were already fundamental problems plaguing British rule in Northern Nigeria. The administrative dysfunction of proxy rule was traceable to the complicated mechanics of delegated colonial guardianship. In the 1930s, this complication was a flashpoint of internal colonial debates among British officials. These debates were elevated to a new deliberative decibel when Donald Cameron became governor of Nigeria in 1931 and outlined his effort to reform what he saw as the autocracy and illegitimacy of Muslim Hausa-Fulani rule. His *Principles of Native Administration and Their Application* was a blueprint of his reformist vision.[97] His envisioned reform was founded on the principle of democratizing indirect rule to give British-supervised administrative sovereignty to non-Muslim communities being colonized through the agency of Hausa-Fulani personnel.

Cameron had attempted to put his theories into practice in Zaria Province in 1933 when he advised the resident to appoint indigenous district heads in most of the Southern Kaduna districts. The resident balked at the idea, contending that it would undermine the authority of the emir of Zazzau and jeopardize the entire edifice of proxy British rule in the province. When consulted on the idea, the emir rejected the proposal outright, arguing that the peoples of Southern Kaduna were too immature for supervised self-governance and that autonomy would channel their civilizational deficits into internecine crises.[98]

The failure of these reformist efforts set the stage for the protests against emirate rule in 1944 and 1946. The Katab and Bajju were not the only ethnic groups to protest against emirate rule; the Kagoma people rose up in 1945 and 1946 to protest Jema'a's suzerainty and to demand a Kagoma chief. The protests were promptly quelled and the organizers detained. In 1945 and 1947, the Chawai refused to pay taxes and provide labor for public works projects, demanding that the Hausa district head of Lere be replaced by a Chawai chief. Sporadic, loosely organized campaigns of civil disobedience continued through the 1940s and 1950s, as did clandestine attacks on the human and material symbols of emirate subcolonial rule.

By this time the politics of pre-independence Northern Nigeria had subsumed the localized struggles of the Southern Kaduna peoples against emirate subcolonial rule. Bigger political ideas percolated among mission-educated Christian converts who constituted the emergent Southern Kaduna elite. One such idea crystallized in the formation of the Non-Muslim League in 1949. The League, whose name was changed in the same year to Middle Zone League (MZL), was a quasi-political party and a forerunner to the better-known United Middle Belt Congress (UMBC), which became a political platform for the wider struggle of Middle Belt peoples against perceived Hausa-Fulani political domination. MZL was a direct product of the Southern Kaduna struggle, having been birthed at a "solidarity meeting" of politically conscious Southern Kaduna mission-educated men in Kafanchan. The organization was formed with the expressed purpose of challenging emirate subcolonial rule and of blunting the politically dominant position of Hausa-Fulani Muslims in the future politics of a decolonized Northern Nigerian region.

While large-scale organized political groups were emerging in opposition to emirate preeminence in colonial Southern Kaduna and in the wider Middle Belt region, the local struggles of ethnic communities against emirate power persisted in the form of petitions and protest letters. The Fatsuam people of Kafanchan were particularly vocal in their opposition to the emirate colonialism of Zazzau's vassal, Jema'a. Their polemical ferocity climaxed in their willingness to accuse British colonial officials of being materially invested in the continuation of what they saw as emirate oppression.

In March 1954, the "Natives of Jemaa" came together to call attention to the foreignness of their Jema'a subcolonial overlords, submitting a petition to the resident of Plateau Province, the supervising province of Jema'a Division. Penned by Yohanah, their appointed scribe, the petition followed the unanswered demand by the Fatsuam people for the removal of the Jema'a-appointed district head. The district head was a holder of the *madaki* title in Jema'a sub-emirate. Also targeted in the petition was the district head's brother, Mallam Nabuja, the district scribe in charge of everyday administrative routines.

Dripping with frustration, the petition reminded the resident of the community's overwhelming opposition to the madaki's rule. "Madakin Jemaa . . . is not right in all his deeds, we the natives of Jemaa have told you that we do not want him," the petitioners wrote.[99] The petitioners further alleged a British-Jema'a plot against the demands and interests of the Fatsuam people, a conspiracy they claimed was consummated by bribes and patronage from the madaki: "You are a topranking officer and you must not receive bribery from Madaki just to treat the lives of the natives of Jemaa, stop as from today receiving bribery from Madaki and his brother Mallam Nabuja just to upset the natives demand."[100] The "natives" of Jema'a accused the madaki of a slew of administrative malpractices including extortion, embezzlement, incompetence, and disdain for his non-Muslim Fatsuam subjects.

The resident, the petitioners claimed, was reluctant to intervene because he had been bribed with "yams, pineapples, fowls, eggs, Bananas, [and] Rams." They claimed to have in their possession a dossier on the madaki's dealings with the resident, asking the latter "to arrange for a better judgment."[101] The resident's ethical infractions would be forgiven if he assented to their demand for the madaki's removal and replacement with a Fatsuam chief, the petitioners stated: "We shall foregive you if you treat the matter as a right Governor of a province." Accusing the resident of condoning and subsidizing the madaki's oppression, the Fatsuam petitioners recalled the influence of his predecessor, Mr. Bell, who "never allow[ed] Madaki to pass injustice to us here."[102] While advancing a conspiracy of "alien" rulers and reiterating their autochthonous legitimacy as "natives," the petitioners also deftly sought to appeal to British self-image as an impartial, overarching colonial authority capable of neutralizing emirate subcolonial oppression. It was a crafty rhetorical and political strategy on the part of the petitioners. They sought to either blackmail or pressure British supervisory officials into removing "oppressive" Hausa-Fulani officials.

Although the immediate goal of the petitioners was to get the colonial authorities to remove the perceived yoke of the district head's delegated rule, the broader import of their struggle emerged when they shifted from making specific allegations of misconduct to expressing a more deep-seated resentment of emirate rule. The Fatsuam simply did not consider the madaki a legitimate colonial agent-chief. He was, in their eyes, a Hausa-Fulani Muslim interloper: "We still say we do not want his ruling in this Jemaa for he is a stranger to this town Jemaa, his father a native of Kabawa in Kano Province his mother a native of Jemaa in a village by name Numana and must follow his father to his town Kano."[103] The foreignness of the madaki appears to have been further heightened by the claim that he was not even of Zazzau ancestry but of more unfamiliar caliphate heritage, which supposedly explained his egregious lack of empathy for the concerns and interests of the Fatsuam. Whether the claim of the madaki's Kano paternal origin was true or not, it functioned to dramatize the ideological distance of emirate subcolonial rule from the interests and aspirations of the non-Muslim peoples they governed with British approval.

The tone of the petition originated in a sense of frustration among the Fatsuam people at seemingly being ignored by colonial authorities who were more inclined to maintain the status quo than to correct injustice. The frustration appeared justified, for this was the second petition to express the Fatsuam people's discomfort with emirate subcolonial rule. The nominal clan and village heads of the seven Fatsuam and Kaningkon villages under the madaki's administrative jurisdiction had submitted a more diplomatic, less accusatory petition to the British district officer of Jema'a Division a month earlier. In that petition, which was written in the Hausa language, they had categorically stated their opposition to the madaki's continuation as district head.[104]

The struggle of Southern Kaduna peoples against British-delegated emirate rule was complicated by the existence of the three Southern Kaduna "independent" districts: Moroa, Kagoro, and Jaba. The "independent" kingdoms inspired nonindependent Southern Kaduna peoples to aspire to futures outside the emirate system. The three districts' autonomy pointed to the possibilities of colonial self-governance for Southern Kaduna peoples placed under the administrative jurisdiction of Zazzau and its vassals at the inception of the British colonial order. In reality, the kingdoms' administrative independence was incomplete as their funds were housed in and controlled by the Zazzau treasury, giving the emirate a fiscally grounded symbolic hegemony over them.[105] Because they began life under British colonialism as third-class chieftaincies, the independent districts were, by the order of colonial precedence, subordinated to the first-class chieftaincy of Zazzau in the colonial administrative hierarchy of traditional leadership. As a result they enjoyed only as much prestige as Zazzau was willing to concede to them.

This political dynamic meant that the three independent Southern Kaduna districts were compelled to patronize the Zazzau subcolonial system to ensure their fiscal and symbolic wellbeing. Throughout the colonial period, the ruling houses of the Southern Kaduna independent chiefdoms bucked the tradition of hostility between Zazzau and its Southern Kaduna frontier. They instead forged patron-client relationships with the royal institution of Zazzau, entering into mutually beneficial relationships that have persisted over several generations to this day.[106] Even so, the nominal independence enjoyed by the three districts heightened the sense of injustice that their neighboring Southern Kaduna communities felt.

The self-interested maneuvers of the independent districts within the Zazzau subcolonial system contrast sharply with the uncompromising protests of the nonindependent districts of Southern Kaduna. This contradiction gave Zazzau leverage in maintaining some symbolic foothold in Southern Kaduna. However, it also produced a bifurcated Southern Kaduna struggle that simultaneously looked to and away from Zazzau in the colonial and postcolonial periods.

British and caliphate ambitions meshed into a common colonial administrative project in convoluted ways. The ensuing system of proxy colonial rule in the non-Muslim Southern Kaduna region extended and formalized a loose, faltering Zazzau precolonial hegemony. British imposition of Zazzau rule in the non-Muslim communities of Southern Kaduna truncated two intertwined precolonial processes: the unraveling of Zazzau's precolonial political presence in the Southern Kaduna area and an increasingly successful effort on the part of Southern Kaduna communities to discontinue their informal political relationship with Zazzau and its surrogates.

Hausa-Fulani subcolonial rule through the political agency of the Zazzau emirate was fraught with complications from the outset, not least because the empowerment of Hausa-Fulani officials with ties to Zazzau occurred against the momentum of recent history. Southern Kaduna communities felt that the advent of Hausa-Fulani subcolonial agency in the aftermath of the British conquest robbed them of their growing independence at a time when Zazzau's outposts were in decline. This perception colored how they related and reacted to the new colonial order. The British, they surmised, were the promoters of what they perceived to be a resurgence of Zazzau hegemony. The messiness of Zazzau's subcolonial rule over the Southern Kaduna peoples reflected and reinforced this anxiety.

The importation of Hausa-Fulani Muslim chiefs and other subcolonial rulers into the Southern Kaduna area authorized a system of political and social oppression that Southern Kaduna peoples sometimes experienced as a British-aided continuation of earlier Zazzau incursions. Southern Kaduna resistance to the indignities of Anglo-Hausa-Fulani colonial rule took the form of escape, migration, self-exile, armed fight-backs, defiance, and, later, with the advent of Western missionary education, formal oppositional mobilization. At the same time, Zazzau officials, especially the powerful emir, consolidated their privileged political positions in the colonial enterprise in Southern Kaduna communities through choreographed tours meant to normalize their subcolonial rule. As part of this process, the emirs even crafted a fairly elaborate narrative of paternal subcolonial tutelage, which they announced passionately to their non-Muslim subjects. These textual and symbolic acts of Hausa-Fulani rule stoked the resentment of Southern Kaduna youth, who availed themselves of the technologies of writing, reading, and political organization to assault delegated Zazzau rule.

Yet, even as Southern Kaduna peoples railed in their petitions against the excesses of Hausa-Fulani colonial officials, calling attention to their foreignness and distance from Southern Kaduna cultural sensibilities, their outrage against the British masterminds of the colonial arrangement they resented remained somewhat ambivalent. Whether they were petition writers or activists using incipient organizational and political resources to articulate anti-caliphate protest, Southern Kaduna protesters struggled to balance a critique of British officials with their desperate faith in a professed British commitment to justice and self-determination. Whether by design or happenstance, then, emirate subcolonial rule among the Southern Kaduna communities enabled the British to occupy the ironic role of noble, compassionate arbiters, capable and willing to undo or moderate the excesses of emirate subcolonial officials. In that sense, they did not merely transfer the quotidian administrative responsibilities of colonization to Zazzau-appointed officials; they also deflected Southern Kaduna criticisms to emirate proxies.

This is significant in its illustration of the advantages of subcolonial rule to fragile colonial orders. If indirect rule allowed colonialists to make and sustain claims about commitment to fairness, justice, self-determination, and other nice-ties of colonial rhetoric, the more volatile subcolonial rule of "foreign" African groups also paradoxically gave them leeway to demonstrate their commitment to those ideals. The position of British supervising officials as mentors and benefac-tors of Hausa-Fulani colonial agents meant that they could escape the direct quo-tidian backlashes of harsh colonial policies. It also meant that Southern Kaduna peoples seeking a third-party mediator with clout to ameliorate grievances had to turn to the British. British officials could theoretically occupy such dual ideologi-cal and moral roles under the indigenous mediation of indirect rule. However, the fact that indigenous mediators, with local empathy and legitimacy, were un-likely to attract the visceral resentment directed at "alien" African colonial agents meant that aggrieved colonial subjects under indirect rule often directed their anger to British officials and institutions rather than to their mediating kinsmen. Herein lies one crucial difference between indirect rule and subcolonialism.

Out of desperation and strategic guile, Southern Kaduna activists against emirate rule invoked the benevolent and moderating capacities of British power in a vain effort to get the British to undo emirate rule. Maintaining a distance from what Southern Kaduna peoples perceived as emirate oppression was impor-tant for the British self-image. However, when emirate subcolonial figureheads resisted moves to grant self-governing powers to Southern Kaduna peoples, Brit-ish officials sided with their emirate allies, proof of the persistence of the con-stellation of ideologies and priorities that converged to authorize Hausa-Fulani subcolonial rule in the first place.

3 Emirate Maneuvers and "Pagan" Resistance in the Plateau-Nasarawa Basin

MORE COMPELLING AND unique examples abound of precolonial caliphate ventures and the ways in which they sparked resistance and adaptations among non-caliphate peoples, eventually contributing to the emergence of a subcolonial system that fobbed off power to Hausa-Fulani personnel. In the Bauchi-Plateau sector, Bauchi emirate's loose precolonial amana-based hegemony applied to some of the non-Muslim ethnic communities. Most, however, enjoyed some form of independence from Bauchi emirate's control. Upon being conquered by the British, however, many of the non-Muslim ethnic groups of the plateau highlands and lowlands found themselves placed under Bauchi's rule, administered through Hausa-Fulani agents. This British policy was founded on a misreading of precolonial relations and on the search for usable conquering groups, whose supposed legitimacy as precolonial political hegemons predisposed them to colonial leadership in non-Muslim communities. This pattern of emirate-centered colonial organization and rule requires a closer examination.

Another proximate example is the vast region encompassing the Niger and Benue littorals. Caliphate military agents and their Hausa-Fulani followers extended caliphate influence to the region and raided nearby non-Muslim communities. Caliphate military control was, however, inchoate, contested, and sporadic by the time of the European scramble for African colonial possessions. In the case of this region, early British travelers and missionaries who witnessed the most violent phase of caliphate incursions helped to give caliphate hegemony a stability and completeness that it lacked on the ground. These early European interlocutors were clearly enamored of the martial capacities of caliphate agents and the centralized political hierarchies of the caliphate system. As a result, their polemical and descriptive writings helped to establish the basis for caliphate preeminence in British colonial administration in the region.

This travel corpus, the claims of caliphate agents and caliphate-affiliated outposts, and British obsessions with the virtues of centralization and Islamic civilizational superiority constituted the tripod on which British colonial administrative policy in this area was supported. The resulting British imposition of Hausa-Fulani and Muslim Kamberi (Kanuri) chiefs and officials as the vanguard of colonial administration on the non-Muslim communities of the region found justification in these claims and in the imperative of fiscal pragmatism.

Emirate subcolonial rule triggered multiple anxieties among the peoples of the Northern Benue and Lafia region. It also elicited multiple protests and violent backlash from the non-Muslim peoples subjected to it. These protests often degenerated into violence. They intensified during the post–World War II period of pre-independence political positioning, as the fear of Hausa-Fulani and Muslim domination took on a new valence, and Hausa colonial agents consolidated and normalized their positions in preparation for independence. These new waves of late colonial protest, often accompanied by violence toward Hausa and Kamberi officials, required careful British intervention. British officials occasionally acknowledged the legitimacy of the struggle for self-administration and of the protest against emirate subcolonial rule among the autochthonous groups of the region. These rare official vindications, however, seldom altered the established British commitment to emirate proxy rule. As a result, the subcolonial initiatives of emirate colonial agents took center stage in the colonial system.

Once officials grew comfortable with a system of subcolonial delegation, they were reluctant to let their occasional critique of its excesses get in the way of their continued support. As the late colonial period wound down, protests escalated, fueled by new anxieties about the position of marginalized ethnic minorities in the future politics of a decolonized Northern Nigeria.

From Amana to Bauchi Colonial Agency on the Plateau

In the Sokoto Caliphate's eastern sphere of influence, the preeminent enforcer and protector of the caliphate's moral, religious, and cartographic boundary was the emirate of Bauchi. Bauchi was a direct product of the Fulani Jihad; the founder of its Muslim Fulani dynasty, Mallam Yakubu, was a jihad flag bearer charged with the "pacification" of a vast frontier peopled by several groups of non-Hausa traditionalists. Attacks carried out by Yakubu's army in the Bauchi-Plateau highlands between 1814 and 1850 brought him and the caliphate directly into contact and conflict with the ethnically plural, non-Muslim hill and plain regions of the Jos Plateau.

Yakubu's southward inroads benefited from the presence of numerous Fulani communities (the Jama'a) among the traditionalist communities of the Bauchi-Plateau plains. Some of these communities had by the time of the jihad morphed into small, self-contained communities with Fulani heads. The cooperation of these preexisting Fulani oligarchies on the Bauchi-Naraguta frontier proved decisive for extending some of Bauchi's influence over the non-Muslim peoples of the region. Of these proto-jihadist Fulani states, Toro stood out and became Bauchi's reliable vassal, policing the Naraguta sector on behalf of the rulers of the emirate.[1]

As Bauchi pushed the caliphate's frontier southward toward Naraguta-Afizere country, Toro helped with mop-up operations and with recruiting new Fulani Jama'a into the jihad. Toro became a bona fide proxy of Bauchi, securing and negotiating peace agreements, or amana, with non-Muslim communities and executing the terms of these accords. Bauchi's imperial hegemony in the Naraguta Plateau rested on the amana system of formalized peace settlement.[2] Amana was consummated through gestures of submission and obligations, such as the payment of an annual tribute to the overlord.

It is not clear when the Anaguta, Bujel, and Loro non-Muslim communities acquiesced to amana, but by the 1830s the relationship between Bauchi and its non-Muslim *dar-al-Harb* to the south was governed by amana conditions. While the Anaguta, one of the most populous of the non-Muslim polities in the region, pragmatically accepted amana to preserve a nominal independence and to save their traditionalist way of life, the Afizere, another major non-Muslim group, rejected the offer of amana from Toro and resisted subsequent efforts to impose

Bauchi rule on them. Several other non-Muslim peoples similarly escaped amana-mediated emirate hegemony.

Yakubu is said to have harassed the Burum people with repeated raids that resulted in a de facto, albeit infrequently enforced, control. His forces raided Ngas groups located on the vulnerable foothills of the Jos Plateau. Further military campaigns took Bauchi's forces to the land of the Tarok (Yergam) and Ankwe, where slave raids intermittently tore through the societies.[3] As Bauchi's expansionist activities stretched deeper in the regions south of the Naraguta hills into the Shendam plains, it became apparent that the forces were worn thin and that for any meaningful enforcement of caliphate influence to occur on that frontier, there had to be a stationed outpost. In 1820, Yakubu's brother, Hassan, who held the title of *madaki,* founded the town of Wase deep in the non-Muslim territory around Shendam. His brother, Yakubu, granted him suzerainty over the entire area as far as he could impose his authority and influence and made him the first emir of Wase.[4] Subsequently, Hassan raided the nearby Montol people. but the Montol fought back and he failed to establish his authority over them. The emergence of Wase was a significant development in the southward expansion of the caliphate realm. Through Wase, the caliphate had a presence—an enforcer and slave raider—in this vast non-Muslim territory.

Bauchi's control was brittle though, needing constant enforcement as amana polities rebelled or refused to fulfill the tributary claims of Toro and Bauchi. Only the smallest plain communities accepted amana outright and consistently kept its conditions. Non-Muslim communities with size and population advantages constantly breached the terms of amana and tested the resolve and might of Bauchi, often successfully. Keeping a restive frontier compliant with the terms of amana was a challenge. This was compounded by the fact that Bauchi was already groaning under the intermittent harassment of Ningi, the state on its northern frontier. Ningi, a formidable military state in its own right, was at this time independent of the caliphate system, was largely non-Muslim, and was pursuing its own territorial, foraging, and slave-raiding ambitions in multiple directions into the caliphate zone.[5]

Bauchi's rulers lacked the personnel to enforce authority or influence over such vast territory, so they began to appoint friendly members of non-Muslim groups who had converted to Islam as chiefs over some of their subject peoples in the hope of exacting tribute while conceding a measure of autonomy. The emirate of Bauchi developed this system of indirect control over time in amana communities by establishing ruling dynasties that were nominally loyal to the emirate. This precolonial form of indirect rule resembled the subsequent British practice in emirate Northern Nigeria in many respects: there were accountable indigenous surrogates and there was tribute collection and supervision. Tribute enforcement and the "maintenance and security of trade routes" trumped direct control in this pragmatic extension of influence.[6] Over time, this system proved difficult, as there were many independent ethnic groups to be dealt with. Nonetheless, Bauchi succeeded intermittently in extracting tributes of slaves, corn, horses, and cloth from some of the non-Muslim peoples. Some of the tribute was formalized; others were irregular—subject to the arbitrary discretion of Bauchi-allied agents.

One of the amana communities with a Bauchi-installed puppet Muslim indigenous chief was Kanam. Kanam emblematizes the advantages and perils of the amana system and its corollary of indirect caliphate control. Most amana societies were persistent in seeking to expand their autonomy and to reduce the extent of their tributary obligations and submission to Bauchi. As John Nengel points out, many of them succeeded. Kanam was one such case. During the reign of Emir Ibrahim (1843–79), the successor to Yakubu, Kanam rebelled successfully, and neither Bauchi nor its vassal on the Shendam lowlands, Wase, was able to resubjugate it. In fact Wase's effectiveness as an enforcer for Bauchi and the caliphate zone was on the decline after the death of Yakubu. Its attacks on several non-Muslim groups floundered. The Montols repelled and at times terrorized them. Other peoples developed mechanisms for standing up to Wase's raids. The outpost shrank in both power and territory in the second half of the nineteenth century, becoming only a symbolic and demographic indicator of the caliphate's reach. As the century drew to a close, "Wase's control over any part of the . . . Province had become nominal," and its role as an imperial outpost of Bauchi and by extension Sokoto gave way to its own quest for survival in a hostile region that was home to an overwhelming plurality of non-Muslim groups.[7]

Elsewhere around the plateau, especially in the Naraguta area, Bauchi's influence was also on the wane. In many areas it had never been strong, and war making and better resistance techniques further eroded its ability to intimidate and force compliance to its will among the non-Muslim groups of the plateau highlands. If Bauchi's hegemony over the Naraguta Plateau was uneven and weak, the most potent—by reason of their invisibility—threats to that control were the many non-Muslim hill communities that ringed small emirate outposts on the frontier. Independent of Bauchi and its vassal, Toro, these communities, among them many Afizere villages, loomed as potential military equalizers in an all-out military confrontation between the emirate and traditionalist polities on the frontier. The laxness of Bauchi's imperial regime was a pragmatic outgrowth of, and response to, this threat. The hill communities were impregnable to the cavalry of Bauchi, and escaped the emirate's slave-raiding campaigns. But they also moderated Bauchi's aggression on the non-Muslim plain communities who could migrate to the hills or call upon their co-traditionalists to aid them in confronting the common threat of Bauchi's war machine.

At the time of the British conquest then, what existed on that frontier was a set of stalemated relations similar to the shaky precolonial caliphate imperialism in other sectors. What remained of caliphate influence was a scattered and waning system of emirate control that nominally oversaw some non-Muslim peoples while pragmatically ignoring others. The hill communities were so entrenched in their "mountain fastnesses" and so independent of emirate tributary control that pioneer British administrators sometimes speculated that colonial interaction with them was the first time the communities were leaving their hill fortresses to engage in relations with outsiders on the plains below.[8]

Early British administrative thinking on the Bauchi-Plateau post-caliphate frontier was a mishmash of an exaggerated notion of the caliphate's prior imperial reach and a measured recognition of the limits of that hegemony. British official thinking was ambivalent. Officials sought to understand precolonial emirate influence and the extent of non-Muslim independence. The formula for discerning these preexisting conditions was less than perfect and sometimes arbitrary. The result was a default exaggeration of Bauchi's prior control, and the equation of amana and other relational modes with emirate conquest. For instance, British colonial officials asserted Bauchi's political control "over the Pagan district of the Plain Angass."[9] This was clearly implausible considering the fact that the Ngas groups were located to the south of the unsubordinated Anaguta and Afizere.

Although some Ngas groups had been raided and had accepted amana, they had managed to retain their autonomy under the system. Because of their distance from the centers of emirate enforcement and the logistical challenges of distant political control, many Ngas groups rejected amana outright and faced no repercussions. In fact one colonial report conceded some prior Ngas autonomy, stating that "the Pagans in the Naraguta Division (other than the plain Angass . . .) were and are independent of Emirate Rule."[10] The exclusion of some Ngas groups from this prior independence was unfaithful to the on-ground relational dynamic, since amana in fact did not preclude de facto independence, which many Ngas communities enjoyed in the face of Wase's inability to enforce Bauchi's wishes.

The ambivalence of early colonial administrative imagination was partly a reflection of the complexity of the preexisting relations between the caliphate zone and its non-Muslim frontier in this region. In reconstructing these relations, colonial observers asserted the familiar anthropological distinctions between the people with religion and the people without, the people with a civilized sensibility and the people without, the people who were organized and stratified and those who were supposedly trapped in primal wildness. In the view of the British, the people of the Central Province, as the region was designated in the colonial bureaucracy, "ranged from high civilization to pagan cannibalism: from the organization of the Bauchi Emirate to the self-law prevailing among the pagans: from devout Mohammedanism to a pagan fetish-worship which requires a newly severed and bleeding head for its drunken orgies: and from the armed horsemen of Bauchi to the slingman of Benguda."[11]

Anthropological assumptions such as this are grounded in the colonial default to precolonial caliphate supremacy and constituted the basis of early colonial administrative arrangements on the plateau highlands and lowlands. The persistence of this template of sociopolitical valuation in Northern Nigerian colonial officialdom meant that it helped frame the perception of non-Muslim peoples in relation to the peoples of the caliphate zone. Administrative expediency and philosophical assumptions about the superior nexus of Islam and centralization gave further impetus to these claims. Once these contrasts were written into colonial discourse as canonical references for administrative innovations, they were replicated for different zones of precolonial contact between the caliphate and Northern Nigeria's non-Muslim peoples.

These simplistic binaries of course elided some of the nuances and instabilities of emirate–non-Muslim relations in the Bauchi-Plateau sector. But even as British officials reified precolonial emirate rule, they recognized the limit of Bauchi's hegemony and the resistance of non-Muslim peoples in former times. This recognition was expressed especially for the most obvious instances where Bauchi had failed to impose its political will on determined non-Muslim communities. British officials recognized that "the influence of the Bauchi and Gombe Emirates stopped short . . . at the hill regions: the pagan preserving his independence where the country is mountainous."[12] The effort to balance the recognition of de facto precolonial non-Muslim independence with official fascination with the administrative utility of emirate political tradition would prove the supreme challenge of colonial governance in this region.

In the end, administrative convenience and the canonical influence of the "emirate model" trumped sensitivity to precolonial "pagan" independence. On the completion of the colonial conquest, administering the region required territorial definition and (re)naming the new conquest. In this, colonial officials defaulted to the doctrine of caliphal supremacy: the colonial provincial entity that emerged was called Bauchi Province, and its territory was defined to capture all the areas that comprised Bauchi emirate's precolonial territory as well as the surrounding non-Muslim territories to the south, east, west, and north within uneven radii. The city of Bauchi was declared the headquarters of the new colonial province. The non-Muslim groups were organized into two administrative units within Bauchi Province in 1908: the Naraguta Division, which included the Kanam, Ngas, Sura, and Berom peoples, and the Bukuru District, which included several other non-Muslim ethnic groups in the broader Jos Plateau region. In 1911, the name of the province was changed to Central Province.[13]

Although the administrative arrangement appeared to recognize the range of independence and freedoms that the non-Muslim peoples of the region enjoyed in precolonial times, in practice, colonial officials recognized Bauchi as the political center of the province and its emir as the figurehead of British rule in the region. More revealingly, in 1912 following a series of administrative adjustments, a new Angass District emerged and was placed under the direct administrative control of Bauchi in what was a clear expression of the erroneous colonial assumption of Bauchi's precolonial sway over the Ngas people. Because of the district's distance from Bauchi, it was supervised by a British administrative officer stationed in the proximate non-Muslim district of Pankshin even while being subject to the emir of Bauchi's rule.[14] This arrangement produced a confusing reality of dual control that starkly illustrated the arbitrariness of emirate subcolonial rule.

In 1912, the resident of the province recognized the egregious oddity of emirate rule among the Ngas and recommended that Angass District be removed from the administrative orbit of Bauchi. His proposal was greeted with hostility and he "left [the unresolved status of Angass District] in abeyance."[15] After consulting the emir of Bauchi and some on-ground colonial officials, the convergence of emirate and British opinion favored the retention of Bauchi's control over the Ngas people. The resident subsequently changed his mind. He not only acquiesced to the existing arrangement of Bauchi control and pragmatic supervision by a nearby British official but also contended that Bauchi should assume direct administrative supervision of the distant district to go with its statutory control. "There is no reason," the resident argued, "why the District cannot now retake its former place in the Bauchi Emirate, and be controlled entirely from Bauchi, instead of from Pankshin."[16] By the resident's logic, the Ngas people and their administrative unit, Angass District, would merely be rejoining the emirate system that they purportedly belonged to in precolonial times. The district would, according to him, be "retake[ing] its place" in the emirate. This was convenient colonial revisionism.

The staying power of pro-emirate assumptions in British administrative practice in the Bauchi-Plateau axis was a compelling factor in the administrative partitioning of Central Province. Other early colonial administrative decisions bore out this simplistic translation of precolonial relations. Between 1901 and 1912, there was considerable British investment in tin mining on the Jos Plateau, triggering the immigration of miners and laborers from across the geographical spectrum of colonial Nigeria, most of them "a mixture of Hausas, Fulanis and Kanuris."[17] The migrants congregated in camps and settlements that quickly evolved into self-contained communities. These communities then gave rise to new commercial dynamics in the non-Muslim Anaguta, Berom, and Afizere country they were located in.[18] Seeking to enforce order and administrative discipline on the fast-urbanizing camps and settlements, British officials arbitrarily pronounced the settlement constellation a colonial administrative district and placed it under the emir of Bauchi. A brother of the emir of Bauchi was then appointed as the first district head (chief) of the new unit.[19]

The pragmatic administrative merits of this action occluded its political awkwardness. The creation by colonial fiat of a Bauchi emirate-administered colonial district in the heart of the non-Muslim region of the province conformed to the philosophy of empowering the emirate sector in territorial, symbolic, and jurisdictional ways. It would, however, be the basis of future political agitation by the Berom for an indigenous chief of metropolitan Jos, the vast city that evolved from the tin economy of the Naraguta-Bukuru plains.[20] It would also help dramatize a future narrative of Hausa-Fulani political dominance and galvanize the non-Muslim peoples of the plateau area.

In other sectors of colonial Plateau Province, as the region was later named when Bauchi emirate became a stand-alone province, the British continued to privilege Hausa-Fulani personnel as the executors of colonial rule in non-Muslim communities. For the Tarok and other non-Muslim groups, what Adam Higazi terms "the transformative effects of colonialism" flowed from Hausa-Fulani agency.[21] The British put Hausa-Fulani colonial agents in charge of dreaded colonial activities such as forced labor and taxation. Subsequently, the spread of Christian missionary activities among the Tarok and other non-Muslim ethnic groups intensified their resentment against Hausa colonial agents, especially those recruited from the proximate and hostile emirate outpost of Wase. Higazi notes that in the colonial plateau lowlands, "Christianity was associated . . . with opposition to Islam, [which] in turn [was] associated with Wase."[22] These colonial realities of emirate subcolonial rule would reconfigure the political aspirations of several plateau non-Muslim ethnic groups, who increasingly saw Hausa-Fulani domination as the visible and proximate face of colonial oppression.

Prelude to Emirate Colonization in the Niger-Benue–Lafia Axis

To the south and southwest of Plateau Province lay the Niger-Benue and Lafia regions, with their own long and convoluted path to emirate subcolonial rule. The mid- to late-nineteenth century was a period of increasing European commercial and exploratory activities in the Niger-Benue region. This occurred as the caliphate was expanding southward or consolidating earlier expansions. The consolidation and spread of caliphate influence generated discernible social fissures, but it also gave rise to some permanent demographic and political reconfigurations. The terror generated by caliphate expansion and by slave raiding and the tribute-taking military adventures of caliphate surrogates such as Nupe, Keffi, Nasarawa, and others is already well documented.[23] The mid-century's pervasive terror produced chaos, upheaval, and displacement. By the century's end, certain regional status quos were evident.

The diary of the freed Yoruba slave and Christian missionary explorer of the Niger-Benue region, Samuel Ajayi Crowther, is an illuminating window into these dynamics. In 1854 when he traversed the area, he saw fresh indicators of forced migrations caused by "the invasions of the Filatas [Fulani jihad-ists]."[24] Tales of non-Muslim groups moving between different sides of the Niger and Benue Rivers and escaping the Fulani raiders by building "houses upon the mountains as places of refuge" are prevalent throughout his recorded observations. No other event in the caliphate's southward expansion elicited as much of a demographic chain reaction as the invasion of Opanda by the forces of caliphate surrogate Nasarawa in 1854.[25] In numerous towns and villages, Samuel Crowther saw "temporary sheds to escape the depredations of the Filatas," and frightened villagers who "[had] taken refuge on Islands" on the opposite side of the river, which were inaccessible to the Fulani warriors.[26] Crowther described the pervasive climate of insecurity, anxiety, and rootlessness as conditions caused by the "fear of the Filatas."[27]

Refugees from Nasarawa's destruction of Opanda and Toto abounded in several sectors of the Niger-Benue confluence region, harassed by other caliphate forces such as Keffi and Nupe. The Bassa and Ebira sought out high grounds, islands, and forested areas on the southern bank of the two rivers to establish new settlements. The caliphate's surrogate warriors had spread their influence as far as Doma, where a procaliphate chief held sway fleetingly in loyalty to Zazzau.[28] Across the vast region, new caliphate-allied mavericks were staking out new claims to raiding territory, hoping to carve out their own sphere of authority and establish valuable trade routes.

By the 1890s, non-Muslim communities in the Niger-Benue region had uneasily settled into a life of paranoid evasion, constructing the details of their lives around the imperative of escape and self-preservation. Their strategies ranged from rational to bizarre in the face of their desperation. Paul Staudinger, who traveled around the river port town of Loko in the 1880s, observed settlements clearly designed to physically and spiritually ward off Hausa slave raiders and aggressive Hausa ivory traders and merchants. Homes along the Benue's banks were tucked away in thick forests "with a narrow path leading up to [them] which could be barred in two places with tree trunks at night." The Agatu hung "elephant skulls" on the entrance to immobilize "any dangerous peoples who should enter." In order to guard the spiritual source of their protection and keep their perennial nemesis far from the sacred instrument of their protection, the "Hausa were not allowed to enter" the shrines.[29]

At other locations, Staudinger and his crew observed new settlement patterns that rendered caliphal control and influence ineffective in many areas beyond the immediate vicinity of caliphate outposts and Hausa-populated subsidiaries. In the Eggon sector, some villages successfully kept slave raiders from Keffi at bay by digging protective trenches around their settlements.[30] They also constantly appealed to a network of protective shrines that I toured during a recent research visit.[31] Other Eggon villages, already protected by the natural barrier of the Eggon hills and by the long, winding Mada River, took additional protective measures to make it impossible for jihadist cavalries to invade them. They built protective stone walls (*ganuwa*) around their settlements, making them inaccessible to jihadist cavalry.[32] They also posted sentries at designated gates around the walls to alert villagers to jihadist activities or spies at the foot of the hill so they could respond, as they often did, by raining down poisoned arrows on the aggressors from Keffi.[33] The remains of these walls are visible around some Eggon settlements to date.[34]

Because of the success of these efforts, a new order of ineffective hegemony characterized the caliphate's engagement with the non-Muslim peoples of its most southerly frontier in the 1880s and 1890s. Emblematic of this state of affairs were the permanent fortresses that mushroomed in the region, which Staudinger described so graphically:

> Several times we noticed in the distance natives peering down into the valley, and a glimpse of thatched roofs betrayed the presence of a village here and there. Such mountainous hideouts are impregnable fortresses and for a last refuge for the pagan population in retreat from the Hausa. The thick forest in the middle of a depression or valley is also a place often sought by these tribes for settlement as the impenetrable wood provides a comparatively safe retreat in case of attack.[35]

Although the fear caused by caliphate raids remained and continued to shape the movements of non-Muslim groups at the end of the nineteenth century, the caliphate's influence was on the decline, and its relationship with the non-Muslim polities of the region most closely resembled a stalemate. The inventive desperation of the non-Muslim peoples had led them to devise effective solutions to caliphate raids. Coupled with the diminishing return of raids, these non-Muslim defensive initiatives had undermined caliphal influence in the region.

By the end of the nineteenth century, the Niger-Benue region was dotted by a few caliphate-allied emirates that were headquartered in evolving urban centers such as Keffi, Bida, Nasarawa, and Lafia. They had occasional alliances with elite Muslim converts in Doma and Keana. Most of the region was, however, a vast rural area populated by politically decentralized and semicentralized non-Muslim peoples. Non-Muslim polities like Igu and Umaisha, whose political aristocracies were beginning to embrace the cultures of caliphate Islam, complicated this demographic collage. The presence of itinerant and sedentary Hausa traders and Fulani herdsmen in the rural sectors added further complexity to this mosaic. Dependent on the goodwill of non-Muslims but politically loyal to the caliphate, the Hausa-Fulani settler communities were a source of constant tensions and ethnic suspicions.

Emirate domination, to the extent that it can be called that, was not accompanied by hegemony in the sense of being normalized or accepted, and many of the caliphate surrogates in the Niger-Benue area had no actual political control beyond the immediate vicinity of their foundational towns. The non-Muslim peoples of the Niger-Benue region adjusted to the reality of insecurity, but most of them did not acquiesce to Islam or the caliphate's political authority. Lacking legitimacy with the people, caliphate influence in the region was uneven, contested, fragile, and largely symbolic. In many areas, the end of the nineteenth century saw either a faded caliphate influence or a successful challenge to its power.

British Reaffirmation of Caliphal Primacy

Late-nineteenth-century European travel and trade in the Niger-Benue area tipped the political situation in favor of the caliphate presence and the people and institutions that embodied it. Acting on the established tradition of European fascination with the caliphate and disregard for the political and social systems of non-Muslim peoples of Northern Nigeria, European travelers and traders sought protection and treaties only from caliphate-allied rulers even when those rulers had no actual or symbolic jurisdiction over the areas of travel and trade. When Paul Staudinger and his group arrived in the Loko area to begin their northward journey, they sought the blessings of the Hausa chief of Loko and his overlord, the emir of Nasarawa, sending letters to them and acknowledging their claimed jurisdiction over the area.[36] They ignored the Agatu chiefs of the area.

Staudinger and his group were doing nothing new but, as many European traders and travelers who came before them had done, acted on the preexisting affinity for caliphate authority to extend recognition and reverence to caliphate-allied rulers. Some of this was a pragmatic acknowledgement of de facto military supremacy. Some of it, however, was dictated by a generic European attraction to centralized, monotheistic polities that were similar to the political systems in Europe. One of the earliest and most influential of these travelers, William Baikie, set the tone when he counseled subsequent British travelers, traders, and colonialists in the Benue area to "never pay any undue or excessive respect to the heathen Chiefs and Kings below the Niger-Benue Confluence; treat them with ordinary courtesy—nothing more, and especially pay no heed to their degrading ceremonies. With the kings of Nupe and Hausa, again, be more particular . . . their superior intelligence, civilization, position, and influence, entitle them to a much larger share of respect and deference."[37] This advice had a canonical effect on the attitude of subsequent British travelers and traders. By the time of Staudinger's journey in the 1880s, the mythologized positions of the emirates and their rulers as the unchallenged lords of Northern Nigeria were fairly established in the European consciousness. Caliphate-allied operatives emerged as preferred allies as the British prepared to conquer the Northern Nigerian territories and establish British rule.

A custom of European deference to the nearest caliphate-allied authority had emerged by the late nineteenth century. The Niger Company, a proto-imperial British trading firm that did much of its business in the Niger-Benue region, had concretized this custom by entering into formal treaties with the Muslim authorities of the region while shunning non-Muslim rulers and elites. The company's patronage of caliphate-ordained authority was dictated by a long British imperial attraction to martial, centralized aristocracies.[38] It was also dictated by a pragmatic quest for territory and spheres of commercial and quasi-political influence. It was easier to sign so-called treaties of protection and friendship with a few centralized Muslim authorities than with numerous fragmented non-Muslim entities scattered throughout the Niger-Benue hinterland. Nonetheless, the attraction to caliphate institutions was self-reflexive in that it mirrored what the British admired in their own high political and religious cultures.

British dealings with the emir of Nasarawa reflected this mix of pragmatism and idealism. The Niger Company signed a treaty with the emir of Nasarawa around 1880. The company would later claim that the treaty ceded both banks of the Benue River to it and by extension to the British Crown.[39] The credibility of this interpretation is suspect, however, since the claim by both the British and their Nasarawa emirate partners that both sides of the Benue were caliphate territories was disputable. The claim represented a textual extension of caliphal jurisdiction. The southern bank of the Benue was clearly beyond the reach of most of the caliphate's cavalries, hence its attraction in the mid-century as a site of refuge. Despite this easily verifiable fact, the British characterization endured. The outlines of a European-designed caliphate rule in Northern Nigeria were emerging in this period of early colonial contact, and complicating factoids could not stand in the way. By the mid-1880s, the Niger Company had an official intermediary from the emir of Nasarawa monitoring its activities and mediating between it and the emir.[40] The Hausa-Fulani rulers happily played the script handed to them by European interlocutors, sending parties to welcome important European traders and travelers, exchanging gifts and letters with them, welcoming the Europeans to "their country," and assuring them of the caliphate's protection.[41] Caliphate-British alliance in this region emerged through the strategic sidelining of indigenous non-Muslim authorities.

British Conquest and the Beginning of Emirate Rule

When the British government bought out the charter of the Royal Niger Company in 1900 and took over the administrative and political jurisdiction of a largely unconquered Northern Nigerian area, they recognized caliphate-allied states as possessors of authority in Central Nigeria. Subsequently, this became the linchpin of British colonial engagements with the peoples of the region. Early British officials, like their Niger Company predecessors, continued to view the entire northeastern bank of the Benue as the domain of the emir of Nasarawa. The actual picture was more ambiguous. Loko was essentially an Agatu and Afo town with a caliphate-backed Hausa aristocracy. However, the British regarded it as an enclave firmly within the jurisdiction of Nasarawa and treated it as such. After the British conquest, the Hausa chief of Loko, a nominal figurehead whose power applied only to the Hausa and Nupe Muslim immigrants in the town, received official colonial recognition as a legitimate political authority over the people of Loko and its surroundings.[42] The British ignored the chief of the Agatu autochthons.

After the British declaration of a protectorate over Northern Nigeria in 1900, the emir of Nasarawa was the first caliphate-allied ruler to submit to the British forces commanded by Frederick Lugard. Not wanting military confrontation with the British, the emir, Umar Danwaji, whose sphere of influence the British had extended by treaty and patronage, pledged allegiance to the Crown in 1901 and formally submitted to British authority in 1902.[43] Subsequently, the headquarters of the Lower Benue Province, as the region had been named, was moved to Nasarawa town and the province's name was changed to Nasarawa Province.[44] These gestures further affirmed the primacy and centrality of the caliphate presence and its corollary institutions to British rule. The emir of Keffi had earlier accommodated a British resident, Captain Maloney, who was sent there as the advance guard of British imperial schemes in the region. Captain Maloney was subsequently murdered by the emir of Zazzau's supervisory intermediary, or *magaji,* the notorious slave raider Yamusa, who then fled northward, triggering the events that led to the British march to Sokoto, headquarters of the caliphate. The ostensible British pursuit of Yamusa culminated in the defeat of the caliphate in 1903, and the surrender of the emirs of Lafia, Jema'a, and Abuja. With the "pacification" of the last caliphate holdouts, the architecture of the colonial administrative province of Nasarawa Province was in place.[45]

In an act that encapsulated the caliphate-centered trajectory of British colonial rule, Frederick Lugard, the high commissioner of Northern Nigeria, visited the province in 1905 and confirmed the positions of the five Muslim caliphate-allied emirs in the province, bureaucratizing their positions and granting them official roles as British allies in the new colonial administration.[46] No non-Muslim figures of traditional authority were accorded the same recognition or bureaucratic role. Instead, they and their non-Muslim kinsmen came under the jurisdiction of various Muslim rulers by default and by colonial fiat. Subsequent administrative reforms expedited both the Hausa-Fulani role in British rule and the directly proportional decline in non-Muslim bureaucratic power. The authority of non-Muslim chiefs was a casualty of the early colonial administrative reforms as they were subsumed under the administrative infrastructures of preferred emirate allies. The Agatu, like the Afo, Bassa, and other non-Muslim peoples, found themselves placed under the Hausa chief of Loko via administrative reforms carried out between 1901 and 1902. This was even before they had been formally "pacified" into British colonial Northern Nigeria.[47]

Occasionally, pro-emirate British fantasies collided with reality. The emir of Keffi's submission to British authority represented a pacification of the entire territory of the new colonial province, British officials assumed. This assumption was rudely shattered when the Mada hill dwellers, who had in precolonial times secured their protection from caliphate raids by moving to hilly high grounds, successfully repelled a British pacification expedition in 1917.[48] As the many politically decentralized, non-Muslim peoples of Northern Nigeria revolted and distracted British officials from administrative tasks, the problem of enforcing centralized rule in regions without centralized political organization plagued the fledgling colonial administration. The sheer number of such communities meant that in order for indirect rule to achieve ubiquity across Northern Nigeria, the absence of preexisting political centralization had to be addressed. Pioneer governor Frederick Lugard articulated a pervasive British colonial problem in his administrative manual *Political Memoranda*: the absence of institutions compatible with indirect rule in the non-Muslim communities. He declared that when confronted with the decentralized political traditions of the Middle Belt, officials were to "endeavor to find a man of influence as chief, and to group under him as many villages and districts as possible."[49] It was an unwritten assumption that such "men of influence" and men of prior leadership pedigree even in non-Muslim zones were to be found among groups with prior ties to the caliphate system. Decentralized non-Muslim polities were not considered reservoirs of men with such administrative inclinations.

Hausa-Emirate Subcolonialism and Its Consequences

The bureaucracy of emirate colonial administration took slightly different shapes in different non-Muslim sectors of this region, but the outline remained similar. Among the Agatu people of Loko, Anglo-caliphate colonial rule came complete with the full repertoire of emirate administrative titles and offices. Subsumed under the administrative jurisdiction of the Hausa chief of Loko, Muhammed Maikandiri (1900–1919), the Agatu witnessed the cultural and political erasure of their political system, which was designed around the figure of the *oche,* or chief, and a council of titled elders known as *igabo.*[50] In place of this system, a myriad of Islamic titles were introduced into Agatu society, and the holders of these titles were assigned to oversee various responsibilities on behalf of the chief of Loko and his superior, the emir of Nasarawa, who in turn reported to the British resident. Early protests by the Agatu against what they perceived as a cultural and political humiliation invited decisive British military reprisals.[51]

Once the emirate administrative institutions began to operate within the larger colonial bureaucracy, their true implications emerged in sharp relief. As officials appointed by the chief of Loko began to assess and collect taxes, the new-ness of the fiscal burdens and their harsh enforcement by Hausa-Fulani colonial personnel heightened the resentments against the new regime. The legitimacy gap between the new Muslim officials and their Agatu, Afo, and Ebira subjects exacerbated the problem. Routine colonial administrative duties such as pun-ishing tax defaulters, enforcing law and order, and convicting and sentencing offenders reinforced the long-festering perception of Hausa-Fulani oppression, which in turn harkened back to precolonial caliphate expansion and raids.

In other parts of Nasarawa Province, the same dynamics played out in di-verse ways. The British farmed out the peoples of Akwanga to the Muslim emir-ates of Lafia, Keffi, and Jema'a as administrative appendages. The Eggon people found themselves tucked into the administrative domain of Lafia and Keffi, and the Mada people were parceled to Jema'a. By 1913, Lugard had rearranged the ethnic groups in the Akwanga region into five districts: South Mada, North Mada, Central Mada, Mama, and Nungu. Although they were still administered through the chiefly authority of Lafia's ruler, the British appointed indigenous subchiefs for some of the districts. Central Mada, the most populous and im-portant of the districts, however, was ruled directly by Isiyaku Bashayi, a Fulani Muslim and son of the emir of Keffi.[52]

Sometimes the desired preparation for the implementation of indirect rule was achieved through the simple imposition of emirate-type administrative for-mulas. Once established, however, the "alien" emirate institutions often took on a life of their own, spawning administrative tentacles that deepened the admin-istrative control of Hausa-Fulani officials. Take the case of Bashayi, the Fulani district head of Central Mada. Without authorization from his British supervi-sors, Bashayi appointed his own agents, or *jekadu,* and assigned them to sev-eral Mada districts where they collected taxes and levies, sat in judgment over disputes, and effectively usurped the role of indigenous Mada village heads.[53] The village heads were by colonial protocol in charge of these responsibilities under the supervision and direction of Bashayi. The discomfort of British of-ficials with Bashayi and other Hausa-Fulani agents' discretionary extensions of control was mitigated by the desire for grassroots despots capable of taming res-tive non-Muslim communities and schooling them in the obligations of colonial governance.

There was a pedagogical intuition at the heart of the British delegation of power to Hausa-Fulani colonial agents among the non-Muslim peoples of Na-sarawa Province. The British envisioned Bashayi as a transitional Hausa-Fulani chief who, as a man of assumed superior intellect, "would inculcate this knowl-edge among the [Mada] village heads, train them in administrative matters and build up their authority, so that in a few years they would be able to assume the administration of the tribe by themselves."[54] Such didactic aims were, however, threatened by excesses, such as Bashayi appointing his own personal jekadu and building a parallel colonial bureaucracy that rendered Mada subchiefs irrelevant.

In 1922, Hugh Clifford, the colonial governor of Nigeria, failed to secure colonial office support for his proposal to gradually abandon the policy of converting the non-Muslim "primitive tribal systems" to centralized, administratively effective rural autocracies through Hausa-Fulani chieftaincy. His failure reinforced the emirate model as the administrative gold standard in colonial Northern Nigeria. More consolidation of the emirate model followed. Bashayi was reassigned from Mada and appointed a district head over the Eggon people, who protested being ruled by a Fulani, to no avail. The assistant resident, Charles Arden-Clarke, subsequently worked to break the ranks of the Eggon opposition to Bashayi by playing Eggon village heads against one another.[55]

Subcolonialism Reaffirmed and Contested

When Richmond Palmer took over as governor of Northern Nigeria in 1925, he pursued a path of administrative reforms that returned to the Lugardian essence of empowering emirate-type rural autocracies to lubricate the wheels of colonial administration. Subsequent reforms confirmed the imposition of "alien" Hausa-Fulani chiefs over non-Muslim groups. The fleeting vision of Hausa-Fulani tutelage was replaced by a more permanent idea of Hausa-borne colonial civilization in "pagan" areas. Political centralization and territorial boundedness became the central idioms of colonial chieftaincy, and non-Muslim districts in Nasarawa Province increasingly mimicked emirate models of political organization. By this logic of studious mimicry, the people of Mama were placed under the Muslim district head of Wamba, Mohammed Kore, who had converted to Islam at the urging of his Muslim subcolonial supervisors at Lafia.[56]

Agitations by some of the indigenous non-Muslim peoples of Nasarawa Province in the 1930s and 1940s for their own indigenous chiefs forced the colonial authorities to acquiesce to their demands and encourage chiefly "men of influence" from among their ranks, while keeping other non-Muslim peoples under emirate rule. This represented a small triumph for the non-Muslim peoples against the subcolonial regime of Hausa-Fulani operatives. The emergence of indigenous chiefs from among the largely decentralized political systems of the non-Muslim peoples, however, served to further the initial colonial vision of engineering institutions of centralized leadership among non-Muslim communities through the preparatory tutelage of Hausa rulers. British officials celebrated this as a success of subcolonial rule, the attainment of its endpoint, even as the ethnic communities allowed to self-administer through their own chiefs celebrated what they saw as their freedom from emirate subcolonial control.

This shift toward centralized, indigenous political institutions fulfilled one of the conditions for a seamlessly functioning indirect rule system. In a sense, political centralization and the engineering of chieftaincy among non-Muslim groups demonstrated the success of the preparatory vision of emirate transitional subcolonialism. Rather than being a departure from the ideals of subcolonial rule, the transition to indigenous subordinate chieftaincy in some districts deemed prepared enough for it was a crystallization of the vision that underpinned emirate-centered colonialism. For British officials the movement toward indigenous, if subordinate, chieftaincy was a validation of their view that caliphate tutelage would culminate in the emergence of self-sustaining and colonially accountable chieftaincies among the non-Muslim peoples.

The gradual evolution of indigenous chieftaincy and centralized traditional leadership in the Nasarawa Province did not, however, erase the legacies of British-aided emirate consolidation over the non-Muslim peoples of the province. These legacies unfolded in dramatic ways in some areas and in subtle ways in others. As the colonial period progressed, British colonial officials encountered strong, lingering resentments toward the emirate administration system. Negotiating this ethno-religious minefield of colonial power relations created new problems and threatened to imperil colonial rule. The tumultuous arena of lower-level administration would reveal just how volatile the caliphate's subcolonial interaction with the non-caliphate sector had become.

Colonial officials confronted a vast rural non-Muslim sector dotted by enclaves of caliphate-aligned power. In some areas, the tensions were as visual as they were conceptual, as Muslim emirate city-states such as Lafia, Nasarawa, and Keffi found themselves surrounded by thriving non-Muslim communities. These communities flourished as the colonial order removed the threat of slave raids and similar harassments. Many of them were sources of potential threats to nearby former caliphate outpost towns and emirates.

The Lafia sector exemplified and dramatized this trend. Lafia, with British support, subsumed many non-Muslim districts and became the area's preeminent subcolonial authority early in the colonial period. Its British-bestowed status, however, contradicted its real status as an insular, ethnic, and religious presence in this vast non-Muslim region. Lafia was a Muslim former outpost of the Sokoto Caliphate surrounded by "four districts [that were] all strongly pagan."[57] This demographic oddity was exacerbated by a British obsession that gave the Muslim emir of Lafia subcolonial jurisdiction over the surrounding non-Muslim districts, all of which were "presided over by forceful pagan District Head[s]."[58] From the outset, British officials worked to subordinate the non-Muslim ethnic groups in the area to the Kamberi Muslim rulers of Lafia.

Lafia was founded, according to most sources, in 1804 by Kanuri immigrants from the kingdom of Bornu, led by a man named Dunama. Oral accounts state that the immigrants were given the current location of Lafia town to settle by the chief of the Gwandara people, whose major ancestral hub is the nearby town of Shaabu. The Kanuri immigrants accumulated goodwill with the chief of the Gwandara by strengthening his hand in local military rivalries. In return they found support and protection among the Gwandara, which inspired them to settle permanently in Lafia.[59]

Once established in the early-nineteenth century, the city-state became the object of Bauchi's interest because of its location in a region teeming with non-Muslims who could be raided for slaves and booty. Emir Yakubu of Bauchi attacked Lafia in 1817, destroying villages on its outskirts. Umar, Lafia's chief at this time, counterattacked, leading to a stalemated outcome in the form of a siege on the town. Thereafter Umar surrendered and a truce was arranged, under which Lafia accepted the suzerainty of Bauchi and pledged to pay tribute and fulfill other customary obligations of membership in the Sokoto Caliphate.[60] Over the course of the late-nineteenth century, Lafia town was consolidated as a caliphate outpost with the arrival of more Kamberi, Hausa, and Fulani immigrants, and its political structures as well as those of other Lafia-affiliated Hausa settlements in the area took on a decidedly emirate sociopolitical character, replete with hereditary offices and theocratic rituals.

Although Lafia conducted intermittent raids in the nearby non-Muslim communities, the results were checkered, and the city-state never controlled or exacted tribute from the Alago, Gwandara, Eggon, Tiv, or any of the other ethnic groups that surrounded the town. Yet in 1903, with the colonial conquest concluded, British officials declared the region, with an overwhelming population of non-Muslim communities, an emirate. The Muslim chief of Lafia town was declared emir and recognized as a second-class colonial chief. The Alago of Doma and Keana, along with the Eggon, Gwandara, and Tiv communities, were organized into districts and placed under the newly created emirate.[61]

Of the subordination of Alago chieftaincy institutions to emirate subcolonial supervision, Dickson Eyoh writes: "Their traditional rulers were sanctioned as district heads with the designation of third class chiefs. They became representatives of their districts in a newly established Lafia Native Authority Council, through which they were to be supervised in the performance of their functions by the emir of Lafia."[62] Eyoh argues that the policy of subordinating the non-Muslim communities of this region to the subcolonial supervision of Lafia "rested on a strained postulation that, first, the Kamberi were conquerors of minor tribes in the region, and, second, under Kamberi leadership the region had become subject to the intermittent 'overlordship' of Bauchi and Zaria emirates in the aftermath of the . . . jihads."[63] The "artificiality and arbitrariness of the political hierarchy newly imposed on the region" reflected a tendency of the British to rework and simplify contested narratives and local histories of political relations as a way of "manufactur[ing] 'conquering groups,' based on the degree of centralization of political authority, who then could be posited as 'natural' rulers of particular areas."[64]

In organizing the communities of the Lafia region in the postconquest peri-od, British officials "appeared driven to imagine isolated pockets of Hausa-Fulani and other Islamized communities . . . as founders, through conquests, of emir-ates which had gone into decline. These imagined emirates were to be revital-ized as frameworks of political rule over more backward 'pagan' communities."[65] In addition to placing them under Lafia, the British appointed ad hoc chiefs for the Eggon, Tiv, and Lindiri peoples, who lacked centralized political authority of even the intermediate type possessed by the Alago. This was a way of making them more amenable to Lafia rule and a strategy of extending the centralized chain of political accountability that led from Lafia to the towns and villages of the region. Although numerically ranked fifth in a census taken in 1938,[66] the privileged Kamberi ethnic group of Lafia quickly established themselves as the dominant African colonial actors in the non-Muslim communities of Lafia Divi-sion. They dominated the Lafia Native Authority Council despite their numerical minority, occupying fifteen of twenty positions reserved for communities that constituted the division.[67]

By British design, the Muslim Kamberi and Hausa officials controlled the consequential institutions of colonial rule in Lafia Division. The non-Muslim communities were even required to consult the rulers of Lafia on the selection of their own district heads, a colonial rule that often enabled Lafia to ensure the ascension of chiefs loyal to its appointed supervisory officials. Such a position of privilege and power had its perks, and some of these perks existed at the expense of subordinate non-Muslim groups, in a colonial system increasingly governed by zero-sum permutations. The vast majority of salaried colonial jobs went to Kamberi and Hausa officials, who in turn used these jobs to create spin-offs that either were paid from the treasury or were subsidized informally by exacting un-authorized fees and taxes from non-Muslim communities. Lafia officials enjoyed the power and privileges of tax collection. As court officials they collected court fees, and as the dominant officials of the Lafia Native Authority they favored themselves in the award of small public works contracts.

Diverging statuses in the colonial system here corresponded to primordial differences. Understandably, then, the "difference in religion" as one colonial official described it, "was the cause of endless difficulty" in administering the region.[68] The difference transcended religion and included ethnic and ideologi-cal impulses. The pattern of historical relations between Lafia and the vast, non-Muslim countryside in which it was nestled is implicated in these tensions. Con-flicts between the different non-Muslim peoples were as intense and frequent in colonial times as they had been in precolonial times. However, while the fluidity of precolonial caliphal overlordship prevented the emergence of a non-Muslim coalition of anti-caliphate resistance, the British colonial order's centralizing im-perative drew these adversaries together, making solidarity possible. This solidarity of non-Muslim peoples was often inchoate and unstable, but it was sustained by a common resentment of the Hausa allies of British colonialism. As the divisional officer of Lafia Division, Lawrence Stephenson, asserted in 1946, the non-Muslim peoples in Lafia Division, "who were administered by the Emir of Lafia," were not always in solidarity with one another, but they were "united in their hearty dislike of their Moslem overlords in Lafia."[69]

The Revolt of the Alago

Non-Muslim peoples' growing resentment of their subordination to nearby emirate entities made the routine colonial practice of touring a particularly dangerous arena of power relations. During tours into the countryside, British officials encountered firsthand the bitterness that non-Muslims harbored against their British-empowered subcolonial overlords. In March 1946, one such encounter unfolded in the Alago town of Keana during the visit of the divisional officer. His observations are a poignant commentary on the state of colonial relations between Hausa officials and the peoples of non-caliphate zones in colonial Northern Nigeria:

> On one of these tours we had planned to stay the night at a place called Arago, the headquarters town of the Arago, a pagan tribe. . . . When we arrived there we found the place in a state of turmoil. Agitators had whipped up the feelings of the people to a state of fury, likely to explode into violence any moment. The target of their threats, and abuse, was the Moslem Emir of Lafia in particular, and all Moslems in general.[70]

Incidents like this were routine occurrences in the frontier regions, where the caliphate came in direct, messy contact with non-Muslim peoples over a long span of time. Often, non-Muslims timed their anti-emirate protests to coincide with the visits of British colonial officials in a desperate effort to be heard. The melodrama was also sometimes choreographed to curry the sympathy of touring officials. Nonetheless, the scene described above was typical in its expression of the depth of anti-caliphate resentment in the predominantly non-Muslim region.

The hostility encountered on the March 1946 tour seemed to have escalated rather dramatically on account of the presence of two senior members of the council of the emir of Lafia, his representatives on the tour who came along "to get a bit of experience."[71] Against the backdrop of the existing anti-caliphate sentiment of the people of the Alago town of Keana, the presence of the two Muslim subcolonial agents had deep implications, as they were seen to represent the dreaded British-Hausa alliance. The seething Keana mob interpreted the visit of Lafia's senior officials as a reaffirmation of British disregard for their quest for colonial self-governance and a reendorsement of Lafia's subcolonial hegemony. The mob openly threatened the divisional officer that if the two Muslim colonial agents spent the night in the town mob members would kill them in their sleep. Only the divisional officer's decision to allow the two terrified Muslim officials to sleep in his official quarters saved their lives.

A long discussion then followed between the divisional officer and elders of the community, who claimed that they were helpless against the overwhelming agitation of their people. The divisional officer's effort to "make [the] excited pagans see some sense" failed as the town was united in rejecting Lafia's subcolonial imposition in any form. The stalemate hung in the air and tension rose through the night until the uneasy calm erupted into full-blown pandemonium when the emir of Lafia suddenly entered the town with a large retinue of his councilors, agents, and bodyguards.

The divisional officer's description of the ensuing drama speaks for itself: "Here, in their midst, were the very people the locals disliked more than anybody else in the world. At one moment I felt sure there would be onslaught, for the Keana men were all armed. . . . I am sure they were itching to get at their traditional enemies."[72] The people of Keana regarded the emir's flamboyant entry into their town as a new affront, a way for the emir to reiterate his power over them. As representatives of the Keana people sat "glowering at the Moslem interlopers," Stephenson moved decisively to defuse the escalating standoff by claiming the entourage as his own and implying that an attack on the Muslim officials or the emir would be an attack on the British crown.[73] The negative, disruptive symbolism of the emir's intrusion, however, registered strongly on him. He would reflect later that the emir had, by his audacious presence and display of chiefly grandeur, almost caused "a serious incident" and "achieved nothing except to show off his superiority in a most tactless and unnecessary manner."[74] Stephenson may have been genuinely shocked at the authoritarian vulgarity of the emir, but such insensitive displays of emirate despotism among resentful non-Muslim subjects were fairly common.

The incident fizzled out as the threats of British power prevailed over the Alago desire for retribution against the emir of Lafia and his officials. But the Alago were not deterred in their contestation of Lafia's subcolonial authority. Rather, their quest for self-government and their resentment of emirate subcolonial rule intensified. In the weeks and months that followed the incident, the Alago people refused to pay taxes to the emir of Lafia and declined to turn law-breaking Alago people over to the colonial native court presided over by the emir's appointees. They would not surrender fugitives to the emir's law enforcers, or *dogarai*. The Alago were "openly rejecting the authority of the Emir and his council" despite the token colonial administrative nicety of having an Alago representative on the council.[75] Matters escalated steadily, and the Alago repudiation of the emir's authority became more brazen. This prompted the divisional officer to intervene decisively, mobilizing hundreds of British troops and policemen to march on Keana in a show of force and intimidation. The invasion cowed the restive Alago, who surrendered two fugitives they were holding in defiance of the emir, in return for the assurance that the men would be tried under the judicial authority of the British, not of the emir as colonial protocol demanded.[76]

Routine administrative "tours" of the Middle Belt grassroots exposed British officials to the layers of resentment that remained against caliphal sociopolitical influence. Far from truncating this influence or its spread in the non-Muslim Middle Belt, colonial conquest extended its frontier territorially and ideologically, emboldening caliphate-allied elites to abuse their colonial privileges by resorting to the raids of old. As late as 1946, the emir of Lafia was still conducting small-scale discretionary raids into Doma, seizing young Doma women as concubines. Once he even made away with several women from the harem of the chief of Doma, a violation of the humanity and dignity of the Doma and their leader, which the chief could only report to a visiting British official.[77]

Intensifying Agitations against Emirate Rule

British support for the prevailing Hausa subcolonial administration caused considerable anxieties among non-Muslim peoples. Non-Muslim communities resented the British for consolidating the caliphate's loose precolonial influence in the Middle Belt, but they also perceived British colonial officials as a buffer against the excesses of emirate colonial agents, and as an outlet for expressing their grievances against emirate rule. As a result of this dynamic, expressions of anti-caliphate resentment intensified in correspondence to the increased vigilance of non-Muslim communities eager to detect and report the excesses of emirate rulers.

The 1940s were years of rising awareness within the colonial bureaucracy of the complications of Hausa subcolonial rule. The post–World War II wave of anticolonial nationalist activity caused dissent of a wide variety and transformed the rhetoric of self-determination into faddish political slogans. For the Alago people of Nasarawa Province, the period brought a new urgency to their quest for freedom from the subcolonial suzerainty of the emir of Lafia. Their political sights focused in the direction of combating the most proximate, visible, and consequential colonial presence: the emir of Lafia and his officials.

The 1950s brought more nationalist activity in Nigeria, as activist mobilization became regionalized. The Northern Peoples Congress (NPC) was a political party representative of the interests and heritage of the northern, largely Muslim elite, which inherited the caliphate's legacy.[78] The party quickly morphed into a regional political behemoth, and with British colonialism visibly winding down, enduring Hausa-Fulani Muslim political clout emerged with unprecedented clarity. For the Alago, the 1950s were the years to force a final showdown in their struggle for self-governance under British colonialism. Accordingly, they escalated their assault on the subcolonial rule of the Lafia emirate. An incident in Keana District on March 29, 1956, illustrates this growing confrontation between caliphate colonial agents and non-Muslim communities.

On that day, the British divisional officer was touring the district and decided to attend the district council meeting. Muslim representatives of the emir of Lafia accompanied him, as was the tradition. At the meeting, the Alago people were united in "voicing their desire for independence" from the caliphate subcolonial agents at Lafia.[79] In response, the divisional officer advised them to "drop such tribal demands" and expressed the familiar British colonial platitudes about the imperative of progress. As the meeting progressed, hundreds of Alago people surrounded the venue, protesting around the windows and doors of the building, refusing to disperse. It soon emerged that the chief of the Alago people, the embodiment of Alago loyalty to Lafia, had endorsed the demonstration and had helped mobilize the crowd in the hope of compelling the divisional officer to act on the Alago demand for self-governance.

The divisional officer left "with no difficulty" after the close of the meeting, but when the madaki and Shehu Usman, the representatives of the emir of Lafia, attempted to leave, the mob of angry anti-Lafia protesters surrounded them, preventing their departure. The standoff lingered until they were able, with the help of colonial security guards and police, to escape as "they were jeered, abused, and [as] sand and stones [were] hurled at their cars."[80] Of all the non-Muslim peoples subordinated to the authority of the emir of Lafia in Nasarawa Province, the Alago proved particularly rebellious toward this order of delegated "alien" rule. On four other occasions, the Alago conducted similar displays of anti-Lafia protest. On November 14 of the previous year, the emir of Lafia, the madaki, and M. Muhammadu Uban Gari, an aide of the emir, were openly insulted by the Alago people when they visited Doma. The Alago people called the emir and his officials names and threw sand at their cars in a symbolic act of disrespect. The present confrontation grew out of the hostility built up from the previous year's incident.

Later that day when the emir and his entourage visited Obi, another Alago town, to consult with the district head, a mob assembled and became disruptive. Fearing the eruption of violence, the entourage abruptly departed without concluding their meeting, leaving in a hail of jeers and abuse.[81] The leaders and members of the Alago State Union, a proto-nationalist ethnic association in the order of many similar organizations that sprang up in the late colonial period of the 1950s, had planned to "disgrace the Emir in public by abuse and [to] damage his car."[82]

In December, when the emir, the divisional officer, and the madaki toured Keana again, one member of the Alago State Union announced that his people had decided that the emir and his entourage should never return to Keana. A hostile crowd assembled as the emir met with the district chief in his chambers.

The crowd surrounded the cars of the emir's entourage, jeering and abusing them with words like *kambari* (mildly derogatory word for caliphate-affined Muslim people from Lafia), *shegu* (bastards), and *barayi* (thieves).[83] Symbolically endorsing the protest of his people and sympathizing with their anti-Lafia agitations, the Alago district chief made "no effort to stop the flow of insults."[84]

While touring Doma on February 19, 1957, the emir made his customary visit to the district chief's chambers. While he was there, an elected representative of the Alago people and member of the district chief's council, Baban Kwata, "informed the Emir . . . that the Aragos [Alago] demanded that neither he nor any other 'kambari' should ever again spend a night in Doma."[85] Subsequently, the Alago became so hostile in all their districts that the emir and his officials were "unable to go on [routine administrative] tour because highly undesirable incidents were almost certain to arise."[86] The escalation of the Alago's campaign for independence morphed into a palpable security threat, a challenge not just to Lafia's subcolonial authority but also to the authority of British colonialists.

The escalation prompted action by Lawrence Stephenson, who was in his second stint as divisional officer. Another incident in March was the tipping point. The divisional officer summoned a meeting between the district head and council of Keana and the emir of Lafia and his officials. He told the district head that the "behavior of [your] people . . . was inexcusable" and that the incidents of protests and anti-Lafia intimidations were increasing in frequency and intensity because he and his council condoned them. Stephenson threatened to send the district chief and his council members to Makurdi to explain their actions to the resident of Benue Province, which was now the supervising province of Lafia Division. The district head apologized and promised to issue proclamations against unruly behavior toward the emir and his officials. The madaki remained unconvinced and, sensing danger, concluded that "they dare not stay the night" in Keana because if they did, he was sure that they would be heckled or their car would be damaged.[87] Still, the divisional officer decided to give the district chief a chance to calm his people down before moving toward punitive intervention.

Subsequently, the divisional officer moved to have the president and two members of the Keana branch of the Alago State Union tried in the Native Court. On March 30, the men were found guilty of "causing a disturbance and ordered to pay punitive fines of various sums."[88] It soon emerged that the Alago State Union had raised nearly £1000 to engage lawyers from Lagos to defend their three members against the charges. The divisional officer blamed this effort on what he termed "paltry fines" imposed on the convicted Alago men. Summoning the district head, he told him that the sentences amounted to condoning the trio's "flagrant disregard for authority" and that the men deserved a more severe punishment. He then ordered the court to retry the case. Later that day, the three men were given prison sentences ranging from one to three months.

This law and order approach only served to further inflame the tensions, turning the situation into a full uprising of the Alago against the subcolonial system. When the three convicted men were handed over to Native Authority policemen to be transported to prison, Alago protesters led by Baban Kwata, one of thirteen men wanted for their roles in the Alago uprisings, snatched them from police custody and whisked them away. Helpless and overwhelmed, the district head requested more police reinforcement. The reinforcements arrived with the emir of Lafia, the madaki, and the divisional officer. The policemen invaded the hideout of the convicted men, dispersing their Alago guards. A large crowd of protesters followed the policemen as they dragged the prisoners away toward their vehicles. Two of the prisoners were put in the truck, but as the third was being placed in it, the agitated crowd breached the police line and charged the vehicle and the policemen guarding the three detainees. The ensuing pandemonium enabled the prisoners to escape.

The policemen then used tear gas grenades to disperse the increasingly violent crowd, and when the fog cleared, the policemen pursued and apprehended Baban Kwata and four other wanted Alago men and placed them in custody. The Alago protesters were not done, however. To prevent the arrested men from being taken away to Lafia, the crowd moved quickly to the bridge on the only road out of Keana and commenced sabotaging it. Another group placed logs and dirt on the road to block the truck's exit from the town. A quick scramble followed, and the truck driver navigated the treacherous road and arrived at the bridge in time for the policemen to disperse the saboteurs, arresting one of them in the melee that followed.[89]

The emir and his party found their paths barricaded by long poles originally intended for use in building the district chief's shrine. As messengers and policemen worked to remove the barricades, the crowd of Alago protesters grew bigger and more violent, attacking the policemen, who used batons to keep them at bay. After a slow, difficult process marred by multiple disruptions, the barricades were cleared. The convoy then made its way out of the town center to the nearby rest house slowly, with the divisional officer and some policemen providing escort on foot. The crowd followed closely "hurling epithets and more solid insults at the police in the lorry."[90]

When the emir, the divisional officer, and the entire party retired safely to the resthouse, the lorry carrying Baban Kwata and the other detainees was sent to Lafia to prevent further effort by the Alago to free them. A small crowd, however, kept the party in view, making sure that the emir and his officials, the targets of the Alago's anger, were still in Keana. Later that evening, a group of fifty Alago young men gathered at a crossroads where the party was sure to pass on their way out of the town. Shouts of "kill the emir" filled the air. When the divisional officer confronted them they declared that "they had been ordered to waylay the

Emir should he try to leave."[91] The divisional officer pleaded with them for "half an hour," after which they dispersed.[92]

The following day, the divisional officer called a series of meetings with the district head, his council, and Alago elders. Meanwhile, the three convicted prisoners who escaped in an earlier chaos had been tracked down, arrested, and placed in a Native Authority truck to be transported to Lafia to join Baban Kwatta and the other detainees. The arrest of the escaped prisoners caused further offense to the Alago, who gathered once more in angry protest, and demanded to know why the five accused Alago men had been taken to Lafia the previous day. The divisional officer offered "numerous explanations," but they did not satisfy the crowd, as they "demanded that the five accused be returned to Keana at once and set free, before they would allow the lorry containing the three convicted prisoners to proceed."[93] The demand for the release of Baban Kwatta and the other detainees in Lafia in exchange for safe passage for the truck conveying the re-arrested convicts had little effect on the divisional officer, who advised the Alago to drop "their present belligerent attitude." He assured them that the Alago men who were being sent to Lafia were being tried and detained in Lafia only because there was a possibility of an uprising if they were tried in Keana.

Long consultations followed between the divisional officer, the district head, and Alago elders as the Alago youth became increasingly implacable. While the elders accepted the inevitability of the three convicted men being taken to Lafia, the young men viewed trying the leaders of their struggle in Lafia as the ultimate humiliation, a symbolic act reaffirming the subordination of the Alago to the dreaded colonial overlordship of Lafia emirate and, by extension, the caliphate. The "fanatical and highly-strong youths" once again blocked the road out of town with logs and stood in the middle of the road, acting as a human barricade. With the district head and the elders failing to control the angry youths, the divisional officer grew impatient. He warned that he might resort to force as his and the emir's patience "would not last much longer." The stalemate continued until evening, when the divisional officer ordered policemen to take positions along their route and to be on alert for crowd trouble. This show of force intimidated the riled-up youths enough that no actual violence ensued. The party made its way gradually out of town, as the youth withdrew from the road to grant them passage. Unable to prevent the departure of the emir's party and secure the release of the three convicted Alago men, the restless youth attacked a Kambari resident of the town, a Muslim Lafia man who was employed by Lafia as the dispensary attendant. The mob set his house on fire, and he and his two wives escaped to a nearby bush, where the emir's party later collected them and whisked them away to safety in Lafia.[94]

Crises of this type plagued the caliphate subcolonial system from the beginning of British rule to its end. Many confrontations between enforcers of

Hausa-Fulani subcolonial rule and non-Muslim resisters were not as dramatic as the one between Lafia and the Alago people. Nonetheless, in each instance, the underlying index of causality remained the same. Colonialism had empowered caliphate-aligned operatives and entities with powers beyond even that of the most successful precolonial caliphate surrogate. The British commitment to the administrative utility of the emirate system and of emirate-originated personnel rarely wavered even as subcolonial rule came under increased strain. The opposition of non-Muslim peoples in the Middle Belt, especially in the Niger-Benue region, remained as resolute as the authoritarian determination of its Hausa-Fulani targets. This was a recipe for continued crisis and tension in the lead-up to independence in the 1950s.

Superintended by Hausa-Fulani and Kamberi officials with British support, subcolonial rule in this region of the Middle Belt solved the quotidian challenges of British rule, but it also generated unforeseen dynamics that the British were ill prepared to manage. Emirate colonial agents, prestigious rulers in their own communities, saw their new positions as enforcers of British colonial order among "backward" ethnic communities as an opportunity to rule the communities as extensions of their domains. They insinuated themselves powerfully into their roles as subcolonial guardians among non-Muslim communities, creating, by virtue of the paucity of British oversight, a subcolonial system that far exceeded the preparatory and civilizational mandates that British officials articulated for them. The British, at least going by the textual outlines of their justification for emirate rule, envisaged a far more modest form of subcolonial agency than what emerged in the region, pointing to the self-interested political creativity of emirate subcolonials.

In the Lafia sector, where the simmering tensions of subcolonial rule boiled over, the goal of preparing and civilizing the non-Muslims for indirect rule through Hausa mediatory contagion dissolved as Lafia's Muslim Kamberi rulers redefined their roles and repositioned themselves as parallel colonial operatives subject only to the oversight of the British. "Alien" mediation morphed into "alien" Muslim rule under the overarching rubric of British colonialism. The intensity of this transformation of emirate supervision into emirate colonial control catalyzed the uniquely violent confrontations that marked the protests of the Alago people against Lafia subcolonial rule. The crudeness of Lafia's subcolonial agency and the intrusiveness of its agents were so glaring that in the 1940s and 1950s when the Alago rose up in revolt against Lafia rule, British officials seem to have been genuinely taken aback by the determination of Lafia's subcolonial rulers to underline their power among the Alago. The subcolonial system here may have been a project of British officials, but its ultimate contours were shaped by the ambition and political savvy of emirate authorities, whose initiatives escalated non-Muslim resistance and paradoxically transformed the British into the unfamiliar role of startled arbiters.

Why was resistance to emirate subcolonial rule violent in this region and why did the intervention of British officials prove less capable of stemming the violence and anger directed at figureheads of emirate rule than it did elsewhere? In answering this question, it is hard to resist a comparison with colonial events in Southern Kaduna. There, non-Muslim communities' precolonial entanglements with caliphate surrogates had been deeper, messier, longer, and more elaborate than they had been in the Plateau-Nasarawa zone. This was a function of geographical proximity to the Hausa states and later the caliphate. As a result, objectionable as emirate subcolonial rule was in the twentieth century, it was somewhat familiar and less of a rupture than it might have otherwise been. Because of this history and the longer tapestry of what one might call Hausa oppression, the peoples of Southern Kaduna had honed their survival mechanism, which they simply modified during colonial times. They had little need for the violent emotional reactions to emirate rule that the people of Alago displayed. In the Nasarawa sector, particularly in Lafia Division, precolonial emirate hegemony among non-Muslim communities had been minimal and ephemeral.

A hypothesis that emerges from this comparative insight and that deserves further exploration is the correlation between distance from the centers of the caliphate and the extent of prior exposure to emirate influence. It seems that the more southerly a region was, the lesser its exposure to precolonial caliphate maneuvers and the less familiar its people were with emirate political culture. Lesser familiarity with caliphate systems of rule produced a more emotional and violent reaction to its mechanics once the people of such a region were exposed to them in colonial times. Emirate rule in whatever form was thus less familiar in Lafia Division, the most southerly sector of Nasarawa Province, than it might have been in areas to the north, which were closer to emirate centers. As a result, the British imposition of Hausa-Kamberi rulers on the non-caliphate ethnic groups had a particularly jarring effect on these communities, unleashing emotions that, in the face of flamboyant displays of power by emirate officials, erupted in violence.

Resistance escalated in the post–World War II period as emirate subcolonial officials consolidated their positions, raising the specter of an emirate-dominated political fait accompli that would endure into the impending post-independence period. Some of these anxieties and tensions persist to this day, not just in the plateau and Lafia-Keffi-Nasarawa axis, but also in the Lower Benue Valley, the geographical focus of the next chapter.

4 Hausa Colonial Agency in the Benue Valley

THE BENUE VALLEY borders Southern Nigeria. It is easy, therefore, to assume that because of its geographical and cultural distance from the defunct caliphate and its proximity to Southern Nigerian culture, the influence of Hausa colonial agents could not have been as profound there. To the contrary, British colonialists assumed that precisely because of the distance between the region and the center of the caliphate it lacked the positive caliphate political institutions and socioeconomic values valorized as the bedrock of indirect rule. This conviction caused British officials to import and rely on hundreds of Hausa colonial agents among the Idoma, Tiv, and Igedde peoples. It was relatively easy for Hausa agents to flock to the Benue Valley: the Benue River, which might have limited the exposure of the Tiv, Idoma, and Igedde peoples to the caliphate and the jihad, now made entry into the region easy for British and Hausa personnel alike.

In the early days of the colonial enterprise, Hausa personnel, as soldiers, guards, and interpreters, shadowed the British and mediated their encounters with the Tiv and Idoma. Trusted to carry out quotidian colonial tasks and viewed as racial and cultural superiors of the Tiv and Idoma, Hausa agents and officials quickly found a niche of authority in the colonial systems of Idoma and Tiv Divisions. They helped to fulfill British colonial demands but also carried out their own self-interested initiatives in the name of the British. Through skillful maneuvers, Hausa colonial agents expanded the depth and scope of their power even as a scanty and stretched British presence failed to define and police their activities.

Given these circumstances, tension and conflicts were inevitable. The Tiv and Idoma preemptively attacked Hausa colonial agents even before colonial rule was consolidated, inaugurating a long cycle of anti-Hausa attacks and overwhelming British military responses.

Growing opposition to Hausa subcolonial rule, violent anticolonial revolts, and attacks on Hausa colonial staff sometimes forced British officials to devise chieftaincy apprenticeships for the Idoma and to suspend Hausa chieftaincy in the Tiv area. Nonetheless, as the colonial period unfolded, the Hausa subcolonial presence actually increased even as British officials tried to use Idoma figure-

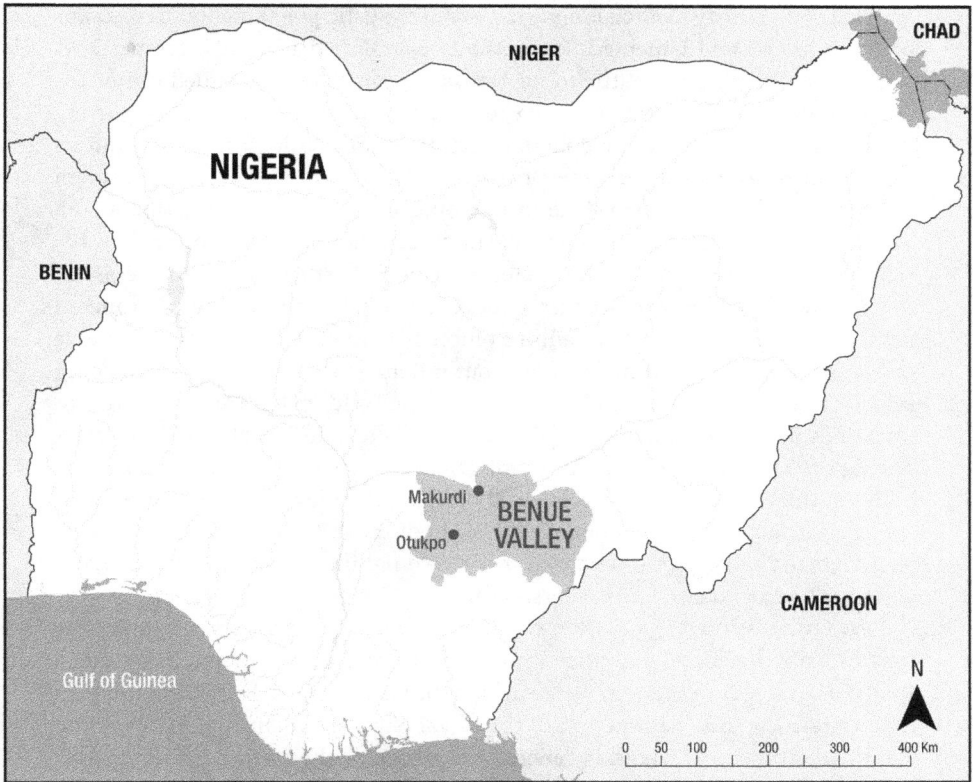

heads to conceal it. As the backlashes against Hausa rule signaled its growing unpopularity, British officials remained unwilling to craft an alternative form of rule or to consider the indirect rule ideal of indigenous colonial agency. Instead they resorted to reinforcing notions of Idoma backwardness as a way of justifying the continuation of Hausa subcolonial rule. The chapter begins with an exploration of the foundational problem of colonial communication and how that opened the way for Hausa interpreters, who, through their activities, reinforced for the British the necessity of Hausa colonial agents.

Hausa Interpreters in the Benue Valley

The adoption of the Hausa language as a colonial lingua franca in Northern Nigeria was regarded in British colonial officialdom as a pragmatic, cheap, and expedient administrative decision.[1] It also necessitated a British reliance on Hausa-speaking intermediaries and interpreters who also knew the local languages of the Middle Belt. For this reason and others, the Hausa language generated ambivalence in British officialdom. As a sociolinguistic phenomenon, Hausa was both celebrated and lamented. In southerly colonial enclaves like Idoma Division, where people spoke little to no Hausa, its imposition as a medium of colonial communication was disruptive, especially since it necessitated importing hundreds of Hausa-speaking colonial operatives. The shift was radical, and its impact on relations between the British and the Idoma was dramatic enough to warrant official comment. One British official described the situation as "an unsatisfactory position [of] the European official having to commune with the Idoma through an [Hausa] interpreter."[2] He went further to record the assertion of one of his Idoma messengers, Itodo: "During his 17 years with Europeans he had not yet worked with an admin officer who knew the language, A couple could say 'come,' 'go,' 'bring,' etc, etc., but no one has been here yet who could understand a complaint or follow a conversation in Idoma."[3] This linguistic conundrum made the Hausa colonial interpreters an indispensable and powerful part of the colonial enterprise in Idoma Division, intensifying the friction both between the British and the Idoma and between the Idoma and Hausa colonial agents. The fact that most Idoma people did not speak Hausa and the Hausa interpreters did not speak Idoma well made colonial interpretation a particularly volatile arena of colonial misunderstanding.[4]

In Tiv Division, the situation was hardly different. Hausa interpreters were part of British colonial activities in the area from the time of the conquest in 1906. For that reason they emerged early as the visible face of British colonialism in Tivland. The 1906 destruction of the Royal Niger Company's (RNC) trading station at Abinsi in Tivland is generally regarded as the trigger for the British conquest of the Tiv.[5] The events that led to the attack on the station are, however, as interesting for our purpose as the British military action that purportedly reacted to the assault. Tiv and Jukun combatants attacked the station. The selective pattern of their attack and the casualties that resulted suggest a clue to the motive. Notably, the combatants spared British personnel. They instead targeted the Hausa personnel and commercial agents allied with the RNC. It was fairly clear that the attackers wanted to uproot the hundreds of Hausa traders, merchants, and agents that had been imported to the station and had formed, through their association with the British company, a visible African "alien" infrastructure of early colonial rule. The British trusted their Hausa allies not just to mediate relations with the Tiv but also to serve as the human tools of colonial administration. Their status as outsiders who knew the local terrain and who supposedly possessed a higher civilizational instinct gave them a central position in the unfolding British colonial order in Tivland. For their part, the Tiv perceived the Hausa traders, workers, and interpreters at Abinsi as opportunists who were taking advantage of the well-armed RNC to exert concessions from Tiv folk.[6] The Hausa partners of the RNC, the Tiv surmised, were acting out their own economic and political agenda in the name of their British employers and protectors.

With precolonial encounters between Hausa-Fulani merchants and the Tiv still fresh in mind, the negative perception of the British-protected Hausa population served as a Tiv rallying point.[7] About 76 Hausa colonial auxiliaries were killed and about 113 were taken captive in the attack on the RNC trading station. Apart from the destruction of the physical structures of the trading station, which was populated largely by the Hausa, there is no record of the combatants targeting British traders.

The attack on the Hausa allies of the British drew the latter into the fray. The subsequent military retaliation against the Tiv was devastating, but more importantly the declarations and activities designed to restore order and establish the rudiments of colonial administration were supervised and mediated by Muslim Hausa interpreters. Some of these agents were the victims of the earlier Tiv-Jukun raid who came back to Tiv territory with the British military, and some of them had vengeance on their minds.

Historian Tesemchi Makar notes that the "interpreters were Hausa, Nupe, and Yoruba."[8] Given the administrative utility of the Hausa language and the utilitarian weight placed on the markers of Hausa identity, interpreters who were of Yoruba and Nupe ancestry would have become sufficiently Hausa through their Islamic faith and proficiency in the Hausa language to qualify for roles in the colonial enterprise. They would have had to demonstrate sufficient familiarity with emirate administration to have been hired as interpreters by the British. The British proclamation of victory, along with the plea for calm after the end of the military action, was written and read in Hausa. The declaration was then translated into Tiv by Mohammed and Maradu, two prominent Hausa interpreters of the period.[9] These were symbolic political acts with implications for colonial power relations in Tiv Division.

Symbolic incidents like the heavy Hausa input into the rituals of Tiv submission to British rule suggest that the Hausa colonial presence in the non-Hausa-speaking Middle Belt was more profound and widespread than the narrow role of linguistic interpreters might suggest. They also imply that the British placed great importance on tutelage-by-residence, an idea that was responsible for the direct importation of Hausa specialists into the so-called backward districts of Northern Nigeria.

The Hausa Colonials in Idoma and Tiv Divisions

The Hausa presence in early colonial Idoma and Tiv Divisions was a complex assemblage of personnel. It included traders, chiefs, interpreters, messengers, clerks, policemen (dogarai), cooks, sanitary inspectors, and other colonial agents. The groups that had the most significant roles, and thus the most volatile impact on these divisions, were perhaps the traders and chiefs.

As stated earlier, the activity of Hausa traders affiliated with the British RNC was the catalyst for the confrontations that led to the conquest of the Tiv area. In Idoma Division, Hausa traders were also at the center of early confrontations. Hundreds of Hausa, most of them traders, came to both Tivland and Idomaland with the British. Historian Mahdi Adamu has shown that in Tiv country, the British actively encouraged both ethnic and assimilated Hausa to settle in Katsina Ala, a town close to the Tiv-Jukun border.[10] This active Hausa recruitment into Tiv country rested on assumptions inherent in the British belief in the positive civilizational impact of Hausa contact with the non-Muslim communities of the Middle Belt. The British assumed that the presence of the supposedly more economically rational and politically sophisticated inheritors of caliphate traditions would have a civilizing economic influence on the Tiv.

In Idoma Division, a more profound version of this logic was at work. Hausa traders came by the hundreds with the British. This caused an immediate economic concern, quite unlike the reception granted the small number of Hausa ivory merchants who used to visit the Idoma heartland in the precolonial period.[11] Unlike the precolonial Hausa traders who came in insignificant trickles, the Hausa who came to Idomaland in the first two decades of the twentieth century were what one colonial official described as "peddlers and rubber dealers."[12] The "opening up" of Idoma Division by the colonial conquest meant that even forests could now be penetrated to extract rubber, ivory, and other products scarcer up north in the savannah. These "peddlers" were visible bearers of the economic logics associated with Hausa identity. They carried the burden of propagating the virtues of economic rationality and of banishing subsistence production and helping to create a monetized and market-oriented economy. The British envisioned them as economic proselytizers, much as other Hausa specialists were expected to propagate their specific skills and attributes.

The British belief that the Idoma, like other non-Hausa Middle Belt peoples, required a cultural and political makeover was elevated to the status of a working orthodoxy within British colonial officialdom. This narrative stemmed, in part, from what was cast as a corpus of empirical observations made by British colonial officers who served in the Middle Belt and who were willing to testify to the region's backwardness. Walter Crocker, an assistant district officer who served in Idoma Division in the 1930s, captured the prevailing British thinking regarding the Idoma economy. Crocker argued that Idoma modes of exchange were grossly underdeveloped, were based not on money but on barter, and thus lagged behind the protocols of economic exchange in the caliphate areas.[13]

The standard motif in the British characterization of the Idoma world had as its referent the emirate model of social, political, and economic organization. This set of ideas and contrasts emerged in the first decade of the twentieth century. Thereafter, the British sought to create an emirate-based economy dominated by cash crops and geared toward monetized exchange in place of the barter-driven trade in Idoma Division. This was an economic vision that the Hausa traders were expected to promote through buying, selling, and extracting. In theory, this system of utilizing Hausa colonials to do the work of civilizing the Idoma made up for the massive personnel requirement that the British plan of a wholesale makeover entailed. And since most of the Hausa traders were not paid a salary but thrived on their profits and trade commissions, it seemed to be a reasonable, cheap way of fulfilling the British desire to make the Idoma amenable to British colonial economics. In practice, it was convoluted, and its consequences were dire for both Idoma-British and Idoma-Hausa relations.

For the British, the presence of the Hausa colonial auxiliaries and their activities contributed to the civilization of the Idoma and prepared them for indirect rule, but the British were in charge and had the job of supervising Hausa colonial personnel. The British monitored the Hausa agents, but not strictly. Consequently, the Hausa traders engaged in trade practices that bordered on economic plunder. Along with the widespread phenomenon of *sojan gona* (unauthorized taxation and exactions by colonial agents), the practices of the Hausa traders took away much of the colonial currency that managed to get into Idoma Division, causing an inability to pay colonial taxes and to replenish the instruments of production.[14] This made the Hausa traders the objects of Idoma resentment, which would morph into open confrontation.[15]

As in the Tiv area, the opposition to the Hausa subcolonial presence triggered the formal British conquest of Idoma Division. The destruction of the village of Odugbeho in 1906, an incident that inaugurated the British conquest, was connected to the murder of a Hausa trader by the Agatu villagers of Odugbeho. As folk historian A. P. Anyebe has argued, the Idoma, particularly the Agatu people, had a preexisting historical grievance against the Hausa, stemming from the attempts of adventurous caliphate flag bearers to capture or loot Idomaland during the Fulani Jihad.[16] Thus the incident at Odugbeho in the Agatu area drew on lingering resentment and on new realities that reinforced old suspicions. At the heart of this political climate lay the economic partnership between the British and Hausa traders, which the Idoma perceived negatively. The Idoma, Anyebe argues, "regarded the Hausa as their old foes returning with a more powerful ally, the British."[17] The crisis reminded the Idoma of their earlier confrontations with the Hausa-Fulani: "when the Idoma saw the Hausa they remembered with nostalgia the Fulani jihad of the nineteenth century."[18] For Anyebe, the new elements of this crisis turned on perceptions. The Idoma were "angry particularly at the Hausa aliens that came with the British."[19] Some of the Hausa traders who came with the British were not Hausa by ethnicity but were simply Muslim and Hausa-speaking men whom the British still adjudged to be socially and economically superior to the Idoma. Whether fueled by the proverbial zeal of the convert or by newfound power, the assimilated Hausa who came to the division as colonial agents tended, in the eyes of the Idoma, to be their worst tormentors.

There is no evidence that the Hausa traders were the targets of Idoma angst merely for *being* Hausa. On that point, Anyebe may be exaggerating the longevity of precolonial grievance. What is implicated in these incidents of hostility toward the Hausa traders is a new regime of partnership between Hausa agents and British officials, which authorized Hausa agents to intrude on several aspects of Idoma life. This alliance is the backdrop of the alleged economic exploitation of the Idoma hinterland by Hausa traders, produce buyers, and colonial currency dealers. The new Idoma perception of the intertwinement between Hausa trading activities and British colonialism in Idomaland fueled suspicion and backlash.

There is also no evidence that Hausaized Muslim Nupe, Ilorin Yoruba, and Gbagyi attracted special suspicion. The fluidity of Hausa identity, which started with the spread of the Hausa trade and religious diaspora in West Africa, was accentuated by the British adoption of Hausa as a regional colonial lingua franca. Thus many Muslim Northern Nigerians originating in non-Hausa caliphate states like Nupe and Ilorin insinuated themselves into the colonial administration by *performing* Hausa identity. Hausa-speaking persons who were not ethnically Hausa were able to pass themselves off as Hausa and were officially regarded as such, a fact that underscores the British obsession with Hausa as a marker of sociopolitical distinction. This did not necessarily exacerbate or mitigate the Idoma perception that "Hausa" traders were conspiring with the British to remove currency and products from Idoma Division, leaving peasants unable to pay taxes or fulfill other colonial obligations. What it shows is that, as Matthew Kukah argues, the Hausa language along with its associative attributes was one of several instruments of a subtle Hausa-Fulani, British-enabled hegemony.[20] In the British administration's tacit, if pragmatic, support for this system, the Hausaized Nupe and Ilorin men who served as British colonial agents in Idomaland were as much co-opted tools as they were agents of an "Anglo-caliphate hegemony."[21]

Once the identity claims of assimilated Hausa persons received colonial blessing, they blended into the colonial functions of Hausa identity, joining ethnic Hausa men recruited by the British as colonial agents. The British regarded them as individuals who embodied certain socioeconomic values bestowed on a person only by way of exposure to the caliphate's traditions and Islam.[22] Within the colonial system therefore, the Idoma saw these assimilated Hausa as *Abakpa* (the Idoma name for Hausa people) and treated them as such. As Anyebe notes, "As far as the Idoma were concerned any black man who came with the British and spoke to the white man in any language which was Hausa . . . straight away became Hausa."[23] The Idoma resentment toward the Hausa colonial presence was profound. Because the British neither acknowledged the problem nor took steps to assuage the suspicions and resentment, attacks on Hausa traders began and proliferated soon after the formal consolidation of colonial rule.

In 1906 a Hausa trader was killed at Aku, a village close to Odugbeho. A British reprisal expedition was quickly assembled, and marched on both Odugbeho and Aku, destroying them both.[24] The following year, eight Hausa traders harvesting rubber in Adoka territory were murdered. As a reprisal in defense of their Hausa allies, the British attacked Adoka, killing more than twenty people, razing twenty-three villages, and confiscating livestock and food to support the fighting force. Adoka oral traditions tend to justify the attacks on the Hausa traders as a form of self-preservation in the face of the unfamiliar pressures of Anglo-caliphate rule. According to this narrative, the Adoka people could not monitor or restrict the Hausa traders, who, supported by British might, defied local traditional authorities and invaded farms and sacred forests in search of rubber and ivory. This "lack of respect for local authority," as one respondent put it, and the lingering memories of the precolonial jihadist raids across the Benue in the dry season, pushed the Adoka people to preemptively attack the Hausa allies of the British "with the slightest provocation."[25] For the British, an attack on Hausa allies was an attack on the British crown, a principle that in turn blinded them to the grievances that might have led to violent Idoma reaction against Hausa agents.

These confrontations were frequent and rife throughout Idoma Division and sustained a cycle of violence that helped establish a negative colonial reputation of Idoma Division as a difficult colonial backwater peopled by violent savages. The Idoma targeted the Hausa colonial auxiliaries, drawing reprisals from the British, leading to the destruction of more Idoma villages and more vengeful targeting of the Hausa agents in a destructive cycle. In 1912, the people of Onyangede were severely punished by the British for an attack on British-backed Hausa traders and colonial scribes, which resulted in the destruction of the latter's houses.[26] The British resident arranged a quick evacuation of the Hausa traders and interpreters to prepare for the British assault on Onyangede so as to remove them from the danger of further Idoma attacks.

Earlier, in 1907, the British installed a Hausa-speaking Muslim Yoruba trader from the caliphate town of Ilorin as the district chief of Ugboju. Alabi, as he was known initially, adopted the Muslim name of Abubakar, a decision likely motivated by a desire to formalize his Hausa identity.[27] The British then appointed an influential Ugboju man, Amanyi, as Abubakar's deputy and understudy. The relationships between Amanyi and his Hausa superior, and between Abubakar and the Ugboju people, deteriorated over the next three years. Abubakar marginalized Amanyi and is remembered in local lore as a despotic chief who exercised a highly centralized form of power, a phenomenon completely unfamiliar to the Ugboju people, who had no prior tradition of centralized executive chieftaincy. In 1910, Amanyi, disillusioned with Hausa subcolonial rule and his subordinate position in it and determined to overthrow the system, led one of the most violent rebellions against the British and their Hausa allies. Amanyi led Ugboju warriors to ambush a British expedition sent to occupy Onyangede and Ugboju. The combatants attacked the bases of the Hausa commercial agents in the district. Many of the Hausa who had escaped earlier attacks then returned with the British forces to crush Amanyi's revolt. The uprising continued with guerilla attacks and British reprisals until Amanyi was captured and deported to Keffi in 1912.[28]

In 1914, the Ugboju people, led by Ameh Oyi Ija, the new deputy to the Hausa colonial chief of the district, attacked the Hausa traders' quarters at Ombi. The attack resulted in the death of "a large number" of Hausa.[29] Like the Amanyi-led revolt, it fizzled out under an overwhelming British military response. Amanyi's travail is an interesting case study in the pitfalls of the implementation of Hausa-centered colonial rule among the Idoma, for his chieftaincy was subjected to the emasculating tutelage of an "alien" Hausa chief. The story of Amanyi is also a good segue to the phenomenon of Hausa chieftaincies in Idoma and Tiv Divisions.

Colonial Hausa Chieftaincy

The most important plank of the British implementation of the cultural and political makeover in the Middle Belt was the cultivation of a chieftaincy deemed amenable to the demands of indirect rule. The aim of creating chieftaincy among non-Muslim communities was to integrate them into what was considered the political mainstream of Northern Nigeria. The centralized chieftaincy system exemplified by the emirate tradition was the most valued feature of this Northern Nigerian colonial mainstream.

In 1933, Walter Crocker, a district officer in Idoma Division, remarked that "in a Hausa emirate" one of the Idoma chiefs he encountered and had the "misfortune" of working with "would not be given the job of a headman on a road-work let alone a District Headship."[30] He went on to describe the native court system as a charade and a poor copy of the emirate prototype. For him, these quasi-colonial institutions in Idoma Division were undermined by an endemic problem of weak chieftaincy, and an innate Idoma disregard for order, legality, and leadership.[31] Another Idoma chief who worked with Crocker was "a dreadful person" who did nothing but "yawn like an animal and scratch himself."[32] Yet another Idoma chief was so ineffective that he was caught "in a much tattered cloth" being beaten by a subject of his. One Idoma chief chased down a man "with his staff of office!" illustrating the "ways and doings of the Idoma nobility."[33] The subtext to all these characterizations was a lamentation about the absence of an emirate-type system of political and social organization, and the resultant difficulty in forging indirect rule among the people of Idoma Division. The empirical referent and silent prescription in these lamentations was the emirate chieftaincy system. The solution, Crocker implied, inhered in the emirate referents.

British officials believed that indirect rule would take root in Idoma Division only when emirate-type political chieftaincy was firmly established. Subsequently, officials began to graft emirate-type instruments of administration onto Idoma Division. The position of *dandoka* (or Native Authority policeman) was created. The British invested this position with a broad mandate as an enforcer of the decisions and whims of an autocratic chief diligently serving colonial ends. This replicated the emirate-type administration inherited and adopted by the British in the emirate zone of Northern Nigeria. In addition, British colonial officials recruited mostly Hausa and Hausa-speaking men into the *yandoka* (pl.) rank, giving the institution a discernibly "foreign" character among the Idoma.[34] The foreignness of the institutions and personnel of British colonial rule combined to perpetually stoke Idoma resistance.

The problem with creating unfamiliar emirate-styled political institutions among the Idoma was that it heightened Idoma resentment and reinforced a growing impression that the perceived oppressions of Hausa colonial personnel enjoyed British approval. Once the British had settled into the notion of the Idoma as an irredeemably decentralized people, they paid little attention to their complaints and grievances while transforming the area along emirate lines. Of all the emirate-style institutions of colonial rule in Idoma Division, the most contentious was perhaps the Native Authority (NA), with all its visual and textual reminders of its emirate origins.

Two factors further complicated this signifier of emirate intrusion. One was the adoption of Hausa text in the official communication of the NA in a division in which Hausa was hardly spoken. The other was the fact that Hausa personnel dominated the staff of the Idoma NA. In addition, produce merchants affiliated with the NA were Hausa, as were NA messengers, interpreters, and so-called *mallams,* who performed a variety of clerical duties.[35] Grafting a Hausa-Fulani NA onto Idoma Division proved particularly unpopular with the Idoma and Igedde people. A retired Idoma NA messenger recalled that "our people did not like this because of their [historical] hatred for the Hausa people."[36] The NA became the most visible symbol of Hausa subcolonial rule in Idoma Division. Subsequently, the Idoma came to associate the obligations and exactions of colonial governance like taxation and forced labor with the NA system and by extension the Hausa subcolonial presence.

As stated earlier, the Tiv were similarly characterized as a chiefless people, lacking order, social cohesion, and political leadership. Makar has described the British attitude as a product of a preconception that was removed from *actual* encounters with the Tiv. This perception, which cast the Tiv as the civilizational antithesis of the Hausa emirates, as well as the initial difficulty of "pacifying" Tivland "frustrated [the British] into neglecting the study of the people's political institutions."[37] At work was the notion of Tiv political backwardness, which was constructed against the backdrop of the accepted perception of Hausa caliphate political superiority.

If Idoma and Tiv Divisions were seen as epitomes of deviation from the preferred caliphate political typology, there was a concomitant belief in the possibility of redeeming these colonial units from their backward political histories, and in the ability of Hausa political tutelage to correct this political deficiency. Thus in both Idoma and Tiv, Hausa chiefs were foisted on the people, saddled with a finite mandate of instilling in their subjects the virtues of political order symbolized by a central chiefly authority.

In 1914, Audu dan Afoda, a Nupe, Hausa-speaking Muslim who had served as an interpreter and political agent for a succession of British district officers, was appointed the *sarkin* Makurdi (chief of Makurdi). The appointment of a Hausaized Nupe Muslim to govern the Makurdi area underlined the British commitment to Hausa identity as a marker of the attributes that British officials valued as political assets in colonial rule. It also validates and puts a new semiotic spin on Mahdi Adamu's assertion that "the Hausa ethnic unit . . . is an assimilating ethnic entity and the Hausa language a colonizing one."[38] Makurdi was a burgeoning colonial town on the Benue River, in Tiv territory. Many Tiv from the adjacent communities and towns migrated to Makurdi in the late-nineteenth and early-twentieth centuries, giving it a Tiv urban character. Between 1914 and 1926, the British government systematically brought the surrounding Tiv districts under dan Afoda's leadership, approving the appointment of his Hausa messenger, Garba, as the village head of the strategic border town of Taraku in 1924.[39]

In appointing dan Afoda to the new supreme position of chief of Makurdi, the British hoped that his chieftaincy would tutor the population in the ways of centralized emirate-type leadership. In 1926, the resident of Benue Province reaffirmed the necessity of this subcolonial tutelage, stating that Audu dan Afoda's chieftaincy was "still useful," since the hope that it "would exert an educational influence [on the Tiv] is being fulfilled."[40] In fact, in 1937 when there was a growing movement in favor of appointing an indigenous "chief of Tiv," the resident at the time echoed a similarly pedagogical view of the presence of Audu as a symbol and instrument of political tutelage. He believed that dan Afoda's politically civilizing mandate was not yet accomplished, since "Central Administration was yet at its infancy" in Tivland. He also believed that "gradually as a higher education marches with a growing feeling of nationality, a real central administration may be evolved" as a culmination of this evolution toward political centralization.[41]

For his part, dan Afoda moved to expand his authority and fulfill the British expectations that led to his appointment. He appointed several officials of his own and sent them to oversee Tiv districts in the vicinity of Makurdi. He also constituted the nucleus of an emirate-type Native Administration. Subsequently, the British accorded dan Afoda further preeminence by requesting him to lead

Tiv delegations to the periodic Northern Nigerian chiefs' meeting in Kaduna, the regional colonial headquarters. By this recognition, the British, many Tiv people surmised cynically, had effectively made a Hausa Muslim chief over the Tiv people.

Audu dan Afoda died in 1945, igniting a firestorm of Tiv agitation for a Tiv to succeed him as the paramount chief of Tiv Division. An initial British attempt to appoint a relation of the deceased chief, another Hausa man, contributed to the outbreak of street riots in Makurdi in 1947. The crisis quickly degenerated into open street clashes between the Hausa and Tiv populations of Makurdi. The riots were the deadly culmination of a long period of Tiv resentment of the imposition of Hausa chiefs and a perceived colonial preference for governing Makurdi with the active participation and consultative input of Hausa auxiliaries. The Tiv, Makar posits, "resented the Hausa influence in Makurdi Town although they did not object to their presence. The Tiv resented the Hausa control of the courts, political power and landed property . . . scarcely could the Tiv secure plots of land or find accommodation in Makurdi when they were in transit."[42]

There was a sense among the Tiv that dan Afoda had used his chieftaincy not only to increase the number of Hausa migrant residents in Makurdi but also to put the most consequential economic institutions and resources in the hands of his Muslim Hausa kinsmen, displacing and economically disenfranchising the Tiv in the process. This feeling of dispossession added to the Tiv resentment and made the violence worse. The British put down the Makurdi clashes with overwhelming force, and the nascent Tiv uprising was crushed. Subsequently, the British decided not to appoint a replacement for dan Afoda, and to gradually move away from the Hausa system of centralized leadership in Tivland in the interest of peace. Makurdi remains without a chief until today, although the Tiv now have a central chief, the *Tor Tiv,* who is based in Gboko.

In Idoma Division, the appointment of Hausa chiefs did not result in widespread uprisings of the scale witnessed in Makurdi, but it was equally contentious. The British reliance on Hausa chiefs in both cases was a clear expression of British commitment to the civilizing influence of emirate-type Hausa chieftaincy and their investment in an administrative philosophy founded on caliphate political values and ideas.

The Hausa Agents

Seated lower in the hierarchy of Hausa colonial specialists in Idoma Division, but almost as influential in colonial power relations as chiefs, were the messengers, clerks, scribes, and policemen. Like Hausa traders and chiefs, they were often Muslim men of emirate origin who were either ethnic Hausa or had "become Hausa" as a matter of choice and self-interest. They were responsible for the everyday routines of the colonial administration, collecting taxes, taking censuses, touring villages to compile agricultural statistics, delivering instructions, arresting and punishing lawbreakers, promoting colonial trade, and carrying out other duties delegated to them by British employers and Hausa chiefs.[43]

As the administrative buffer between the British and the Idoma, these groups of Hausa colonials exerted enormous influence on colonial power relations. In many districts they were put in charge of tax collection, the most volatile colonial task in much of colonial Northern Nigeria. Many oral traditions affirm that the Idoma particularly despised taxation. By the late 1920s, most of the Hausa chieftaincies in Idoma Division had given way to the ascension of trusted and apprenticed Idoma chiefs and headmen. The Hausa clerks—the so-called mallams, messengers, and scribes—however, remained the bedrock of colonial administration until the economic depression of the 1930s, when the imperative of cost cutting led to the replacement of many of them by cheaper Idoma colonial auxiliaries.[44]

Hausa clerks' involvement in tax collection exacerbated their already charged subcolonial presence and complicated the peculiar difficulties that the Idoma experienced with British taxation. This difficulty was caused mainly by their need-based system of commercial agricultural production and the Idoma's cultivation of food crops that were much less marketable than the cash crops cultivated in the emirate sector of Northern Nigeria.[45] The Hausa clerks did not disrupt the economic lives of the Idoma, but their role in British taxation was a dreaded one. As a result they, too, attracted a measure of hostility from the Idoma. To understand how the Idoma's distaste for taxation grounded their resentments toward visible symbols of colonial authority like the Hausa mallams, one has to understand the disruption caused by the unfamiliar routine of taxation among the Idoma. A history of the painful relationship the Idoma had with colonial taxation and its traumas is preserved in the oral narratives of many Idoma communities and passed down through generations.

The Native Authority was a symbol of the pain inflicted by taxation. Its Hausa operatives and their Idoma staff terrorized the division with uniquely humiliating tax enforcement tactics. A former Otukpo community leader and other informants in Otukpo recalled the taxation experience thus: "When a defaulter was identified, members of the Akpantla [secret masquerade society] would assemble in front of his wife's hut and chant abusive songs. The woman could not come out because if she saw the Akpantla with her eyes, she would be barren. Her screams and cries would then force her husband to pay."[46] Other tax enforcers employed an even higher degree of humiliation as a tactic. They would "shave [a defaulter's] hair and flog him on his buttocks and back in front of his wife and children."[47]

When a defaulter absconded, the tax collectors would direct the *yandoka* to confiscate and detain his "domestic animals, farm implements, wives, and children."[48] In the early 1930s, when locusts invaded farms and destroyed crops all over Northern Nigeria, making it virtually impossible to earn cash and pay tax, "many people committed suicide," recall some Otukpo oral traditions.[49] Unable to pay taxes in the locust and Depression years, thousands of Idoma young men, some traveling with their wives and children, fled to the cocoa fields of south-western Nigeria.[50]

Many Idoma NA staff participated in these tax operations as subordinate officials and as assistants to the Hausa officials. Even so, the NA's essentially Hausa character, and the fact that those who directed and oversaw tax enforcement were often Hausa officials, solidified the perception among the Idoma that colonialism was a Hausa-driven project and that its pains amounted to Hausa oppression. Another source of friction between the Hausa subcolonials and the Idoma was that, like the Hausa traders, the scribes and clerks led lives that were removed from their host milieus. The British set them up in separate, relatively elegant residential quarters funded by Idoma taxpayer money and built by Idoma labor. Anyebe claims that the Hausa colonial agents also exhibited an air of superiority that was coextensive with the declared superiority of the British. Anyebe's description of the situation in the Igedde area is revealing, if a little too polemical:

> There was another strange element—the messengers, scribes or clerks who manned the courts and the administration. They were not even Igedde but "Hausa" and Muslim. Like the white colonialist these black imperialists would not live amongst and mix with the people. They stayed on their own. They had their own quarters just as the Whiteman had his own Government Reservation Area. . . . In Oju I was shown the former abode of these colonial agents near the site of Ihyo market. It is now fully overgrown with trees and grass. The Igedde hated this "Hausa" class most. They looked upon them as collaborators with the British.[51]

Anyebe perhaps overstates the Hausa agency in the de facto social segregation between them and the people of Oju. The arrangements resulted from the British reliance on, and perception of, the Hausa colonials as civilizational superiors who deserved prestige in the eyes of the Idoma. The Hausa subcolonials did not author the policy of segregated residency, they merely benefited from it. Anyebe also ignores the fact that in many ways the Hausa auxiliaries too were victims of a colonial administrative policy shaped by a racist notion of more-civilized "natives" helping to civilize the less-civilized ones. Nonetheless, the hostility that he describes was real. It prompted the Igedde people to take up arms against the British and their Hausa allies in 1926. The rebellion was led by Ogbuloko Inawo, a young man reputed to have possessed magical powers.

Ogbuloko had briefly deputized for a Hausa colonial tax collector, a job that exposed him to the resentments that colonial taxation generated among the Igedde people. Subsequently he became an antitax agitator, relinquishing his employment with the British to begin plotting an uprising. The Ogbuloko uprising of 1926–29 was the bloody outcome of pent-up anticolonial grievances. Its aim was to overthrow the British colonial presence, but its targets were the Hausa co-lonial personnel who were the visible representatives of that presence. The Hausa colonials were the ubiquitous symbols and reminders of British colonialism, es-pecially since the negative reputation of Idoma Division meant that only a few British officials were present in the area at any time. Thus the Hausa officials, whether by intent or incidence, were the main targets of Ogbuloko and his armed protesters.[52] The uprising was so popular that it took a massive British military operation to crush it.

In the Agatu area, the encounter with Hausa colonial agents was equally fraught with tension from the outset. Located on the southern bank of the Benue, Agatuland had been physically separated from the upheaval of the nineteenth-century jihad. The river had, however, proven to be a poor defense, as jihadists from Nasarawa and Keffi on the north bank of the river attacked several Agatu communities, especially those nearest to the bank of the Benue.[53] Attacks oc-curred during the dry season when the water level dropped and portions of the river dried up and formed cataracts accessible to horses.[54] Opinions remain di-vided on the leaders of the various jihadist raids that lasted for several decades in the mid- to late 1800s. There is unanimity, however, on the devastation of *Efu-Onya* (Horse War), as the jihad is known in the oral tradition of Idoma com-munities.[55] Many Idoma communities remember the raids, enslavements, forced migration, destruction, and dispossession that marked the jihadist intrusions as a seminal moment in their relations with the Hausa and Fulani from the north bank of the Benue. Agatu colonial subjects, because of their location and greater exposure to these events, would have entered the colonial order with residual anxieties and resentments against the Hausa.

The era of quasi-colonial trading relations with European companies and merchants stoked old tensions. Agatu people recall how the British came to their land promising to end war and slavery. The British won the Agatu's commercial and political cooperation because Agatu people believed the Europeans' procla-mation that they harbored a "hatred for war and slavery."[56] Trade with Europeans on the Benue boomed, but the Agatu struggled to reconcile the dependence of the Europeans on Hausa middlemen and enforcers.

The presence of armed Hausa enforcers and traders during these commer-cial encounters of the early colonial period spooked the Agatu and rekindled old memories of jihadist raids. An Agatu source cast the dilemma in these terms: "What our elders could not understand was why the Europeans who claimed hatred for war and slavery, fraternized with the biggest war-mongers and slavers in the region—the Abakpa [Hausa]."[57] Some Agatu remember how Hausa trade enforcers and armed guards accompanying early European officials to Agatu-land moonlighted by raiding isolated Agatu villages. They also remembered that Europeans hardly honored treaties that required them to "protect Agatu people from [Hausa] slavers and warriors."[58] Instead of offering protection to the Agatu, the treaties seem to have opened the way for hundreds of well-armed Hausa traders and ivory hunters to flood Agatuland.

Marching through the Agatu hinterland in groups of between fifty and one hundred, the early Hausa hunter-trader groups usually consisted of "a hunt master, his assistants, carriers, women who doubled as cooks and prostitutes, drummers, and slaves."[59] The ensuing visuals resembled the jihadist invasions of old, and Agatu people, paranoid about raids and probably unable to distinguish between genuine trader-hunters and slavers, began to attack the Hausa agents.[60] The partnership between British traders and Hausa colonial agents would deepen in the first three decades of the colonial period, heightening the anxieties of the Agatu and increasing the incidence of anti-Hausa attacks. It also seems that as the Hausa agents settled into their role as trusted colonial officials, they began to take independent commercial and political initiatives, believing that their partnership with British colonialists provided protection from backlash.

Agatu sources claim that the Hausa ivory hunters and traders "had very little respect for our people and our customs" and that they invaded the Agatu countryside indiscriminately, claiming to act "on behalf of the white men."[61] Other oral traditions recall that the Hausa colonial agents polluted fishing ponds and rivers in the process of trapping elephants and crocodiles, declining to pay compensation to the Agatu because they claimed that they were acting in the name of the feared British.[62] Hausa rubber tappers, Agatu sources also recall, tapped rubber trees to death, depriving yam seedlings of shade that shielded them from excessive heat, which caused rotting.[63] With dead rubber trees and rotting yams, some Agatu demanded compensation from the Hausa rubber merchants and were routinely turned down.[64] When the Agatu complained to the British, they were referred to Hausa officials, who, understandably, had little empathy for their cause.

True or not, the claim of the Hausa subcolonials that their actions, including those that offended Idoma customs, were authorized by the British, seemed credible to the Agatu for one reason: British military retaliations for attacks on Hausa agents. Whenever the Agatu people attacked the Hausa, "the white men would come during the wet season and shoot their big guns on fishing villages along the river."[65] It was in this colonial context that Odugbeho, Adoka, and other Idoma communities suffered British attacks in retaliation for their attacks on Hausa colonial agents.

With colonial rule consolidated in the first decade of the twentieth century, the British-Hausa partnership began to shape new experiences of the Agatu people with British colonization. British colonizers recruited Hausa agricultural advisers from Loko, Keffi, and Nasarawa and from more far-flung emirate zones to promote the cultivation of cotton among the Agatu. This was a radical agricultural proposition that caused distress to the Agatu, but that some of them reluctantly embraced as a way of earning cash to meet new tax obligations.

Before 1946, when cotton depots were built in Oshigbudu and Obagaji, the Agatu had no proximate outlet for their cotton crop and had to transport their cotton on boats to Aloko. There, Hausa traders and buying agents employed by British firms acted as de facto trade brokers, preventing the Agatu from selling directly to European merchants and the Ebira weavers who also bought cotton occasionally. The Hausa buying agents paid such low prices that many Agatu abandoned cotton cultivation and began selling yams to Igbo traders instead.[66] The Hausa buyers would resell the cotton to their European trading partners, a chain of arbitrage that British colonial officials praised as a commercial revolution that would socialize the subsistent Idoma into an ethic of trade- and market-oriented production but that intensified the Agatu sense of loss and exploitation in the hands of Hausa colonial agents. "If you attempted to bypass the [Hausa]," recalls an Agatu source, "they would arrest you and confiscate your cotton."[67] Hausa agents allegedly applied the same buying practices to other Agatu products such as sesame and rubber.[68]

The British dependence on Hausa traders to economically reorient the Idoma generated several unforeseen outcomes and empowered Hausa agents to a degree that was sure to stoke trouble. The British trusted the Hausa colonial agents to propagate the virtues of market-oriented production among the Idoma. Hausa agents who could speak some Idoma were particularly valued in this role as they could communicate their way into the deepest parts of the vast Idoma countryside. British faith in their Hausa partners also rested on the latter's indispensability to the marketing of European manufactured goods among the Idoma. The Hausa helped British firms market their goods inland away from their berthing stations on the Benue. To the Agatu, the Hausa traders were bearers of European goods, particularly European cloth, which was the most demanded British product in Idomaland.[69] In addition to the protection and support of the British, this position of controlling the flow of colonial goods to the Agatu area gave Hausa colonial agents enormous political and social capital, which they deployed deftly in their own interests, much to the resentment of the Agatu.

In other sectors of Idoma Division, Hausa officials played an equally central role in colonization. In Ugboju, the colonial presence consisted of a lone British officer and a retinue of Hausa policemen and mallams stationed at Icho.[70] Here, the Hausa agents seemed to possess almost complete control of the colonial system. As a result, they exerted a much greater influence than they did in Agatu district. The disaster of Hausa chieftaincy and the violent end to the rebellion led by apprentice chief Amanyi did little to dissuade British officials from putting the Hausa in charge of all aspects of colonial rule among the Ugboju people. The prevailing wisdom among British colonial officials was that Hausa subcolonial rule could be concealed beneath a veneer of an Idoma figurehead, who had no real power. To achieve this, the divisional officer (DO) of Idoma Division decided to appoint a chief from among the Ugboju. He brought back the exiled Amanyi in late 1912 when Ugboju elders, defying the effort of the DO to discredit the popular former apprentice chief, recommended his return and his installation in the new chieftaincy.[71]

Amanyi's ascension to the chieftaincy of Ugboju seemed to provide the perfect alibi for Hausa rule, a foil to deflect the people's concerns about Hausa rule. Apart from Amanyi, no other Idoma occupied any position in the Ugboju district administration. Hausa officials, some of them former soldiers in the colonial infantry, others new recruits from the emirates, held all the consequential colonial positions. One Ugboju source recalls the situation rather vividly: "In those days, communication was by Abakpa [Hausa] because no Idoma person understood the white man's language. Most of the police, interpreters and clerks were Abakpa. During this period, Abakpa elements increased their number in Ugboju. Those who were not with the administration were traders and hunters."[72]

So overwhelming was the infrastructure of Hausa rule that Amanyi was effectively sidelined. He had no real power. In the absence of the DO, who resided in Otukpo Icho, the Hausa officials ran the colonial bureaucracy, only rendering occasional account to the DO during his rare tours to the district. Amanyi, no longer willing to undermine the Hausa agents, settled quietly into a life of trading and left the native court in the hands of the Hausa colonial agents.[73] Of the many Hausa officials, three men are said to have been particularly instrumental to the expansion of Hausa subcolonial rule among the Ugboju people. They are Umaru, Salihu, and Abubakar.[74] The three men are remembered in Ugboju folklore as having been particularly notorious for extracting arbitrary fees from the Ugboju people, fees that they allegedly used to enrich themselves. They were also known for insisting on their personal needs being met by the Ugboju people. Abubakar, in particular, remains a point of reference for the oppression of Hausa subcolonial rule in Idoma Division. The Ugboju people remember him as one of the Hausa officials who recruited young men to build roads, bridges, and to "carry the white man's load."[75] Abubakar is said to have imposed the forced labor regime so aggressively that "some households lost all their men folk" to the labor gangs working on several colonial projects.[76]

When Amanyi died in 1928, Abubakar "virtually became district head and president of the Native Court," remembers an Ugboju source.[77] Amanyi's death led to a consolidation of Hausa subcolonial rule, marked most starkly by a new influx of Hausa and Muslim Ilorin men from emirate centers up north to enforce colonial policy and control the now restive Ugboju people. Rarely seen in Ugboju, the British DO remained largely oblivious to this unauthorized expansion of Hausa rule. When the Ugboju people rebelled, it came as a surprise to him and prompted immediate action. In response to the protest, the British decided to once again apprentice three Ugboju men from the three main lineages for the position of district head. After spending one year under a de facto Hausa district head, one of the apprentices, Ujo, was made acting district head.[78]

The Padding of a Social Construct

British understandings of the non-emirate sector of Northern Nigeria were founded on a self-replicating and self-fulfilling rhetoric of backwardness. Backwardness was not a *thing* that was there to be understood and acted upon; rather it was largely produced and replenished by the power of British discursive claims. The case of Idoma Division is instructive because of the area's southerly location and its minimal contact with the caliphate in the previous century. Physical and ideological distance from the caliphate, for the British, provided a basis to posit and reinforce a colonial theory of the Idoma people's peculiar backwardness. British officials believed that this peculiar genre of backwardness necessitated Hausa tutelage. This perhaps explains the depth of Hausa subcolonialism in the division. An understanding of how this trope of Idoma backwardness emerged and grew is germane to any understanding of the scope of Hausa subcolonial rule among the Idoma, for the division's supposed divergence from the emirate and the absence of emirate-type political institutions were the alibis for imposing Hausa rule.

The construction of Idoma Division as a peripheral unit of colonial Northern Nigeria was an elaborate activity, requiring constant nurturing and replenishment. British officials who served in the division participated actively in the discourse of Idoma exceptionalism even in a supposedly backward Middle Belt. These officials helped reinforce existing British perceptions of the division and its people. Officials who participated in the "pacification" of the division and those who administered it were responsible for conferring ethnological and bureaucratic credibility on the mantra of Idoma backwardness. Those who came after them helped solidify and reproduce this narrative. Walter Crocker and Hugh Elliot, two British officers who served in Idoma Division in the 1930s, provided detailed ethnographic descriptions of Idoma society, which further helped to make the reproduction of Idoma backwardness a continuous exercise of the colonial bureaucracy in Northern Nigeria.

In his tour diary, which was published with extensive editorial changes in 1936, Crocker strains to demonstrate that the Idoma people were indeed one of the most economically and socially backward people in Northern Nigeria. Of the Idoma economy, Crocker has this to say:

> Trading in the local markets—and there is little such market trading in comparison with what is done throughout the Moslem parts of the country—is, saving a few cheap trinkets and cloths hawked by Hausa peddlers, a matter of one household exchanging its surplusses [sic] (e.g tomatoes) for those of

another (e.g. paw paws), and with the exception of pennies and tenths legal currency is little (if ever) used. The normal exchange media are brass.[79]

Crocker's explication of the Idoma's supposed economic backwardness invoked the emirate economy as a reference, upholding the contention that the Idoma economy was an economic exception, and discounting the possibility that it was an economy governed by its own logics. For Crocker, the challenge of British colonialism was thus to facilitate the assimilation of the Idoma into the paradigmatic economic modernity of the caliphate system. Similarly, Crocker posits an elaborate notion of Idoma social backwardness, in which the reference and remedy was not British modernity but caliphal modernity.

The ethnological canvas painted by Crocker was elaborate, as was his landscape of descriptive assumptions. Claiming to derive his information from his Idoma cooks and servants, Crocker asserted, for instance, that there was hardly an Idoma over the age of thirty who had not committed at least one murder.[80] The Idoma were known to murder Hausa traders and rubber peddlers, and the corpses of non-Idoma people were a common sight all over the division, Crocker claimed.[81] Crocker profiled the Idoma as a people who were "distrustful [and] suspicious," confirming for distant colonial officials the long-held notion that the Idoma were xenophobes, unwelcoming not only to the British and their ideas, but also to other Africans, especially the Hausa traders who were seen by the British as agents of economic progress.[82]

The Idoma were not just purveyors of xenophobic violence, however. Their entire social world was suffused, colonial bureaucratic communications claimed, in violence and killings, and violence was a recurring medium of social communication and relations. Violence, according to Crocker, was a way of life for the Idoma, and this underscored a fundamental evolutionary lag, which he illustrated by comparing them to the Hausa Muslims to the north: "Within the kindred itself a number of personal relationship tangles could be and were normally settled by killing (e.g adultery, blood debts), and kindred and clans warring with one another. The Idoma tribe, in a word, lived in a complete state of nature."[83] Crocker's aim here was to present the Idoma as savages, a people whose existence was underwritten by the seemingly contradictory impulses of barbarism and originary evolutionary purity. The reproduction of these perceptions was central to the justification of Hausa subcolonial rule among the Idoma.

Like Crocker, Hugh Elliot, who served in Idoma Division as an assistant district officer in 1935, believed that the Idoma were the most evolutionarily inadequate of the Northern Nigerian ethnic groups. For him they were a people trapped in superstition and fetish. Such was the extent of the Idoma obsession with traditional African religious practice, opined Elliot, that even at the threat of being cut off from each other by rising flood water, some Idoma groups would prefer isolation to building a boat, which a commitment to *tsafi* (Hausa: derogatory word for ancestral shrine and traditional religious observances and objects) supposedly forbade.[84]

Such administrative reportage ultimately found its way into the official anthropological compilations about so-called ethnic cultures, reinforcing and lending empirical weight to the official ethnologies of C. K. Meek, Northern Nigeria's official ethnologist in the mid-colonial period.[85] More importantly, the reproduction of Idoma alterity worked simultaneously to reiterate the status of Hausa and all its supposed social qualities as the prototypical sociopolitical formation and worldview in colonial Northern Nigeria. The result of this social reengineering was twofold.

First, by constantly reinforcing the discourses of Idoma backwardness, British officials were assured of an ever-present ideological justification for their commitment to the goal of assimilating the Idoma into Hausa culture through a process of cultural and political erasure. So strong was this belief that colonial administrative reports of Idoma Division and the journals of British officials are filled with judgmental comparative references to the emirate sector of the colony. Also, these private and official administrative documents appear to have been so trapped in the social categories of Hausa society that they routinely used Hausa terms to describe Idoma realities and to present them as poor copies of Hausa prototypes. British officials used Hausa linguistic and semiotic indices to describe phenomena observed among the Idoma, deploying suggestive Hausa words such as *rikici* or rikichi (conflict or litigation), *sarauta* (kingship), *zaure* (royal compound), *salga* (latrine), and others to describe situations, objects, and institutions that, in their jaundiced eyes, imitated the Hausa prototypes.

Second, the reproduction of the notion of Idoma deviation from the Hausa model influenced administrative practices in the Northern Nigerian colonial bureaucracy, further marginalizing non-Hausa speaking peoples. It worked like a self-fulfilling prognosis, as Idoma Division quickly became the division to which no decent British officials were posted or wanted to go, and where officials were sent as punishment. This perception was widespread in the Northern Nigerian British bureaucracy, as Hugh Elliot asserted in his memoir.[86] This characterization of Idoma Division as an "unimportant" backwater of British colonial rule transcended the division. It may have been overstressed for the Idoma, but it started out as an elaborate hierarchy of importance and sociopolitical sophistication in which Middle Belt communities emerged as marginal colonial districts. As early as 1908, Sir Percy Girouard, the governor of Northern Nigeria, had, in a letter to his predecessor Frederick Lugard, described the non-Hausa speaking, non-Muslim Kabba Province as "the most unimportant province" in the protectorate.[87] Girouard explained to Lugard that an officer whom the governor had "strongly recommended" to him, Featherston Cargill, was "banished" from Kano to Kabba because his mental state no longer made it "possible to send him to the most important post in the Protectorate [Kano]."[88] Once broached as the authorizing idiom for preparatory Hausa subcolonialism, the rhetoric of non-Muslim backwardness was constantly reproduced through colonial commentary and text.

For southern areas of the Middle Belt like the Benue Valley, where precolonial relations with the caliphate zone could not be manipulated to make a case for continued Hausa colonial agency, the discourse of non-Muslim backwardness had to be reinforced to justify Hausa subcolonial rule.

This chapter examined one aspect of a very complex historical problem: the colonial administrative motivations for the consequential presence of Muslim, Hausa colonial agents in the Benue Valley. While the presence of Hausa and Hausaized Muslims in Idoma and Tiv Divisions predated formal British colonialism, Hausa operatives were reified and elevated by British colonial administrative practices into a quasi-colonial community. Recruited into multiple roles as chiefs, trading agents, policemen, scribes, and messengers, Hausa subcolonials consolidated their positions and expanded the scope of their engagement with the Tiv and Idoma through deft maneuvers. Hausa colonial agents' work complicated Idoma and Tiv engagements with British colonialism. The immediate targets and victims of this proxy colonial system were the Idoma and Tiv people. Subsequently, Hausa officials suffered retaliatory harm because they were seen as the face of British colonization.

The Hausa subcolonial system in the Benue Valley differed from that of other regions in two key respects. First, in this southernmost region of the Middle Belt, with no direct territorial connection to the caliphate zone, the influx of Hausa colonial personnel, Hausa institutions of chieftaincy, Hausa political symbols, and other aspects of Hausa subcolonial rule was uniquely disruptive. Second, the cast of Hausa characters in the British colonial enterprise in the region was larger than in other regions of the Middle Belt, reflecting perhaps a British belief that a greater Hausa input in colonization was necessary to overcome the supposedly greater "backwardness" of the region.

The Hausa subcolonial presence in the Benue Valley was more versatile than in other regions. The community of Hausa colonial officials was made up of not just colonial administrative operatives; it included Hausa traders, commercial agents, rubber tappers, and hunters, all of whom the British propped up as part of a holistic effort to bring emirate economic and sociopolitical values to a region perceived to be the quintessential "pagan" province of the Middle Belt. The sheer breadth of the Hausa subcolonial project here is a strong indicator of the British commitment to the notion of Hausa subcolonial tutelage and pedagogical intervention. As a result of this profundity of Hausa subcolonial agency, the interactions between the Tiv, Idoma, and Igedde peoples on one side and Hausa colonial agents on the other were more frequent and fraught than in other regions.

Another factor that contributed to the depth and scope of the Hausa subcolonial presence was the British perception of the Benue Valley as a difficult colonial backwater deserving little of European administrative attention. The idea that Idoma and Tiv Divisions were the worst postings that any British colonial official could get and the allied notion of Idoma Division in particular being a "punishment division" for incompetent, indifferent, and out-of-favor colonial officials were well known and often discussed by colonial officials. As a result of this reputation, the number of European officials in the region was often small even by the standard of the general scantiness of the European human presence in colonial Nigeria and Africa. Benue Province, especially Idoma Division, was sparsely and sporadically supervised and left largely to the initiatives and improvisations of colonial agents—most of them Hausa and Hausaized Muslims from far and near emirate enclaves.

The egregious colonial neglect of Idoma Division conduced to a deeper experience with Hausa colonial agency. It also emboldened Hausa colonial chiefs, tax scribes, commercial agents, and policemen to take quotidian ownership of the colonial project in ways that they did not in other regions. Unlike in other regions, then, those who resented Hausa subcolonial preeminence and lashed out against it had few British officials to appeal to. Stretched thin, the few officials on the ground were often overwhelmed and were thus unable to consistently play the accidental role of arbiters that their colleagues were thrust into elsewhere. Absent British colonial arbitration between the Idoma and Hausa colonial officials, the former often took out their frustrations on the latter in violent attacks that then fed into the extant colonial narratives of Idoma savagery, which in turn reinforced and prolonged Hausa subcolonial rule beyond its finite mandate.

Difference, produced and reinforced by British discourse, and a notion of the Benue Valley as the quintessential non-caliphate zone, helped authorize an unwavering British investment in the efficacy of Hausa tutelage and rule. In Idoma and Tiv Divisions, the British did not so much seek to formalize and codify difference as they used it to achieve a measure of sameness and uniformity in colonial administration. The ideological aim of the British project of socializing the Idoma and Tiv into the administrative mainstream in Northern Nigeria was to achieve the highest possible degree of indirect rule, even if this ideological fine point quickly gave way to pragmatic improvisation that surrendered more power to Hausa agents. British magnification of ethnic and cultural difference congealed into the goal of using it as a basis for eventually establishing a firm foundation for indirect rule.

5 Fulani Expansion and Subcolonial Rule in Early Colonial Adamawa Province

In July 2011, the Nigerian federal government announced a decision to change the name of the Federal University of Technology in Yola to Moddibo Adama University of Technology. The change was made, the government claimed, to honor the most prominent leader of the Fulani jihad in the Upper Benue Valley and Alantika Mountains and founder of the precolonial Fombina (Adamawa) Emirate. The territorial span of the defunct emirate corresponds to a big chunk of postcolonial Adamawa State. In a unit of Nigeria that already bore the name of Adama (Adamawa is derived from Adama and became the name of the state in 1991, when Taraba State was created out of the old Gongola State), the name change riled the state's non-Fulani population, who constitute, by some estimates, 80 percent of the entire population of the state.[1]

A former governor of the old Gongola State, Wilberforce Juta, a Bachama Christian and chairman of the Adamawa Elders Forum, resolutely opposed the renaming, arguing that there were several deceased Christian indigenes of the state who deserved the honor and should have been "immortalized" in the process of renaming the university.[2] Juta declared that Modibbo Adama had already been honored enough since the entire state bore his name. By approving the renaming, President Goodluck Jonathan, a Southern Nigerian Christian, had "exhibit[ed] insensitivity to the struggle of northern minorities," Juta stated. Juta contended that, "there are also late Christian leaders" who had helped to develop the state but who were "sleeping in their graves without being immortalized."[3] In the course of the debate over the renaming, it emerged that the Fulani lamido of Fombina, Muhammadu Barkindo Aliyu Musdafa, a descendant of Adama, had used his respected chiefly political clout to lobby the president intensely for the name change.

The debate over the naming of a federal university in the Adamawa state capital awakened old tensions between the privileged Fulani Muslim oligarchy of Adamawa and the vast population of non-Muslim peoples over whom they exercised various degrees of delegated control in the Upper Benue Valley and

Alantika Mountains region in colonial times. In declaring support for or opposition to the renaming, Adamawa State indigenes betrayed their investments in old colonial-era identifications and their political consequences. They also demonstrated the staying power and lingering postcolonial relevance of categories that animated political life in precolonial and colonial Adamawa. Implicated in this seemingly innocuous struggle over names and naming are the familiar tropes of perceived Fulani Muslim domination and non-Muslim victimhood and resistance. Unsaid in the public debate is the subtle, long-running subject of contention: whether the construct of Fulani power and political privilege was still a valid frame of reference for non-Muslim politics and oppositional mobilization or whether the stakes had leveled off for both sides.

Non-Fulani opposition to the renaming was intense, and may become the subject of political fisticuffs in the future. Yet it did not resonate in ways that it might be expected to in a region where history and memory are deeply implicated in the terms on which contemporary political struggles are fought. The state authorities moved on from the controversy and, save for lingering ill will, no serious crisis occurred. For non-Muslims, it was not as easy to move on from this position of perceived political vulnerability, a vulnerability whose history, however convoluted, is traceable to British-backed Fulani rule over non-Muslim ethnicities in the Adamawa area.

This chapter reconstructs this turbulent history as a backdrop to the dueling political contentions of today. More crucially, the story foregrounds much of today's dueling identity formulations. These identity claims are often anchored on memories forged in neat metanarratives that approximate but do not always accurately reflect the messiness of colonial rule in this volatile borderland of caliphate–Middle Belt interactions. Because it straddled multiple fault lines in the caliphate–Middle Belt divide, Adamawa Province played host to the same tensions and interactions analyzed in previous chapters. One key distinction, however, is the extent to which Fulani subcolonial rule appeared to have been naturalized among the non-Muslim ethnicities of the Upper and Middle Benue and the Alantika Mountain regions.

Here, like elsewhere, the British put Muslim Fulani officials with caliphate pedigree in charge of the colonial administrative infrastructure as a preparatory civilizing influence over the many non-Muslim ethnicities of the region. In this respect, their role in British colonization was consistent with the ideological and administrative positions articulated for Hausa-Fulani subcolonials in other parts of the Middle Belt. The difference between Adamawa Province and other efforts lies in the profundity of the mandate of Fulani administrative personnel and in the response of non-Muslim communities to Fulani rule. Although they were clearly implementing a British colonial script birthed by administrative and ideological motivations, Fulani chiefs and officials administering non-

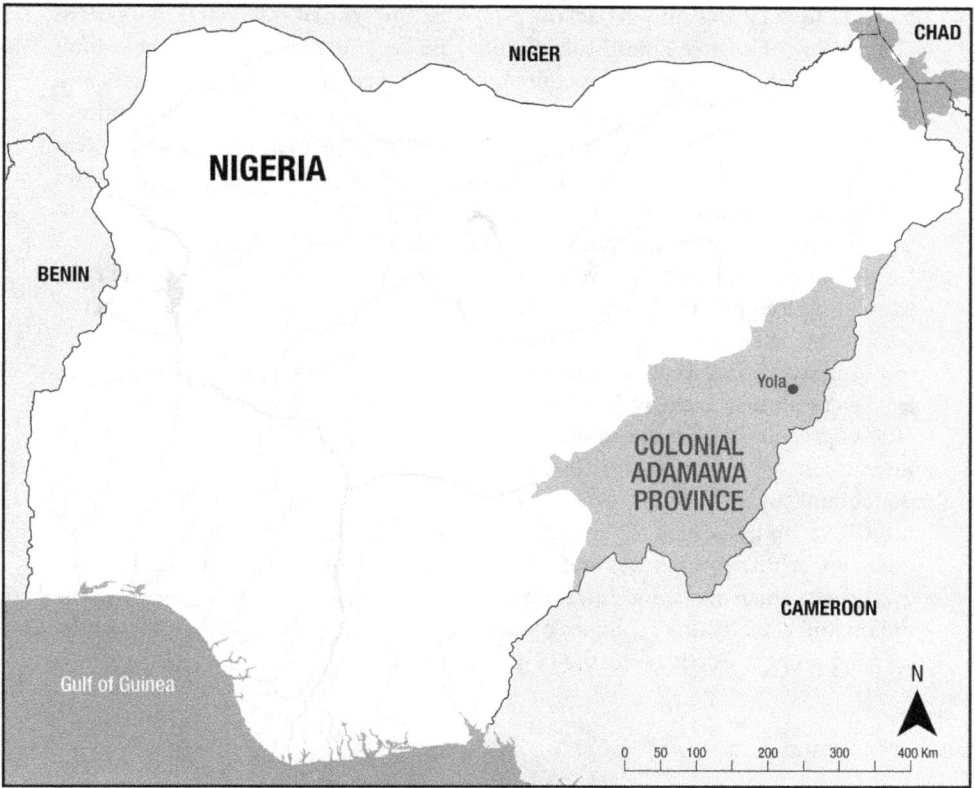

Muslim communities in Adamawa gradually came to assert themselves in their privileged political positions. They came to own the quotidian initiatives of the colonial enterprise, only consulting the British for guidance and, occasionally, for coercive assistance. The British in turn came to depend on the efficient if unorthodox policy of Fulani "alien" rule and subsequently fought to preserve it when problems emerged. This elevated subcolonial system was extreme even by the standard of the Nigerian Middle Belt.

The foundations of this system of subcolonial rule, and the problematic British assumptions that birthed it, call for a profound rereading of the relationship between precolonial sociopolitical and economic dynamics and colonial-era events. Highlighting the sociopolitical peculiarities of Adamawa Province, the existing paradigms that made the imposition of Fulani chiefs and officials possible, and the early problems that Fulani officials encountered as they struggled to insinuate themselves into the political lives of non-Muslim communities requires an excursion into the shifting realities of precolonial relations. But precolonial history was only a backdrop to what burgeoned into a fraught system of colonial rule. Once Fulani subcolonial rule became established, trouble soon followed, eliciting British efforts to reform the system in the face of excesses and abuses of Fulani subcolonial power. The reform sought to devolve more administrative autonomy to the non-Muslim communities. However, the limited success of this reform indicates the continued investment of both the Fulani rulers and the British in the elaborate system of proxy rule. The desire of the Fulani rulers to preserve their political perches converged with a British fondness for cheap, effective colonial rule. This convergence dissolved the finer points of indirect rule, which required community insiders, not ethnic and religious outsiders, to act as colonial go-betweens.

Adamawa is a uniquely interesting case, not only because the colonial agents here were almost exclusively ethnic Fulani but also because of two important facts of precolonial Adamawa society. First, precolonial Fulani migrations to and interactions with non-Muslim societies on both sides of the Upper and Middle Benue and around the Alantika Mountains rarely followed the jihad-military model. Second, because the relationship between migrant Fulani clans and indigenous ethnic groups was not one characterized by imperial control or hegemonic maneuvers, some intermarriage did occur, further domesticating the Fulani and establishing ecologies of identity and codependence. This precolonial starting point is worth exploring in greater detail.

Precolonial Adamawa

Fulani migrations to the Adamawa hinterland began, historians believe, as early as the late-seventeenth century, when groups of Fulbe clans of various sizes began migrating there from Bornu via Hausaland.[4] By this period, Fulani migrant populations in Hausaland and Bornu, themselves produced by waves of migration from the Senegambia region and specifically from the Futa Toro and the Macina plains, had peaked and were spilling over from the Western Sudan to the northeastern part of what is today Nigeria. The contiguous areas to the east of Bornu, and stretching all the way to the north and south banks of the Upper Benue, attracted several waves of Fulani migrants up to the mid-nineteenth century. At least eight Fulani clans, united by the fairly mutually intelligible dialects of the Fulfulde language and by their pastoral and nominally Islamic lifestyles, have been identified as participating in these waves of migration to the Adamawa area, with the largest of them, the Kiri'en, settling among one of the largest of the Adamawa Basin's indigenous ethnic groups, the Chamba.[5]

These migrations brought the Fulani clans into the land of the Kilba, the Higi, and the Marghi, some of whom the Fulani intermarried with to produce a new hybrid ethnic category that came to be known as the Kilba'en Fulani.[6]

The migrations also brought the Fulani groups into the lands of the Bachama on the Benue, and into contact with the Bata, the most politically organized group among the non-Muslim communities of Adamawa. The Bata had a centralized priest-king institution and a fairly discernible military capacity that, combined with their traditional religious skills, enabled them to ingratiate themselves into politically powerful positions among the Kilba, Marghi, Lunguda, Bachama, Bura, Uba, and other ethnic groups of the Adamawa area.[7]

In the 1780s, another wave of Fulani migrants from Gombe, led by Hamman Ruwa, brother of famed jihadist leader in Gombe, Buba Yero, flocked into various sectors of Adamawa.[8] These secondary migrations as well as others that followed a generation or two later pushed deeper into the Adamawa hinterland as Fulani migrants searched for new grazing land beyond locales already grazed by earlier groups of migrants. These later migrations completed the inland push of the Fulani into Bachama, Verre, Chamba, Tikar, Gudur, Gude, Hona, Lala, Ga'anda, Uba, and Jukun countries. They also established or helped to consolidate an increasingly politicized network of Fulani settlements in Song, Gurin, and Malabu. The pattern of Fulani settlements in the vast region of Adamawa was discernible by the mid-eighteenth century. Njuema posits that "by the second half of the eighteenth century, Fulani settlements dotted all along the courses of the Benue and its tributaries."[9] The transformation of makeshift camps and nomadic settlements into sedentary communities was the climax of Fulani demographic consolidation in Adamawa.

This long-drawn pattern of Fulani migration and settlement produced little conflict. In fact, apart from the Kiri'en Fulani clan, who forced their way into Jukun and Chamba countries, there is no record in the oral traditions, of either the Fulani or the indigenous groups, of widespread conflicts between the former and the latter prior to the jihad of the early-nineteenth century.[10] With presents and promises, Fulani groups would often seek the permission of non-Muslim communities to settle and graze cattle in their midst.[11] It was in the interest of the migrating Fulani communities to court and acknowledge "autochthonous authority" even if this authority required them to "abide by customs which were against *pulaku* [the Fulani code of conduct and social relations]."[12] These compromises helped the Fulani avoid conflict with their non-Muslim hosts and enabled them to "graze their herds without fear of theft or molestation."[13] Some Fulani groups resented abiding by conditions that violated pulaku and Islam, and this caused occasional tensions in relations between them and their non-Muslim hosts, but many endured the conditions partly because their commitment to Islam in this period was weak and partly because they needed the land of their non-Muslim hosts to sustain their means of livelihood, cattle herding.[14] A few disenchanted groups migrated to other areas where their hosts had more acceptable conditions of residency and grazing.

In the pre-jihad period, therefore, conflict was minimal, Fulani hegemony nonexistent. The Fulani groups' minority status and the fragmented nature of their settlements caused them to actively, if sometimes reluctantly, cultivate the goodwill of their non-Muslim hosts and neighbors. These were the conditions of relations until the Fulani jihad broke out and spread quickly to the northeastern corridor, already home to several clans of Fulani migrant communities. These communities saw the jihad as an opportunity to improve their status and independence in an area in which they had been compelled to abide by unfamiliar codes and restrictive socioeconomic conditions. Islamic scholars among the pastoralist Fulani of Adamawa shared the religious fervor that drove the jihad, but they were few and succeeded only because the Fulani masses saw militarized defense and offense as the most efficient guarantees of their ability to graze cattle as they pleased under their own conditions without having to answer to non-Fulani, non-Muslim authorities.

The ensuing jihad in this sector was thus more about self-preservation than it was about expanding the Islamic realm or conquering and holding territory on behalf of the caliphate. The jihad here was largely a social movement that sought to limit the control of non-Fulani entities and to compel the latter to accept Fulani independence and right to coexist on equal economic, cultural, and political footing. Fulani jihadists in this sector rarely commandeered territory, content to win independence for Fulani enclaves through slave raids and guerilla attacks that intimidated hosts and neighbors into accepting Fulani occupation of their lands.[15] The raids produced slaves, which the Fombina (or Adamawa) and Muri, two major emirates that resulted from the jihad, used to participate in the economy and patronage politics of the caliphate, but other than intermittently raiding for slaves and intimidating the surrounding, heavily populated non-Muslim states into de facto acceptance of Fulani independence, the jihad produced nothing resembling the caliphate and emirate imperialism of other areas of the Middle Belt. What the jihad did was to destroy some of the trust and codependence of the pre-jihad period. The jihad, in short, accomplished little beyond creating autonomous and mutually suspicious communities of non-Muslims—an overwhelming demographic majority—and Fulani Muslims, who constituted a fragmented but now fairly politically cooperative minority.

Relations continued to be tense across the ethno-religious divide into the late-nineteenth and early-twentieth century, when German and British imperialists began conquering the Adamawa area and jostling for control. Interdependence necessitated by the specializations of the Fulani in cattle herding and the non-Muslims in farming continued. In isolated spots political alliances between Fulani communities and indigenous groups emerged occasionally, and some intermarriage continued, along with linguistic and cultural borrowings between Fulani pastoralists and indigenous communities. This was how things stood at the time of the British conquest of Adamawa, an uneven process that lasted from approximately 1898 to about 1910. British conquest immediately recast the positions of the Fulani and the indigenous non-Muslim communities. The former settled into British colonial communication and early administrative arrangements as precolonial imperial lords, the latter as imperial subjects of the Fulani emirates of Fombina (Adamawa) and Muri. This early colonial historical interpretation laid the foundation of Fulani subcolonial rule, but the process of actually explaining, justifying, and establishing Fulani rule over the non-Muslim communities of Adamawa entailed long discursive and practical gestures on the part of the British.

Making the Case for Fulani Rule

Ronald MacAlister, the colonial district officer of Muri District of Adamawa Province, articulated a province-specific variant of the prevailing British opinion on the non-Muslim ethnicities of Northern Nigeria in an August 1920 tour report. In crudely blunt yet instructive terms, MacAlister constructed his treatise concerning the non-Muslim communities of the Adamawa Basin.

The contrast between the "pagan" peoples and the Fulani of Adamawa was an obsession among British colonials from the inception of colonization at the turn of the twentieth century, but MacAlister sought to proceed from this baseline to produce a usable manual of observations on what one, following his own taxonomy, might call the "pagan" character in Adamawa. He sought to establish the terms of interaction between "pagan" "backwardness," Fulani hegemony, and British overlordship. The "pagans," MacAlister affirmed, were "before our advent . . . confined to . . . hill fastness and had no outlet," circumscribed by Fulani slave raids and harassment that sowed insecurity and prevented external economic contact.[16] The non-Muslim communities "for years before the advent of the British Government have been raided, harried and carried off into slavery."[17] In the same precolonial context, the "pagans" interrupted their flights from the Fulani harassment with "intertribal war."

Although these claims about the precolonial relations between Fulani jihadists and migrants and the non-Muslim ethnicities of the Adamawa area were embellished to fit a paradigm of liberation via colonial occupation, they provide insight into the contrasting British perceptions of Fulani and "pagan" in Northern Nigeria. MacAlister developed these topical anthropological observations into substantive instructional manuals on how to deal with "pagans" who, because of their precolonial encounters with Fulani power, were "nervous and suspicious of all newcomers." Essentially, he framed the British occupation as a glorious intervention that restored the freedom of the "pagans" by taming the aggression of the Fulani. The "pagan," he remarked, "in most cases has not been slow to avail himself of the extension of this liberty."[18]

With self-adulatory niceties out of the way, the district officer's motives revealed themselves. The 1920s were years of both consolidation and experimentation for British colonizers in Adamawa. Many districts in Adamawa Province and the Mandated Territories of Northern Cameroon were being integrated into the apparatus of British rule for the first time. In other parts of Adamawa, however, colonial rule had already been consolidated in the hands of Fulani elites and their appointees, with mixed outcomes. These ideas about "pagan" backwardness and Fulani political acumen highlighted previously learned lessons on the administrative efficacy of extending Fulani subcolonial rule over "pagans." MacAlister thus advanced this treatise not simply as an illumination of the Fulani-"pagan" sociopolitical dynamic but also as something of a blueprint for engaging with the non-Muslim communities through Fulani chiefs and officials.

Echoing the familiar Lugardian indirect rule principles of chieftaincy and political centralization, MacAlister contended that non-Muslims should be organized into a cohesive Native Administration where there was a compatible preexisting political infrastructure. In the absence of such a system, MacAlister suggested that chiefs and other personnel should be recruited from African groups "nearest in sympathy and type to the people to be governed."[19] Theoretically, this opened the way to non-Fulani subcolonials who could be relied on to govern non-Muslim communities on behalf of the British in low-priority districts. But British attention, as MacAlister himself outlined, was fixated on the Fulani as internal civilizers whose long interactions with the non-Muslims supposedly prepared them for this new role as preparatory colonial agents.

MacAlister's logic was that although the non-Muslims were wary of Fulani control, the Fulani were more familiar to them than the British could ever be. This familiarity would, he believed, make the Fulani more effective, if imperfect, colonial agents. The "Africanness" of the Fulani offset their foreignness to the "pagans" and made them good candidates for staffing the Native Administration of non-Muslim districts: "The personnel of such Native Administration may be foreign in race to the 'pagans' concerned but they will be African and very much nearer to them in ideas, instincts, and way of thinking, than any European could be."[20] In this thinking, the Fulani's instrumentality to colonial administration in Adamawa Province turned, in short, on their political competence and African identity. Their status as a "foreign race" with superior instincts and political skills distinguished them and could be the fulcrum of their authority among non-Muslims. Their political craftsmanship distinguished them from non-Muslim elites and aristocrats, while their "Africanness" conferred a measure of authenticity, making their subcolonial rule legitimate. The justificatory groundwork of Fulani subcolonial rule was being laid.

MacAlister believed that there were problems with imposing Fulani chiefs and political personnel on "pagans," but he also believed that such problems would persist only if the Fulani colonials were perceived strictly in political terms. The ideal of Fulani rule under British colonialism was a far more ambitious enterprise in which the end goal was a socially reengineered society elevated and shaped by Fulani culture. Through intermarriage with their non-Muslim subjects the Fulani "foreign" presence would mesh with the non-Muslim peoples, producing a hybrid community of African British subjects "with each succeeding generation." The endpoint was a society in which "pagans" and Fulani "would weld into one nation, self-governed under British supervision."[21] This advocacy of civilization through Fulani-"pagan" miscegenation was an extreme, Darwinist version of a familiar trope of Fulani civilizational influence on autochthonous non-Muslim ethnicities.

MacAlister contended that the functioning idiom was not religion but the immutable civilizational instinct of the Fulani. As such he argued that there was no need to impose Muslim law and institutions on the non-Muslim communities. The religion of the "pagans" should be preserved, but the Fulani should be empowered to influence their sociopolitical lives. This distinction underscores the simple, functional British interest in harnessing the political heritage of the Fulani among the non-Muslims, and their concomitant unease with the messy politics of religion. As long as Fulani rule guaranteed "pagan" participation and the "pagans" were a part of their own administration, "I do not see how the 'pagan' can complain of loss of liberty," contended MacAlister.

Non-Muslim participation in Fulani subcolonial rule was desirable as a safeguard against the predictable backlash of delegated Fulani colonial agency. To achieve this, MacAlister counseled a slight departure from the purity of Fulani-superintended preparatory rule by recruiting as understudies "intelligent non-Muhamadans who would be quite satisfactory" in their role as political apprentices of the Fulani. "Intelligent" non-Muslim participation in the British-supervised rule was the most effective way of ensuring the viability of outsourced colonialism because it "avoid[ed] the appearance of bringing the 'pagan' under his hereditary [precolonial] enemy."[22] This complex set of justifications retroactively intellectualized Fulani rule while making the case for its continuation into the future.

In the Beginning

MacAlister's effort to mitigate the increasingly apparent oddity of Fulani subcolonial rule belied earlier British enthusiastic embrace of the Fulani system as a viable option for colonial rule in Adamawa Province. During the first few years of the British administration, Adamawa Province, which at the time excluded the mandated territories of German Cameroon, was partitioned into several divisions. Each of them fell under the authority of the Fulani lamido of Adamawa, whom the British recognized as having a symbolic right to the vast Adamawa non-Muslim hinterland.

Having thus fit this conclusion into a preexisting ideology of caliphate administrative utility, British officials struggled to walk back from their belief that the Fulani should preside on their behalf over the non-Muslim ethnic communities of the province. Once the lamido's symbolic authority was recognized over Adamawa, the British invoked it to justify delegated Fulani rule over the non-Muslim peoples of the province. This was the beginning of a long messy process to formulate a workable administrative template under Fulani leadership. Fulani rule was then gradually and haphazardly extended to the various non-Muslim communities through Yola-affiliated satellite Fulani entities such as Muri, Goila, and Song.

The case of the so-called no. 2 Division, which comprised the Kilba, Bura, Hona, and Lala ethnic groups, is particularly illustrative of the functional coexistence of Fulani-centered colonial rule and quotidian administrative imperatives. The problem of how to administer the non-Muslim peoples of the province, especially those of the lamido's symbolic realm of influence, haunted the early colonial administration. The British found that the Bura, for instance, had never been conquered or compelled into consistent vassalage by the Fulani, so the argument for subjecting them to the authority of the nearby Fulani district of Song was weak at best. Lacking concrete historical claims, the British proceeded nonetheless to put the Bura under a "Fulani chief" from Song on the basis of tenuous ethnographic references to reciprocal tributary contacts between Song and the Bura.[23] In 1912, the appointed Fulani chief was endowed with the title of district head of Bura.

A similar scheme of Fulani chieftaincy was crafted for the Lala people. Yerima Iyawa, a Fulani of Song, got the nod of the colonial administration.[24] The Hona, Marghi, and Uba similarly came under the authority of Fulani chiefs appointed by the Fulani sub-emirate of Goila or Yola directly. The appointment of these Fulani aristocrats as chiefs over the non-Muslim Bura and Lala fleshed out the colonial administration's long-standing adherence to the ideology of Anglo-Fulani rule.

These appointments followed long discussions within the colonial bureaucracy. The debate, however, skirted the question of whether imposing Fulani administrators over non-Muslim ethnic groups with or without histories of subservience to the Fulani power constituted colonial wisdom. Instead the exchanges focused on whether the Fulani entities of Song and Goila should have the symbolic right to independently control the Bura, Lala, and Hona on the lamido's behalf or if Fulani chiefs appointed by Song and Goila should administer the three communities under the direct supervision of the lamido. Similarly, colonial authorities considered the merits of the Fulani subcolonial chiefs paying symbolic tribute to Song and Goila or directly to Yola, and whether or not they should remit their taxes as "subdistricts" of Song and Goila or directly to the lamido.

While these questions were ultimately resolved on a case-by-case basis, the civilizational imperative of Fulani chieftaincy remained the driving force behind these administrative arrangements, since the constant referents in these discussions were the lamido's powers vis-à-vis those of his subordinate Fulani chiefs, and not the preferences of the non-Muslim communities they presided over.

The administrative ideal, the British resident of Yola Province posited, was an arrangement in which Fulani "resident heads" presided over the affairs of non-Muslim districts with the assistance of "pagan heads" whom the former would "supervise and guide."[25] The projected endpoint, as one colonial memo outlined, was a system in which a "pagan" would "rule the country under the guidance of the Filani [sic] Head, and later on, a pagan District Head directly under the Emir."[26] It was an ideal that preserved the centrality of Fulani emirate rule, but one that would also gradually restore relative self-rule and self-determination to the non-Muslim communities.

This ideal would prove elusive. Nonetheless, its articulation by the resident produced two actionable versions of how the non-Muslim communities of the Adamawa hinterland should be governed. It led to a new administrative configuration founded on the utility of resident Fulani chiefs in non-Muslim communities. The idea of Fulani chiefs residing among the non-Muslim peoples contrasted with the notion of a Fulani chief remaining in Song, Goila, Mubi, or Yola and paying visits to the non-Muslim communities for purposes of tax collection, judicial enforcement, and other colonial tasks. In this respect, Fulani resident chieftaincy in Adamawa departed slightly from the model of Hausa-Fulani subcolonial rule practiced in Southern Kaduna and Nasarawa Province. The new idealism was embraced with some pragmatism, leading to a formal system of chiefly apprenticeship in which resident Fulani chiefs in non-Muslim communities gradually mentored a cadre of indigenous quasi-chiefs and aristocrats who then assisted the Fulani in administering their own people, constituting a kind of miniature indirect rule system within the larger colonial system.

The advent of resident Fulani chieftaincy among the non-Muslim communities of Adamawa was inaugurated discursively as British officials bemoaned "the evil effects of a [Fulani] District Chief who is non resident, and the abuses that occur when he merely visits the tribe for the purpose of tax collection."[27] The contention became more compelling as the Fulani chiefs' distant residency accentuated their foreignness to their non-Muslim subjects, making the implementation of colonial mandates difficult and contentious.

The legitimacy deficit that plagued Fulani colonial chieftaincy among the non-Muslim groups of Adamawa was exacerbated by physical alienation, officials claimed. This problem contrasted with "the advance made by resident [Fulani] chiefs in pagan districts."[28] Residency, it was argued, was imperative to the process of cultivating legitimacy because the Fulani were "of a different race." The

Otherness of the Fulani chiefs was, however, supposedly mitigated by their history with non-Muslim communities in the Adamawa sector. Colonial officials repeatedly asserted that the Fulani had "hereditary right" over the non-Muslim communities and as such carried some residual legitimacy that would serve them well in their colonial duties among non-Muslims. The operative ideology here was the idea of a Fulani zone of influence formed primarily by the demographic shifts caused by the Fulani Jihad of the early-nineteenth century. In 1912, this idea was already a widely held axiom in Northern Nigerian official circles.

The Marghi, Kilba, and Uba were the first to have resident Fulani chiefs. This gesture of colonial administrative convenience inverted the prevailing logic in that part of northeast Adamawa, where before and after the jihad, Fulani communities and aristocrats had to intermarry with the locals "with the aim of obtaining better conditions for the Fulbe [Fulani] community and their cattle."[29] This was because the Fulani jihad in those areas had been at best inconclusive, requiring nonhegemonic coexistence of cultures and religions.[30] Colonial officials believed that the resident Fulani chiefs were instrumental in stabilizing and civilizing these communities. In 1912, the three districts were said to be "working satisfactorily" as a result of the work of the resident Fulani chiefs. By contrast, officials claimed that Lala, Hona, and Bura, all headed by nonresident Fulani chiefs "who only visit[ed] the 'pagan' Districts for the collection of tax," were the sites of abuses. Making the case for the implementation of resident Fulani chieftaincy in the three non-Muslim areas to the secretary of the Northern Provinces, the resident of Yola Province invoked the hereditary right of the Fulani of Song and Goila, a right that he claimed the "pagans" themselves acknowledged.

Officials believed that, if hereditary right legitimized resident Fulani chieftaincy, the absence of chieftaincies in the non-Muslim communities and the assumption that the "pagans" were eager to "look up to and follow a Fulani chief" made Fulani rule inevitable. For these reasons, the resident argued that "the Fulani Heads of these three pagan tribes must be resident."[31] Only a resident Fulani chief could accomplish the civilizational and paternal outcomes anticipated for the Fulani subcolonial system. A visiting Fulani chief might fulfill colonial obligations but could not civilize and prepare non-Muslims for eventual self-administration. A resident Fulani chief would visit his non-Muslim subjects frequently, "listen to their complaints, and advise and help them," the resident claimed. The paternal tutelage implied in these assertions bore out the British philosophical view of Fulani aristocrats acting as empowered African civilizing agents.

The transition from nonresident to resident Fulani chieftaincy preserved the control that the lamido, through his appointees in Song and Goila, exercised over the Bura, Hona, and Lala. But the lamido's colonially aided control extended to several other non-Muslim communities, even to those that comprised the so-called "pagan" Independent Division consisting of Kanakuru, Lunguda, Chamba,

Mumuye, Waka, Bachama, Bata, Mbula, Yendam Yakoko, Zinna, and Piri. For these groups, British officials articulated political centralization and strong chieftaincy as linchpins for pushing forward with the model of Fulani colonial agency.

The Case of the Chamba

The Chamba, perhaps the most populous of the non-Muslim groups in the Middle Benue hinterland, are a composite ethnic community formed through a long process of migrations and coalescing in the hinterland of the Upper and Middle Benue.[32] Its many parts, as Richard Fardon has shown, constructed several occasionally confrontational but largely harmonious relationships with Fulani communities in the late-eighteenth and early-nineteenth centuries.[33] By the time of the British conquest of Chamba country in 1907—1909, the Chamba's many towns and settlements were interspersed with many Adamawa-allied Fulani settlements. While intermarriage and commercial interactions increased between the Fulani and the Chamba in the nineteenth century, very few Chamba communities were in a clearly subordinate relationship with Yola or were tributary vassals of its rulers.[34]

The relationship between the Chamba and the Fulani was complicated by miscegenation, cultural and political overlap, and a series of stalemated confrontations. While the Fulani and Chamba influenced each other, the Chamba remained largely non-Muslim and outside the control of the Yola Fulani and their agents. This was the predominant configuration during the precolonial era. The belief that this system legitimized the policy of empowering Fulani rulers over the Chamba rested on British officials' slanted interpretations of Chamba-Fulani relations. Contrary to notions of precolonial Fulani rule over the Chamba, some of the Chamba forced the Fulani to pay grazing fees to underscore their proprietary rights over the land. Other Chamba groups preferred more reciprocal and symbiotic exchanges with Fulani clans resident in their areas.[35]

Upon the conquest of Chamba country, British administrators produced a new climate for the Chamba's administrative subordination to the Fulani. In this new semiotic universe, even politically innocuous acts like friendly exchanges of gifts, or *gaisuwa,* assumed new meanings for the British as signifiers of the Fulani conquest of the vast complex of Chamba-speaking peoples of the greater Middle Benue region. This belief in precolonial Fulani control over the Chamba autochthons persisted into the 1930s, when British officials still invoked a Fulani right of conquest to explain the provenance of Fulani sociolinguistic and cultural elements among the disparate communities of Chamba-speaking peoples.[36]

It was in the context of this complex maze of British sociological and historical conclusions about the Chamba that Fulani rule came to form a scaffold around the superstructure of British colonization in Adamawa Province. In 1909, the British formalized this subordination when Yola, with British encouragement, appointed one of its aristocrats, Usumanu, as chief over all the Chamba groups of the Central Adamawa plains. Originally the chief of Faran, Usumanu had been put in charge of Binyeri District in 1907. Then Binyeri, acquired in 1903 after the delineation of the Anglo-German boundary, was removed from the non-Muslim Numan Division and included in Yola Emirate. It was returned to Numan Division, along with Gurumpawo and Yebbi, after a revolt against Usumanu's "propensity to extortion" forced his removal in 1920.[37] Binyeri was again reintegrated into Yola Emirate in 1926. The Mumuye, another major non-Muslim ethnic community in the region, found themselves amalgamated to the Chamba under Usumanu's chieftaincy even as the British asserted that they were an "independent" district.

Pragmatism and the Limit of Fulani-Centric Colonialism

The Yakokos and Zinna constituted a source of complication for the burgeoning system of Fulani subcolonial rule. The British had put them under the direct control of the Fulani district head of Mayo Faran, an appointee of Yola. But having a non-Muslim community under the direct authority of the Yola Emirate contradicted the pedagogical underpinning of Fulani colonial chieftaincy because it practically annexed the community to the emirate instead of transforming it through Fulani agency. More importantly, officials reckoned that such an arrangement would defeat the essence of residency as a mitigation of "foreign" Fulani subcolonial rule. The Fulani district head of Mayo Faran would be more loyal to his Fulani benefactors in Yola than to the needs of his non-Muslim constituency. Subsequently, the two peoples were amalgamated and politically centralized as an independent district under the chieftaincy of Ajiya, a resident Fulani chief appointed by the lamido.[38]

During this time, a measure of administrative pragmatism seemed to be prevailing over ideological investments in a Fulani system even as Fulani rule was being consolidated. Pragmatic arrangements outside the idealized script of Fulani rule occurred even in the context of a firm belief in the overall utility of Fulani agency in the colonization of non-Muslim societies. The commitment to Fulani subcolonial rule remained fairly strong, yet subtle reform was occurring as non-Muslim understudies were recruited in districts where resentment against the Fulani threatened the entire edifice of Fulani rule. The British insistence on nominal independence from direct emirate control for several non-Muslim communities also demonstrated a new realist sensitivity to non-Muslim anxieties. This tone of pragmatism only increased as the British encountered communities that did not fit into any of the convenient justificatory templates for precolonial Fulani hegemony.

For non-Muslim groups like Yendam and Waka, colonial administration proved complicated and necessitated new forms of readjustment. Authority in these areas belonged to a localized non-Muslim collective, the Bata, whose chief had sporadically and unevenly exercised influence there. Prior to 1912, the Fulani chief of Mayo Belwa ruled the two peoples on behalf of the British. But this situation, like that of the pre-reform Yakoko and Zinna, quickly became unacceptable because it violated the nominal independence of the Yendam and Waka people. The Yendam and Waka were subsequently reorganized under a Bata chieftaincy. The precolonial relationship between the Bata and these two communities was analogous to the Fulani relationship with the Chamba and other non-Muslim groups, as it was marked more by tense coexistence and stalemates than by conquest and vassalage. The British commitment to locating and empowering precolonial claimants to hereditary rights as a basis for creating accountable chiefs did not waver. This generic commitment ensured that the Bata, too, had a fairly prominent position in the colonial system in some non-Muslim communities. This consistency in British policy underscores the primacy of a utilitarian administrative ethic in British deployments of Hausa-Fulani colonial agents.

British officials believed in the hierarchy of African peoples. This hierarchy was marked most sharply by the dualisms of monotheism and polytheism, and political centralization and decentralization. African societies were also valued or devalued according to the degree to which they possessed or lacked external trading traditions, surplus-producing agriculture, and subsistence. Of all these indicators, the existence of a usable prior tradition of chieftaincy was something of a fetish that trumped all other signifiers. The Bata chief was not Fulani or Muslim, and he lacked the revered caliphate pedigree, but he was a chief of a fairly centralized people, accustomed to the rituals of kingship. For the British, this made the Bata suitable as political civilizers and models for politically decentralized non-Muslim peoples. This found practical expression when Atatenji, a member of the Bata royal family, was appointed as the resident chief of the new independent district comprising the Yendam and Waka.[39]

At work here were many of the same principles that advanced positive tutelage and civilization as the products of centralized chieftaincy. The difference was the ethnic and religious identity of the Fulani Muslim and Bata traditionalist. The same principles of using centralized non-Muslim entities to administer decentralized non-Muslim communities where Fulani rule was considered too risky or logistically impracticable also authorized the merger of the Piri people with the Bachama. The Bachama, like the Bata, had an established tradition of chieftaincy and political centralization. The centralization imperative, informed by emirate influence on colonial administrative policy, also facilitated the Lunguda being placed, for a time, under the subcolonial oversight of Mijibona, the chief of the Kanakuru.

The limited empowerment of non-Muslim subcolonial political entities over other non-Muslim communities intermittently interrupted Fulani subcolonial supremacy in certain areas of Adamawa. But it also affirmed the broader ideology of subcolonial civilizational tutelage under which Fulani rule was rationalized. These non-Muslim subcolonial experiments thus reflected a deeper, more urgent set of priorities than the narrower idea of a Fulani administrative imaginary would imply. Such arrangements were possible, however, because of prior administrative experience with the pitfalls of wholesale Fulani rule. Another reason for the appeal of non-Muslim subcolonial rule in the few cases where it occurred was a lack of a credible basis for making historical and anthropological extrapolations in order to legitimize Fulani chieftaincy in certain non-Muslim communities. Such arrangements reflected the practical limits of Fulani subcolonial rule as well as British anxieties about non-Muslim backlash.

Anglo-Fulani Rule amid Anxieties of Early Colonization

Like other contemporary British administrative officers, MacAlister, the author of the colonial blueprint for Fulani subcolonial rule in Adamawa, recognized both the utility of the Fulani model and its dangers. His main cautions were the risk of rejection and upheaval, dangers that necessitated recruiting non-Muslim understudies who would help translate Fulani rule to their kinsmen while portraying the mitigating aura of participatory representation. The ideal configuration of this Fulani-superintended system would be one in which the British overlords recruited Fulani administrators who were willing and capable of implementing "both Muhamadan Law and Native [non-Muslim] customs for a salary." If "pagan" objection to Muslim law disturbed the cohesion of the system, subordinate "'pagan' courts could be established." This elaboration came in response to the recognition that Fulani rule imposed religious and cultural burdens that non-Muslims were already subtly rejecting on the ground.

This recipe was perhaps the most pragmatic of all the visions of emirate subcolonial rule that percolated within the colonial bureaucracy of Adamawa Province. This pragmatism constituted a departure from the unquestioning belief in the efficacy of Fulani-delegated rule. It took more than a decade of Fulani rule to sift idealism from messy administrative realities. The new realism appeared genuine, actuated by the complications of reinvented Fulani rule. British critique of Fulani rule, was, in some respects, as irrational as their prior ideological investments in the transformative capacity of Fulani administrative agency. But it signaled a coming to terms with the fact that Fulani rule created as many problems as it purportedly solved.

British critical reevaluation of the Fulani was not restricted to simple administrative matters. It extended to the everyday dynamics of the relations between the Muslim Fulani and their non-Muslim neighbors and subjects. British officials operating in grassroots districts, and observing quotidian interactions from close quarters, commented on the frequent crises between the Fulani and non-

Muslim communities extensively in the 1920s, their judgments tilting against the Fulani with every new report. Some of them outright blamed Fulani herdsmen for provoking "pagans" even while pointing lamentably to "pagan" retaliation and aggression: "In nine of ten [cases] the Fulani are to blame. They leave small children to act as herdsmen and the cattle get into the farms," the district officer of Numan Division claimed in 1926.[40] Reports like this stoked the fear that outright Fulani proxy rule might worsen these problems by emboldening the Fulani masses while exacerbating non-Muslim resentment.

The multiple arbitrary levies that Fulani colonial figureheads placed on non-Muslim traders and farmers had by the mid-1920s amounted to administrative extortion according to some colonial memos. Complaints poured in from non-Muslims who felt that Fulani rule overstepped its colonial mandate and had transformed into a parallel bureaucracy of exploitation. British officials began to take sides in these disputes, increasingly in favor of the non-Muslim groups. They condemned excessive and multiple "market tolls, Zango [rest stop] fees, extortionate ferry tolls, and finally the Jimeta Dillali, who grabs from [the pagan] his load of ground-nuts etc and gives him half the price that he would get by going another quarter of a mile to the Niger store."[41] British condemnation of Fulani extortion of the non-Muslim peasant was anything but altruistic. Supervising British officials wanted agricultural produce delivered to European-owned Niger Company stores steadily and resented the exploitative system that discouraged many non-Muslim farmers from producing for the market or making the dangerous journey to the buying stations. For the British the system allowed a Fulani colonial revenue official, or *dillali,* to sit in an exalted position "like a spider in the center of his web" and "pounce on the 'pagan' fly."[42] This system was a threat to the export-crop economic mainstay of the colonial state and needed to be confronted.

There was also an occupational dynamic to the British defense of non-Muslims against the oppressions of Fulani subcolonial rule. The nonaristocratic Fulani population of the province was a cattle-herding community while the non-Muslims were farmers. The latter were invaluable economic assets to be shielded from the excesses of Fulani subcolonial authority. In the district officer of Numan Division's patronizing rhetoric, "the 'pagan' is the greatest productive asset of the province in contrast with the non-productive Fulani."[43] As a result of this clarity in the British economic valuation of the non-Muslim population, and at the urging of the British the supreme Fulani traditional authority in the province, the lamido, minced no words in demanding that non-Muslim traders and farmers from the vast non-Muslim hinterland be protected from Fulani extortion. In 1926, the lamido abolished market dues in the non-Muslim districts of Adamawa Division in deference to British officials' validation of the non-Muslim outcry. This was a token symbolic gesture, but it proved the merit of non-Muslim grievance.

The move was a culmination of a steady decline in the fortunes of Fulani rule among the Adamawa non-Muslim communities, which looked increasingly to the British as a counterweight against the excess of Fulani rule. Administrative observations reoriented British officials' attitude toward the Fulani-"pagan" relationship. During the heyday of British obsession with Fulani subcolonial rule in the first years of British rule, officials fantasized about compassionate and good-tempered Fulani administrators who would civilize the Adamawa "pagans." As one British official articulated this prevailing colonial sentiment, Fulani colonial officials possessed a certain "Fulani instinct to rule when settled among 'pagans,'" and that the "pagan" had the subservient instinct of followership, what he described as "the pagan instinct to leave everything to the Fulani."[44]

Many years of Fulani rule later, officials seemed to be less sure about the attitude and temperament of the Fulani colonial agent in regard to the non-Muslim peoples of the province. Officials were not just concerned that an overbearing Fulani bureaucracy might stifle non-Muslim farmers' ability to satiate the British appetite for agricultural exports. They now feared that, by administratively empowering the Fulani over the non-Muslims, they might have helped consolidate the conceited disposition of the Fulani toward the non-Muslim ethnicities of the Adamawa area: "It is quite obvious in Adamawa Division that the Fulani view of the pagan is that he is a person whom half a brick should always be heaved on sight."[45] In the understanding of British officials, the problems were not economic per se. To be sure, Fulani officials expressed a tendency to improve themselves economically on the backs of non-Muslims.

Increasingly, British supervisors singled out Fulani colonial agents' attitude to non-Muslim colonial subjects as a factor in strained colonial relations. Officials argued that a condescending Fulani attitude toward non-Muslim communities, reinforced by the establishment of a Fulani-centered colonial system, was responsible for the economic oppression of the "pagan." This attitude of the Fulani came under increased scrutiny in the 1920s as British officials sought to contain the unforeseen fallouts of Fulani subcolonial rule.

Delegated Fulani colonial rule functioned surprisingly smoothly in several districts, generating few if any problems and bearing out the colonial wisdom of "foreign" subcolonial agency. In many other districts, however, Fulani rule proved tumultuous, marked by implacable non-Muslim dissent, rebellion, and virulent anti-Fulani resistance. Within a few years of several Fulani chieftaincies being established, non-Muslim complaints about the abuse of authority, oppression, and extortion began to reach superintending British officials. A long history of cultural misunderstanding between the Fulani and the non-Muslim autochthons and a prevailing climate of suspicion between the two zones produced tensions and crisis.[46] As the colonial period progressed, this mutual cultural ignorance of each other persisted among the Fulani and their non-Muslim subject communities. The Goila-appointed Fulani chief of Hona, for instance, was described in colonial records as knowing "little about the Honas," a fact that dramatized the foreignness of his subcolonial chieftaincy.

This gap of knowledge spelled administrative disaster and bred distrust among the non-Muslims. The district officer in charge of the Hona-Bura-Lala cluster of districts described a "persistently distrustful and hostile attitude of . . . pagans towards their Khalifa [Fulani chief]."[47] Such a dismissive description of non-Muslim resentment was slightly misleading because it belied multiple British acknowledgments of Fulani chiefs' abuse of their subcolonial authority, which in turn provoked a disdainful reaction from the non-Muslim peoples. The district officer's indictment of the Fulani *khalifa* of Lala and a subsequent recommendation of his termination encapsulates this acknowledgment and also points to the connection between the hostility of non-Muslim subjects and the insecurity of their Fulani chiefs:

> I suggest the immediate abolishing of the Khalifa of Lala, upon whom I have already reported, as worse than merely useless. A further proof of his uselessness is given in the fact that two days ago I had an urgent message from him, asking me to send police or return myself to town, as he . . . feared the pagans "might" next attack him, finally suggesting he should "run" to Song.[48]

There was also trouble in Yungeru and M'Boi, where non-Muslim groups revolted in response to Fulani oppression and extortion. The Hona people complained persistently about "how the Fulani spoil their country," confiscating goats and sheep even "after a village has finished paying its tax."[49] They claimed that excessive fees collected by agents of Fulani chiefs prevented them from profiting at the markets and that Fulani buyers paid them only a fraction of the market price. Endorsing the grievances of the Hona, the resident warned that any Fulani colonial agent who engaged in any acts of extortion would be held accountable. The intervention of the resident hardly reassured the Hona, who refused to pay any more taxes to the Fulani. Subsequently, they demanded that one of their own be appointed their chief and promised to resume tax payment if this was done.[50]

In some cases, the problems of cultural misunderstanding, lack of legitimacy, and overestimation of the administrative abilities of Fulani officials came together in one systemic breakdown of governmental structure. This threatened the coherence of Anglo-Fulani rule as well as the lamido's nebulous hold on the large, widely dispersed clan of Fulani district heads in non-Muslim communities. In Marghi, the cohesion between the appointed Fulani head and his handlers in Yola came unglued, complicated by the contradictions of Fulani subcolonial rule. The lamido's constant interference in the affairs of non-Muslim groups sometimes snowballed into power tussles between him and the Fulani district heads overseeing these groups. Such squabbles alternately resulted in administrative paralysis and loss of revenue. The lamido's insistence on remotely controlling the affairs of the Marghi through his own representatives, or jekadu, conflicted with British desires to allow the Fulani district head, Iyawa, the latitude crucial for executing everyday administrative tasks. When Iyawa asserted himself in his role as colonial chief of the Marghi, the lamido removed him and began shopping for a replacement.[51] This drew the disapproval of British officials, but they moved gingerly around the issue so as not to undermine the lamido, who sat atop the entire edifice of Fulani subcolonial rule and represented its symbolic authority in Adamawa.

In the case of the Kilba, the lamido's appointed chief proved an incompetent administrator who constantly needed to be prodded by the district officer to carry out routine administrative tasks. When he did work, he preferred a method that stoked more resentment among his Kilba subjects. He farmed out his administrative tasks to yet another Fulani representative, "a foolish old man who . . . [was] unable to carry . . . out [standard administrative instructions] because he [had] no hold over the people for whom he [was] supposed to be responsible."[52] This was a common problem as Fulani officials would sometimes appoint lesser Fulani officials, who in turn appointed their own set of officials. The result was a constantly expanding infrastructure of Fulani rule as well as multiple layers of revenue generation, which non-Muslim groups experienced as Fulani oppression. The problems of illegitimacy and non-Muslim resentment proved combustive and in some cases derailed the Fulani subcolonial system.

These troubles compelled officials to embrace more substantively the idea of appointing non-Muslims to act over their own peoples in districts where Fulani chieftaincy clearly faltered and was counterproductive. Discussions about appointing indigenous chiefs to rule over the non-Muslim communities spiked in correspondence to the intensity of the troubles plaguing Fulani chieftaincies in the non-Muslim areas of the province. As the chieftaincies began to unravel, colonial discourse returned to the issue of appointing non-Muslim figureheads over the administrative affairs of the non-Muslim districts even if supervisory jurisdiction technically resided with the lamido.

Discussions over the possible appointment of so-called pagan chiefs began as early as March 1914, when the district officer of Yola Division suggested appointing Mallu, a Bura apprentice of the Fulani official titleholder, Jauro, to oversee the Bura-Hona district. Mallu's appointment was, however, vetoed when the Hona rejected him because they viewed him as a "tool of Jauro Goila." The Hona wanted an indigenous chief, but not one beholden to the Fulani chief of Goila. Finally, a man called Giyaiya was appointed as chief over the Hona in an experimental capacity. If he proved himself worthy by collecting taxes diligently and maintaining order for a year, he would be confirmed in the position, the resident decreed.[53] Now, officials discussed the possibility of replicating this experiment in the province's many non-Muslim districts.

Reform and Regression in Fulani Rule

British colonial officials in Adamawa experimented extensively with various models and modifications of the Fulani system. It was a system in constant flux and in permanent reform. Some of the reforms were progressive, driven by a sensitivity to the resentment of non-Muslim communities under Fulani colonial chieftaincies. Others seemed to regress to the days when the British believed that the non-Muslim communities belonged under the administrative jurisdiction of proximate emirate enclaves by default.

By 1926, the administrative setbacks caused by the reported maladministration of several Fulani chiefs and the resentments and protests of subordinate non-Muslim communities had resulted in the outright appointment of indigenous, non-Muslim chiefs for the Lala, Hona, and Yungur. The three districts were also officially excised from the control of the lamido in order to rid them of "the shadowy control which the Emir exercised over them prior to their removal from his jurisdiction."[54] Other non-Muslim districts seemed on the cusp of similar transitions. The appointment of indigenous district chiefs was a step above the transitional apprenticeship of experimental non-Muslim subchiefs of the previous decade.

These reforms notwithstanding, most non-Muslim districts remained under Fulani administrative control. In a move that demonstrated the persistence of the long-held belief in the need for emirate tutelage over non-Muslim communities, officials outlined proposals that, while proclaiming reformist intent, would effectively deepen and restore Yola's control over the non-Muslims of the Middle Benue and Adamawa hinterlands. Unfurled in 1926, the proposals would see Yungur, Hona, Lala, Yendam-Waka, and other independent districts reincorporated into Yola Emirate and/or into Yola Division.[55] Even districts that were firmly in the non-Muslim Division of Numan like Gurumpawo and Yebbi were slated for incorporation into Yola Division. Before being officially outlined for the secretary of the Northern Provinces in Kaduna, the proposals had been the subject of considerable deliberation and correspondence in the bureaucracy of Yola Province.

The district officer in charge of Yola first advanced these proposals in August 1926. In a confidential memo written less than a month later, the assistant district officer reported that Yungur, Lala, and Hona did not realize that they would be reincorporated into Yola Emirate and were hostile to the proposal. The people of Yungur "[would] not welcome being included in the Emirate," he submitted. They were satisfied with the performance of their indigenous district chief and saw little sense in the transfer.[56] The Lala were also content with their indigenous village heads. The assistant district officer reported that the Hona "[would] certainly not welcome going back into the Emirate," although they equally resented the symbolic control that the Fulani authority in Goila, "whom they hate," exercised over their district and signaled that they might be willing to embrace incorporation into a distant Fulani entity if that would free them from the oppression of a proximate one.[57]

In Gurumpawo and Yebbi districts of the autonomous non-Muslim Numan Division, the people objected to being subordinated to the lamido because they "fear[ed] that they [would] be expected to pay tribute to the Emir and his subordinates and that their district [would] be 'invaded' by many Fulani who will not respect the customs."[58] The people of the two districts argued that Fulani exactions in the form of unauthorized fees, fines, and taxes "will hamper their prosperity." This was a deeply felt protest against the practice of the lamido "sending Jekadu or tax collectors from Yola" to the non-Muslim districts in what effectively amounted to double taxation, since the peoples of the various districts would already have paid their taxes to their districts chiefs, whether Fulani or autochthons.[59] The rampant problem of unauthorized exaction cast unwanted attention on the excesses of the Fulani system, much to the embarrassment of British colonial officialdom. Citing a punitive raid into Gurumpawo territory by the lamido when he was the Fulani district head of Nassarawo, the people of Gurumpawo rejected their proposed subordination to Yola, likening it to being placed under an old enemy.

The people of Yebbi expressed a similarly implacable objection to the proposal. Their objections found anchor in colonial relational histories of antagonism and hostility, compelling officials to propose a merger with the southerly Fulani emirate of Muri. This recommendation was explained through the rhetoric of administrative efficiency. The resident claimed that their transfer from the non-Muslim Numan Division to the emirate of Muri was pragmatic because "they would be more easily and more frequently visited by the Officer in the Southern Emirate, than by the Officer in Numan Division."[60] He also claimed that the proposed merger would preserve their "independence," as "they would remain under their own Heads as individual units." Such a middle position, while removing the dreaded Yola Fulani hegemony from the debate, reiterated the continued appeal of Fulani rule as an inherently central institution of British colonization in Adamawa. Moreover, the emir of Muri, it was widely acknowledged, fell under Yola's authoritative jurisdiction, so moving from Numan to Muri amounted to reentering the orbit of Fulani rule at a time when there was widespread resentment against it.

Like the Gurumpawo and Yebbi, the people of Yendam-Waka resented the proposal to include them in either of the two Fulani emirates. Yendam-Waka District had been an independent district, albeit under the symbolic purview of Yola, for thirteen consecutive years by 1926, so the proposal to reintegrate it into the emirate was met with particularly strong hostility.

The case of Chamba District was complex in its own peculiar foundational details. Chamba District had a checkered, messy history with Yola. In recognition of its overwhelmingly non-Muslim population the British placed it in Numan Division at the conclusion of the colonial conquest. In 1917, the district was transferred to Yola because officials, in a reference to the precolonial symbolic gestures that had preserved a tentative stalemate in the zone, concluded that the people of the district had a "traditional allegiance to Yola." Several years later, it was transferred to Numan Division and placed under an indigenous, non-Muslim district chief in recognition of the Chamba resentment of Fulani rule and because of what officials described as the "maladministration by the Fulani District Head."[61]

Administrative Expediency and the Persistence of Fulani-Centric Rule

The convoluted history of Chamba District's movement between multiple statuses indicates the experimentation and uncertainties that underpinned the implementation of Fulani subcolonial rule. The fluctuating fate of Chamba District materialized most clearly in the circular reforms that now culminated in a proposal to transfer it yet again to Yola. This also illustrates the fact that when the colonial administration ran into unforeseen trouble and expected outcomes failed to materialize, it defaulted to delegated Fulani rule in spite of earlier acknowledgments of its foundational problems. British officials seemed to prefer the comfort of the familiar to the uncertainty of real change.

The most consequential motive behind these reforms was administrative expediency, not the self-critical acknowledgment of flawed colonial assumptions. Although critiques of Fulani rule proliferated in colonial correspondence in the province, concerns about non-Muslim self-determination seemed to have played a relatively minor, if any, role in shaping reforms to Fulani rule. Officials in fact occasionally strained to discredit the grievances of non-Muslim communities against Fulani rule. The opinion of the resident bears this hypothesis out. Responding to Lala, Hona, and Yungur's objections to the incorporation proposals, he invoked their prior inclusion in the emirate to discredit their present resentment of emirate control:

> I have not the same sympathy with the desire for self-determination expressed by these Districts as I have with Yendam-Waka. All three of them were at one time part of the Yola Emirate and with the enlightened views on pagan administration held by the present Emir I do not think their freedom of local self-government will be in any way impaired by re-inclusion in it.[62]

Although an acknowledgment of the right of self-determination as it pertained to the three districts was not the resident's intention, his use of the self-determination register and its application to the grievance of the Yendam-Waka

District gave effective official recognition to the lingering questions of Fulani legitimacy and non-Muslim resentment. The resident effectively conceded to the three districts a limited, theoretical right to self-government within the administrative rubric of British rule. The non-Muslim communities' struggle for administrative self-determination under British colonization lived more in the denial and silences of colonial officials than it did in their actions. Nonetheless, it was an ever-present irritant, constantly needing to be addressed, even if dismissively. The struggle involved the invocation of dueling understandings of history. British officials, for practical reasons, were prone to lend greater political support to Yola's political hegemony and to give it deterministic weight in the search for a workable administrative model. Non-Muslim communities, on the other hand, glossed over the emirate's assumed precolonial hegemony. Instead they referenced the two interrelated realities of Yola's sporadic military maneuvers and the mutuality of precolonial arrangements that could be misunderstood as hegemony.

In the end, a mishmash of different arrangements emerged. Many non-Muslim districts were placed under Yola with mitigating discretionary safeguards against arbitrary exactions. Others were left "independent" under the symbolic controls exercised by Yola and Muri. Gurumpawo and Yebbi were saved from being placed under the Fulani rulers of Muri by their status as mandated territories of the League of Nations, which insisted on them retaining control over their own affairs with British colonial oversight. As the resident concluded, "their inclusion in the Emirate would almost certainly have resulted in questions being asked which might be difficult to answer."[63]

Chamba "Reorganization" and the Revival of Fulani Rule

Although officials knew when to halt a restoration of emirate suzerainty for pragmatic reasons, the facade of progressive reform hid a deeply entrenched commitment to the emirate model of colonial rule. New, extensive reform, touted as "reorganization," created new opportunities for Yola and its vast network of Fulani officials to reassert control. Conversely the reforms hurt the efforts of the Chamba-speaking peoples and districts to reclaim their administrative independence.

Theoretically, the so-called Chamba reorganization reforms of 1937–38 seemed focused on weakening emirate control and opening doors to Chamba administrative self-assertion. The reorganization essentially birthed the five Chamba "chieftaincies" of Binyeri, Gurumpawo, Yebbi, Tsugu, and Nassarawo. Each of the chieftaincies would be headed by an indigenous Chamba, in an innovation that clearly fit with the British desire to transition from Fulani rule to some measure of autochthonous control. The only exception to this arrangement was Nassarawo, which would continue to be headed by a Fulani appointee,

Haman Tukur, until "it [became] possible to replace him with a local man."[64] Nassarawo was a somewhat peculiar case in that half of its 18,126 inhabitants were Fulani, who had long settled in the area. This contrasted with the demographic information from other Chamba districts, where the Fulani population, made up of mostly nomadic grazers and administrative officials, numbered only in the hundreds.[65] Further complicating things, the district's headquarter town, Jada, may have started out as a Fulani village, settled in the late-eighteenth and early-nineteenth century by migrants, like nine other small village settlements in the area.[66] Although several competing proposals about the creation of multiple purely Chamba districts from Nassarawo were at different times articulated, none materialized. An alternative proposal to replace Haman Tukur with a ruling council comprising Chamba and Fulani also faltered. As a result, the rule of Haman Tukur and his large coterie of Fulani officials continued over the next two decades.

Haman Tukur's retention as district head of Nassarawo went against the spirit of the unfolding reform, but it was legitimized by the logic of pragmatism as British officials preferred to retain a functioning status quo instead of creating a new, potentially costly one. They also still saw the possibility for Fulani rule to fulfill the imperative of civilizational tutelage that the British had articulated for it among the non-Muslim communities. Haman Tukur was not only to serve as the district chief of Nassarawo, he was also to head a new Chamba District Council, an administrative body comprised of Chamba chiefs. The primary justification for his appointment as president of this new Chamba District Council was that it would give him a platform to "continue his task of educating the [Chamba] council [members]," who, British officials believed, were still poorly schooled in the art of administration. The Chamba Council appeared in name to represent a new British sensitivity to the grievances and demands of the Chamba for self-administration, which turned essentially on the need to be released from Fulani control. In reality, the council had the status of a "subordinate Native Authority" or sub-NA, under the general purview of the Yola Native Authority, the institutional pivot of Fulani subcolonial rule in Adamawa.

The reform created a jumble of institutions and generated new dilemmas. How, for instance, would colonial courts operate—by Chamba traditional customs or by the Muslim legal corpus governing the judicial affairs of the Fulani? The response to this conundrum seemed, again, to be driven more by administrative expedience than by a fundamental retreat from the centrality of the Fulani to colonial rule. A customary court was established for each Chamba district, to be headed by Chamba chiefs and to hear cases involving their non-Muslim populations. However, in addition to having their judicial mandate limited in matters involving Fulani and Muslims, the courts' adjudicatory powers were subsumed under a Fulani-controlled judicial infrastructure. The Federated Chamba Subordinate Native Authority, as it was called, was given superior, overriding judicial authority, which included the presence within the Native Authority of a superior court with appellate powers. Located in Jada, in Fulani sociopolitical territory and headed by Haman Tukur, the superior court would hear cases involving both Muslim Fulani and non-Muslim Chamba.

The new Chamba Area Court did not just possess a superior judicial purview, it was also the appellate court to which all verdicts from the various Chamba courts automatically reverted. In addition, the court was empowered to hear appeals in cases involving Muslims and non-Muslims, corresponding in most cases to the Fulani-Chamba demographic dichotomy. Reforms in the judicial arena illustrated that the political anxieties of Yola and its Fulani agents drove the reform process more than did Chamba grievance. Nothing encapsulates this contention more than the fact that in all cases emanating from the Chamba Federation or from its constitutive chieftaincies, the lamido's court in Yola had the final appellate word, subject to review only by the British resident.

By intent, the reform was meant to give the Chamba a taste of self-governance under the Anglo-Fulani system. Instead it created new judicial and political bureaucracies that remained under the control of Yola. British officials outlined the 1937—38 reform as a long-desired effort to unify the many Chamba-speaking peoples of Yola Division into a coherent federation of self-governing chieftaincies. The changes were necessary, officials argued, as part of a broader "search for more effective administration of the Southern [non-Muslim] districts of Adamawa Division."[67] Over the next two decades, however, the messiness of the reform process would unravel. Subsequent contradictions and problems surfaced in the reformers' failure to undermine the edifice of Fulani rule or weaken Yola's hold on the Chamba. British pragmatic reliance on a group of entrenched Fulani officials and concomitant anxieties about embracing a radically new system of Chamba-controlled institutions were also revealed.

Officials' reluctance to move decisively away from the Fulani model even as they espoused the need for Chamba authority pivoted on a foundational British narrative on Fulani precolonial hegemony. The 1930s were years in which, all over Northern Nigeria, administrative reform was occurring to give a measure of administrative autonomy to non-Muslim ethnic groups, the so-called northern minorities. Governor Donald Cameron had made this reform his signature project. In Yola Province, however, reform was half-hearted at best, moderated by prior assumptions of Fulani-caliphate precolonial control and by resistance to alternative colonial arrangements that more closely resembled the British indirect rule idea of ruling through indigenous elites and institutions. Even in the period of reform, an official report on the proposed reorganization among the Chamba repeated the claim that the "tribe was conquered by the Adamawa Fulani during the [Fulani] Jihad" of the early-nineteenth century. The evidence for this assumption was the provenance of Fulfulde as a second language among several Chamba groups and the flimsy conclusion that "many of the Chamba have been considerably affected by the Fulani in dress and manners."[68]

Clinging to a notion of precolonial Fulani hegemony in Adamawa Province as a mark of the province's exceptionalism helped officials escape the obligation of implementing a 1935 memo crafted from the regional colonial headquarters in Kaduna as a manual for the reform of Fulani emirate rule among the non-Muslims of Adamawa Province.[69] The memo recommended a radical transition from a caliphate- and Fulani-centered rule to decentralized self-administration in non-Muslim districts. It failed to influence the tenor of the 1937 Chamba reforms.

In the ideological and bureaucratic evolution of Fulani subcolonial rule in Adamawa Province, two main factors actuated Fulani rule among the non-Muslim, seemingly low-priority colonial territories in the province and made it possible for Fulani chiefs and their numerous appointees to effectively rule the areas on behalf of the British. The first factor was the familiar exigency of finance and personnel. The other was a British obsession with a Fulani governing imaginary founded on interpretations of the precolonial history of Adamawa.

In Adamawa Province, precolonial relational patterns were less dichotomous than they were in other provinces. The ability of Fulani migrants to embed themselves in and around non-Muslim communities, and the extensively symbiotic, although occasionally fractious, relations between the two groups of people meant that there was no prior tradition of loose caliphate imperialism here. Moreover, the jihad in the Adamawa area had left much of the preexisting sociological realities intact because fragmented Fulani communities were nestled between non-Muslim groups, and no clear frontiers emerged that could be policed and used to separate dar-al-Islam from dar-al-harb. In a pattern that demonstrates a trend of less teleological state formations in zones of contact, a coherent Fombina state never emerged until the contentious contact with indigenous non-Muslim communities and the latter's resistance made Fulani political unity imperative.[70] Even so, Fombina remained fragmented into semi-autonomous Fulani communities and was never the fairly bounded emirate that emirates in the northwest were. It was able to sustain its political authority largely on the strength of its ties with the Sokoto Caliphate. The result was a fairly unique relational flux that did not mirror the situation in other regions, where Muslim states had coherent polities with clear frontiers that they used as a basis to stake intermittent claims to tribute from some non-Muslim communities.

These peculiarities made the British imposition of Fulani rule on Adamawa's non-Muslim ethnic groups particularly disruptive. The colonial system that emerged endured clumsily, and it became clear that doctrinal coherence was a casualty of the everyday challenges of maintaining a semblance of colonial order.

Fulani subcolonial rule here, even in its mutating forms, represented a level of co-lonial improvisation that not only departed from the doctrine of indirect rule but also contradicts the widely held notion of the imperial universality of indigenous mediation. In the rough quotidian grind of colonial rule, what seemed to matter was getting the job done, whatever that was, and the grand claims of bestowing the blessings of guided self-rule (indirect rule) took on a secondary importance.

The bureaucracy that the Fulani and British built in the non-Muslim com-munities became so central to colonial rule in Adamawa that British officials came to rely fully on them. Subsequently, they became resistant to alternative ad-ministrative arrangements that better expressed British colonial rhetoric about administrative self-determination, the very ideational foundation of indirect rule. An indication of this symbiosis is the fact that, even as British officials ac-knowledged oppression and abuse of power by Fulani rulers and their Fulani ap-pointees and recognized the need to move the non-Muslim communities toward "pure" indirect rule in which they would be ruled by their own personnel and institutions, the pragmatic reliance on the institutions and personnel of Fulani rule scuttled efforts at reform.

Fulani rule created many problems for all parties involved. The British, the Fulani emirate of Yola and its administrative tentacles in non-Muslim districts, and the non-Muslim communities all struggled to contain and manage its un-foreseen fallouts. Complaints and protests came frequently from non-Muslim subjects, who desired control over their own affairs and resented the excesses of delegated Fulani rule. When reform came in 1937, along with a surprising set of British indictments against Fulani rule, it was half-hearted, compromised by the degree to which Fulani institutions and personnel had become the fulcrum of colonial rule in the province.

The failure of the 1937—38 reforms to dismantle the consequential aspects of Fulani rule and the rise of organized, coherently articulated Middle Belt political agitation crystallized in a determined and widespread opposition to Anglo-Fu-lani rule in Adamawa. New anti-caliphate agitation seized on the colonial idioms of self-determination and indirect rule and recalibrated them as the intellectual anchor of a renewed, fiercer demand for colonial self-rule. These new, aggressive non-Muslim protest politics erupted in Adamawa in the period following the failed reforms.

6 Non-Muslim Revolt against Fulani Rule in Adamawa

THE IMPLEMENTATION OF a Fulani-centered colonial rule in Adamawa Province among the Chamba people in particular highlighted several foundational problems while eliciting backlash and intermittent, largely cosmetic, reform. As Fulani rule in the province transitioned into the second half of the colonial period, new problems emerged. These problems included increased protests by non-Muslim subjects of the Anglo-Fulani system, the volatile interplay of late colonial anxieties and fears, and aggressive political positioning by both the Fulani and non-Muslims. This chapter explores this gradual descent into conflict, botched reform, and failed colonial crisis management. It also analyzes the organic and organizational connection between, on one side, the struggle of non-Muslim groups and Western-educated youth against Fulani domination, and, on the other side, a broader struggle against caliphate political hegemony in Northern Nigeria in the late colonial period.

The impact of Fulani rule on the socioeconomic and political life of non-Muslim communities accumulated over time. As a result, reaction to Fulani colonial schemes and what non-Muslim groups regarded as oppressive policies developed gradually until it reached a crescendo in the 1940s and 1950s. By then, British officials would discover, other political forces beyond Adamawa had intervened to complicate both non-Muslim agitation and the Fulani's expanding role in colonization. The late colonial period brought new confrontations between the British and the Fulani on one side and a proliferating array of non-Muslim groups on the other side. These encounters were animated by conflicting Fulani and non-Muslim political aspirations, as decolonization appeared imminent. The struggles of this period were as much about the dualism of anticipated privilege and oppression as they were about the grievances of the present. But their immediate roots lay in the failure of much-touted reforms and in the ironic consolidation of Fulani rule in the age of professed departure from its excesses.

Prelude to Revolt

The 1937–38 reforms discussed in the last chapter were designed, British officials claimed, to devolve more administrative self-determination to non-Muslim communities in response to their grievances against Fulani subcolonial rule. The reforms floundered partly because they went against the prevailing administrative orthodoxy, which privileged ruling through Fulani officials. Had the reforms lived up to their declared intent, they likely would have set the non-Muslim districts on the path to true indirect rule, that is, colonial rule through non-Muslim indigenous chiefs and institutions. In the end, apart from some cosmetic changes and a few experimental non-Muslim chieftaincies and apprenticeships, the reforms altered little in the system of Fulani rule. These mixed outcomes and, in some cases, outright failures did not register strongly in the colonial bureaucracy until the early 1950s, when non-Muslim agitation for freedom from Fulani subcolonial rule assumed new, charged dimensions. Events during the interval between Chamba "reorganization" and the late colonial period of the early to mid-1950s proved crucial in giving new expressions to the familiar problems associated with British-engineered Fulani rule.

The reforms of 1937 had many goals. The delegation of administrative power and initiative from Fulani to Chamba and other non-Muslim groups was one of them. By 1951, however, many of these goals remained unrealized, as components of non-Muslim administrative self-determination were ignored in favor of the Fulani-centered status quo. As part of the reform, Haman Tukur, the Yola-appointed district head of Nassarawo, had been appointed the president of the Chamba Council. By colonial declaration his mandate was temporary and preparatory as "he was appointed to demonstrate [to the Chamba Chiefs] efficient and honest District administration."[1] Tukur's secondary mandate was to help establish the bureaucracy of a "federal executive authority" for the five-member council. The crux of the reform was for Tukur to "help the Chamba to reach these goals, and when they had he would retire from the scene."[2] The finite pedagogical premise of Fulani authority over a federated Chamba bureaucracy was clear in this vision.

In the period between 1938 and 1951 "not the slightest progress" was made toward the avowed goals, a fact attested to by colonial memos and reports.[3] One of the starkest indicators of this failure to advance toward Chamba self-governance is the fact that Haman Tukur, in addition to holding his position as president of the Chamba Federation, also held on to his temporary position as the chief of Nassarawo District. This represented a clear departure from one of the cardinal goals of the 1937 "reorganization" reform: the declaration "that Nassarawo District should in due course have either a Chamba as Head or a Council."[4] Officials declared in 1951 that "the 1937 [reforms] envisioned, as authority for this District, either a local [Chamba] man or a council."[5] The same memo lamented, however, that, "no progress has been made towards this." This was one example of how the feeble commitment to reform dissipated in the interval between 1938 and 1951.

In that same period, several intersecting and mutually reinforcing developments occurred, stoking Chamba and non-Muslim grievances against Fulani rule. Haman Tukur had consolidated his position, transmuting to a de facto authoritarian ruler over the Chamba, and now had the final say, save for British review, over their judicial and administrative matters. The British attributed this unexpected consolidation of Fulani rule to the absence of British administrative touring for twelve years. This, they claimed, "spoilt the 1938 [re]organization." It was clear even to British observers, long in denial of their own creation of a Fulani colonial oligarchy, that "there was now less administration of the Chamba by the Chamba than there was before [the] 1938 [reform]."⁶ Acknowledging the failure of reform and the paradoxical institutionalization of Fulani rule against prevailing official rhetoric, the district officer of Yola was uncharacteristically blunt: "Haman Tukur, who was [under "reorganization"] intended to be a sort of guide and helper and chairman, has become a District-Head-in-Chief of the five [Chamba] Districts, and is officially responsible for the administration of all of them."⁷ Because the reforms established a Native Authority subordinate to the Yola Native Authority, the titular protocols and political symbols of Yola (Fombina) Emirate found their way into the Chamba Council. The lamido formalized this reality by renaming the office of the president of the Chamba Council as the *wakili,* or emir's representative, with all the trappings and responsibilities of the office.

Haman Tukur, as a representative of the lamido, worked quietly to entrench and institutionalize Fulani rule. With Yola's blessing, he appointed more Fulani district scribes for all the Chamba chieftaincies, swelling the existing number of Fulani officials and undercutting the Chamba apprentice chiefs. The district scribes, in turn, appointed other Fulani subordinate colonial auxiliaries. Together, these cadres of Fulani personnel constituted the hands, eyes, and ears of British colonialism in Chambaland. They ran the colonial bureaucracy, and the indigenous Chamba peoples encountered many more Fulani officials than they did Chamba subordinate officials in their relationship with the colonial state.

The 1937–38 reorganization exercise was intended, officials admitted, to replace Fulani colonial agents with Chamba auxiliaries in all four Chamba districts of Binyeri, Yebbi, Gurumpawo, and Sugu. They further acknowledged that "this could have been carried out and completed long ago." However, the district officer now lamented that "no attempt has been made to" accomplish this goal. As a practical matter, then, the 1937–38 "reorganization" firmly reinstated the Chamba and other subordinated non-Muslim peoples into the Yola Emirate system.

Self-Determination in Limbo?

Officials' political aims to pursue their avowed commitment to eventual self-administration for non-Muslim communities collided and competed consistently with an even more compelling reality: Fulani rule *worked.* Unlike the putative infrastructure of Chamba rule, Fulani rule was already in functional existence and was cheaper than constructing a new, multilayered administration that would assuage the non-Muslim agitation for self-determination. This functional violation of indirect rule proved more appealing and practical than a rigid insistence on ruling through indigenous colonial agents.

The struggle to effectively administer the colonial possession and to regard all competing sentiments as being of secondary importance constantly complicated the desire for devolution. Nonetheless, the two pressures of effective administration and fidelity to the indirect-rule ideology of indigenous rule tugged simultaneously at the colonial enterprise, dueling for space in the colonial bureaucracy. More often than not officials confronted the two possibilities by taking the path of least resistance, and settling for the status quo, pushing off genuine devolution into the future. When the pressure for non-Muslim self-determination caught up with them, they repeated the routine of artful postponement. This was how things stood in the early 1950s.

British sensitivity to this problem of hardening Fulani subcolonial rule was slow to emerge, but when it did it was surprisingly candid and self-indicting. The district officer of Yola had this to say in his confidential memo to the resident on the matter in September 1951: "I have discussed the matter on several occasions with the Waziri, and more recently with the Wakilin Chamba himself. All of us are agreed that no progress whatsoever is being made towards the obvious and correct goal of the administration of the Chamba by the Chamba and that the office of Wakilin Chamba is redundant, having long outlived its usefulness."[8] In another section of the memo, the district officer stated pointedly that "Haman Tukur should go," but he argued that before he was relieved, another position be found for him in the Yola Emirate to reward him for his service to the British administration.[9] He advised that the "first step" in returning to the goal of restoring self-administration to the Chamba was to "move Haman Tukur and abolish the post of Wakilin Chamba." This office and Haman Tukur had become, in the period between 1937 and 1951, the two most potent symbols of Fulani subcolonial rule in Chambaland.

Officials conceded that, like the wakili, the Fulani District scribes and their Fulani appointees were detrimental to the goal of Chamba self-administration and called for their replacement by Chamba agents.[10] Even as officials took a more self-critical look at the nature and reception of Fulani rule among non-Muslim groups, they still trusted the administrative utility of Fulani officials and sought to retain some of them, even in Chambaland. The argument was made for appointing a Fulani official to replace Haman Tukur as the district head of Nassarawo pending the appointment of a Chamba district chief for the district in the future. The new Fulani district head, it was argued, should be appointed as an "administrative official only," "on the understanding that he is to conduct the routine of the district pending possible reorganization."[11]

It was clear, as officials would later acknowledge in a secret memo, that "with signs that [non-Muslim] people wanted more say in their own affairs, the Yola Native Authority must sooner or later delegate and could not go on ignoring that in this area a subordinate native authority had been constituted."[12] British officials subtly criticized the lamido for being "hesitant about delegation," but time was no longer on the side of either. Already, by 1951, "there [were] signs of restlessness under this Fulani domination," a colonial memo proclaimed in an unusually blunt description of Fulani rule.[13] The official acknowledgment of the idea of "Fulani domination," long the rhetorical refrain of Chamba anti-Fulani grievance, amounted to an inadvertent endorsement. It was also an indication of the urgency and inescapability of Chamba self-determination, and the growing political mobilization of non-Muslim grievances.

The Revolt of the Non-Muslims

In February of 1951, the much-feared specter of an enlightened non-Muslim agitation materialized. A man identified in the records simply as Simon, a Christian convert and mission-educated Chamba man, penned a petition and call to action to the district head of Yebbi. Simon railed against what he termed the betrayal of Chamba chiefs, who would rather keep their positions than confront Fulani rule and the lamido. "I have heard that the Chief of Tola the Chief of Gurum and the Chief of Sugu have agreed to do all within their power to follow the Fulani," Simon charged.[14]

The chiefs were oblivious to the political import of their flirtation with the infrastructure of Fulani rule, argued Simon. Their decision to side with the Fulani and snub the political aspirations of the Chamba was sustained by fear and self-interest, he argued further: "On account of fear they have ignored the feelings of their peoples; their fear of Fulani is such that they think that if they refuse to accept the Lamido as their . . . chief he will remove them from their offices; they have no thoughts for anything except fear."[15] In making these declarations, Simon was establishing the template for a new tactic in the Chamba struggle for administrative self-determination. This tactic rested with Chamba young men, the demographic most resentful of Fulani rule. They seemed to believe now that their best chance of undermining Fulani subcolonial hegemony was not the familiar reactionary but ineffective attacks on the Fulani. Their new tactic, Simon's letter shows, was a campaign that sought to target the Chamba subordinate district heads who were the legitimizing enablers of Fulani rule among the Chamba communities. The goal was to do one of two things, either emotionally blackmail Chamba apprentices into reconsidering their cooperation with Fulani rule, or discredit them as illegitimate representatives of Chamba cultural values.

In writing to the district head of Yebbi, Simon was focused on the fact that the latter had not yet taken a public position on the Chamba agitation for self-determination nor pledged allegiance to the Fulani. "I have heard that you have not yet made a statement to the Fulani," the author opened his letter. Simon wanted to get to the chief of Yebbi before the Fulani did, seeing in him a malleable, undecided chief who could anchor the struggle for Chamba self-determination or at least refuse to legitimize Fulani rule. Simon was also directing this campaign toward the head of his own district, as he was from Yebbi. He urged the chief to take the lead in the struggle, assuring him that the Chamba would "never refuse your lead."[16]

In imploring the chief of Yebbi to side with his Chamba kinsmen and to abandon his statutory loyalty to the Fulani, Simon employed both flattery and subtle threats, invoking the reward of solidarity and the repercussions of betrayal. He also stressed the virtue of nativist legitimacy and the shame of embracing short-term political favors dispensed by the Anglo-Fulani colonial alliance: "Don't depart from what our forefathers used to do; if you allow the Fulani to absorb the Chamba country you have acted wrongly. It is not right for you to sell the people to the Lamido because of fear; but your steadfastness that I have heard of is good."[17] Simon appealed to the chief's rumored "steadfastness" while pointing to the possibility that his eventual position on the Chamba struggle could erase or affirm his goodwill with the Chamba. He also introduced the quasi-religious reference to ancestral obligation to further pressure the chief into aligning with the burgeoning struggle for Chamba independence.

As for Chamba chiefs who had shown opposition to the struggle or had resolved to continue to cooperate with Fulani rule, Simon was unsparing in his indictment: "Those other chiefs who think they have made themselves popular with the Chiefs of the Fulani do not know that they have sold themselves to the Fulani; don't you do this to your people."[18] The gist of Simon's letter was the deployment of a new tactic of shaming Chamba chiefs who would not support the agitation for Chamba independence while ennobling those who did. Yet, Simon's effort did not represent a wholly novel approach to the struggle. It was part of a broad strategic continuum challenging the pillars of Fulani subcolonial hegemony in a way that summoned both political and intellectual logic.

The insistence on civil activism through appeals and deliberation rested on the desire to avoid being labeled irrational troublemakers, a label that was a predictable colonial recourse to discredit such struggles. The strategy was also designed to resolve the contradictory fact that Chamba chiefs and their aides were invested in the Anglo-Fulani colonial system and saw their economic and political fates intertwined with it. A less civil methodology of struggle might have forced the Chamba to deal with that uncomfortable political reality in ways that would ultimately highlight the divisions among the Chamba, undermining the long-term goals of the movement.

Christian Literacy and Anti-Fulani Consciousness

As it turned out, Simon's letter was the latest in a series of efforts by increasingly militant Chamba youth to have their grievances and demands heard by the Anglo-Fulani colonial system in Adamawa Province. On several other fronts, young Chamba men resorted to other unconventional but civil methods to bring official attention to Chamba self-determination, a struggle complicated by the status of much of the territory covered by the Chamba Federation as a UN mandated territory. The Chamba agitation was representative of similar struggles brewing in other non-Muslim districts in Adamawa Province. Years of official laxity toward the Chamba problem caused non-Muslim anger to fester underground across the province.

Another significant development occurred in the years between 1937 and the early 1950s when both Fulani and British operatives in the colonial system bucked their own reformist rhetoric and firmed up the apparatuses of Fulani rule. Christian missionary activities like evangelization and the dissemination of mission-mediated Western education intensified during this time. Niels Kastfelt and Andrew Barnes have painstakingly documented the successes of the Sudan United Mission, or SUM, and the Sudan Interior Mission, or SIM, among the non-Muslim people of the Upper and Middle Benue hinterland.[19] Much of that success was recorded in the late 1930s and 1940s, a period in which a combination of the Great Depression and the inflationary economy of the war and postwar years saw a surge in the number of non-Muslims flocking to mission schools. They did this in order to establish more secure economic foundations and to acquire the educational prerequisites for accessing lucrative employment in colonial and quasi-colonial enterprises.

Yusufu Turaki, Matthew Kukah, Chunun Logams, Andrew Barnes, and Niels Kastfelt have also documented the transformative political impact of missionary education and sustained Christian conversions on identity formation and political mobilization in non-Muslim societies of Northern Nigeria.[20] The impact mirrors similar ones in Southern Nigeria, where missionary education produced a colonial intelligentsia that grew increasingly political in its demands and public expressions.[21] There was, however, a key difference between the intellectual ferments in the two regions and their political implications. In the south, the political intellectualism of the new urban, largely coastal intelligentsia was directed at colonial policies and was aimed at securing rights and resources under the colonial system. For the most part, the main concern of the northern, mission-produced intelligentsia was more the displacement of a local Hausa-Fulani hegemony than a preoccupation with colonial policy. Even when mobilization turned to the question of independence from Britain, the fear of Hausa-Fulani domination mediated the involvement of Adamawa non-Muslims in nationalist activities.

By the early 1950s, the meshing of Christian education and the emergence of new political anxieties among the non-Muslim communities of Adamawa had fully begun. Non-Muslim, Western-educated intellectuals with varying degrees of adherence to Christianity began to entertain new fears about their place in the emerging politics of the late colonial period. The heady politics of this period activated multiple social, cultural, and political anxieties among the elites of various communities in the Middle Belt. These fears found expressions in diverse ways, corresponding to the location, priorities, and aspirations of the elites.[22] The embryonic non-Muslim elites, fearing their potential marginality with the onset of national political independence, remained fairly constant factors in all these expressions, as they sought to reposition themselves on better bargaining pedestals. The constitution-making and revision processes that dominated the political arena in the late colonial period exacerbated the fear of non-Muslim elites, necessitating new tactics of political expression. These processes encouraged political consultation, town-hall public hearings, petitioning, and civil protest. Political pressure groups with aspirations and stakes in the unfolding political order adopted one or more of these strategies to force their issues and grievances into the public consciousness.

The emerging non-Muslim elites of Adamawa Province were not inoculated from these late colonial political trends. They were active participants in them, crafting new tactics to advance their struggle against Fulani rule and to articulate their late colonial and post-independence aspirations. As transitional political rituals intensified, pointing to imminent decolonization, the elites of Chamba, Bata, Kilba, and other non-Muslim communities of Adamawa Province became more distressed. This caused their tactical repertoires to expand and embrace new ways of publicizing their struggle.

Although petition writing was a key component of these tactical shifts, it was not its defining feature. Simon's letter caused a stir in the colonial bureaucracy when the chief of Yebbi shared it with colonial authorities. It triggered a flurry of urgent secret correspondence between British and Fulani officials. It elicited that reaction, however, only because it represented an escalation of a familiar struggle and not necessarily because it was new.

Simon's effort was a legal and skillful utilization of methods of civil protest that were being endorsed by colonial authorities trying to mobilize Nigerians for their input into the constitution-making process. Other non-Muslim young men deftly inverted this colonial political environment to their advantage. As the resident put it in a secret memo: "The Mission youth technique is simple and difficult to counter: get at older people, be orderly, and use as justification for asking for changes the fact that Government consulted the people on the form of constitution they wished."[23] The broad tactics of the Chamba agitators confounded colonial officials who were eager to criminalize complaint in order to discredit it.

Simon's letter was a culmination of previous efforts and was effective in capturing official attention because it followed previous strategies of public complaint.
One strategy adopted by Simon's contemporaries and kinsmen was face-to-face
confrontation with British officials to present lists of demands.

Tactical Creativity in the Chamba Revolt

In December 1950, a few months before Simon penned his petitions, the first of
many face-to-face confrontations between Chamba youth and British officials
took place. A delegation of five Chamba youths sought and obtained audience
with the assistant divisional officer, or ADO, Mr. Phelps, to inquire about the
implications of the ongoing constitutional debates for the Chamba area.[24] The
delegation, a group of mission-educated young men, wanted to know what the
government's endgame was on the old question of Chamba separation from Fulani rule represented by Yola. The visit was produced by the familiar late colonial
anxieties of minority groups in the politics of transition to national independence. These anxieties motivated many other minority groups to send petitions
and presentations to government-appointed minority rights panels, notably the
Willink Commission on minority grievances and rights.[25] Apparently, the delegation's core inquiries were lost on the ADO and the DO, who misunderstood
the group to be inquiring about development projects for their area. Whether
this was a deliberate misunderstanding is not clear as officials would later blame
the misunderstanding on the delegation's inarticulateness. After listening to the
delegation, Phelps promised to tour the Chamba communities and discuss the
government's plans, but no official response on the substantive issue of constitutional guarantees of Chamba independence came.

One month later, the delegation, now expanded, wrote a joint letter to the
resident about the Chamba's place and rights in the unfolding constitutional order. This petition seemed to have been provoked by the ADO's inattention to the
delegation's previous inquiries, and by the absence of official acknowledgment of
their concern. The petition "made it quite clear that the writers considered that
the Camba [Chamba] should be made independent of the Fulani," one memo
stated.[26] The petitioners protested vehemently against the existence of the office
of a Fulani wakilin Chamba, the overbearing face of Yola's subcolonial control.
They labeled the office and its occupant symbols of the Chamba's subjugation
under the Fulani.

The Chamba delegation traveled to Yola a few days later to follow up their petition, where they met with the resident and elaborated on their earlier demands.
They moderated their earlier demand for outright separation from the administrative domain of the Yola Emirate. They would, they submitted, be content
with the modest change of having a Chamba in the position of wakilin Chamba
instead of a Fulani.[27] Because colonial officials transcribed the records of this

meeting, the veracity of this positional shift is suspect. If the shift were true it would suggest a measure of pragmatism on the part of the Chamba agitators. Even so, it highlights a growing contradiction within the movement between the Western-educated leaders, who wanted to project an image of civility, and the more militant young Chamba men from the countryside.

The divide between the moderate, civil face of the agitation and its more militant incarnation surfaced a few days after the Yola meeting, when a public protest took place in Gurumpawo calling for the overthrow of Fulani rule. The rally was extensive and enjoyed the support of the Gurumpawo district head, a Chamba subordinate of the Fulani wakili. Although he pledged his support for the movement, he promised that he would do so only privately, as his public position in the colonial administration compelled him to publicly disavow the goals of the agitators.

The rally seemed to have been a spontaneous outgrowth from the widely attended Christmas celebrations organized by the SUM mission at Gurumpawo. Chamba youths, many of them mission-educated teachers, clerks, and mission workers, took turns addressing the attendees on the subject of Chamba administrative independence. Several of the speakers called strongly for separation and urged attendees to tell touring European officers in unison that the Chamba desired independence from Fulani rule. In a development illustrating the way in which the burgeoning Middle Belt struggle was impacting the localized agitation of non-Muslim communities around Northern Nigeria, the local organizing secretary of the nascent Middle Zone League (MZL), the precursor to the United Middle Belt Congress (UMBC), Jonah Assadugu, a Bachama veteran of the Second World War, addressed the rally at Gurumpawo and toured several Christian missions in Chambaland and other non-Muslim sectors in Adamawa Province. Everywhere he went, Assadugu fired up his audience with anti-Fulani, anti-emirate rhetoric and encouraged people to fight for emancipation from Fulani subcolonial control.

Colonial Paranoia and the Non-Muslim Awakening

Reports of Assadugu's rallies reached colonial officials just a few days after the meeting with the Chamba delegation in Yola, provoking a frenzied response that saw the dispatch of a touring party to Jada led by a colonial official identified simply as Mr. Rickford, who soon discovered how deeply entrenched the desire for separation was. His strategy for dealing with the crisis was twofold. First he confronted the district head of Gurumpawo with evidence of his support for the movement for Chamba independence. Although the latter denied supporting the agitation, he received a stern warning that continued support for the demands of independence would cost him his job and probably lead to other punitive repercussions. The second aspect of Rickford's plan to undermine the movement was to isolate and discredit its principal leaders. He did this by identifying at least five of them by name in a shaming campaign that also carried veiled threats.

Another focus of the official inquiry into the new, militant identity of the Chamba struggle was the degree to which missionary ideology and the rhetoric of Middle Belt activists such as Jonah Assadugu were responsible for stirring up a new, more threatening wave of Chamba agitations for independence from Fulani rule. Assadugu's motivational imprint had already been identified, as he was a ubiquitous activist presence in the political circuits of non-Muslim communities in the province. But lesser-known agitators from other parts of the province also caused officials anxiety. One of them was Amos Yerima Balla, who only months earlier had mobilized his Kilba kinsmen to fight for independence from Fulani rule.[28] Niels Kastfelt has documented Balla's polyvalent effort in inspiring Kilba opposition to Fulani rule. These efforts included his leadership of the Kilba State Union, or KSU. Balla led several anti-Fulani demonstrations drawing hundreds of Kilba marchers to Mubi, seat of both the local colonial bureaucracy and the proximate Fulani authority. Balla initiated an audacious fund-raising effort in 1951 to "collect money for their political movement against Fulani dominance."[29] He was also deeply involved in vigorous mobilization among the Kilba to ensure that the KSU produced a representative for the Kilba in the house of representatives elections in 1954.[30]

As a solution to the growing agitation, Rickford recommended eliminating what he called "outside influences" brought to bear on the Chamba and other non-Muslim peoples by activists, mission-affiliated people, and other organizers. He also acknowledged the intractability of the sentiment of Fulani domination, which was being disseminated among students at missionary schools in Adamawa Province. In particular, he feared that the commingling of non-Muslim students from "the 'free' tribes of Numan Division," with those from the Chamba, Kilba, Mumuye, Marghi, and areas still under Fulani rule was a catalyst for "political discussion" of the type that fueled emancipatory agitation. Before he left Jada, Rickford made the district heads of Gurumpawo and Binyeri, the two district heads suspected of being sympathizers of the Chamba agitation, address a large audience of regular Chamba folk and mission-educated young men. The two chiefs issued public disavowals of the self-determination movement and made platitudinous proclamations about the mutual benefits of Fulani-Chamba relations.

A resurgent "Chamba Movement," as it was now routinely called in official correspondence, rattled a complacent colonial officialdom accustomed to postponing inevitable confrontations. The movement might have been silenced yet again if not for a confluence of multiple incidents that reinforced one another. In February 1951, the Bata communities in Yola Division conducted rallies and meetings at which the call for independence from Fulani rule rang loud. Whether this was coordinated with the Chamba or not, the parallel was not lost on colonial officials, who were quick to relate the campaign of the Bata people to the Chamba's. The agitation seemed to have begun with the personal activism of a Bata mission-educated teacher simply named Peter, who taught at the SUM mission school in the village of Jobolio. Under pressure from colonial authorities, the mission threatened him with dismissal for "being involved in political matters."[31] It appears that once this threat was carried out, the movement ignited, attracting many other Bata young men to the cause.

On February 12, a delegation of seven Bata men visited the DO in Yola, claiming to speak on behalf of all the Bata, having "been authorized by some 14 of the Bata headmen."[32] Most of them were from Peter's home village of Jobolio. Distilled to its essential elements, the demand of the delegation was that the Bata people be allowed to constitute their own district under their own headman. The headman, they conceded, could operate under the authority of the lamido. This was a modest demand by the standard of the ongoing non-Muslim agitations, but officials took a derisive attitude to it, questioning the representational authority of the delegation and asking them for proof that they indeed spoke for all of their kinsmen. The delegation, described as "very courteous and restrained and simple in speech," departed, then returned the next day with what an official described as an "illiterate and anonymous document" to prove that they were authorized spokesmen for the Bata in Yola division. The DO rejected the proof and again questioned their legitimacy on account of what he saw as a dubious mandate.[33]

Content that the movement was small, officials sought to curtail its spread rather than take it seriously. Although Jonah Assadugu had visited Jobolio and may have met with Peter and some of the other members of the delegation, officials decided to watch the movement rather than take action against its members. The DO summed up the government's attitude: "I do not see that any of these . . . mission followers are committing any offence, since they are at liberty to discuss Batta tribal government with anyone so long as they do not engage in anything subversive."[34] The contagion of anti-Fulani, pro-autonomy rhetoric was difficult to halt because it traveled through multiple sources. The colonially sanctioned unevenness of Fulani subcolonial rule in Adamawa Province was an important, if unrecognized, vector. It meant that with the self-administering non-Muslim peoples of Numan Division in close proximity to Yola-administered non-Muslim peoples, it was easy for those under Fulani rule to see the possibilities of colonial self-governance, indirect rule in its "pure" form. This heightened the frustrations of Fulani rule for the Chamba, Kilba, Marghi, Mumuye, and the Bata who were arbitrarily placed under Yola Division, far from their Numan Division kinsmen.

In dealing with the rising wave of anti-Fulani agitation, colonial officials undertook two significant actions that would have deep ramifications for the movements. First, they foreclosed discussion on Fulani subcolonial rule and

Chamba separatism. The resident routinely issued instructions to his staff to "make it clear to members of the [Chamba] Native Authority that there was no question of separation and that it was a serious offense to seek to undermine the Lamido's authority."[35] This directive effectively criminalized a wide range of actions and narratives that questioned British-supervised Fulani colonial rule. The result of this censorious move was that much of the agitation went underground and continued to fester unseen. In displaying rigid intolerance for anti-Fulani dissent among non-Muslim communities, colonial officials were reaffirming the administrative fetish of Fulani authority. The lionization of Fulani authority was dependent on a corresponding criminalization of dissent against it among non-Muslim groups.

The second strand of official response proved equally crucial in shaping the outlines of the emerging political order in Adamawa Province. British officials effectively let the lamido drive official reactions to non-Muslim agitations. The lamido had argued that if he did not take a "strong" stance on the Chamba struggle, his position in the British colonial system in the province might become difficult to sustain and that if his authority was weakened, the Chamba and other non-Muslim groups would be emboldened to try to wean themselves off the control of the colonial state. Officials acquiesced, as the resident reiterated in his correspondence with the secretary to the Northern Provinces in Kaduna: "I agree with the Lamido that if such movements as the one in the Camba area are not to arise among all the [non-Muslim] tribes in the Emirate, active steps must be taken to check them (by active steps prosecution is meant)."[36] In principle, then, the congruence between the lamido's position and that of the government remained strong. The lamido was able to assert his wishes on the government's handling of the non-Muslim aspiration for autonomy.

There were, however, points of divergence between the lamido's uncompromising position and British efforts to seem attentive to the sentiments of both the lamido and the non-Muslim communities. British officials' concern about inadvertently validating the case of the "separatist" movement moderated their commitment to the implacable high-handedness recommended by the lamido. Thus, despite agreeing that prosecution could be a deterrent to further protest, the resident feared that such a harsh response, especially against non-Muslim traditional authorities, would produce blowback. Such a reaction "will result in making the movement really popular," he argued. Official caution about harsh persecution also rested on the status of the Chamba area as a United Nations mandate. This concern, colonial correspondence shows, proved decisive in mitigating official intolerance for the escalation of the non-Muslim agitations for independence.

The international status of the Chamba area clearly played a role in withholding official support for the lamido's suggested counter measures: "In order to counter these movements there is the added complication in the Camba area that it is in Trust Territory and any action by the Lamido which could be represented or held to be high-handed might lead to repercussions elsewhere and prove difficult to explain away under the terms of the Trusteeship agreement."[37] These concerns resonated with new clarity in late 1951 because the United Nations Trusteeship Visiting Mission was scheduled to visit the Chamba area the following year as part of its oversight of the former German colonies parceled out to Britain, Belgium, and France as Trust territories in the aftermath of World War I. The divergence of the administration's position from the lamido's reflected the immediate anxieties of each party in the Anglo-Fulani system. The lamido worried about quotidian administrative matters, specifically how the Chamba struggle threatened his legitimacy and effectiveness. British officials worried more about the international reverberations and perceptions of their approach to the Chamba struggle in the context of trusteeship obligations.

If officials thought that persecuting the Chamba movement's secret chiefly backers would confer undeserved populist appeal on the struggle, no such concern permeated their thinking regarding operatives of the MZL such as Assadugu. For this group of people, the resident wondered whether they could be charged "under section 41 of the Native Authority Ordinance," especially if there was evidence that the activists "went around advocating throwing off Fulani rule."[38] Although the resident sought advice from Kaduna on this possibility, there is no evidence that any was offered, and formal legal criminalization through judicial precedence seems to have been discounted in favor of the de facto criminalization urged in several instructions to the province's political staff.

Subsequent touring of the Chamba area, the most volatile site of anti-Fulani agitation in the province, revealed that the sentiments that underpinned the Chamba movement were alive. When touring officer Mr. Cassidy returned to Jada to tour Chambaland again, the Chamba youth had turned on their chiefs. In Gurumpawo, restive youths insulted and ridiculed the chief when he returned from a meeting with Mr. Rickford in Jada. One youth threatened to hit the chief with a stick. Helpless, the chief, an early supporter of the Chamba autonomy movement, who, having, "seen which way the wind was blowing and not having the character to support an officially disapproved movement," appealed to the wakilin Chamba for help.[39] The wakili directed him to arrest the culprit, who was then put on trial in Jada.[40] During Mr. Cassidy's tour, youth restlessness had become even more pronounced. He presided over a meeting between Chamba youth and a representative of the lamido, during which the youth outlined their case against Yola and Fulani rule as well as their political demands.

Chamba Youth and Anti-Fulani Militancy

In what sounded like a carefully prepared manifesto, Chamba youth stated that they were acting in the spirit of the ongoing constitution-making consultations, citing a Hausa-language document circulated by the colonial authorities in Northern Nigeria. The document, "Jawabin Babban Sakataren Nijeriya a Majalisar Dokoki 11th March 1949," encouraged Northern Nigerian groups to consult and articulate their aspirations in the unfolding constitution debate. The youth claimed to have done exactly that, pushing their case up through the administrative hierarchy of village heads and district chiefs to no avail. Their decision to bring their grievances to the attention of the resident through the touring officer was a desperate quest for official attention, they claimed, since "they had been forbidden to discuss these matters by their chiefs on pain of punishment."[41]

The political naïveté of the youth led them to assume that the censorship was a decision of their chiefs and not of the Anglo-Fulani colonial authorities. The youth repeated the familiar grievances of the Chamba against Fulani rule, albeit with a few new accents. They were not rejecting Fulani rule just in order to assert their right to self-determination. Fulani rule, they claimed, had not benefited the Chamba. Blaming the British for "subject[ing] them to Fulani rule," the youth argued that "after more than thirty years of [Fulani rule] there was no evidence of progress in their districts. The Chamba area had been ignored by the Fulani administration at Yola while other districts received some benefits in the way of education etc. As a result of this the Chamba now wanted to sever all connection with the Fulani."[42] The new critique of Fulani rule echoed the familiar rhetoric from earlier periods, but it advanced more pragmatic concerns about the responsibilities of leadership than it did a generic resentment of Fulani domination. Their list of demands included the familiar demand for the creation of a paramount chieftaincy for the entire Chamba area to replace the wakilin Chamba.[43]

In addition to the familiar menu of demands, however, the Chamba youth lamented the absence of "roads, schools, wells, dispensaries," and other concrete benefits of colonial modernity. This suggested that their resentment of Fulani rule grew from its failure to deliver these benefits and not necessarily from a cultivated primordial hostility toward the Fulani. Even so, they made it clear that there was a hierarchy to their list of demands and that self-determination trumped a beneficial Fulani rule. A firsthand colonial account recalled the youth declaring that "they would rather live in poverty without the things requested [schools, dispensaries, roads, etc.] than live much longer under the Fulani."[44]

In the clearest enunciation of their political aspirations and anxieties yet, the Chamba youth argued that their activism was founded on the fear that "unless [non-Muslim] tribes form a separate Division from the Fulani Emirate they cannot hope to be represented at all in the House of Assembly under the revised constitution."[45] This fear had a basis. The provincial representative in the Northern House of Assembly was a Fulani from Yola. In future elections under the revised constitution, the colonially aided political dominance of the Fulani was almost certain to guarantee the reemergence of a Fulani representative for all of the division.

The prospect of having a Fulani voice speaking for the Chamba in the emerging political order riled the youth. They also feared, without much evidence, that once the new constitution took effect, British officials acting as a buffer between the Fulani political formation and the Chamba would be withdrawn and "there will be no one to guard the interests of the [non-Muslims] vis-à-vis the Fulani." Officials blamed mission propaganda and the feisty rhetoric of the MZL for the proliferation of such fears and rumors, singling out one European SUM missionary, Mr. Hansen, in particular for criticism because he reportedly admitted to having sympathies for the cause of the Chamba youth. Confronted, Hansen denied encouraging the Chamba Christians or engaging them in political discussions.[46] Hansen, however, told several officials about what he observed to be the Fulani subcolonial rulers' attitude of disdain toward the non-Muslims, with one official agreeing that much of what the missionary said "concerning the attitude of the Fulani to the Chamba and other pagan tribes is . . . unfortunately true."[47] While mission sympathy and the underground campaign of the MZL may have helped stoke the anxieties of the Chamba and other non-Muslim groups, there were underlying concerns about a transformational perpetuation of Fulani domination, which enabled fear mongering to thrive.

In the end, officials could do little more than warn European missionaries suspected of political meddling to return to an apolitical stance. Because some of the Chamba movement's fears were founded on exaggerations and misinformation, officials briefly considered the idea of sending the provincial representative in the Northern Nigerian House of Assembly to reeducate the Chamba youth on the political process. They decided against it, however, because "being a Fulani he will not altogether be believed by the mission followers."[48] Events were unfolding faster than officials could track and confront them.

Ethno-Religious Affirmation and Anti-Fulani Revolt

By the end of March 1951, the Chamba movement had become an established platform of political mobilization for a separate political and administrative identity. A clear leader had also emerged in an SUM teacher in Gurum named Dauda. He had recently traveled to Bukuru on the Jos Plateau to attend a conference of the MZL along with Jonah Assadugu, the local organizing secretary, as representatives from Kilba and Bata respectively.[49] The delegation returned to Adamawa resolved to formally establish a chapter of the MZL in each of the non-Muslim areas.

Assadugu remained an inspiration and a hardworking organizer. He gave speeches in villages and in churches all over Numan Division urging his audience to fight against Fulani domination, claiming that Fulani control permeated all spheres of life in the division and the entire province. Assadugu even connected the need for non-Muslim economic nationalism and Fulani oppression. He told audiences in Guyuk and in the Lunguda countryside that the Fulani were exploiters who used their favored position in the colonial system to buy groundnuts from them at arbitrarily low prices and sold it back to them in processed form at high prices.[50] Dauda, one of the anti-Fulani activists who attended the MZL convention, led the renewed initiative for the Chamba area. On March 30, he approached the touring officer, Mr. Cassidy, for approval to start a quasi-political body and to recruit members among the mission-educated Chamba men. Unsure of how to proceed, Cassidy sought advice from the DO and also promised to submit the request to the Chamba Council, which, given its disposition toward the Chamba struggle, was sure to veto it.

In 1952, the Chamba "problem" seems to have metastasized enough to necessitate some cosmetic changes, the highlight of which was a firm instruction to the Fulani wakilin Chamba to limit his activities to being district head of Nassarawo. No Chamba replacement was announced, however, as demanded by the agitators. The administration seemed unwilling to radically reshape the fundaments of Fulani rule and seemed more interested in carrying out showy, inconsequential measures. These actions effectively preserved a status quo in which no central Chamba political authority existed, and in which the Fulani wakilin Chamba acted in that capacity as needed.

This was the state of affairs for the next three years. In the meantime, the constitutional debates had been concluded and a new constitution, the so-called Lyttelton Constitution, became law in 1954. The new developments on the national constitutional front and the political contests that they unleashed raised the stakes in the discussions over how to address Chamba aspirations for independence. Frustration escalated among the Chamba, while colonial pragmatism prevented decisive action. By 1955, the Chamba "problem," as an example of the larger issue of non-Muslim agitation, resurfaced as a major concern for the fading colonial enterprise in Adamawa. Officials began to unequivocally admit that their previous efforts at addressing concerns, the 1937–38 reforms in particular, were regrettable failures. As the resident disclosed in a secret memo to the permanent secretary of the Ministry of Local Government in Kaduna,

> except for the setting up of an Area Native Court, the arrangements provided seem to have defeated to a great extent the original aim of reorganization, namely, to give the Chamba more say in their affairs even though a subordinate Native Authority was created. In the event the subordinate Native Authority was nothing more than a paper creation and the area continued to be administered virtually as five districts but with a Supra-District Head (Fulani) set over the four Chamba District Heads (Chamba Chiefs).[51]

In the years leading to national independence, this self-critical analysis signaled a new British appreciation for the backlash created by delegated Fulani rule. The new approach clearly focused less on punishing or discouraging Chamba agitation and more on the lamido and other levers of Fulani authority, pressuring them to make concessions on the question of devolving more self-government to the Chamba and other non-Muslim groups. There was a recognition that the matter had acquired a new urgency and that the strategy of postponement was no longer tenable.[52] Subordination to Yola was the single most defining character of Fulani rule among the Chamba. Officials' willingness to broach the subject of mitigating that subordination was thus a significant departure from the previous commitment to protecting this essential character of Fulani rule.

The Chamba versus the Lamido

Predictably, the lamido was "hesitant about delegation," and when British officials managed to convince him to accept its inevitability, he preferred the circuitous process of setting up committees of his officials to recommend devolution models. The actual recommendation from Yola substantiated the reluctance of the lamido and his Fulani administrative officials to surrender their privileged subcolonial positions to the demands of the Chamba. The recommendations proposed a new council comprised of the various districts to replace the Subordinate Native Authority system. It represented nothing new, and promised no meaningful political concessions to the Chamba. The proposed council was not even slated to hold equal power to a Subordinate Native Authority, let alone the desired powers of an independent Chamba chiefdom. The suggested administrative model would create something new to replace the dreaded subordinate authority system, but it would essentially preserve, if not consolidate, the present system of Fulani rule. It promised to devolve no power or independence to the Chamba.

Officials balked at the lamido's recommendations, rejecting them outright. They declared that "delegations must be made if local government is to be a reality" and that powers of self-government "must be given if the aspirations of the peoples . . . are to be satisfied." The fear of validating the Chamba struggle and undoing the infrastructure of Fulani rule, however, prevented concrete action. As the resident put it, the necessity for redress and ameliorative action was not in question; rather, "the problem is how to do this in Adamawa Emirate without giving unnecessary encouragement to separatist tendencies."[53] This dual concern about Chamba political restiveness and the potential for reform having the unintended consequence of stimulating further agitation coexisted uneasily throughout the mid-1950s.

The lack of resolution to these dueling concerns meant that the status quo endured, leading to a measure of willful denial regarding the Chamba struggle for self-determination. This reluctance to confront the problem manifested itself on several fronts. When the government of the Northern Region submitted its report to the Willink Commission on Minority Rights, it made "no reference to the existence in Adamawa Province of any problems of minorities," only parenthetically referring to the Kilba protest against Fulani rule.[54] This was symptomatic of a larger, growing neglect of a problem that plagued the Anglo-Fulani colonial system from its inception. In late 1957, the administration commissioned a comprehensive report on the anti-Fulani, non-Muslim movement for self-determination to be written for the visit of the Willink Minorities Commission to Adamawa in 1958. This report also sought to understand Chamba grievance and to function as a last-ditch effort to develop a policy on the issue.

A Last Push against Anglo-Fulani Rule

Released on the eve of national independence in February 1958, the commissioned report sought to unearth the cultural, historical, and sociological roots of Chamba-Fulani antagonism as well as establish the basic outlines of present resentment. The excavation of antecedents rested on a new realization on the part of officials that "the legacy of the past . . . cannot be treated as irrelevant in the disdain of the Chamba for the Fulani."[55] It identified divergent notions of chieftaincy, boundaries, and land usage as foundations of discord between Chamba autochthons and Fulani immigrants.[56] It also highlighted the unintended consequences of colonially established platforms of political sociability and how they had, over the years, acted as catalysts for the emergence of Chamba political unity and consciousness, crystalizing in some instances in anti-Fulani political mobilizations. Such platforms included markets attended by all Chamba, a common colonial treasury, officially organized annual agricultural shows, and athletics competitions at Jada.[57] These formal and informal associational interactions morphed into political conversations that channeled the Chamba's common political imaginations into new anti-caliphate political organizations like the MZL, the Chamba State Union, and the United Middle Belt Congress.

The report made it clear that as the political landscape had shifted, so had the demands and rhetoric of the Chamba struggle changed. The inquiries conducted by the investigators revealed this change with clarity. In addition to familiar demands, the Chamba now complained about the physical and symbolic burdens of Fulani rule and about the place of the Chamba and other non-Muslim groups in the emerging politics of late colonialism. Their complaints now included their objection to being called "arna," or pagans, by the Fulani, a name that they claimed encapsulated "the Fulani attitude towards them."[58] They also complained about the lack of Chamba employees in the Native Authority, and about reluctance on the part of the Native Authority to hire Christian Chamba because the latter would not work on Sundays. They alleged subtle efforts on the part of the Fulani subcolonial rulers to "make Islam the 'official religion'" in the Yola Native Authority through the denial of permission for the expansion of Christian mediums of instruction such as churches and schools. There was a tacit official support for the spread of "Moslem propaganda" in their districts, the Chamba alleged.[59]

The expansion of the Chamba's complaints notwithstanding, the fundamental concerns of the long Chamba struggle against Fulani rule remained. As the report found, the Chamba

> resent the fact that their chiefs become willy-nilly tools of the Fulani, encouraging the Moslem faith and exerting their influence to secure the election of district councils which will do as they are told and of electoral colleges which will elect the Yola nominees to the Federal and regional legislatures. This the chiefs do through fear or because they are themselves corrupt and depend upon the favor of Yola for their continuance in office.[60]

This was essentially the latest manifesto in the long struggle, a "good summary of the grievances of all the Adamawa minorities," as one official commented.[61] The report concluded that "after 40 years of British rule the Chamba despair of obtaining freedom of religion and equality of opportunity with the Fulani within the Yola Emirate," and that they yearned for "the creation of a separate division within a Middle Belt state or, failing that, the continuance of British Trusteeship until they are prepared to join the Northern region as a separate division."[62]

The report's tone was decidedly sympathetic to the Chamba cause, and its conclusions reflected this pro-Chamba slant. To be sure, the authors of the report sympathized with the anxieties of the Fulani, whose interests and political estate would be adversely affected by Chamba separation. They contended, however, that granting the Chamba a separate division not only would redress a colonial wrong compelled by administrative expediency, but also would alleviate the frustrations caused by the failure of Fulani rule to foster inclusion and a sense of belonging for the Chamba. "The feelings of the Fulani cannot be ignored but it must be admitted that while their influence over the Chamba has been greatly extended by the European Administrations, the Fulani have so far failed to rise to the opportunity by rewarding the Chamba with impartial government."[63]

The report warned that this could be the last chance for resolving the Chamba struggle "by peaceful means." It recommended the establishment of a Southern Trust Territory Division for the Chamba. This recommendation made clear that if the goal was to "delegate real powers," officials had to recognize that "the best solution would be separation from Yola."[64] On the other hand, the authors argued that there was room yet for a midway solution that retained a measure of control for Yola over the Chamba, or at least "permit[ted] a token relationship of allegiance between an independent [Chamba] Division and the Lamido of Adamawa."[65] This reasoning was predicated on the observation that, the tensions of "past history" notwithstanding, "relations between Chamba and Fulani are not yet hopelessly embittered."[66] Nonetheless, the author contended that for such a compromise to be viable, Yola had to undertake willful gestures to guarantee certain baselines of rights and privileges to the Chamba, including proportionate representation in the Yola Native Authority, "freedom of religion and equality of opportunity with the Fulani," the right to conduct free elections of district officials, and the granting of real powers to Chamba district and village administrative authorities. The report also emphasized the need for judicial reform as a way of accommodating the sensibilities of non-Muslims.

There is no indication that these recommendations found favor in Yola or in the departing colonial officialdom. For the Fulani power structure in Yola Division, the recommendations stood in opposition to the on-ground Anglo-Fulani expediency of consolidating the emirate's hold over the division. For the British, the overwhelming desire was to fend off the messy political complications of colonial rule, and to transfer the challenge of addressing lingering political grievances and aspirations to Nigerians, along with political independence. These two imperatives in the waning Anglo-Fulani system ultimately overwhelmed and displaced the strong case for reform advanced by the report.

As the colonial period sputtered to a tense end, the non-Muslim colonial subjects of Adamawa Province found their voice and began to revolt openly against the proxy colonial rule of Muslim Fulani officials. Western education and the Christian missionary enterprise proved to be catalysts for a wave of anti-Fulani agitation that began in earnest in the late 1930s and climaxed in the 1950s. But non-Muslim rebellion also stemmed from subordinate non-Muslim chiefs who subtly engaged in subversive activities designed to undermine Fulani control. As insurgent anti-Fulani agitations proliferated, British colonial overlords, having previously taken a back seat to Fulani colonials, found themselves involved in a fast-moving political environment that threatened the very functionality of the colonial system. Having failed in 1937–38 to broker indirect rule for Adamawa's non-Muslim ethnic constituencies, British officials were drawn to the scenes of these new confrontations to mediate the growing rift between Fulani subcolonial chiefs and their increasingly restive non-Fulani subjects.

Soon, new talks of reforms and the need to restore self-determination to the non-Muslim communities gripped the colonial bureaucracy. Officials talked about scaling back Fulani rule over non-Muslims, while at the same time acknowledging the simultaneous utility and indispensability of Fulani rule, as well as their own entrenched reliance on its inexpensive infrastructure. This latter consideration thwarted any radical reform in support of the much-vaunted imperative of non-Muslim self-determination. Fulani officials, fearful of losing their privilege in the colonial system, also fought back and resisted reform proposals that they deemed too radical a departure from the status quo. Hesitant to reform Fulani rule over the objection of Fulani colonial officials, British colonialists balked at many of the reform proposals. The success of Fulani officials in fending off any meaningful transition to non-Muslim self-rule is a good indicator of the functional centrality—some might say indispensability—of Fulani officials in the British colonial enterprise in Adamawa.

The British reluctance to reform Fulani rule illustrates two important points. First, once the components of Fulani subcolonial rule were in place, Fulani personnel, with the backing of the British, gradually built a functional colonial routine that was hard to break, giving permanence and momentum to a system designed to be transitional. Fulani rule endured because the Anglo-Fulani colonial partnership seems to have generated its own alternative logic, a logic that British colonial officials on the ground defended when distant colonial authorities urged them to move toward indigenous non-Muslim self-rule. Second, transitional colonial rule through "alien" elites might not have fulfilled a theoretical British colonial desire for "uplifting" backward non-Muslims through European-supervised "alien" rule, but it *worked* and resonated functionally and broadly with the generic idea of a hands-off British rule. Fulani rule endured to national independence in 1960 and weathered waves of non-Muslim political agitation because it worked and because British officials were not sure that non-Muslim self-rule was practical. Colonial authorities formulated and defended workable alternatives to indirect rule in the field, allowing actual experiences on the ground to enrich their colonial repertoires rather than be hamstrung by doctrines formulated by metropolitan colonial idealists. Scholarly analyses of colonial repertoires will have to reflect the infinite innovativeness and constant improvisations that sometimes displaced the logic of indigenous mediation on the ground.

The colonial debate on the reform of Fulani proxy rule and the non-Muslim quest for self-administration were rooted in a colonial doctrine that officials deemed impractical for their quotidian colonial priorities. In the end, only a half-hearted reform effort took shape, and attention turned, once more, to a law and order approach that alternately dismissed and suppressed non-Muslim agitation. Paradoxically, official persecution and Fulani opposition to reform only confirmed the fears of non-Muslim groups. In this atmosphere, frustration against perceived Fulani domination in the 1950s only increased, aided by the advent of late colonial nationalist politics and by the regionalization of non-Muslim, anti-caliphate politics in Nigeria in the form of the MZL and the UMBC. The surreptitious entry of the MZL and its successor, the UMBC, into Adamawa Province raised the stakes of non-Muslim protest. It also hardened the resolve of Fulani subcolonials, determined to maintain their political privileges and to stall any movement toward non-Muslim self-determination.

7 Middle Belt Self-Determination and Caliphate Political Resurgence in the Transition to National Independence

As NATIONAL POLITICAL independence drew closer, the anxieties of regional minorities erupted into the political arena with unprecedented intensity. In Northern Nigeria, Middle Belt separatist mobilization reached a new height. The struggles of the Chamba, Alago, Katab, Kilba, Batta, Marghi, and other non-Muslim groups were being replicated across several Middle Belt provinces even as the pendulum of privilege appeared to swing discernibly in the direction of entrenched inheritors of caliphate political capital.

This late-colonial resentment against Hausa-Fulani domination was partly a product of the visible march toward self-government in Northern Nigeria, which was a prelude to and part of the messy march to national independence. The significance of this political moment was evident in the fears of Middle Belt elites. As preparations for self-government advanced, the political uncertainties plaguing Middle Belt communities increased. Middle Belt elites were searching for their place in the politics of an emerging Nigerian state and now understood the agenda of Hausa-Fulani Muslims to be a threat to their aspirations. Their prevalent fear, however exaggerated, was that if the British left the North as one political bloc at the time of national independence, the political fate of the Middle Belt would be sealed as a fief of an emerging political caliphate.

There was a new militancy to the vernacular of this phase of the old fragmented struggle for Middle Belt autonomy in Northern Nigeria. Nonetheless, many of the old platitudes discussed in the last several chapters remained a mainstay of the struggle, reemerging in a new language of entitlement and victimhood, and recalibrated to serve new, more urgent political ends. For instance, the new regional struggle for a separate Middle Belt political identity reached back to the familiar premises of precolonial caliphate oppressions, the British investment in caliphate administrative control, and Hausa-Fulani abuse of colonial power, but it also invoked and mobilized political anxieties with novel anchors in present politics and expectations for the future.

Political battles were being fought in terms of familiar historical binaries in several parts of Northern Nigeria where the caliphate–Middle Belt divide was now a discernible factor of political positioning. Because of the charged political climate of the time, even local disputes and political debates quickly took on the familiar emirate versus Middle Belt, Muslim versus non-Muslim, character. In this chapter I analyze the rise of these politics of Middle Belt self-determination in the shadow of national independence and their constraints. Multiple variables erupted into Nigerian politics in the late-colonial and early-independence periods, complicating the Middle Belt struggle against the political legacies of the caliphate. These struggles witnessed the unraveling of the very idea of the Middle Belt as much as it validated the many political battles fought under its rubric. The Middle Belt struggle suffered from a foundational contradiction. The bases for its oppositional politics found empirical validation across Northern Nigeria. However, continuing to respond to these new challenges outside the Northern Nigerian political mainstream heightened the marginality of Middle Belt elites and paradoxically diminished their capacity to effectively challenge Hausa-Fulani power and privilege.

The Struggle for Jos and the Middle Belt Movement

The long-standing controversy over administrating the Jos Plateau, especially Jos city, acquired new political salience in the escalating late-colonial duel between Middle Belt separatism and Muslim-caliphate hegemony. The contest over Jos pitted the autochthonous ethno-religious groups of the Plateau highlands against the Hausa migrant community. This conflict was a microcosm of the larger struggle over whether complaints of Hausa-Fulani domination necessitated separation or political redress within the emerging political community of Northern Nigeria.

Jos was a colonial town founded on tin mining, which at the turn of the twentieth century attracted a plethora of ethnic communities from all over Nigeria. Seeking economic work and entrepreneurial opportunities, young men and women flocked to the highlands of Jos, to the south of Bukuru. Jos was surrounded by Afizere, Anaguta, Buji, and Berom villages. Hausa-speaking Muslim migrants mainly from the caliphate areas of Kano and neighboring Bauchi had flocked to the town, encouraged by the aggressive recruiting of mining companies in far northern provinces. In recognition of the town's cosmopolitan character, and in a decision that probably reflected the British investment in Hausa chieftaincy, the colonial authorities appointed a Hausa *magajin gari,* or town overseer, who was assisted by a multiethnic advisory council.

This arrangement applied only to the town center and not to the surrounding areas that now constitute the postcolonial city of Jos. As the population of Berom, Anaguta, Afizere, and other indigenous non-Muslim ethnic groups contiguous to the city increased, so did their agitation against ad hoc Hausa Muslim rule, however nominal and symbolic this rule might be. Following the magajin gari's death in 1947, a fierce struggle ensued between the Hausa residents of Jos and the multiethnic group of indigenes. The Hausa population of Jos was, properly speaking, a composite community of Hausa, Kanuri, Nupe, and Fulani Muslims, all of whom spoke Hausa as a first or second language.[1] The conflict between the Hausa and the indigenous communities led by the Berom was fought over the question of who had a legitimate authority to administer Jos. The latter claimed authority on the basis of indigeneity, the former on the basis of residency and the colonial precedence of the Hausa magajin gari.

Subsequently, Jos was administered by an elected multiethnic council without a political figurehead until 1952, when Rwang Pam, a Berom, was appointed the first *gbong gwom* (paramount chief) of Jos, much to the disappointment of the Hausa community. Ahmadu Bello, the holder of the prestigious *Sardaunan Sokoto* title, the leader of the dominant Northern Peoples Congress (NPC), and the most influential political embodiment of the caliphate political heritage in late-colonial Nigeria, supported the Berom demand for a Berom chief with jurisdiction over Jos town. He did so mainly because the Hausa political establishment in Jos belonged to the radical Northern Elements Progressive Union (NEPU). The party's membership in Jos was predominantly comprised of migrants from its stronghold of Kano.[2] NEPU also dominated the elected city council in the interim between the death of the magajin gari and Rwang Pam's appointment as gbong gwom. To appease the Hausa community in Jos, the colonial authorities gave its representative a prominent role in the Jos Native Authority.

This appeasement did little, however, to quell the crisis. The Hausa community persisted in clamoring for a return to the era of the Hausa magajin gari in this growing bastion of Middle Belt political militancy. The ferocity of Hausa agitation was matched only by the determination of the Berom to prevent a return to Hausa chieftaincy. In the meantime, the gbong gwom Jos consolidated his position as paramount ruler of the city and its suburbs, undermining and sometimes antagonizing the Native Authority, which was the only platform of administrative representation and participation for the Hausa and other migrant ethnic communities in Jos.[3]

The dueling ideologies of Hausa chieftaincy and indigenous self-determination continued to coexist in the mid-1950s, canceling each other out, and effectively preserving the political status quo of Berom political consolidation and Hausa insecurity. Into this preexisting political cauldron entered the equally volatile brew of regional Middle Belt advocacy and the effort of dominant Hausa-Fulani politicians to strengthen their stance against separatism in Northern Nigeria. Regional politics, as the non-Muslim struggle for administrative autonomy in Adamawa and other provinces shows, had become invested with material privileges and concrete political advantages. Access to these advantages sometimes required zero-sum representational and participatory calculations. As political stakes fed into regional and national arenas of struggle, scattered and seemingly isolated struggles in many corners of Northern Nigeria began to coalesce into a regional political aggregate that then crystallized into the struggle for a separate Middle Belt region.

In Jos, the politics of chieftaincy, administrative participation, and ethno-religious maneuvering intersected with the new configurations, birthing decidedly higher stakes than the largely localized maneuvers of the late 1940s and early 1950s. The second half of the 1950s brought more posturing on both sides of the Jos political divide, fueled by the successes of the NPC and growing fears of political marginalization in the Middle Belt provinces. In 1957 the Hausa community managed to revive the chieftaincy issue by renewing their demand for a Hausa chief. The response of Bitrus Rwang Pam, the United Middle Belt Congress member for Jos districts in the Northern House of Assembly and son of the gbong gwom Jos, contained clear references to the charged tropes of pre-independence Middle Belt politics.[4] In opposition to a speech given by Isiaku Gwamna, a NEPU member of the House for Jos town, calling on the Northern regional government to appoint a magajin gari for Jos town, Pam warned that if the government gave in to the demand it would substantiate the long-held suspicion of an Anglo-caliphate conspiracy to subdue the non-Muslim communities of Northern Nigeria under Hausa-Fulani rule. Pam argued that such a shift would prove that the pronouncements of colonial officials suggesting that "the ultimate aim of the Muslim North was to dominate other tribes in the Region at all costs" was not mere rhetoric but a plan of action.[5]

The back and forth between the Hausa community and members of the Plateau Middle Belt activist circle continued in the ensuing months and years, with both sides trying to recruit allies while appealing for official redress. In December 1957 the Jos Native Authority Council appointed Bitrus Rwang Pam as the *chiroma* of Jos. Most observers, Hausa and Berom alike, saw this as a way of positioning him as the heir apparent to the Jos chieftaincy, even though Pam and the Native Authority (NA) rejected this inference. In its collective response, the Hausa community went further, interpreting the action as a deft maneuver by the gbong gwom–controlled NA to foreclose its demand for a magajin gari for Jos municipality. By positioning a successor, the Hausa community argued, the Jos NA was perpetuating the office of the gbong gwom and thus closing the door on Hausa chieftaincy. The Hausa took their complaint to the senior resident of Plateau Province, A. T. Weatherhead, presenting him with a formal petition that alleged nonconsultation of the Hausa community over the creation of the office of chiroma.[6]

The UMBC "Complication"

The emergence of the United Middle Belt Congress (UMBC) transformed the political dynamics of Northern Nigeria in the 1950s. Several scholars have documented the convoluted history of the UMBC from the founding of the Non-Muslim League in 1949 to its transmutation into the Middle Zone League (MZL) in 1950 and the eventual merger of the MZL and the Middle Belt People's Party to form the UMBC in 1952.[7] Several emerging elites from non-Muslim locales found themselves drawn to the activism of the so-called tribal unions that preceded the UMBC. In many ways, platforms of non-Muslim ethnic associational life were the building blocks of the UMBC.

The "tribal" associations in non-Muslim areas began to function as feeder organizations to the MZL founded by Patrick Dokotri and other Middle Belt activists in Bukuru. When it emerged, the UMBC became a catalyst and platform for many diverse forms of anti-caliphate sentiments emanating from several areas in the Middle Belt. It became the platform for centralizing the disparate struggles of many non-Muslim peoples across Northern Nigeria. The fragmented struggles had a common denominator, which made organizational unity possible. They all demanded recognition, political patronage, and a separate political identity for non-Hausa-Fulani peoples in Northern Nigeria. Even non-Muslim peoples located in Muslim-majority provinces with no geographical proximity to the centers of Middle Belt activism constructed emotional connections to the UMBC and its cause.

With the political moment aligned in its favor, the UMBC grew rapidly. The party was a victim of its own success though, growing faster than its leaders could manage. In 1954 it broke up into at least three factions over the decision of Pastor David Lot and his supporters to enter into an alliance with the Northern Peoples Congress (NPC), widely regarded as the party of Hausa-Fulani privilege and oppression. When the party was formally and ceremoniously inaugurated in 1955, the fissures over approach and outreach did not completely abate. Nonetheless, on the question of the creation of a Middle Belt state, the resolve of the movement's increasingly fractious elements remained steadfast and united. This determination was tested in 1957 and 1958 during the regionwide hearings of the Willink Commission on Minority Rights. The commission itself was a product of petitions by minority groups alleging marginalization by regional ethnic or ethno-religious majorities. The public hearings, half political theater and half legal duel, dramatized the content of the Middle Belt struggle. Remarkably, the hearings failed to showcase the internal divisions in the UMBC, indicating instead the ability of the cause to temporarily heal the divisions in the organization. In fact the two main factions had come together in 1956 when David Lot and his constituency withdrew from the alliance with the NPC, taking exception to the NPC's alleged failure to honor an agreement that barred it from fielding candidates against UMBC incumbents in the 1956 general elections.[8] The January 1957 congress of the party in Lafia, at which Joseph Tarka was elected president, cemented, at least for the moment, this renewed unity.

The Jos Willink Commission Hearings

The Jos hearings of the Willink Commission in February 1958 were particularly volatile, displaying both the depth of the Middle Belt cause and the opposition to it by an alliance of Hausa-Fulani and British officials. The testimonies and submissions were informative windows into the prevailing grievances of the peoples of the Middle Belt. The event was also significant because several important and founding members of the UMBC testified, including Pastor David Lot, Moses Rwang, and Patrick Dokotri.

In his testimony, David Lot indicated that the defining anxiety in the Middle Belt was that if the region remained one political entity after the departure of the British, non-Muslim peoples would be further excluded from its political and economic privileges, and that Christians would be compelled to obtain permission to build churches "while Muslims would build Mosques as they liked without permits."[9] But like many supporters of the creation of a Middle Belt state, Lot had to confront the contradictions of Middle Belt political rhetoric. At one point during the hearing he was forced under cross-examination to admit that in 1956, while he was a minister in the Northern Nigerian government as a representative of his UMBC faction, he had opposed a motion moved by an NPC member of the Northern House for the creation of a Middle Belt state. His explanation that his opposition was to the political identity and motive of the originator of the motion rather than the motion's content was less than convincing. This exchange presented an insight into how the pendulum of Middle Belt advocacy in this period sometimes swung according to the mutating political identities of advocates.

Other people who testified on behalf of Middle Belt state creation rehashed the complaint of Hausa-Fulani Muslim domination. George Yelgwen, the general secretary of the Goemai Youth Association, lamented the "neglect of chiefs in his Shendam area," which he blamed on the dominant caliphate political infrastructure's contempt for non-caliphate peoples. Even being Muslim, he argued, was not a guarantee of dignity and recognition for the Goemai people as "[Goemai] people who were Muslims were not regarded as such by the Hausas."[10] He advanced the conspiratorial rumor that on the departure of the British, the sultan of Sokoto would seek to recruit the people of the Middle Belt "to do manual work." When challenged by the chairman of the commission to substantiate the fears he had outlined, Yelgwen cited a case of the alleged snub of the ruler of the Goemai of Shendam by the sultan of Sokoto. The latter allegedly refused to shake the hand of the former because he was not a Muslim.[11]

Yelgwen, for all his seemingly shaky complaints, advanced the serious theme of neglect, alleging that the NPC-controlled Northern Nigerian government had not funded education in Shendam and that what educational activity took place in the area was funded and run by Christian missionaries. Other witnesses similarly transitioned between the mundane and the substantive, between impulsively quotidian complaints and grievances bordering on high politics. Addressing the commission on February 22, R. A. Fani-Kayode, the counsel to the UMBC, revealed what he said were the many facets of his clients' grievances, among them the imposition of the Hausa language on non-Hausa speaking areas.[12]

A few days earlier, Patrick Dokotri, a founding member of the UMBC, had attributed the separatist movement to historical events that culminated in the UMBC making the creation of a Middle Belt state the party's central preoccupation. The demand acquired political significance beyond Northern Nigeria in October 1957 when Dokotri announced that the party had formed an alliance with the Action Group, or AG, the dominant political party in Western Nigeria, which supported the Middle Belt state creation movement.[13]

Dokotri had contended that the alliance between the NPC and the National Council of Nigerian Citizens (NCNC) was "trifl[ing] with" the political "fate of millions of people in the Middle Belt."[14] His testimony at the Jos hearing fleshed out this allegation, supplying political references for his claims. Dokotri alleged systematic discrimination against the peoples of the Middle Belt in civil service recruitment, claiming that "most of the top jobs in the civil service were given to Hausas and Fulanis."[15] In advancing this allegation, he was echoing the official UMBC memorandum presented to the commission. He also cited the prevalence of Muslim *Alkali* (lower) courts in Jos, which tried cases involving Christians, as evidence of Hausa-Fulani domination. He declared that the Northern Nigerian government did not care about the welfare and education of the peoples of the Middle Belt, and, like other witnesses, attributed educational development in the Middle Belt provinces to missionaries.

These testimonies mixed the experiential and apocryphal with the substantive and political. Dokotri's testimony followed the same script, as he alleged that a failure to give even perfunctory loyalty to Hausa-Fulani culture elicited religious and cultural discrimination. His argument was one that many Middle Belt elites and commoners repeated during this time, as they had to try to conform to popular markers of Hausa identity in order to access the routine entitlements of regional citizenship: "You must dress like the Hausas if you want to be respected," Dokotri claimed.[16] The notion of "Hausa dress" had a political resonance that the people of the Middle Belt, long accustomed to their own style of dress and to European dress introduced by the missionaries, struggled to understand. European dress increasingly marked one out simultaneously as a Christian and as a nonconformist in the emerging political ideology of "one-North, one destiny" that the NPC championed.[17]

Another UMBC leader, Moses Rwang, echoed the testimony of Dokotri, arguing that the case for the creation of a Middle Belt state was not simply political but was also a cause that relied on what he termed "scientific facts." Other witnesses pointed to elements of religious discrimination, such as the failure of the Northern Nigerian government in Kaduna to provide food in the Northern Nigerian House of Chiefs when the House sat during the Muslim Ramadan fast. This was advanced as evidence of both religious discrimination and the unreflective nature of Hausa-Fulani Muslim attitudes toward non-Muslims in the region.[18]

Mary Princewill, the president of the Berom Women's Association, claimed that Christian women were disenfranchised from the region's politics and educational patrimony. She accused the educational institutions funded by the Northern Nigerian government of excluding the Berom language in favor of Hausa. Princewill claimed that although the Hausa language was a language of commercial interaction in the public square, "my people speak their native language at home" and preferred not to have their children instructed in Hausa. She alleged that in "schools at Jos and Bukuru their children were being taught Mohammedanism though they were Christians." The Hausa language, for all its utility in social and commercial contexts, drew suspicion from many people in the non-Muslim areas of Northern Nigeria, who saw it as a linguistic tool of Islamization. Rational or not, the fear, already stoked by the adoption of Hausa as the language of official communication in the Native Authority system across the North, grew apace with the growth of Hausa instruction in schools. Other aspects of Princewill's testimony included the claim that, even in Jos, Hausa women "did not associate with [Berom women] as they regarded them as pagans."[19]

Other witnesses included members of Jos' Tribal Party, whose leader, Choji Bott, claimed that the goal of his party was "to resist the Hausas who came some years ago into the division for the purpose of mining" and whose current political aim was to dominate the indigenous peoples.[20] Bott gave voice to the sentiment long held in the Middle Belt areas that, for all its pan-regional outreach and rhetoric, the NPC was a party of Hausas and Fulanis, who "would suppress" Middle Belt peoples after national independence. Bott declared the Hausa community in Jos and their political activism a legacy of British colonialism. He argued that because of the NPC's political dominance and its perceived loyalty to the cause of Muslims and the Hausa, the maintenance of this domination was at the root of the Jos Hausa community's restiveness. The undertone of the testimony was clear: the colonial authorities, having encouraged the migration of Hausa into the Jos colonial settlement, were responsible for ensuring that the community did not become a new class of oppressors, a political outpost of the NPC in the heart of the Middle Belt. The gist of Bott's polemical testimony, as reported by the *Nigerian Citizen,* was that the indigenous groups "were afraid of the Hausas who were brought to Jos by the British and it would be unfair for the British to leave them there when they left."[21]

The trouble with this pre-independence phase of Middle Belt political activism was that opposition and contradictions plagued it throughout. Opposition to the struggle for a separate Middle Belt state was particularly fierce when it came from non-Middle Belt peoples, and devastating when it was cultivated within the Middle Belt. Both types of opposition dogged the UMBC and individual Middle Belt elites that embodied the struggle. UMBC leaders, as spokespeople for the separatist movement, had to explain the recurring divisions within the leadership of the UMBC.

The hallmark of this ongoing fragmentation was that, in spite of the united front put up at the Willink Commission, another faction, led by Achiga Abuul, broke off and renamed itself the Middle Belt State Party. Even the core message of a Middle Belt identity that was neutral on religion and ethnicity was occasionally muddled by indiscipline and opposing loyalties and visions. There were those on the margins of the Middle Belt struggle, such as Chief H. O. Abaagu, a Tiv, who considered the UMBC manifesto too restrained; he launched his own localized struggle defined in religious terms. Under Abaagu's Benue Freedom Party, the few Middle Belt locales with Muslim majorities would be excluded from a future Middle Belt state.[22] Although such narrow conceptualizations of the Middle Belt struggle were overshadowed by the religious and ethnic ecumenism of various UMBC factions, they highlighted the lingering absence of definitional consensus in the struggle. In the midst of the division, a discernible, fairly inclusive struggle coalesced.

This political cosmopolitanism was demonstrated most visibly by the Moses Rwang faction, which emerged in 1955 and was led by a team of multireligious and multiethnic leaders such as Chief Abaagu, Abdul Ado Ibrahim, Bello Ijumu, and Jonah Assadugu. Nonetheless, factional and rhetorical differences incubated and festered even as Middle Belt activism intensified. One of the lingering catalysts for friction was the lack of precision and consistency in the ethnic and religious definitions of the Middle Belt as a geographical and political unit. This imprecision continued to plague the cause. In addition to confronting this legacy, Middle Belt activists and politicians faced persistent critics who confronted them with the contradictions of their struggle. Individual Middle Belt politicians, increasingly ensconced in political institutions superintended by the NPC, also had to reconcile their separatist agitation with their participation, however marginal, in the emerging political mainstream of the North.

The Middle Belt Struggle and Its Opponents

Daunting as they were, contradictions were the least of the UMBC's troubles, as opposition to the Middle Belt struggle came from multiple quarters. Fierce resistance came from hardnosed NPC lawyers in the Willink Commission hearings. They dismissed the UMBC's allegation of religious and ethnic marginalization, questioned the viability of a putative Middle Belt state with such a dizzying array of ethnic and linguistic plurality, and pointed to linguistic, cultural, historical, and pragmatic political affinities between the caliphate and non-caliphate zones. The lawyers absolved the caliphate zone of the often-cited oppression of emirate-modeled colonial administration in Middle Belt societies.[23] Opposition to the struggle during the contentious Willink Commission hearings also had the force of colonial officialdom behind it. A skittish colonial officialdom, already defensive about the allegations of systemic colonial preference for caliphate administrative hegemony, was eager to defend itself against such charges.

In several hearings, the chairman of the commission, Sir Willink, would call upon an "expert" witness, the attorney general of the Northern Region, H. H. Marshall, to adjudicate the authenticity of the UMBC's allegations. On each occasion, Marshall not only dismissed the claims but used the platform to espouse the fairness and balance of the Northern Nigerian colonial system. The commission also called upon several British district officers to testify on grievances as "experts." Predictably, each avoided indicting pro-caliphate British administrative policies. Instead, they sought to discredit each alleged case of discrimination, marginalization, and oppression that implicated caliphate colonial agents.[24]

Opposition to the Middle Belt struggle had several dimensions, some articulated in the context of the Willink Commission hearings, others in the public domain. Ahmadu Bello set the tone for the anxieties and hostility that underpinned the typical caliphate response to the Middle Belt cause. His presentation before the commission hit the familiar notes in the standard response of the Hausa-Fulani aristocracy to separatist agitations founded on narratives of British-aided caliphal oppression. Bello argued that the NPC government, which came to power in the 1954 elections, was a magnanimous protector of the rights of Northern Nigeria's ethnic and religious minorities. This protection, he contended, was complemented by a generous policy of minority ethnic and religious representation that went beyond what the population of minorities in the region would require. He promised, nonetheless, to extend the policy of chiefly representation and patronage to Middle Belt provinces by giving more representation to chiefs of non-Muslim groups in the Northern Nigerian House of Chiefs.[25]

Ahmadu Bello dismissed the allegation of ethno-religious preference and discrimination and proclaimed the NPC's controversial commitment to the symbiosis of faith, worship, and work as a creed rather than an ideology directed at Christians and traditionalists. Although Bello eloquently reiterated the commitment of the NPC government to religious freedom, the significations of the government's overt display of Islamic favoritism had a political resonance in the Middle Belt. This perception filtered through to Middle Belt elites, Hausa-Fulani politicians, and bureaucrats alike, giving rise to unofficial acts of discrimination such as loss of entitlements and alienation from patrimonies to which Middle Belt individuals felt entitled. Ahmadu Bello's assurances did little to calm the fears of religious discrimination. Nor did it mitigate Muslim officials' overzealous translation of the premier's bureaucratization of Islam to promote their own narrow goal of constructing the parameters of exclusion.

Ahmadu Bello's submission seemed overly insensitive to the demands of the Middle Belt struggle. It mirrored a prevailing proclivity in the caliphate provinces to delegitimize Middle Belt aspirations by denying the basis for the expressed grievances and by pointing to the repercussions of the creation of a Middle Belt state. Bello argued that "the shock to an economy of such shattering proportions as would result by the creation of a Middle Belt state could well produce such effects that both parties would find themselves hard put to survive."[26] The general outline of Bello's opposition made its way into the rhetorical arsenal of other Hausa-Fulani Muslim politicians of the NPC. Muhammadu Ribadu, the second vice president of the NPC and federal minister of mines, power, and Lagos affairs, echoed Bello's core themes but escalated the rhetoric by threatening bloodshed in the event of the creation of a Middle Belt state.[27]

Ribadu, like other critics of Middle Belt activism, repeated the belief that the Middle Belt struggle was an external political project driven by the Action Group (AG) to break the national political dominance of the North. Although this was true to the extent that the UMBC was in formal alliance with the AG, this reality became an elastic rhetoric allowing critics to cheapen the Middle Belt struggle by simply invoking the specter of external political manipulation. Caliphate critics externalized the origins of Middle Belt separatism while sidestepping the local grievances that animated it. The UMBC-AG alliance served to embolden the perception that multiple forces were combining to dismember the North. The uncompromisingly hostile attitude that politicians of caliphal heritage adopted toward vocal Middle Belt activism reflected this suspicion.

Opposition from Within

The fulcrum of the opposition to the Middle Belt movement was not the caliphal origin of its critics or the fact that they controlled bureaucratic power in late-colonial Nigeria. The real strengths of the opposition were uncertainty and fear. These two sentiments gripped not only Hausa-Fulani Muslims but also individuals from the Middle Belt who had grown accustomed to the patronage networks of the North and the relative certainties that they carried. Northern Nigerians studying in the United Kingdom published an op-ed in the context of the Willink Commission hearings arguing that the creation of a Middle Belt state would undermine the foundational solidarities of the North and threaten the secured futures they imagined for themselves as bureaucrats, teachers, and leaders, and participants in the Northern regional government.[28] They feared, like other Northerners, that the emergence of a Middle Belt state would at the very least reduce the capacity of the Northern Nigerian government to accommodate and subsidize their economic and professional aspirations.

Many members of the Middle Belt elite exhibited this self-preservationist instinct in their attitude to the Middle Belt struggle. As a result, many of them declared their opposition to the effort to the Middle Belt state lobby, even if they shared the underlying sentiment against caliphal hegemony. As in earlier periods, chiefs continued to experience this bifurcated loyalty arising from individuals' desires to sustain their foothold in the Northern patronage system while lamenting its unfairness. One example of this trend is that the Kagoro and Jos chiefs, both Christians with Middle Belt sympathies and sensibilities, were instrumental in persuading Pastor David Lot to take his faction of the UMBC into alliance with the NPC in 1954.

In rationalizing their decision to urge the alliance, the chiefs showed that they were struggling to reconcile their Middle Belt identity and loyalties and their functional roles in the NPC-controlled government. Their declaration indicates the unsettled pragmatism that continued to mark their two loyalties. Their reason for supporting the alliance between the UMBC and NPC was that "they [Muslim emirate peoples] are the leaders, we are their junior brothers," a position that should be understood in the context of the paternal political relationship that evolved over the long period of colonization between caliphate agents (and subsequently the caliphate-dominated NPC regional government) and the peoples of the Middle Belt areas.[29]

Other chiefs in the Middle Belt struggled to balance their expected loyalty to the NPC government, which funded their salaries and perks, and the yearnings of their people for redress and fairness, especially in situations in which the performance of such loyalty might displease constituents. When the *attah* of Igala, Aliyu Obaje, addressed the Willink Commission in Lokoja, he claimed that he had addressed twenty thousand subjects in Anyangba and that they all resolved that they did not want a Middle Belt state. But Alhassan Layemi, a community leader from Lokoja Division, contradicted the attah, claiming that the movement for Middle Belt state enjoyed overwhelming support in Kabba Province. Coming short of accusing the attah of lying to the commission, he contended that the venue in Anyangba, in which the attah claimed to have addressed the crowd, could not hold even one thousand people.[30]

Other Middle Belt insiders of the Northern Nigerian government were less nuanced in their opposition to Middle Belt activism, partly because they had fewer anxieties about being seen to be empathetic to their kinsmen's aspirations or about their loyalty to the government. G. U. Ohikere, an Ebira, the Northern regional minister of works, proclaimed opposition to the movement because he claimed that in the view of his people it would weaken the political unity of the North.[31] Abutu Obekpa, a member of the Northern House of Assembly representing Idoma Division, also declared that his constituency opposed the creation of a Middle Belt state. Only the Tiv in Benue Province, he argued, supported the

Middle Belt state creation cause.[32] This was partly true, as the official Willink Commission submissions from Idoma Division and Wukari, which was represented in the Northern House by an NPC politician, Jolly Tanko Yusufu, were against the creation of a Middle Belt state, even if, as we saw in chapter 4, the Idoma peoples' resentment of perceived Hausa domination was deep.

Obekpa and Yusufu, as two of the most powerful politicians from the two divisions, may have influenced the submissions in favor of their party's position, although the fear of Tiv political domination in a Middle Belt state may also have played a role. Still, there were dueling supportive and opposing tendencies in Idoma Division as the influence of the NPC's patronage network made unanimity of opinion in favor of the Middle Belt cause impossible. Obekpa's position was one of several similar positions adopted by visible figures from Middle Belt constituents in the NPC-controlled Northern government, which consciously used patronage to blunt the UMBC's appeal and to cultivate support for Northern Nigerian unity.[33] The divergence of attitudes to the Middle Belt cause and the absence of a clear consensus are indicators of the depth and breadth of the NPC's political influence as much as of divergent political aspirations in the Middle Belt struggle.

Weary Agitation and "Fulani Domination" in the Years of Independence

After many hearings, newspaper duels, debates, and competing claims that inflamed passions and raised awareness to new heights, the Willink Commission decided not to recommend the creation of any new states. Meanwhile Nigeria marched to independence with the existing structure of three regional governments in the north, west, and east. Official national independence on October 1, 1960, brought new fears to Northern Nigeria. Old tensions, suspicions, and complaints endured as the NPC assumed full, unsupervised control of the Northern regional government and its vast infrastructure of resource mobilization and distribution.

Feelings of Middle Belt alienation grew even as pragmatic engagement with the NPC by previously oppositional Middle Belt politicians increased. Middle Belt activists such as Joseph Tarka who chose to stay on the path of separatism intensified the vehemence of their anti-caliphate rhetoric, while those who chose to find their niche within the Northern Nigerian government did so with equal determination. No matter where they stood in relation to the Middle Belt struggle and to what the UMBC called Fulani domination, for many educated Middle Belt peoples, independence cast a new spotlight on the promises of accommodation espoused by Ahmadu Bello in his address to the Willink Commission.

For those resolved to continue the struggle for a new state in the face of the new scramble for the political spoils of independence, the test of independence lay in the extent to which religious discrimination against non-Muslims abated. These issues took on new political significance in the early 1960s. The policies of the NPC government, now free of colonial constraints, were scrutinized carefully and compared to existing suspicions of anti-Christian, anti–Middle Belt bias.

The first five years of independence witnessed an aggressive extension of the NPC's patronage network. More Western-educated Middle Belt people were co-opted into the Northern Nigerian government as bureaucrats and appointees. The NPC government's willingness to use the North's post-independence revenues to solidify its One-North ideology proved effective in reducing the ferocity of the Middle Belt struggle. More Western-educated Middle Belt people, seeing their kinsmen operate and prosper in the admittedly restricted and arguably discriminatory Northern political system, gradually moved away from Middle Belt political militancy and began to pursue their political futures in the NPC government. As George Kwanashie has argued, the main reason for the dwindling appeal of the Middle Belt struggle in the post-independence period was the "success of the Northern regional Government in using the resources available to it either to suppress opposition or to win people, by incorporation, over to its idea of One-North."[34]

Patronage, though, had its limits, and brute politics sometimes proved a more effective tactic for the NPC. Suppressing the opposition sometimes involved denying opportunities, privileges, and access to resources; at other times it involved meting out subtle punishment to unyielding political adversaries. The cumulative effect was a trend of increased engagement with the NPC government by Middle Belt elites who only a few years earlier were campaigning for a Middle Belt state. Some of those who refused to engage with the government as a matter of principle retired quietly from active politics. For those who embraced pragmatism and sought their place in the Northern bureaucracy, the rewards were immediate, albeit limited because they were either Christians or non-caliphate Muslims. Some non-Muslims desirous of even greater privileges found that they could access them by converting to Islam and did so.

Middle Belt Holdouts and the Fear of Theocracy

For the holdouts in the Middle Belt struggle, NPC patronage definitively answered the question of who really dominated political and economic life in the North. For them, this was a vindication, as it substantiated their claims that Middle Belt people were to be paternally coddled and recruited into a system of privilege controlled by people with caliphate heritage. For uncompromising separatists, NPC's tokenistic gestures proved that postcolonial Northern Nigerian politics was still dominated by the historical political adversaries of Middle Belt peoples. Conversion to Islam by individual members of the Middle Belt elite proved to the separatists that the NPC rhetoric of religion-neutral opportunities was just that, and that resource distribution was being leveraged to achieve an Islamization agenda.

In the early 1960s, Ahmadu Bello's conversion and preaching campaigns throughout the North provided fodder to Middle Belt activists because they seemed to belie his declarations at the Willink Commission. The campaigns suggested a blurring of the secular institutions of the government and the religious commitments of its key figures, most of whom were Muslims. Throughout the early 1960s, Ahmadu Bello personally led many preaching tours in the region, at which thousands of non-Muslims converted to Islam. At each event the converts were given gifts funded by the government and assigned Islamic advisers. For many Middle Belters, even those who were embedded in the government, it was an uncomfortable spectacle to behold.

The Southern Nigerian press sensationalized the conversions as a prelude to the Islamization of Nigeria. The Northern Nigerian press, especially the NPC-aligned *Nigerian Citizen,* celebrated the conversions and preaching tours with provocative headlines, such as "Islamic Campaign breaks through Christian Fortress . . . 9,000 become Muslims in Jos," "Sardauna Declares Holy War," "Sardauna's Crusade," and "Islamic Conversion Campaign Hots Up."[35] One report on the campaigns even predicted that "the percentage of converts into Islam will continue to grow until we have a one hundred percent Islamic state."[36] Whether this was the official position of the NPC government or not, the realities of Bello's personal leadership of the conversion campaigns and the NPC loyalties of the *Nigerian Citizen* and its parent company, the Gaskiya Corporation, lit a fire under Middle Belt activists, for whom these were vindications of their anxieties and fears.[37]

In reporting on the scale and success of the conversion campaigns one edition of the *Nigerian Citizen* even invoked the most dreaded idiom of caliphate domination, the Fulani jihad. It declared that Ahmadu Bello was following "in the footsteps of Sheikh Othman Dan Fodio," a statement that was sure to be interpreted in many parts of the Middle Belt as indicating a continuation of the Fulani jihad of the nineteenth century. The jihad and its many myths had been the rhetorical idiom of victimhood in many non-caliphate areas, especially frontier communities. Justified or not, these narratives on the jihad were still animating struggles as historical baselines and referents.

The same report declared that the NPC government was committed to the "total elimination of Paganism in Northern Nigeria."[38] "Pagan" had long functioned as a derisive code word for Christians and traditionalists in the taxonomy of British colonial texts and in caliphal discourses. One of the recurring complaints of Middle Belt submissions during the Willink Commission hearings was that caliphate Muslims who dominated the emerging political order were fond of calling Christians and traditionalists "pagans," a term that offended non-Muslims and that illustrated the contempt in which Hausa-Fulani Muslims allegedly held peoples of the Middle Belt. Given these realities, the import of the newspaper reports was hardly missed among the Christians and traditionalists of the North. For Middle Belt activists, the growing government commitment to Islamic conversion portended a threat to their communities and their ways of life. The conversion campaigns and the ways in which they were covered in the NPC-beholden regional media inflamed the polity and added a new layer of political tension to a region already gripped by ethno-religious anxieties. It also emboldened Joseph Tarka, Patrick Dokotri, and others who were still actively pursuing the cause of Middle Belt separatism.

The Gains of Patronage and the Foil of Otherness

The conversion campaigns alone would not have stoked the angst and suspicion that many non-Muslim elites increasingly came to harbor. Ahmadu Bello reinforced the perception that the Northern Nigerian government was transforming into an Islamic state with his decidedly pro-Islam foreign policy when he aggressively cultivated ties across the Islamic world in North Africa, the Middle East, and Asia, and took steps to forge a pan-African Islamic solidarity.[39] As Ousmane Kane notes, Ahmadu Bello pursued both Islamic conversion and international Islamic solidarity on behalf of Northern Nigeria because he "had undertaken to unify Northern Nigeria and made Islam the central element of his unification policy."[40]

Many Northern non-Muslims, even those loyal to the NPC, felt that the government represented only Muslims and projected their worldview internationally. Many in the Middle Belt came to believe that only conversion to Islam could confer on them access to and inclusion in the North's vast political patrimony. This conclusion took hold partly because Ahmadu Bello's government's obsession with Islamic proselytization diminished the populist distribution of political largess for which the NPC was known in the Middle Belt. As Joseph Garba puts it, "the Sardauna's rule had . . . become oppressive . . . paradoxically because his preoccupation was with spiritual rather than temporal affairs . . . [as] he embarked on a region-wide tour to amass new converts to Islam."[41] For many Middle Belt people, reconciling Bello's extension of patronage and access to Middle Belt people with his investment in Islam proved particularly confusing. When a delegation of Northern Christian associations visited Bello in October 1965, this ambivalence marked their interaction. While they thanked the premier for his outreach to non-Muslim provinces of the North, they expressed their concern about the fact that Northern politics still favored caliphal Muslims, Middle Belt Muslims, and Middle Belt converts to Islam, in that concentric order. In particular, they drew the premier's attention to the activities of local Muslim political figures in Middle Belt provinces, alleging that the latter were urging local elites, through blackmail and promises, to convert to Islam as a way of earning respect and privileges in the Northern political system.[42]

The delegation gave voice to prevalent concerns about the semiofficial policy of the NPC government, which sought to blunt Middle Belt activism by encouraging and in some cases pressuring chiefs and aristocratic members of several non-Muslim ethnic groups to convert to Islam. Several non-Muslim chiefs converted as a way of attracting political recognition, prestige, and patronage from the NPC government headed by Ahmadu Bello.[43] Anecdotal evidence proliferated about pressures brought to bear on several chiefs to convert. Some chiefs, the most prominent among whom was the attah of Igala, converted to Islam, spurring more conversions among his people as a mark of deference to their traditional ruler. Such exemplary conversions often took on their own lives as Islamic identity became increasingly linked with privilege and recognition. Often, overzealous caliphate migrants and residents in those locales exaggerated the prestige that conversion conferred. Such narratives sometimes evolved into folk wisdom, which then was reinforced by the upward sociopolitical mobility of those who converted.

During the first five years of Nigerian independence, this climate of new suspicions and evidence of caliphate hegemony and Middle Belt subordination lent new life to the politics of the UMBC. The perceptions that this official politics of religion spawned gave new validity to the claims of the UMBC in a period in which its political clout was in decline. Thus, even as the party decreased in numbers and saw the NPC make inroads into its bases in Benue, Plateau, Kabba, Zaria, and Adamawa provinces, its demands became fiercer and its rhetoric sharper. In March 1964, when the party, still under the leadership of Joseph Tarka, held its convention in Jos, it renewed its call for the creation of a Middle Belt state.[44] Not even the decision of NEPU only a few weeks earlier to oppose the creation of a Middle Belt state dampened the UMBC's commitment to their long-held objective. A more skeptical view is that the creation of a Middle Belt state was the raison d'être of the party, the endpoint of its aspirations, and as such it could not justify its existence without publicly repeating this goal. In some ways, the party was a prisoner to its own foundational commitments.

The NPC Machine and the UMBC's Last Stronghold

As sympathy for Middle Belt separatism waned in proportion to the NPC's expanding machine of political patronage, UMBC leaders grew increasingly more militant in their quest to retain a base of support from which to continue their struggle and grow the party's influence. For a variety of reasons Tiv Division in Benue Province became the operational base for the new UMBC, the site of its fiercest struggle. The Jos Plateau was still ideologically a UMBC cradle, and Jos remained the scene of the dueling claims of non-Muslim indigenous entitlement and Hausa-Fulani settler anxieties, but the theater of the broader struggle shifted to Tiv Division.

The tension between Hausa migrant anxieties and aspirations on one hand and indigenous political self-determination on the other lingered into the 1960s, as the indigenous groups of the Plateau and the Jos area were able to consolidate and normalize their control of the contentious politics of Jos metropolis. Many of the plateau's chiefs and politicians had become beholden in one form or another to the NPC government, however, and could not see gains in continued opposition on the basis of Middle Belt separatism. As a result the UMBC's influence in its bastion became diluted. In Tiv Division, the NPC government also successfully courted many politicians, blunting the influence of the UMBC. Weakening influence did not, however, lead to diminished popularity and appeal among the Tiv, the third largest ethno-linguistic group in Northern Nigeria. The difference in Tiv Division was that, due to the leadership of Joseph Tarka, and also to the NPC's overly aggressive targeting of this locale, a backlash developed, which in turn imposed a ceiling on NPC penetration and assured the UMBC of steady support.

Tiv Division became the organizational base and ideological stronghold of the UMBC in the post-independence period. The reasons for this go beyond Joseph Tarka's Tiv identity, or the geographical distance of Benue Province from the center of Hausa-Fulani power in Kaduna, although these factors may have also played a role in the party's renewed popularity among the Tiv. The sociology and history of colonial Tivland had something do with its emergence as the hotbed of postcolonial anti-caliphate political ferment. Tivland was a collection of fiercely republican, antiauthoritarian, and willfully decentralized polities held together by language and culture. The Tiv, like many decentralized peoples in Africa, cherished their "radical political autonomy," which British colonialists and Hausa-Fulani politicians misunderstood as political backwardness and social anarchy.[45] The encounter between this relatively peculiar historical sociology and emirate-modeled colonial centralization proved a catalytic development in the formation of an implacable opposition to the NPC and its Hausa-Fulani hegemonic heritage.

Why Tiv Division?

The Tiv colonial encounter with political, administrative, and judicial institutions derived from the emirate system was disastrous. It generated a culture of suspicion regarding even the most remote indication of subordination to the caliphate zone. The encounter with colonial rule convinced Tiv folk that the emirate political model was alien and oppressive and conditioned them to protect their way of life and identity from its perceived political residue in postcolonial Tivland.

Colonial application of emirate-type centralized rule in this milieu of non-hierarchical social organization served to sharpen the self-narrative of the Tiv and their sense of difference from the caliphate zone further north. The most authoritative documentation of this encounter comes to us via the semiautobiographical chronicle of Akiga Sai, titled *Akiga's Story*.[46] Akiga Sai was one of the first Western-educated Tiv Christians. In this work, he narrates the many forms of corruption practiced by colonial agents appointed by colonial officials who professed a desire to see Tivland mirror an emirate-type society compatible with indirect rule. The colonial personnel who oversaw this emirate system were a mix of Tiv and Hausa officials. The template was, however, decidedly caliphate in origin, and the preparatory African colonial staff that helped to implement political centralization in Tivland was largely Hausa.

To govern the decentralized Tiv in the period following their conquest, the British appointed staff-chiefs. The staff-chiefs were appointed arbitrarily based on perceived character and charisma, as the Tiv had no preexisting chiefly tradition or a culture of centralized governance. Each district chief was put in charge of several Tiv clans grouped together to form districts. The British appointed a council for the chiefs and assigned them policemen, or dogarai in Hausa. This British political reform unleashed a new set of sociopolitical dynamics that resulted in several forms of corruption, Akiga argues. This corruption was, in turn, underwritten by supervising British colonial officials for whom the stability of colonial rule was more important than policing the moral conduct of African colonial agents. The beginning of colonial chieftaincy in Tivland ushered in an era of unfamiliar exaction and unethical conduct that was carried out in the name of British colonialism.

This reform was profound and so was its impact. The invention of colonial policemen as operational appendages of colonial staff-chiefs was particularly important, as it authorized a new regime of corruption and oppression. According to Akiga, the centralizing reform "was the beginning of the Tiv's troubles. After that it was not only staff-chiefs who beat the people and seized their possessions by force, but also council members, policemen, and messengers."[47] The new colonial agents acquired more wives, a key marker of wealth in Tiv society, at the expense of the Tiv peasantry: "As soon as they obtained posts under the European, this was the object on which they first set their hearts; the work for which they had been appointed held little interest for them."[48] Chiefs "would take [wives] for nothing, and the owner of the ingol [bride] would be afraid to take action against the white man's scribe." Outright confiscation of property by colonial chiefs and their agents was a common practice: "If any one reared a particularly fat bull and the chief heard of it, it was as good as his. He sent a policeman to tell the owner to catch it, and bring it to him, and also to pay the cost of the oil with which to cook it. All the best of the livestock was confiscated by the staff-chiefs for their own use."[49] Once appointed, a policeman "did what he liked"; he looked upon his appointment as an investment and felt entitled to a reward. This feeling underwrote colonial police corruption as the dogarai "laid hands on people's property, saying, 'you can't play the fool with me. I was not made policeman for nothing; it cost me a cow!'"[50]

Given the depth of the Tiv's commitment to decentralized living, their experience with imposed emirate-type centralization was especially disruptive, triggering antiauthoritarian protest and uprising. Besides scattered but frequent localized revolts, the Tiv had embarked on two major widespread revolts during the colonial period. The Haakaa revolt of 1929 and the Nyambua uprising of 1939 targeted the infrastructure and personnel of centralized colonial rule, particularly taxation.[51] The Native Authority system, a visible reminder of emirate administrative influence, and the native courts came under particular attack.

This legacy of political oppression, extortion, and corruption forged a rhetorical link between the institutions of colonial rule and the emirate inspiration for them in the minds of many Tiv. In the heady political period of the 1960s, memories of colonial hardship soured the Tiv on the aristocratic tradition that was the base of the NPC. The NPC and its organic affinity with the emirate system raised concerns among the Tiv. The egalitarian, anti-emirate rhetoric of the UMBC found a natural home among the Tiv as a result. UMBC political activists opportunistically latched onto the perception that the source of the Tiv's pains under colonial rule was a system of administration imported from the Fulani-ruled emirates. This solidified the association of the NPC with the dreaded hierarchical organization of social, economic, and political life, which was anathema to Tiv traditions of functional republicanism.

Migration, Urbanization, and Militancy

The construction of the Makurdi Railway and Benue River Bridge from 1929 to 1932 created a new demographic reality in Tivland. The project saw migrants from many ethnicities, including the Hausa-Fulani, take up residence in Makurdi and its surrounding Tiv country, many of them staying after the completion of the project.[52] Already resentful of the role that Hausa dogarai played in spreading the reach of colonial power in Tivland and wary of the implementation of an emirate-inspired system of rule in the division, many Tiv young men seethed with unease at the influx of Hausa-Fulani migrants into Makurdi and the surrounding Tiv towns and villages of Igbor, Aliade, Taraku, Moigbo, Paka, and others.[53] When the headquarters of Benue Province was moved from Abinsi to Makurdi in 1936, the sleepy town on the banks of the Benue River became a bigger magnet for migrant Hausa traders. Because Benue Province included such caliphate-affiliated towns and kingdoms as Keffi and Lafia, the influx of Hausa personnel affiliated with the colonial government soared. In addition, as a result of the arrival of private Hausa citizens trying to avail themselves of new opportunities in a growing provincial railway and administrative hub, the Makurdi metropolitan area enjoyed an unprecedented population boost.

Migrants from other provincial areas outside of Tivland, such as the Jukun, also flocked to Makurdi. The change in Makurdi's administrative status and the migratory flow that it generated produced a major political and demographic outcome. Hausa-Fulani "interpreters, cooks, messengers, clerks, policemen, sanitary inspectors, and other motley auxiliary colonial staff" fanned out across the town and the surrounding areas of Tiv Division.[54] Tiv sources remember a rapid growth in Hausa-Fulani influence in Makurdi and other parts of Tiv Division, to the dismay of many politically conscious young Tiv men.[55] The growth of Hausa-Fulani populations in Tivland in the mid-colonial period fed a growing, implacable narrative of Hausa oppression. Tiv Division was awash with sensational accounts of Hausa produce buyers' price manipulation at several rural locations. Hausa produce buyers are said to have "fixed prices at which they would buy [sesame seeds]; introduced all kinds of levies and manipulated the weighing machine to cheat the local farmer."[56] Such stories were probably sensationalized and subsequently hardened into usable political truths in correspondence to the growing ubiquity of the Hausa presence and influence in Tivland. Nonetheless, they provide a window into the growing centrality of Hausa-Fulani influence in the Tiv's oppositional political texts.

This history of opposition to Anglo-Hausa colonial rule provided referents to UMBC politicians and activists who sought to mobilize Tiv political opinion against the NPC and Hausa-Fulani Muslims in postcolonial Tivland. The effort to rediscover the historical essence of Tiv independence and republican consciousness often involved a critique of alleged Hausa-Fulani domination purportedly executed through the NPC. Post-independence Tiv opposition to the NPC government was an epic struggle steeped in a complicated history. At the same time the political conquest of Tivland, the UMBC's last formidable stronghold, became an obsession for the NPC, a symbolic milestone that would cement the party's political preeminence in the North.

Elections, Political Power, and the Tiv Uprising

As the December 1964 general elections drew close, the contending political objectives of the UMBC and the NPC increasingly headed toward a collision, and a showdown seemed inevitable. The two sides exchanged heated rhetoric. Encouraged by the electoral campaign language of the commissioner for Benue Province in the Northern government, Jolly Tanko Yusufu, Tiv and Idoma supporters of the NPC used regional media outlets sympathetic to the government to make declarations of support for the NPC government and to predict the defeat of the UMBC.[57] Abutu Obekpa, the representative for Idoma Division, boasted that Idomaland was a base of support for the NPC, although the influential Idoma Hope Rising Union (IHRU) had presented a strong pro-UMBC position calling for the creation of a Middle Belt state to the Willink Commission.[58] Well-funded and desperate to retain their perch in the NPC government, pro-NPC forces in the province were very vocal in their media campaign. They sometimes took out full-page newspaper advertorials to campaign for the Nigerian National Alliance

(NNA), the joint platform of the NPC and the National Council of Nigerian Citizens (NCNC).[59]

Triumphant and provocative in tone, NPC-friendly headlines in the *Nigerian Citizen* included "NNA Storms UMBC Stronghold—Tivs Are Changing as Manifesto Is launched"; "Benue Must be Won: Tanko on the Offensive"; and "Tivs Declare for NPC."[60] The last headline also functioned as a caption for a large photo showing a sea of Tiv people flanked by prominent NPC officials who had allegedly crossed over to the NPC from the UMBC. Superior publicity aside, the Tiv Division NPC machinery was a party challenged by the on-ground dominance of the UMBC and by the negative associations that it conjured in the minds of many Tiv people. In fact, the postcolonial bureaucratic records of Benue Province are replete with complaints from NPC party activists and supporters who felt that they were contending against an intimidating groundswell of support for the UMBC and pleaded for resources and protection in propagating the NPC in Tivland.[61] What the NPC lacked in grassroots support, however, it made up for in the savvy use of its media clout and resources to project a sense of visibility, strength, and inevitability.

The tensions that led up to the elections received additional momentum from the series of uprisings that took place between 1960 and 1964. The Tiv riots, as they would later be known in media and official reports, were both spontaneous and organized protests targeting a plethora of institutions and personnel. Anyone associated with the NPC, Hausa-Fulani people, and those carrying out routine official tasks such as tax collection and census on behalf of the NPC government were attacked, leaving many dead and maimed. Houses of prominent NPC supporters and appointees in Tivland were attacked, and regular Tiv folk who showed support for the NPC were assaulted.

Makurdi town was home to a subordinate Native Authority under the Tiv Native Authority presided over by the central Tiv chief, Gondo Aluor. The town was hit particularly hard. Makurdi's unusual ethno-religious alchemy made it the epicenter of the crisis. There, the political might of the NPC and its ability to appoint people of Hausa-Fulani and Muslim heritage into Native Authority positions in the Middle Belt clashed with the determination of Tiv nationalists in the UMBC to resist NPC-engineered Hausa domination. To this cauldron must be added the legacy and memories of the 1945 Makurdi uprising, in which the Tiv protested against plans to install a Hausa Muslim as successor to Audu dan Afoda, the British-appointed Hausaized Muslim chief of Makurdi, when he died that year.[62] All of these factors came together to make Makurdi a hotbed of the NPC-UMBC rivalry, a rivalry often fought, from the UMBC perspective, as a struggle to uproot Hausa-Fulani Muslim domination.

The Hausa-NPC Struggle for Makurdi

At the time of the uprisings, Makurdi was still a cosmopolitan railway town, with many Hausa-Fulani residents who were supporters of the ruling NPC. The head of the Makurdi Sub-Native Authority, Alhaji Ari, was a Hausa Muslim appointed to the position by the NPC government. In the ensuing political debates and dueling propagandas over how to deal with the disturbances and their political fallouts, Makurdi came to occupy a central position because of its history as a site of Hausa-Tiv confrontation. The prevalence of Hausa personnel in the colonial administrative bureaucracy of Makurdi heightened ethno-religious tensions, but the influence of Hausa-Fulani traders and business owners trumped that of colonial administrators. Traders bought up land and property and came to control the political, economic, and social life of Makurdi.

This Hausa influence, along with that of Jukun migrants, was reflected in the names of some the neighborhoods in Makurdi, which had clear Hausa and Jukun etymologies.[63] Many Tiv, apolitical in their effort to survive in the colonial system, had made peace with the dominance of colonial Hausa administrative personnel and traders. One indicator of this reluctant acquiescence was that many Tiv farmers, seduced by the power of Audu dan Afoda, the Hausa chief of Makurdi in the 1930s and early 1940s, in fact called Makurdi *Gari u Audu* (Audu's town).[64] This nomenclature reflected both the brute reach of Audu's power and the extent to which delegated Hausa colonial power had become normalized in Makurdi. The political crisis of the post-independence period thus opened a new phase in the old ethnic confrontation between the Tiv and the influential, colonially backed Hausa power formation. The new crisis in Makurdi threw yet another complication into the tense brew of troubles plaguing Tivland in the 1960s.

When clashes broke out, the dreaded NA system became both a target and a fulcrum of the political crisis, as the Tiv called for its abolition and for the appointment of a Tiv chief for Makurdi. On the other hand, the Hausa residents of Makurdi, surrounded by Tiv villages and towns on all sides, felt under siege and relied on the might of the NPC government, which controlled the instruments of law enforcement, for protection. Adding to this conflict, the Makurdi Sub-NA, led by its president, Alhaji Ari, waged a spirited struggle of its own. It protested what it saw as the imposition of Tiv staff on the Makurdi Sub-NA by the Tiv NA in Gboko and the inadequate representation of the town's non-Tiv population, mainly Hausa-Fulani Muslims, in the Sub-NA's bureaucracy.[65] Ari petitioned both the provincial and regional authorities to remove the Makurdi sub-NA from the control of the Tor Tiv in Gboko. He argued that with a predominantly Tiv staff "imposed" on it by the Tiv NA, the Sub-NA could not effectively protect the town's NPC-supporting residents, the main targets of UMBC rage.[66] Finally, Ari asked the NPC-controlled authorities to transform the sub-NA into an independent chieftaincy, an effective return of the contentious colonial Hausa chieftaincy that was rested in 1945 after the death of dan Afoda and the ensuing Tiv protests. Ari argued that "all over the town" sentiments were in favor of "resuscitating the [Hausa] chieftaincy."[67]

The struggle of the NPC-aligned Hausa-Fulani community in Tivland to re-vive the dan Afoda chieftaincy of colonial times stoked the disdain with which militant UMBC supporters regarded the NPC. The intensity of the disturbances, especially in Makurdi town, reflected this angst. But if the violent crisis escalated the NPC-UMBC rivalry, its handling by the NPC government and its support-ers made reconciliation less likely. The NPC government applied the harshest punitive measures judicially possible to some of those arrested and charged for breaching public peace. At least nine of the arrested rioters were sentenced to death by hanging in November 1964.⁶⁸ The NPC government also deployed po-licemen across Tiv Division to put down the uprisings in a show of force that displayed its authority but also paradoxically validated UMBC's narratives of Tiv victimhood.

In a move of collective punishment, the NPC government imposed a "Riot Damage" tax on the inhabitants of areas where the disturbances took place, who were mostly UMBC supporters.⁶⁹ The move was clearly designed to discourage support for the rival UMBC even among the less militant, grassroots support-ers of the party. As documented petitions and pressures from the NPC's own supporters show, indiscriminate punitive fines amounted to overkill that both punished UMBC's supporters and undermined the NPC's incipient base of sup-port among the Tiv.⁷⁰

When the government panel set up to investigate the disturbances and advise ways of addressing the fallouts submitted its report in April 1965, a few months after the NPC swept the December 1964 elections, it rejected any suggestion that the violence was a product of a Tiv resentment of caliphate or NPC domination. Instead, the report blamed a plethora of factors ranging from what it termed a Tiv cultural proclivity for rejecting authority and organization, to missteps in colonial administration, to the instigation of opportunistic UMBC politicians and its external partners, the Action Group.⁷¹ The report's overarching conclu-sion was that "the disturbances were engineered by the UMBC/AG exploiting the local tribal tension" among the Tiv.⁷² The report surmised that political trouble, in essence, flowed from the stirring up of old "tribal tensions" marked by dueling cultural rituals.⁷³ It followed its diagnostics with recommendations for adminis-trative reforms in the Native Authority system.

The NPC government did not act alone in imposing collective punish-ment on riot-prone areas of Tiv Division. Before the 1964 elections, many NPC-supporting politicians in the minority in Benue Province and Tivland urged stronger action against the UMBC and its grassroots enforcers and ac-tivists. Three of these politicians won seats in the 1964 election as the NPC performed above expectations because some people in Tivland preferred to join an established political mainstream rather than insist on the unreward-ing ideological purity of the UMBC.

The victorious NPC politicians, still swimming largely against the Tiv's current of resentment, moved to consolidate their positions and to improve the fortunes of their party through a combination clandestine scorched-earth advocacy and public appeals for peace and development. Publicly, they appealed for calm and promised to use their newfound power to steer development and patronage to the troubled division.[74] Privately, the NPC leadership in Tivland called for more prosecutions of UMBC supporters and suspected rioters. They complained when detained UMBC supporters were let off or granted bail.[75]

The Paradoxes of Middle Belt Engagements in the Northern Mainstream

The 1960s were years of political contradictions in Northern Nigeria. For members of the Middle Belt elite, the de facto dominance of the NPC and the popularity of its patronage politics was something to be accepted and engaged with. Yet the Far North/Middle Belt divide, marked most starkly by religious difference, manifested in several arenas of interaction. This was a persistent source of dilemma for many young, Western-educated men and women from the Middle Belt who sought to protect their way of life from the overwhelming presence of the caliphate while entering the Northern political system.

By this time, many of those who fought in the Middle Belt struggle of the 1950s had decided to engage with the NPC mainstream or to retire to less fractious, more secure political institutions in their home areas. Joseph Tarka and his few holdouts represented a waning political tradition of militant Middle Belt self-assertion. As they tried to reignite the Middle Belt struggle in the early '60s, they had to convince not just those who had assimilated to the political mainstream but also a third group of political actors in the Middle Belt that the struggle was still relevant. This group of Middle Belt political actors was comprised of those whose political pedigree predisposed them to skepticism on the Middle Belt struggle and to pragmatic relational connections to the emirate system. These people subscribed in principle to the premise of the Middle Belt struggle and the UMBC's articulation of it, but they could not reconcile their political ecumenism with the party's separatist and exclusivist message.

No one exemplified this group's central anxieties and positions more than the chief of Moroa, Malam Tagwai Sambo. Sambo was raised in part by his uncle, Kazah Boman, whom he succeeded, and who was a close ally of the Zazzau ruling house. Because of this relationship, as a child and young man Sambo visited the Zazzau palace frequently and was welcomed and accorded the privileges of a royal son. He also befriended several members of the Zazzau royal lineage of his age, notably the current emir, Alhaji Shehu Idris, with whom he attended primary school.[76]

Sambo's career followed the trajectory of other Western-educated royal sons who were groomed to assume leadership positions in the political mainstream,

away from the centers of radical ideological or ethno-religious dissent and mobilization. Sambo was appointed the divisional secretary of the NPC in 1958, in
charge of the party's mobilization in Jaba, Kagoro, and Moroa, before succeeding his uncle as chief of Moroa. With a pedigree steeped in the emirate tradition
in the frontier areas of the Middle Belt, Sambo was an unlikely target for the
UMBC, which attempted to recruit him in the early 1960s to help reinvigorate a
challenged struggle. Joseph Tarka personally visited Sambo's palace to urge him
to take up an executive appointment in the UMBC secretariat in Jos.[77] Sambo
rejected the appointment because, as he would reminisce years later, he was uncomfortable with the narrative of "tribal and religious difference" at the heart of
the UMBC's identity as a political party.[78]

Outside the chieftaincy domain, other Middle Belt elites wrestled with what
it meant to be a Northerner and to participate in an emerging Northern Nigerian
political system. Zamani Lekwot, a retired general of the Nigerian army, and
Adamu Mbaka, a retired air vice marshal of the Nigerian Air Force, both epito-
mize this burgeoning dilemma of identity. Like Sambo, both are from Southern
Kaduna. Lekwot's biography is particularly intriguing. Ahmadu Bello inspired a
young Lekwot to join the army with the unifying regional rhetoric that it was a
way of constructing a counterweight to the Southern Nigerian head start in several Nigerian institutions, including the armed forces.

Ahmadu Bello's model of Northern empowerment, which was largely blind
to religion and ethnic identity, appealed to many Western-educated Middle
Belt young men, Lekwot included. Lekwot remembers Bello as a broad-minded
champion of Northern interests who constantly overruled his own close caliphate associates' efforts to enforce a second-class status on non-Muslim Northerners, and as a dynamic leader who forged a diverse region into a fairly unified
political entity. Yet he, like many young men from frontier communities, had "as
a young child observed a lot of the [emirate] oppression—how the Zazzau NA police dealt with our parents," and had witnessed and experienced discrimination
outside the mitigating influence of Ahmadu Bello.[79] It took military discipline
and the relative absence of overt discrimination in the armed forces to erase these
memories and to reassure Middle Belt young men like Lekwot of the oneness of
the North, a favorite mantra of the NPC.[80]

Similarly, Adamu Mbaka remembers a Northern Nigerian political arena
united by Ahmadu Bello's rhetoric and gestures. The premier, he recollects,
preached and persuaded but never insisted on conversion to Islam as a precondition for access and privilege in the NPC government.[81] Mbaka also remembers
Bello as an unwavering architect of Northern ascendancy who, on one occasion,
personally intervened to release money to enable him and his fellow Northern
Air Force cadets travel overseas for their training.[82] Yet he, too, struggled to reconcile the Sardauna's pan-Northern activism with the ubiquitous reality of Mid-

dle Belt marginality and with the insidious discrimination that he experienced in the hands of dominant caliphate forces in the air force top hierarchy.[83]

Such stories proliferated in the 1960s among Western-educated non-Muslim Northerners, especially as the politics of resource distribution and bureaucratic access degenerated into cutthroat, zero-sum maneuvers.

The late-colonial and early-independence periods witnessed the regionalization and aggregation of multiple strands of Middle Belt political and social resentment against perceived caliphate domination. Given the intensity and ubiquity of non-Muslim protests against Hausa-Fulani subcolonialism, it was only a matter of time before these disparate movements across the Middle Belt congealed into a fairly coherent movement for the political emancipation of the Middle Belt. The emergence of the UMBC crystallized this expectation.

In some ways the late-colonial and early-independence periods were seminal moments in the engagement of Middle Belt peoples with what they perceived to be a consolidation and political capitalization of Hausa-Fulani subcolonial clout. Across the Middle Belt, non-Muslim ethnic communities became anxious as Hausa-Fulani elites with privileged perches in the colonial system subtly but discernibly converted their preeminence into usable political capital in preparation for Nigeria's independence. Much of this anxiety exaggerated the intentionality of Hausa-Fulani political maneuvers. Many Hausa-Fulani subcolonial groups, like Middle Belt peoples, were simply struggling to find their place in the late-colonial order and in the process may have appeared more deliberate and ruthless than they actually were in their effort to ride their colonial privileges to postcolonial political preeminence. Nonetheless, emergent Middle Belt elites, bolstered by Western education and the resulting financial security of paid employment, moved to prevent a feared transition from Hausa-Fulani subcolonial privilege to postcolonial Hausa-Fulani political domination of the Middle Belt both in the local politics of Middle Belt areas and in the general politics of the larger northern region of Nigeria.

The result was that in the period under review, the Middle Belt region was thrown into political convulsion as anti-caliphate activists sought to carve out political niches independent of caliphate control while Hausa-Fulani elites worked to preserve a unified region and a common regional destiny as a firewall against their own anxieties of Southern Nigerian domination. The development of a politically consequential, if fragmented, Middle Belt consciousness continued apace with the high-stakes politics of the pre-independence period. This late-colonial and early-independence Middle Belt consciousness continued to feed off memories and histories of precolonial and colonial practices that Middle Belt political activists now conveniently distilled into a resonant slogan of Hausa-Fulani domination.

This phase of anti-caliphate mobilization and the political impulses that it activated owe a rhetorical debt to the struggles of earlier Middle Belt protesters against emirate subcolonial rule. But the strategies, anxieties, and priorities of Middle Belt elites in the 1950s and early 1960s took on decidedly novel characteristics. The Middle Belt struggle benefited from the uncertain trajectory of independence and from the combustive commingling of multiple factors at the moment of national independence. This produced a seemingly intractable brew of conflicts pitting Middle Belt peoples and their political demands against the dominant mainstream Hausa-Fulani political tradition.

The politics of the period also revealed the contradictions and dilemmas of the Middle Belt struggle in the context of Nigerian national politics. Opposition to the UMBC's agenda from the Hausa-Fulani–dominated NPC in Northern Nigeria was articulated in a vocabulary of patronage that seduced many Middle Belt Western-educated folk. Additionally, the NPC's vast patronage machine relied on networks and structures emplaced in the heyday of Hausa-Fulani subcolonial preeminence in many Middle Belt regions. This, and the failure and increasing marginality of oppositional mobilization in national politics, made the NPC effort to co-opt and isolate the UMBC largely successful.

Where patronage and co-optation failed, the NPC did not hesitate to deploy a ruthless stratagem of political enforcement. The NPC resorted to this method to confront a waning UMBC in its last remaining strongholds in Tivland, where the Middle Belt struggle for self-determination against perceived Hausa-Fulani domination made its last stand. The NPC-controlled regional government did not hesitate to deploy its political muscle where necessary to further its interests. It demonstrated this tactical versatility in its response to the UMBC-inspired Tiv uprisings that engulfed Tiv Division in 1963–64 and in its position on the Tiv-Hausa conflict over the control of the politics of Makurdi.

Away from the sites of high politics, many Middle Belt elites began to quietly assimilate into the Northern political and bureaucratic mainstream even as they struggled to reconcile the NPC's stated vision of regional ecumenical politics to the reality of a tiered citizenship that corresponded to access and entitlements in the Northern Nigerian patrimonial system.

Conclusion

Subcolonialism, Ethnicity, and Memory

THERE IS, at least in the field of African studies, a rich and growing literature on imperial mediation, on the political repertoires of indigenous colonial elites, and on their brokerage of colonial relations. But we have yet to articulate in a coherent conceptual or empirical vocabulary colonial administrative arrangements that devolved colonial control to non-autochthonous groups of Africans. The analyses in the foregoing chapters fill this gap by positing subcolonialism as a poorly understood but consequential colonial administrative form. At the same time, I have wrestled here with, but have not fully resolved, the epistemological and political legacies that subcolonialism birthed or reinforced.

Since the emergence of professional African history in the late 1950s and early 1960s, scholars have grown gradually familiar with how European colonizers implemented their colonial visions and how African communities responded to, recalibrated, instrumentalized, and inverted these visions of control. Studies of the colonial experience have furnished empirical evidence from different corners of the continent about the governing repertoires of colonizers, notably the use of indigenous—and thus supposedly legitimate—colonial insiders as mediators. This is an important epistemological baseline.

However, when colonization is viewed exclusively through this lens, it leads to the inadvertent reproduction of the supreme rhetoric of indirect rule: that British colonizers tampered little with African societies and that the deployment of indigenous insiders as mediators ensured that life continued for Africa's colonized people as before. We know now that this rhetoric is at best misleading, and that colonization, regardless of the shape it took, was much more disruptive of African lives than colonial texts admit. A willingness to contemplate the ruptures of colonial rule leads to a corresponding reflection on colonial arrangements that were less legitimate and thus more volatile than indigenous mediation or indirect rule.

In the early period of professional African history writing, historians of colonial Africa posited a dualist, Manichean conceptualization, which in turn informed the reconstruction of the African colonial past. In this narrative, omnipotent European colonizers executed their administrative, economic, and social fantasies on the blank canvas of African societies and on the backs of passive African colonial subjects. Africans, in this paradigm, were squeezed into three categories: oppressed African subjects, collaborating elites, and resistant nationalist heroes.[1] Implicit in this analytical frame are notions of African colonial subjects as docile or resistant participants in colonial endeavors, and of European colonizers as the consistent and quotidian drivers of the colonial enterprise.

This reading of the African colonial experience has since come under sustained critique mainly because it flattens the complex roles of African groups in colonial society. One mainstay of this critique is to call attention to the simplistic, dichotomous assumptions that underlie nationalist historiography. Scholars have since faulted its two premises: European political ubiquity and omnipotence in colonial rule, and a blanket assumption about African marginality in the mechanics of colonial rule.[2] Critique notwithstanding, this much is true by consensus: Africans were marginalized by colonial rule because conquest and occupation gave European actors overwhelming primacy in colonial affairs. Europeans tended to be the drivers and architects of the overarching colonial ideology at work in a given context. Colonial rule would not be so colonial if it were different. Ultimate agenda-setting power resided with European colonialists. Even so, colonial authorities did not exercise quotidian administrative control everywhere or at every stage of the colonial encounter. They also did not always possess the physical capacity to consistently and evenly enforce their ideologies. This logistical handicap enabled some African groups to populate and drive the institutions of colonial rule in some contexts. It also gave them the leverage to author sociopolitical scripts useful to their own objectives.

Empowered African elites deftly filled the gaps revealed by colonial personnel and logistical challenges. Yet, to posit certain groups of Africans as drivers of colonial rule in certain contexts is not to contend that African subcolonial actors replaced European colonialists as the ideologues of colonial rule, or that ultimate power and authority did not reside with Europeans even in regions like the Middle Belt where British colonizers preferred "alien" African colonial agents to indigenous mediators. In fact, in several instances discussed in this book, the invisible but powerful hands of European officials could be seen in the encounters between Hausa-Fulani subcolonials and Middle Belt communities.

It is also true that the position of the Hausa colonials, their initiatives, and the political acts they carried out for themselves or on behalf of the colonial administration flowed from the ideological space into which British discourses and preferences thrust them. Nonetheless, there was a vast field of power and political privilege between the British and the Middle Belt communities where Hausa-Fulani colonial agents operated with remarkable agency and administrative assertiveness. Through their initiatives and through the creative deployment of the power vested in them by British authorities, Hausa subcolonials came to own this space and used it to exert an influence on the colonial experience in the Middle Belt that went beyond mere mediation and brokerage. It is in this liminal colonial interstice than one can locate subcolonialism.

As a form of colonial praxis, subcolonialism was not a far-fetched proposition. As some scholars have argued, there were several impediments to effective European control and presence, and, of course, to direct European rule.[3] This reality provided an opening for indigenous African intermediaries, whose agency and initiatives as trusted insiders in colonized communities are increasingly being recognized in the literature on colonial mediation and indirect rule. It also created opportunities for lettered Africans, indigenous or not, who filled roles in the colonial bureaucracy as clerks. More crucially for the arguments in this book, the problem of extending and sustaining European rule necessitated, in several colonial domains, outsourcing colonial business to a cadre of nonindigenous colonizers, whose mandate was much wider than that of the typical African colonial intermediary. European colonizers saw these groups of subcolonizers as civilizers ruling over "backward" Africans on behalf of European colonial officials who had determined that the communities lacked the capacity to rule themselves under European supervision as dictated by the ideology of indirect rule.

The stories in this book illustrate how this type of layered colonial system worked in several provinces and districts of the vast Nigerian Middle Belt. Collectively, these stories make the corrective epistemological point that not only did Africans self-consciously and strategically mediate colonial rule, they were, in some instances, colonizers in their own rights, subject only to the sporadic and nominal supervisory oversight of European officials. I have argued here that Hausa-Fulani subcolonial rule was implemented at the Middle Belt colonial grass roots with a heavy European policy input but that many of the priorities and quotidian initiatives were informed and shaped by the interests of Muslim subcolonials with ties to the Sokoto Caliphate. Outside the overarching discursive and administrative oversight of European officials, British colonization in much of the Nigerian Middle Belt pivoted on Hausa-Fulani subcolonial initiatives and ideas. As a result, the colonial everyday in the Middle Belt had an unmistakable imprimatur of Anglo-caliphate colonialism.

Toward a Recognition of African Colonizing Agency

The concept of colonial mediation is inadequate in capturing the depth and breadth of "alien" African participation in the processes of colonization in the Nigerian Middle Belt. Subcolonial rule is a coinage more suited to the subordinate but robust roles played by Hausa colonials outside their home districts. The concept accounts for the unique decision-making agency of the Hausa-Fulani colonials discussed in the preceding chapters while also recognizing the overall political and ideological orbit in which they operated, as well as the limits of their authority in matters in which European colonial prestige was at stake.

Northern Nigeria was not the only area that played host to this brand of colonization in British colonial Africa. Uganda hosted a colonial system in which ethnic and, in some cases, religious Others superintended the colonial enterprise in certain regions of the colony. This system meant that ruling by proxy went beyond mere administrative delegation or mediation; it meant that privileged "native aliens" had the autonomy and latitude to craft their own discernible imperial agendas, some of them corresponding to precolonial imperial traditions and priorities. Nor was subcolonialism, broadly understood, an exclusively British imperial innovation. In Rwanda the Belgian colonizers succeeded in establishing the Tutsis as a separate ethnic entity. Tutsi elite administrators in Hutu communities could be understood as an "alien African" subcolonial presence, although their actual role in Belgian colonial rule in Rwanda straddles the murky boundary between colonial mediation and subcolonial rule.[4]

Some scholars have explored the empirical manifestations of subcolonial arrangements but have not posited a case for conceptually designating this type of colonization, which was characterized by the charged tropes of preparation, pedagogical administration, and African-to-African civilizational influence. What I have done here is to supply yet another set of empirical examples while letting the case studies congeal into a fairly coherent conceptual schema. The imperial strategy of subcolonial rule deserves its own conceptual and analytical space. Insider mediators in a classic indirect-rule colony brought certain advantages to colonization while facing the peculiar challenges thrown up by being perceived by some kinfolk as treasonous agents of a foreign power. From the pragmatic perspective of European officials, outsider civilizers in a subcolonial system also brought a unique set of advantages to colonization, but their rule and initiatives were similarly fraught with unfamiliar and in some cases seemingly intractable problems of power relations. The conceptual tools we use to analyze colonial relations need to reflect these contrasts and convergences between different formulas of colonization.

Can the Subaltern (Sub)Colonize?

The nationalist historiographical reluctance to acknowledge the self-conscious role of Africans in colonization is premised on a legitimate point that recalls the famous Gayatri Spivak question and title: *Can the subaltern speak?*[5] Many years after this question was provocatively posed we know fairly definitively that the subaltern can indeed speak and act, but that his gestures are inflected and constrained by the ambience of colonialism, if not by its crude physicality. With this insight in mind, we now recognize the conceptual limitation of Spivak's foundational question. A more productive inquiry might thus be a search for *how* the subaltern acts or what colonial conditions allow him to act and to what extent.

In our case, it is a question of whether the subaltern can act as a semi-sovereign colonial agent in the orbit of European imperial hegemony, and whether we can ascribe a rational, fairly autonomous colonial agency to Africans inside the deterministic ambit of colonial subjugation. Can the subaltern subcolonize, and if so how might we explain or theorize his colonizing initiatives without obscuring the overarching European colonial framework that enabled and constrained his initiatives? This is a conundrum that haunts discourses of African mediation in colonization, and appears to undercut the very notion that African groups like the Hausa-Fulani Muslim subcolonials discussed here could be posited as having displayed a colonial administrative agency unencumbered by the strictures of a European-created system.

The subcolonial rule discussed in this book does not, however, presuppose an absence of European colonial oversight or encumbrance. Rather, the argument that sustains the validity of the concept of subcolonialism rests on two facts: that in subcolonial situations European colonial supervision was at a negligible minimum except when conflicts erupted and required European intervention, and that Europeans had ab initio surrendered much administrative control and initiative to their preferred African "alien" civilizers as a conscious policy. The symbiosis of these two realities conferred leverage and power on subcolonial agents.

The agency of African outsiders who acted as colonial agents among groups considered too backward for self-rule was a product of British ideological design, albeit aided in this particular case by caliphal imperial discourses. However, once ideology became administrative policy on the ground, the British could not control what Hausa-Fulani agents did, nor did they want to, unless there was a crisis to be managed or suppressed. Overarching European control and ideological cover was an ever-present factor, but it did not preclude the creativity and, in some cases, independent initiatives of Hausa-Fulani agents. Because European colonizers consciously built their governing enterprise around detached administrative mercenaries, the self-assertion and self-interested initiatives of these empowered rulers should be regarded as predictable outcomes rather than as aberrations. Hausa colonials were aware of their indispensability to colonial rule and used this awareness to blackmail British officials into submitting to their preferences as well as to initiate wide-ranging administrative innovations that sometimes directly contradicted the professed goals of British colonizers.

The question of the ability of subaltern groups, privileged or not, to speak and act outside the confines of the colonial state structure is a crucial one. But it is also one that has been muddled by the paradigmatic influence of nationalist history and its anxieties, which tend to forbid the ascription of autonomous scripts of ethno-religious or racial exclusivity to subaltern groups, no matter how powerful and privileged these groups may have been in colonialism. Historian Jonathon Glassman has begun to trouble this orthodoxy, pointing to indigenous Zanzibari elite scripts that sought to justify Arab political hegemony and its antipode, a subordinate black racial subjectivity. These scripts, he argues, were not mere mimicries of parallel British colonial racial discourses. They were remarkable as much for their originality as for their audacious proclamation of racial and civilizational superiority.[6] My argument aligns with Glassman's, and the chapters of this book contain evidence of fascinating registers of manifest imperial destiny, ethno-religious exclusivity, and civilizational superiority, which were developed and expressed, with little or no prompting, by Hausa-Fulani subcolonials. Hausa subcolonials developed these precolonial and colonial narratives not as simple imitations or strategic inversions of British discourses but as a way of drawing on their own caliphate imperial self-narration to justify their subcolonial rule over the non-Muslim peoples of the Middle Belt.

A hard look at areas where colonial chiefs were put in charge of communities outside their home areas, communities earlier affected by the hegemonic practices of the ancestors of the new subcolonial chiefs, will reveal the existence of fairly autonomous indigenous colonial scripts. These imperial agendas did not always rival or contradict European ones; they were imbricated in them. They were, in short, parallel imperial agendas that in some cases exerted a more profound sway on colonial subjects than did the actions of European colonizers and indigenous African intermediaries. As this book has demonstrated, the Hausa-Fulani colonials went to their Middle Belt colonial administrative jurisdictions with prepared political agendas that often had more constitutive input from their emirate origins than from British imperial instruction. In this way, they insinuated themselves consciously and strategically into the colonial enterprise in ways that the familiar concept of mediation and colonial administrative hierarchies cannot capture, and in ways that render irrelevant dead-end debates about the ability of the subaltern to speak and act in the confines of colonization.

In many districts of the Middle Belt, Hausa-Fulani subcolonials were in charge of the various spheres of colonial rule in their areas of administrative jurisdiction. They hired their own staff and paid them from the revenue they generated. More crucially, they shaped the contours of the colonial enterprise, setting the parameters of economic, political, and social policies and changes. Unlike indigenous intermediaries, whose work was clouded by an overwhelmingly constant European presence and by the pressures of kinship, the clout of the Hausa-Fulani subcolonials reached deep into colonial policies crafted by nominal European supervisors. As chapters 6 and 7 show, Fulani officials not only influenced decisions about how the non-Muslim districts of Adamawa Province were administered, they also were able to shape the extent to which British officials could respond to the complaints and agitations of the non-Muslim peoples of the province against Fulani rule.

Fulani officials, led by the lamido, frequently established limits to changes and reforms that British officials wanted to make in the interest of increased self-rule for the non-Muslim autochthons. Thus, even when non-Muslim peoples sought reprieve in the context of colonial relations between them and their Hausa-Fulani colonial administrators, the political clout of the latter intruded powerfully into the processes of European colonial oversight. European colonial intervention, already nominal and sporadic, was circumscribed in effect and consequence because of the foundational centrality of Hausa-Fulani personnel to colonial rule. Despite appearances to the contrary, then, Hausa subcolonials were able, in some instances, to limit the depth and scope of European officials' administrative actions more than the latter were able to curtail the agency of Hausa-Fulani officials.

Colonial Administrative Diversity

The imperial repertoires of European colonizers in Africa combined deliberate strategies with those thrust upon them by the pragmatic impossibility of direct European rule. The trajectory and flow of colonial power was discernibly linear in some cases, as Frederick Cooper has argued to demarcate the limits of Foucauldian postulations in understanding the diffusion of power and control in colonial contexts.[7] However, the fiscal and logistical realities of colonial rule often entailed the devolution of various degrees of power to layers of the administrative infrastructure through which colonial control was experienced.

The vernacular of colonial power was also constrained by discourses of racial and civilizational hierarchies constructed on the spot but with inspiration from preexisting texts of metropolitan self-image. By mapping these metropolitan racial pathologies onto perceptions of African cultures, European colonial officials found openings for a corresponding but locally specific racial and ethnic hierarchy. Such a hierarchy was usable as a political object, authorizing administrative innovations that sometimes departed from established colonial orthodoxies. This is the context in which Hausa-Fulani subcolonial rule was birthed as a solution to a seemingly intractable administrative problem. The fixation on caliphate civilizational agency and utility in the Middle Belt was both a product of British understandings of difference and a remedy for that difference.

The nexus of practical administrative constraints and devotion to influential metropolitan theories about race and cultural sophistication meant that European colonial authorities often enlisted culturally validated groups of Africans to be the eyes, ears, and mouths of colonial rule among African communities considered in need of social and political tutelage. The question of who would fill this role and how much operational autonomy they would possess is the juncture that separates colonial mediation from subcolonialism. It is the point of divergence between the rich corpus of studies dealing with colonial mediation and the analytical trajectory pursued in this book.

Subcolonial rule was a distinctly problematic and volatile genre of colonization. I have not just documented the way it worked (or did not work), but also
analyzed the peculiar tensions that it generated at the colonial grass roots, and
the postcolonial legacies it spawned. It was an exception and not the rule, a departure from the standard colonial practice of indirect rule. Thus it lacks the
clearly articulated doctrinal corpus that we find in abundance in the archive of
British colonial discourse for indirect rule. The system was neither enunciated
in a coherent body of text nor acknowledged officially as a substantive colonial
template. Improvisational and heterodox colonial systems rarely find space in
self-congratulatory metropolitan documents.

Nonetheless, Frederick Lugard's two canonical indirect-rule manuals, *The
Dual Mandate* and *Political Memoranda,* cleared the theoretical space for the exception of subcolonial rule. Lugard argued that departures from indirect rule in
the form of Hausa-Fulani emirate rule among non-Muslim peoples were permit-
ted as a way of preparing them for indirect rule through the tutelage of culturally
superior Hausa-Fulani Muslims. Still, the system was never fully inscribed in
the canons of British colonial discourse. It was discussed only as a finite, temporary civilizational intervention that would facilitate entry into the mainstream of
indirect-rule colonialism. Because of this informal status, when subcolonial rule
persisted beyond its initial preparatory and temporal mandate, change was slow
and in some cases never came. Hausa-Fulani subcolonial rule lasted through the
dawn of independence in 1960 in several provinces and beyond in some districts.
The system acquired its own political momentum, making its dismantling unap-
pealing. The Hausa-Fulani colonials acquired robust political personas that expanded their centrality to colonial rule in the Middle Belt. They became invested
firmly in colonial grassroots infrastructures that they helped build in the non-
Muslim areas. In turn, the British, despite prior declarations about the preparatory and transitional character of subcolonial rule, grew comfortable with this
stable, if deviant, form of colonial rule.

The import of this British willingness to stick to unorthodox administrative
models that *worked* is twofold. First, it indicates that functionality sometimes
trumped colonial doctrine, no matter how elaborate or canonical such a doctrine
had become. This is an insight familiar to Africanists who study colonization, but
it is one that bears restating and can benefit from additional empirical illustration
because improvised colonial administrative genres continue to confound scholars
of empire who are schooled to identify colonial administrative typologies practiced with greater temporal and spatial regularity. Second, the case of the Nigerian
Middle Belt should serve to sensitize scholars of empire to the infinite variety that
may be housed under the generic category of indirect colonization.

As the subcolonial system persisted largely undisturbed, its Hausa-Fulani
architects gradually assimilated into the role of confident, influential subcolo-

nials. And as British proprietary investments in the system expanded, so did the vast colonial anthropological justification of subcolonialism as a mechanism for dissolving differences that stood in the way of uniform colonial administration. Differences between the caliphate Muslim zone and the non-Muslim Middle Belt in particular proved a sticking point of early colonial administration. Officials fumbled their way around a variety of possibilities for dealing with difference even as they envisioned a Northern Nigerian protectorate administered within a uniform indirect-rule system. Once they concluded that the caliphate zone possessed the prerequisites for indirect rule while the Middle Belt lacked them, one option stood out. The British sought to erase to the extent possible the functional markers of Middle Belt cultural alterity and to disseminate treasured caliphal values and cultures among the peoples of the Middle Belt as a way of forging political uniformity across Northern Nigeria.

Colonialism, Subcolonialism, and Ethnicity

The relationship between colonization and ethnic difference is another arena in which the difference between conventional colonialism marked by indirect rule and the colonial system discussed in this book emerges with clarity. Scholars of African ethnicity correctly link colonial obsessions about nativism and the customary with a surge in the embrace of fixed, unyielding ethnic identities by Africans. But as this book's conceptual and empirical analyses have illustrated, the notion that European colonizers sought to preserve and reinforce ethnic and religious differences everywhere in Africa is a stretch.

Clearly, in a few eccentric colonial domains such as Northern Nigeria, where there was a *longue durée* of ethnic and religious diversity, difference was not an asset to be cultivated and preserved. In these contexts, difference was a problem to be solved in the interest of establishing a uniform, cheap colonial administration throughout the colonial territory. The development of a caliphate-centered administrative system and its extension to the non-Muslim Middle Belt represented an audacious British intervention to overcome the burden of ethno-religious bifurcation that divided the caliphate zone and the Middle Belt and threatened the imposition of a uniform administrative system. The object was to bring the ethnic and religious communities of the Middle Belt culturally closer to the caliphate realm, so that caliphate-inspired indirect rule could be applied across the entire colonial region.

The implication of Northern Nigeria's divergence from the dominant paradigm of colonialism and ethnicity is weighty. As political and social crises involving ethnicity have proliferated in postcolonial Africa, scholarly discourses on them have returned intermittently to the idiom of colonial ethnicity. This perspective regained traction in the wake of the Rwanda genocide as scholars struggled to understand the roots of the horror. Historical explorations into the crisis devolved to Belgian colonial politicization and racialization of ethnic categories.[8] Subsequent ethnic conflicts across Africa have rekindled the appeal of this explanation. Scholars wrestling with the causal aspects of the crisis in Sudan have stressed the lingering utility of old animosities created by colonial obsessions with ethnic homelands and with the enforcement of a nativist ethos.[9]

This trope is illuminating, but it has limited explanatory power, for it fails to account for the prior existence of the markers and boundaries of difference, which exacerbated the political instrumentality of the "tribal" communities created by colonialists. It also, more crucially, fails to explain colonial histories and tensions of regions like Northern Nigeria, where colonial authorities frowned upon difference instead of reinforcing it, and improvised administratively to reduce, not increase, difference. In Northern Nigeria, ethnic—and religious—difference was sometimes highlighted, sensationalized, and codified in official colonial discourse but largely as a way to authorize its erasure in "backward" Middle Belt communities.

Ethnicity, Conflict, Memory

British colonial power did not accentuate ethnic and cultural differences everywhere in Britain's African empire. In Northern Nigeria the erasure of the cultural singularities of Middle Belt communities through the civilizational agency of Hausa-Fulani colonials engendered and foreshadowed tensions that were not rooted in colonial ethnicity per se but in the dueling struggles of Anglo-caliphate administrators and Middle Belt peoples. The former sought to extend caliphate cultural consciousness, and the latter were determined to retain their cultural and religious attributes.

The conflicts between caliphate-originated colonial agents and Middle Belt colonial subjects bear out my contention that conflicts caused by colonial ethnic erasure were as charged as those inspired by colonial reinforcement of previously permissive ethnic categories. In the colonial climate of dueling agendas, ethnicity and ethno-religious cultural symbols were targeted for both erasure and perpetuation, depending on the end-goal of colonialists. The relationship between colonialism and ethnicity was thus a much more complex dynamic than the argument about the colonial creation of African ethnicity allows.

Because of this somewhat peculiar history, the perennial postcolonial ethno-religious crises in the Nigerian Middle Belt call for a different set of reflections on the connections between colonization and postcolonial political ethnicity. These crises have many dimensions. There is a resource-access element to them, in which Fulani nomads battle for space and pasture with autochthonous farmers. There is also a political dimension. In this scenario, Hausa-Fulani migrants and settlers in the Middle Belt consider the Middle Belt their home and frown upon being denied political recognitions and rights there. Autochthonous Middle Belt ethnic groups, on the other hand, resent the assertive political demands of their "guests." They point to the unsettled national constitutional questions of indigene/settler dichotomies and to the unresolved issue of what role, if any, residency and migration should play in determining the rights and privileges of national citizenship. Then there is a clear law and order aspect to the crises as armed citizens latch on to these tensions as linchpins for criminal violence.

As complex as these crises are, however, they are united by the recurring idioms of memory and history. Middle Belt autochthons and Hausa-Fulani migrants alike invoke colonial and colonial-era texts to support their dueling claims. Middle Belt peoples recall historical injuries inflicted on their cultures, languages, and religions by Anglo-caliphate colonials seeking to extend their influence and power. Depending on the political context, this narrative of victimhood is conjoined to a coterminous script of heroic resistance against Anglo-caliphate colonial oppression. Hausa-Fulani elites, on the other hand, invoke colonial anthropological evidence that dramatizes Middle Belt cultural "backwardness" and Hausa-Fulani civilizational influence on peoples of the Middle Belt. In the ensuing debate, Hausa-Fulani communities in the Middle Belt posit the dominant political and economic position of caliphate subcolonials in Middle Belt colonial societies as a basis for postcolonial political claims and as an anchor for laying claims to the patrimony of some Middle Belt constituencies.

Whether made up on the go as needed or archived away as usable referents, both the Middle Belt narrative of noble, heroic victimhood and the Hausa-Fulani claim to political primacy and manifest destiny rest on an acknowledgment of the depth and profundity of the Hausa subcolonial project in Middle Belt communities. This acknowledgment works even in strategic denial. The two ethnoreligious formations differ only in their interpretations of this foundational factoid of Middle Belt history. Sometimes, Hausa-Fulani intellectuals and oral historians exaggerate and romanticize Hausa-Fulani hegemony in the Middle Belt. At other times, they deny that hegemony altogether or seek to sanitize it of negative attributes widely imputed to it among the Middle Belt's non-Muslim peoples. For Middle Belt intellectuals and memory makers, the narrative oscillates between an exaggerated and vilified Hausa-Fulani hegemonic imprint in the Middle Belt and a denial of that imprint. The frequency with which these dueling narratives have been summoned and acted upon in the last two decades has defined the intensity and frequency of violent ethno-religious clashes in the Middle Belt.

The original conditions featured in the narratives of postcolonial Hausa-Fulani and Middle Belt claim makers include the precolonial interactions between the two zones in the form of wars, slave raids, conquests, stalemates, and other confrontations. Indeed, the trope of jihad and resistance, often expressed in its most vulgar and provocative form, has found its way into charged political debates in the Middle Belt, especially as ethno-religious violence has escalated in recent years. These debates often elide the nuances of how precolonial caliphate adventures sometimes informed or constrained subsequent subcolonial initiatives in the Middle Belt. Instead debaters settle for the simplistic certainties of causality and teleology. Nonetheless, the fact that these connections are part of the range of references that combatants mobilize to legitimize their struggles calls for scholarly sensitivity to how imperial systems and struggles of the past complicate and animate postcolonial claim making and magnify the stakes in current political conflicts.

The notion that European colonization divided Africans in order to administer them is valid to the extent that European colonial authorities began their colonial projects from baselines of ethnic difference, which in turn informed the "production" of customs and traditions that sometimes ossified over time. Yet this theory of the growth of ethnic difference and the proliferation of politicized, even violent, ethnicity presents a bromide that is too neat and linear to account for the convoluted movement from colonial ethnic obsessions to tense ethnic interactions and relatively fixed ethnic identities in the postcolonial period. If European colonial authorities established the symbolic frames for ethnic politics, the self-conscious, rational deployment of ethno-religious difference and exclusivity by privileged African colonial elites and their postcolonial inheritors should also be recognized as a catalyst for postcolonial eruptions of identity conflicts.

Africans were not simply compelled by colonial practices to subscribe to created ethnic categories. For pragmatic purposes, many African colonial subjects had to proclaim and embrace ethnic identities that were far more rigid than they had been in precolonial times. However, already existing outlines and boundaries of ethnic communities made this transition easier and are cautions against the valorization of colonial causality in ethnicity. Yet other Africans, privileged, powerful, and ambitious colonials, strategically created their own myths and props of ethno-religious exclusivity that complemented colonial enunciation of difference.

Hausa-Fulani subcolonial personnel were skillful producers of ethnic scripts that not only reinforced British colonial narratives on ethnicity in Northern Nigeria but also marked and policed the boundaries of ethnic and religious exclusivity more vigorously. To describe these narratives and gestures as simply the outcomes of colonial "divide and rule" is to dismiss the subcolonial agency and creativity of Hausa-Fulani "civilizers" and to accord colonial discourse and praxis powers that they lacked in reality. More crucially, it is to ignore the immense seepage of precolonial hegemonic discourses emanating from the caliphate and its canons into early colonial assumptions on ethnicity, religion, civilization, culture, and domination in Northern Nigeria. Colonization in the Nigerian Middle Belt involved complex transactions between Middle Belt peoples and Hausa colonial agents. These negotiations produced and necessitated multiple claims of identity and exclusivity on both sides, claims that have sometimes endured into present struggles. However, for reasons that we have seen, the constructed self-images of Hausa-Fulani colonials entered the postcolonial political space with more power and capital.

Narratives of ethno-religious exclusivity and difference have no inherent teleological power to shape behavior or produce violent attempts at identity claims. Whether authored by Hausa-Fulani postcolonial intellectuals or by Middle Belt operatives, narratives of ethno-religious privilege do not empower or authorize political practices in a vacuum. Thus the development of Middle Belt political and social consciousness and its practical expression in organized anti-caliphate politics was not simply a reinvention of the old politics of resistance. Middle Belt politics, represented most visibly by the UMBC and its various mutations and predecessors, thrived in the context of new struggles for power and privilege in an emergent postcolonial state. Middle Belt political mobilization, as Matthew Hassan Kukah argues, is a product of opposition—opposition to perceived Anglo-caliphate conspiracy aimed supposedly at placing "the instruments of power in the hands" of caliphate-aligned groups.[10] The conventional Nigerian explanation that the British favored the Hausa-Fulani is a simplistic rendering of how Anglo-caliphate practices and Middle Belt anxieties commingled to produce memories and perceptions that have perpetuated the oppositional narratives of Middle Belt peoples to date.

The colonial state project and the subsequent emergence of the Nigerian postcolonial state raised the stakes for both hegemonic and oppositional politics in Northern Nigeria. The postcolonial Nigerian state emerged as a powerful site of privilege, where groups staked out organizational political territories for the purpose of securing power.[11] Middle Belt struggles for redistributive and symbolic benefits and Hausa-Fulani struggles to secure their privilege against the encroachment of Middle Belt elites found a new resonance in the combustive politics of the late-colonial and early-independence periods. This resonance of contending instrumental identity claims has since been revived intermittently as the Nigerian state has moved from one regime to another and from one set of political debates to another.

In the early post-independence period, the equalizing idiom of Western education, which Obafemi Awolowo, the political leader of Southwestern Nigeria in the colonial and immediate postcolonial period, used to effectively dissolve dichotomies and create solidarities across his region, proved inadequate to suppress Middle Belt agitation for recognition and access to Northern Nigeria's political and economic resources.

Ahmadu Bello, the most prominent political leader in late-colonial and postcolonial Northern Nigeria, failed to harness Western education to serve as political glue for his region for two reasons. First, a combination of British colonial policy and a preexisting system of Arabic and Ajami literacy created a postcolonial condition in the caliphate areas of Northern Nigeria in which Western education struggled for positive reception.[12] Second, in the Middle Belt, Western education proved to be a catalyst for an ameliorative, even revolutionary, politics anchored in anti-caliphate grievance. Another variable is that the postcolonial Nigerian state has operated largely as a feudal entity, which is lubricated by resources that are deployed sporadically and as needed to hold people together. This ad hoc management of the postcolonial Nigerian state and a corresponding failure to develop more enduring, less contentious signifiers of national unity have created conditions in which group self-help and intergroup conflicts serve as legitimate planks for pursuing power and resources.

Colonialism left far-reaching legacies in the Nigerian Middle Belt and in the larger Northern Nigerian region in which it was situated. Whatever their limitations then, discourses of neocolonialism and neocolonial instrumentality in postcolonial Africa are essentially correct in attributing most of the political, economic, and social upheavals in postcolonial Africa to the fallouts of the colonial encounter and to colonial structural bequests. To the extent that Northern Nigeria's postcolonial troubles are connected to the struggles, claims, and counterclaims unleashed by subcolonial rule earlier, the story of this book might fit into the classic frame of neocolonialism—that is, it illustrates the aftershocks of colonial arrangements produced for the colonizer's convenience and comfort, however important some Africans may have been in these systems. Nonetheless, for Northern Nigeria, the question of which of these legacies are the result of what British colonizers engineered and which are the outcomes or fallouts of the initiatives of Hausa subcolonials is still up in the air, and a faithful historical accounting has to consider African agencies and frames of reference beyond the neocolonial grid.

Certainly, many of the questions and claims that stoke today's debates and crises in the Middle Belt are articulated in terms that invoke the roles of Hausa-Fulani entities and the reactions and deprivations of Middle Belt subalterns. Doing scholarly justice to the legacies of colonization, at least in the Middle Belt, is thus not a simple matter of accounting for the damage done by European colonialists. Rather, to the extent that the initiatives of the British and their privileged Hausa-Fulani partners commingled to produce diverse outcomes, the ledger of colonial legacy in the Middle Belt will have to include the cultural, economic, and political disruptions of Hausa subcolonial rule, and the equally disruptive reactions of Middle Belt communities and groups.

The Hausa-Fulani and the non-Muslim communities of the Middle Belt were instrumental subalterns. Hausa instrumentality in colonial rule was largely proactive while Middle Belt peoples' initiatives were mostly reactive. In this sense, subalternity took different forms and was expressed differently by both groups.

This difference corresponds to the different sociopolitical stations in which colonial authorities placed the two groups. The homogenizing category of subalternity, often posited without differentiation and nuance, suggests that all subalterns were marginalized or privileged uniformly in the colonial system. The story told in this book calls for the unpacking of subalternity to reveal the hierarchies that existed within colonized communities as well as the differential colonial experiences and narratives of privilege and victimhood that these hierarchies activate. All subalterns were obviously not created equal. Some had more leverage and maneuvering room than others. Some happened to belong to ethno-religious communities that attracted the political and cultural patronage of colonial authorities and ended up occupying the highest positions that subaltern status allowed. Others had the misfortune of belonging to groups whose political and cultural heritage and histories colonial authorities devalued, an accident of identity that allowed colonial discourses and practices to consign them to marginal positions and to subordinate them to more privileged subaltern groups. But colonial marginality can be rearticulated as postcolonial victimhood, which confers political capital in certain contexts and in national political contests for finite resources and privileges, and for zero-sum rights.

Chronology

1400–1804 Hausa States flourish in the Sahel-Savannah regions; small kingdoms, proto states, and communities of decentralized peoples proliferate to the south of the Hausa States and Bornu

1804–1808 Fulani jihad (establishment of the Sokoto Caliphate)

1830–1888 Efforts to expand the caliphate's realm to areas beyond its southern frontiers

1808–1903 Sokoto Caliphate Rule

1900 Declaration of British Protectorate of Northern Nigeria by Frederick Lugard

1903 British defeat of the Sokoto Caliphate at the Battle of Burmi

1898–1908 British conquest of Northern Nigeria

1900–1960 Colonial period

1954 General elections in Nigeria (caliphate-dominated NPC wins in the North and forms a regional government)

1954 Beginning of self-rule in preparation for independence in northern region of Nigeria

1954 Ahmadu Bello, NPC leader, becomes leader of government business in Northern Nigeria

1955 Emergence of the United Middle Belt Congress (UMBC) through a merger of the Middle Zone League (MZL) and the Middle Belt Peoples Party (MBPP)

1959 General pre-independence parliamentary elections in Nigeria (NPC wins and retains power in Northern Nigeria)

October 1960 Independence from Great Britain (NPC assumes full, unsupervised political power in Northern Nigeria and, along with Nnamdi Azikiwe's NCNC, forms a national government at the center)

1963–1964 So-called Tiv riots (UMBC supporters attack NPC supporters, symbols, and Hausa-Fulani residents of Tivland)

1964 General parliamentary elections (NPC wins an election marred by violence and allegations of rigging)

Glossary

abakpa Idoma name for Hausa people and Hausa-speaking Muslims.

ajami Hausa language text written in modified Arabic script.

amana Trust, entente, agreement, friendship.

attah Paramount ruler of the Igala people.

ciroma or chiroma A prestigious royal title usually given to the son of emirs and some northern Nigerian paramount chiefs who are widely believed to be favored as possible successors.

dandoka or dan doka (pl. yan doka) Emirate/Native Authority policeman/law enforcer.

dar-al-Harb An Islamic term for the abode of unbelief, or areas outside an Islamic realm or state; usually a contiguous territory where Islam had not been established.

dar-al-Islam The abode of Islam, an Islamic state or territory.

dhimi In the context of the Fulani Jihad, a protected community of non-Muslims performing loyalty and paying tribute to the caliphate or its emirates in exchange for protection.

dillali (pl., dillalai) Emirate/colonial revenue official.

district A unit of colonial administration comprising several villages; usually headed by an African district head (DH) and supervised by a British assistant district officer (ADO).

division A unit of colonial administration comprising several districts; sometimes headed by a paramount chief, emir, or divisional chief and supervised by a British district officer (DO) or assistant resident (AR).

dogarai (sing. dogari) Colonial policemen attached to the Native Authority (NA) in Northern Nigeria. Inherited from the emirate system of the Sokoto Caliphate.

efu-onya A compound, descriptive word used by the Idoma people to refer to the Fulani jihad and the wars it spawned in the nineteenth century.

fatake Makeshift settlements usually associated with long-distance trade.

gaisuwa Literally greeting, but often denotes friendly exchanges of gifts between patrons and clients, which could be individuals or communities/states.

ganuwa Stone or mound rampart usually built around a town, city, or village as protection.

gbong gwom Paramount chief of the Berom people and supreme traditional ruler of Jos municipality.

igabo A council of title holders or chiefs advising the king (oche) in Idoma-speaking communities of the Benue Valley and the Nasarawa Basin.

jama'a (Fulani jama'a) Fulani masses, commoners, and cattle herders scattered across many settlements.

jekada (pl. jekadu) A messenger, go-between, or enforcer for a ruler among subordinate communities.

jizya Tributes paid by protected non-Muslim communities to the Muslim states under whose jurisdiction they find themselves.

kamberi Descriptive and quasi-derogatory name used among the Alago and Afo people of Lafia Division to refer to Hausa and Hausa-speaking Muslims.

khalifa (of Lala) From the Arabic "caliph," a title used by a few Fulani rulers in Adamawa/Fombina Emirate.

kofa Appointed emirate official who represented Zazzau's interest in vassal states and satellite emirates. The kofa oversaw the activities of Zazzau-appointed vassal officials, conveyed Zazzau's directives, and conducted fact-finding missions for the emir about the dealings of vassals with non-Muslim communities.

katuka (pl. katukai) An official emirate position that was later transformed (in Zazzau emirate) and used as a title for emirate officials given vassalage and fief-holding privileges among Southern Kaduna non-Muslim communities.

lamido Title analogous to "emir" held by the leader of the Adamawa/Fombina emirate of Northern Nigeria and Northern Cameroon.

madaki An important traditional title derived from emirate titular traditions. In emirate political tradition, the madaki is usually deputy to the emir, a trusted inner-circle aide, and often third in the hierarchy of precedence.

magaji An important title usually conferring the status of an overseer of a territory or an administrative unit.

magajin gari Town overseer.

maguzawa Non-Muslim Hausa people; descendants of pre-Islamic Hausa communities, traditionalists who held out against the wave of Islamic conversions that swept Hausaland over several centuries.

makama Royal title whose bearer is often charged with supervising lesser, subordinate chiefs such as district heads (hakimai) on behalf of the emir.

mallam(s) (also malam or pl., malamai) Literally teacher and/or scholar. Used in the context of colonial relations in Idoma Division to refer

to Muslim colonial officials: clerks, scribes, revenue officers, etc.

munci or munchi Derogatory Hausa name for Tiv people.

oche King or chief among the Idoma people.

province A large unit of colonial administration usually headed by a high-profile chief, emir, or a group of chiefs and emirs and supervised by a British resident.

pulaku Fulani code of conduct, behavior, and relations.

resident A senior British colonial official in charge of a province.

rumada Slave-worked farm where slaves also lived, usually located away from the city where the king or aristocratic master lived.

sarki (pl. sarakuna) Generic term for "king" in the Hausa language.

sojan gona Literally a farm raider. A phenomenon in which colonial agents and their impersonators (mostly dressed as colonial soldiers or policemen) raided farms and storerooms of people in remote colonial areas either under threat of arrest or simply because they believed that colonial service—or pretensions to it—inoculated them against resistance or retaliation. The term then morphed into a fairly generic description of any type of unauthorized revenue collection, swindle, deceptive extortion, or oppression in the name of the colonial state.

tor tiv Paramount traditional ruler of the Tiv.

tsafi Quasi-derogatory Hausa word for ancestral shrines and traditional religious observances, rituals, and objects.

wakili (pl. wakilai) A representative, caretaker, or guardian acting on behalf of the emir, usually among non-Muslim communities.

Notes

Introduction

1. Jane Burbank and Frederick Cooper, *Empires in World History: Power and the Politics of Difference* (Princeton, N.J.: Princeton University Press, 2010).

2. Adiele Afigbo, *The Warrant Chief: Indirect Rule in Southeastern Nigeria* (London: Longman, 1972); Mahmood Mamdani, *Citizen and Subject: Contemporary Africa and the Legacy of Late Colonialism* (Princeton, N.J.: Princeton University Press, 1996).

3. Mamdani, *Citizen and Subject*.

4. Examples of influential works that assume a default to indirect rule at the moment of conquest include Mamdani's *Citizen and Subject*; Afigbo's *Warrant Chiefs*; and Jason C. Myers's *Indirect Rule in South Africa: Tradition, Modernity, and the Costuming of Political Power* (Rochester, N.Y.: University of Rochester Press, 2008).

5. Burbank and Cooper, *Empires in World History*, 8.

6. Ibid., 14.

7. Achille Mbembe, *On the Postcolony* (Berkeley: University of California Press, 2001), 26, 31.

8. See Patrick Chabal and Jean-Pascal Deloz, *Disorder Works: Disorder as Political Instrument* (Bloomington: Indiana University Press, 1999).

9. Charles Lindsay Temple, *Native Races and Their Rulers: Sketches and Studies of Official Life and Administrative Problems in Nigeria* (Cape Town: Argus, 1918), chap. 1. One could argue that Temple supplied the racial and civilizational classifications that constituted the bedrock of Hausa-Fulani subcolonialism, for it was he who enunciated the history of Northern Nigeria in terms of civilized, light-skinned migrants from northeast Africa displacing, and ultimately dominating, so-called negroid autochthons.

10. Frederick Lugard, *The Dual Mandate in British Tropical Africa* (Hamden, Conn.: Archon Books, 1965); Frederick Lugard, *Political Memoranda, Revision of Instructions to Political Officers on Subjects Chiefly Political and Administrative 1913–1918* (London: Frank Cass, 1970); Tony Kaye, "Civilizing (the) Chiefs: Islam and Indirect Rule in the Northern Territories of the Gold Coast Colony" (MA Thesis, University of Saskatchewan, 2011); Marion Johnson, *Salaga Papers* (Legon: Institute of African Studies, University of Ghana, 1965).

11. Catherine Hall, *Civilizing Subjects: Metropole and Colony in the English Imagination, 1830–1867* (Chicago: University of Chicago Press, 2002), 18.

12. P. Daley, "Ethnicity and Political Violence in Africa: The Challenges to the Burundi State," *Political Geography* 25 (n.d.): 657–679; Bruce Berman, "Ethnicity, Patronage and the African State: The Politics of Uncivil Nationalism," *African Affairs* 97, no. 388 (1998): 305–341.

13. Okwudiba Nnoli, ed., *Ethnic Conflicts in Africa* (Dakar, Senegal: Codesria Book Series, 2000); Okwudiba Nnoli, *Ethnicity and Development in Nigeria* (Aldershot, England: Avebury, 1995); Jean Marie Allman, *The Quills of the Porcupine: Asante Nationalism in an Emergent Ghana* (Madison: University of Wisconsin Press, 1993).

14. Mahmood Mamdani, *When Victims Become Killers: Colonialism, Nativism, and the Genocide in Rwanda* (Princeton N.J.: Princeton University Press, 2001).

15. Ibid., Introduction and ch. 1.

16. James S. Coleman, *Nigeria: Background to Nationalism* (Berkeley: University of California Press, 1958), 194.

17. Emmy Godwin Irobi, "Ethnic Conflict Management in Africa: A Comparative Case Study of Nigeria and South Africa," *Beyond Intractability*, 2005, http://www.beyondintracta bility.org/casestudy/irobi-ethnic.

18. Thomas J. Davis and Azubike Kalu-Nwiwu, "Education, Ethnicity and National Integration in the History of Nigeria: Continuing Problems of Africa's Colonial Legacy," *Journal of Negro History* 86, no. 1 (January 1, 2001): 1–11.

19. Lloyd A. Fallers, *Bantu Bureaucracy: A Century of Political Evolution Among the Basoga of Uganda* (Chicago: University of Chicago Press, 1965); A. D. Roberts, "The Sub-Imperialism of the Baganda," *Journal of African History* 3, no. 3 (January 1, 1962): 435–450; Twaddle, *Kakungulu and the Creation of Uganda*.

20. Mamdani, *Citizen and Subject*, 39, 41.

21. Simon Gikandi, *Maps of Englishness: Writing Identity in the Culture of Colonialism* (New York: Columbia University Press, 1996), 34–36.

22. Mamdani, *Citizen and Subject*, 43.

23. The term "middle figures" is used by Nancy Hunt to capture the functional in-between-ness of African colonial brokers. See Nancy Rose Hunt, *A Colonial Lexicon of Birth Ritual, Medicalization, and Mobility in the Congo* (Durham, N.C.: Duke University Press, 1999); Quotation from Benjamin Nicholas Lawrance, Emily Osborne, and Richard Roberts, eds., *Intermediaries, Interpreters, and Clerks: African Employees in the Making of Colonial Africa* (Madison: University of Wisconsin Press, 2006), 4.

24. These anxieties, familiar to historians of colonial Africa, turn on the declared and undeclared imperative of casting African colonial actors and subjects as resisters or collaborators and European colonizers as omniscient hegemons determining the actions and agendas of Africans. For illuminating analyses of the constraints and anxieties of nationalist historiography, see Frederick Cooper, "Conflict and Connections: Rethinking Colonial African History," *American Historical Review* 99, no. 5 (1994): 1516–1545; Achille Mbembe, "African Modes of Self-Writing," *Public Culture* 14, no. 1 (2002): 239–273; Toyin Falola, *Nationalism and African Intellectuals* (Rochester, N.Y.: University of Rochester Press, 2001).

25. Amadou Hampate Ba, *The Fortunes of Wangrin* (Bloomington: Indiana University Press, 1999); Philip Afeadie, *Brokering Colonial Rule: Political Agents in Northern Nigeria, 1886–1914* (Saarbrücken: VDM Verlag Dr. Müller, 2008); Lawrance, Osborne, and Roberts, *Intermediaries, Interpreters, and Clerks: African Employees in the Making of Colonial Africa;* Emily Lynn Osborn, "'Circle of Iron': African Colonial Employees and the Interpretation of Colonial Rule in French West Africa," *Journal of African History* 44, no. 1 (January 1, 2003): 29–50; Ralph Austen, "Colonialism from the Middle: African Clerks as Historical Actors and Discursive Subjects," *History in Africa* 38 (2011): 21–33; Ralph Austen, "Who Was Wangrin and Why Does it Matter?" *Mande Studies* 9 (1997): 149–164; Tamba E. M'bayo, "African Interpreters, Mediation, and the Production of Knowledge in Colonial Senegal: the Low Land Middle Senegal Valley, ca. 1850s to ca. 1920s" (PhD dissertation, Michigan State University, 2009); Femi Kolapo and Kwabena Akurang-Parry, eds., *African Agency and European Colonialism: Latitudes of Negotiation* (Lanham, Md.: University Press of America, 2007); Colin Walter Newbury, *Patrons, Clients, and Empire: Chieftaincy and Over-Rule in Asia, Africa, and the Pacific* (Oxford: Oxford University Press, 2003); Afeadie, *Brokering Colonial Rule;* Peter K. Tibenderana, "British Administration and the Decline of the Patronage-Clientage System in Northwestern Nigeria, 1900–1934," *African Studies Review* 32, no. 1 (April 1, 1989): 71–95.

26. John Edward Philips, *Spurious Arabic: Hausa and Colonial Nigeria* (Madison: University of Wisconsin, 2000).

27. Michael Twaddle, *Kakungulu and the Creation of Uganda, 1868–1928* (Athens: Ohio University Press, 1993), 225–234.

28. T. O. Beidelman, *The Culture of Colonialism: The Cultural Subjection of the Ukaguru* (Bloomington: Indiana University Press, 2012). This quote is from the book's back cover blurb.

29. Timothy Mitchell, *Rule of Experts: Egypt, Techno-Politics, Modernity* (Berkeley: University of California Press, 2002).

30. Jonathon Glassman, "Sorting out the Tribes: The Creation of Racial Identities in Colonial Zanzibar's Newspaper Wars," *Journal of African History* 41, no. 3 (January 1, 2000): 395–428.

31. Anthony Clayton, *The Zanzibar Revolution and Its Aftermath* (Hamden, Conn.: Archon Books, 1981), 2.

32. Jonathon Glassman has developed his argument about locally embedded, if dynamic, racial ideas and claims about racial difference as political capital into a full-fledged book. See Jonathon Glassman, War of Words, War of Stones: Racial Thought and Violence in Zanzibar (Bloomington: Indiana University Press, 2011).

33. See, for instance, Bruce Hall, A History of Race in Muslim West Africa 1600–1960 (Cambridge: Cambridge University Press, 2011).

34. Roberts, "The Sub-Imperialism of the Baganda."

35. For a synthetic exploration of the Indian princely states and the princes who oversaw them under British supervision, see Barbara Ramusack, *The Indian Princes and Their States* (Cambridge: Cambridge University Press, 2004). See also Karen Leonard, "Reassessing Indirect Rule in Hyderabad: Rule, Rulers, or Sons-in-Laws of the State," *Modern Asian Studies* 37, no. 2 (2003): 363–379.

36. Thomas Metcalf, *Ideologies of the Raj* (Cambridge: Cambridge University Press, 1997).

37. Myles Osborn, "The Kamba and Mau Mau: Ethnicity, Development, and Chiefship, 1952–1960," *International Journal of African Historical Studies* 43, no. 1 (2010): 63–87.

38. Sam C. Ukpabi, *The Origins of the Nigerian Army: A History of the West African Frontier Force, 1897–1914* (Zaria, Nigeria: Gaskiya, 1987); David Killingray, "Imagined Martial Communities: Recruiting for the Military and Police in Colonial Ghana, 1860–1960," in *Ethnicity in Ghana: The Limits of Invention,* ed. Carola Lentz and Paul Nugent (New York: Palgrave Macmillan, 2000); Johnson, *Salaga Papers.*

39. Osborn, "The Kamba and Mau Mau."

40. The term "becoming Hausa" was coined by Frank Salamone in an article of the same title, in which he argued that Hausa identity became a more inclusive and allowable category once Islam became its most defining attribute, and that the Sokoto jihad and the utility of Hausa as an idiom of colonial privilege in the twentieth century gave the identity more currency, making "becoming Hausa" even more attractive to Muslims who were not ethnically Hausa. See Frank Salamone, "Becoming Hausa: Ethnic Identity Change and its Implications for the Study of Ethnic Pluralism and Stratification," *Africa: Journal of the International African Institute* 45, no. 4 (1975): 410–424. See also Frank A. Salamone, *The Hausa of Nigeria* (Lanham, Md.: University Press of America, 2010).

41. See Ukpabi, *The Origins of the Nigerian Army; David Killingray, "Guarding the Extending Frontier: Policing the Gold Coast, 1865–1913," in Policing the Empire: Government, Authority, and Control, 1830–1940,* ed. David M. Anderson and David Killingray (Manchester: Manchester University Press, 1991), 106–125; see also the introduction to that volume: "Consent, Coercion and Colonial Control: Policing the Empire, 1830–1940," by David Anderson and David Killingray.

42. Ibid.

43. Twaddle, *Kakungulu and the Creation of Uganda,* 226.

44. For Ghana, see Sean Hawkins, *Writing and Colonialism in Northern Ghana: The Encounter between the LoDagaa and "the World on Paper"* (Toronto: University of Toronto Press, 2002), 108–109.

45. Kaye, "Civilizing (the) Chiefs." See also Carola Lentz, *Ethnicity and the Making of History in Northern Ghana* (Edinburgh: Edinburgh University Press, 2006); Hawkins, *Writing and Colonialism in Northern Ghana,* introduction and chap. 3.

1. The Hausa-Caliphate Imaginary and Ideological Foundations of Proxy Colonialism

1. The Hausa-caliphate imaginary is, properly speaking, a Hausa-Fulani caliphate imaginary. Starting from the late-eighteenth century when commingling and intermarriage between the Hausa and the Fulani increased, a new ethnic category effectively emerged. This category is linguistically Hausa, but it is a hybrid of Fulani and Hausa culture. After the Othman bin Fodio Islamic jihad, the mutual assimilation of the Hausa and Fulani accelerated. Presently, apart from small pockets of ethnic Fulani in the Adamawa area, smaller pockets of transhumant Fulani all over Northern Nigeria, and the Maguzawa non-Muslim Hausa in the northwestern states of modern Nigeria, much of the population of the pre-jihad territory of Hausaland is made up of people who can be called Hausa-Fulani. Indeed, this is the term in use in contemporary Nigerian political and ethnic taxonomies and discussions.

2. Several competing definitions of the Middle Belt abound, especially since the entity so designated has a geographically fluid existence. In general it is agreed that a conservative territorial estimation of the Middle Belt (as opposed to the idea of a Greater Middle Belt, which is a largely political construct appropriating all non-Hausa-Fulani and non-Kanuri peoples of Northern Nigeria) comprises Benue, Plateau, Kwara, Kogi, Southern Kaduna, FCT, parts of Niger, Adamawa, and Taraba states. Even this territorial definition is imperfect, since in all these states, there are significant numbers of Muslim non-Hausa as well Muslim Hausa peoples, who may or may not be captured by specific delineations of the Middle Belt. Similarly, "Muslim Hausa" states like Kebbi, Gombe, Bauchi, Borno, and even Katsina and Kano contain pockets of non-Hausa, non-Muslim populations that may qualify as Middle Belters in the political sense of the word, since Middle Belt identity is often politically constructed against Hausa-Fulani, Sokoto Caliphate Muslim identity. There were and still are non-Hausa, non-Muslim peoples in the Jos Plateau, parts of Bauchi, Taraba, Adamawa, and Southern Borno who historically spoke Hausa as second or third language, and these non-caliphate people who did/do not share in Hausa ethnicity by either inheritance or assimilation were also subjected to the British policy of subordination through Muslim rule. The non-Hausa-speaking, non-Muslim sector of Northern Nigeria, on the other hand, is a narrower descriptive category that consists of districts in the former Benue, Ilorin, and Kabba Provinces, whose populations, for the most part, did not speak Hausa at all. For the purpose of my analysis here, the Middle Belt refers to the predominantly non-Muslim, non-Hausa areas of Southern Kaduna, Plateau, Nasarawa, Adamawa, and Benue. For no reason other than to keep the project manageable, I excluded the Kogi sector, another predominantly non-Muslim and non-caliphate zone.

3. Hawkins, *Writing and Colonialism in Northern Ghana,* 10.

4. Ali Al'Amin Mazrui and Ali A. Mazrui, *The Power of Babel: Language and Governance in the African Experience* (Oxford: James Currey, 1998).

5. For the scope of Hausa as a linguistic category, and for a discussion of its origins and spread in West Africa and in Northern Nigeria, see Philips, *Spurious Arabic;* for a history of the Hausa ethnic group and of the spread of Hausa identity and influence in Nigeria and West Africa, see Mahdi Adamu, *The Hausa Factor in West African History* (Zaria, Nigeria: Ahmadu Bello University Press, 1978).

6. For instance, see M. Hiskett, "Kitab Al-farq: 'A Work on the Habe Kingdoms Attributed to Uthman dan Fodio,'" *Bulletin of the School of Oriental and African Studies* 23, no. 3 (1960): 558–579; see also Bivar, "The Wathiqat Ahl Al-Sudan: A Manifesto of the Fulani Jihad," *Journal of African History* 2, no. 2 (1961): 235–243. This document, a chancery letter written by Othman bin Fodio himself to the Fulani flagbearer of the jihad in the Daura area, uses "Sudan" and "Hausa States" interchangeably to refer to the geographical area we now call Hausaland.

7. Edward John Arnett, *The Rise of the Sokoto Fulani: Being a Paraphrase and in Some Parts a Translation of the Infaku'l Maisuri of Sultan Mohammed Bello* (London: School of Oriental and African Studies, 1922) hereafter *Infakul Maisuri*; see also Hugh Clapperton, *Hugh Clapperton into the Interior of Africa: Records of the Second Expedition, 1825–1827*, ed. Jamie Bruce-Lockhart and Paul E. Lovejoy (Leiden: Brill, 2005), which contains Mohammed Bello's cartographic and discursive efforts to delineate a Hausa-Islamic political and geographic entity and its frontiers and others.

8. Philips, *Spurious Arabic*, v.

9. See for instance the *Infakul Maisuri* of Mohammed Bello. His own testimonies and the many earlier texts that he quotes and consults attest to this history of ethnic Hausa-Fulani intermingling in the Western Sudan.

10. The maguzawa can still be found in small communities in Kano, Jigawa, and Katsina States of northwestern Nigeria. Their unique, non-Islamic culture has come under sustained assault from the governments of these states in recent years; they are a constant target of Islamization campaigns, which have converted many of them to Islam, especially many of their young ones, who see Islamization as an access to urban life and to socioeconomic opportunities that would otherwise be closed to them. This author has observed these Islamization campaigns. Islamization has also eroded many aspects of the maguzawa's culture. The adoption of the Sharia criminal legal code in many Northern Nigerian states in the last seven years has had a devastating effect on their way of life as several aspects of their culture, including the brewing of grain beer, were deemed un-Islamic and banned.

11. "Maguzawa" was a term used to denote non-Muslim Hausa people who submitted to the authority of the Sokoto Caliphate and paid tribute in exchange for being allowed to keep their identity and culture. The word itself is a Hausa version of *majus* or *magian*, one of the peoples of the book that, according to the ethics of jihad in Islamic doctrine, could be accorded protection in an Islamic state in exchange for loyalty and the jizya. See Murray Last, *The Sokoto Caliphate* (London: Longman, 1967), 67n18. The term "majus" was also used by the jihad leaders to refer to the Zamfarawa (the people of Zamfara), before the jihad because they were seen as mostly non-Muslims as opposed to the people of other Hausa states who were constructed as nominal Muslims. See Mohammed Tukur b. Muhammad, *Qira al-ahibba* (1908), cited in Last, *The Sokoto Caliphate*, 67.

12. See Anne Haour and Benedetta Rossi, eds., Being and Becoming Hausa: Interdisciplinary Perspectives (Leiden and Boston: Brill, 2010).

13. See Frank A. Salamone, "Becoming Hausa: Ethnic Identity Change and Its Implications for the Study of Ethnic Pluralism and Stratification," *Africa: Journal of the International African Institute* 45, no. 4 (January 1, 1975): 410–424; see also Michael Garfield Smith, *The Affairs of Daura* (Berkeley: University of California Press, 1978); Abner Cohen, *Custom and Politics in Urban Africa: A Study of Hausa Migrants in Yoruba Towns*, 2nd ed. (London: Routledge, 2004).

14. Steven Pierce, *Farmers and the State in Colonial Kano: Land Tenure and the Legal Imagination* (Bloomington: Indiana University Press, 2005), 27.

15. Salamone, "Becoming Hausa," *The Hausa of Nigeria*, chaps. 1 and 4.

16. Alvin Magid, *Men in the Middle: Leadership and Role Conflict in a Nigerian Society* (New York: Africana Publishing, 1976), 45.

17. Richard Fardon, *Raiders and Refugees: Trends in Chamba Political Development, 1750–1950* (Washington, D.C.: Smithsonian Institution Press, 1988), 147.

18. Obaro Ikime, *The Fall of Nigeria: The British Conquest* (London: Heinemann, 1977).

19. Arnett, *Infaku'l Maisuri*. Mohammed Bello's narrative on the expeditions on the Doma-Keana axis is a rather triumphalist rendering of the encounters between the people of this region and the Fulani raiders in that it masks the stalemated outcome of the wars. The wars produced uneasy stalemates and fluid triumphs for Keffi, the Zazzau-controlled raiding sub-emirate in the area. The stalemates nonetheless resulted in the partial adoption of Islam and Hausa-Fulani culture as a strategy of survival and accommodation in small pockets.

20. This is an Arabic-derived Hausa term that denotes trust but that, according to John Nengel, was enunciated into a political doctrine that allowed expanding Muslim polities and migrants from different parts of the Sokoto Caliphate to coexist peacefully with the non-Muslim peoples of the Central Nigerian Highlands. The terms of amana included stipulated tributes paid to the neighboring Muslim polities of Bauchi and Zazzau by the non-Muslim states and mini-states on the southern frontiers of the caliphate as well as the reciprocal offer of protection from the emirates and sub-emirates. See John G. Nengel, *Precolonial African Intergroup Relations in the Kauru and Pengana Polities of the Central Nigerian Highlands 1800–1900* (Frankfurt: Peter Lang, 1999). Although the works of Professor Ibrahim James cast some doubt on the extent to which the amana system was the normative relational model on the non-Muslim southern frontier of the caliphate, there is evidence to suggest that amana did hold informally and sporadically in some areas and over certain periods.

21. I owe this point to Professor Murray Last, who drew my attention to it in a personal conversation. Also see Professor Last's essay "The Idea of 'Frontier' in the Nigerian Context," presented at the conference on Political Crisis on West Africa's Islamic Frontier, SAOS London, 1982.

22. M. H. Kukah, *Religion, Politics and Power in Northern Nigeria* (Ibadan, Nigeria: Spectrum Books, 1993), 2.

23. Ibrahim James, *Studies in the History, Politics, and Cultures of Southern Kaduna Peoples Groups* (Jos, Nigeria: Crest, 1997), 17.

24. See Heather Streets-Salter, *Martial Races: The Military, Race and Masculinity in British Imperial Culture, 1857–1914* (Manchester: Manchester University Press, 2004); Pradeep Barua, "Inventing Race: The British and India's Martial Races," *Historian: Journal of History* 58 (1995): 107–116; Joan Leopold, "British Applications of the Aryan Theory of Race to India, 1850–1870," *English Historical Review* 89, no. 352 (July 1, 1974): 578–603.

25. Arnett, *Infaku'l Maisuri*, 2.

26. Ibid.

27. Far from being controlled formally or informally by the caliphate zone, the Idah court was in fact building and consolidating its control over the Nsukka Igbo and other peoples within its vicinity. In fact, as Shelton argues, the Igala were, like the Sokoto Caliphate, an imperial power in their own right. See Austin J. Shelton, *The Igbo-Igala Borderland: Religion and Social Control in Indigenous African Colonialism* (Albany: State University of New York Press, 1971).

28. E. W. Bovill, *The Niger Explored* (London: Oxford University Press, 1968), 132–134.

29. Clapperton, *Hugh Clapperton into the Interior of Africa*.

30. Arnette, *Infaku'l Maisuri*, introduction (i).

31. See Clapperton, *Hugh Clapperton into the Interior of Africa*, appendixes v–vi, 485–486, 493. Much information came from Mohammed Bello himself or members of his household. The map of the caliphate's Hausa core given to Clapperton and published in his journal, for instance, came from one Musa, a member of Mohammed Bello's household.

32. Ibid., appendix v, 485, 491, 493.

33. Ibid., 515. See 488–511 for the maps used by Clapperton to represent the Sokoto Caliphate, its many emirates, trade routes, and Borno.

34. Ibid., 396, 487.

35. Ibid., appendix 5: "Contemporary Maps."

36. William Balfour Baikie, *Narrative of an Exploring Voyage up the Rivers Kwóra and Bínue (Commonly Known as the Niger and Tsádda) in 1854* (London: J. Murray, 1856), 105.

37. The word "munci" or "munchi" means "We have eaten [the cattle]." It is a Hausa expression that the Tiv allegedly used to explain to the Hausa-speaking Fulani pastoralists that their cattle had been taken. The etymology of the munci label is a poignant metaphor for the troubled and tense encounters that the Hausa-Fulani presence in the Tiv area produced.

38. William Balfour Baikie, "Inclosure 1 No. 74 (General Rules for Dealing with the Natives along the River Niger) Rule 14," in *Accounts and Papers of the House of Commons*, vol. 43 (London: Harrison and Sons, 1863), 91.

39. Baikie, *Narrative of an Exploring Voyage*, 393.

40. Ibid.

41. For a full account of Clapperton's two-phase travels in the Sokoto Caliphate, see his published journal, *Journal of a Second Expedition into the Interior of Africa from the Bight of Benin to Soccatoo* (Philadelphia: Carey, Lea and Carey, 1829). Clapperton made his first journey to the Hausa States, the core of the Sokoto Caliphate, in 1822–1825. He met with the Shehu, with whom he exchanged gifts and signed "a treaty of trade and friendship." He died on his second expedition, which he described as a quest to discover the mouth of the Niger River. His death occurred near Sokoto on April 13, 1827, before he could accomplish this mission.

42. See Heinrich Barth, *Travels and Discoveries in North and Central Africa: Being a Journal of an Expedition Undertaken under the Auspices of H.B.M.'s Government in the Years 1849–1855.* (London, 1857).

43. For a full account of the Lander brothers' travels, see their published journal *Journal of an Expedition to Explore the Course and Termination of the Niger, with a Narrative of a Voyage Down That River to Its Termination* (New York: J. & J. Harper, 1832).

44. E. P. T. Crampton, *Christianity in Northern Nigeria* (London: Macmillan Publishing Company, 1975), 53.

45. Kukah, *Religion, Politics and Power in Northern Nigeria*, 3.

46. For a comprehensive discussion of the process of British declaration of imperial intent and subsequent conquests in Northern Nigeria, see Ikime, *The Fall of Nigeria*; and R. A. Adeleye, *Power and Diplomacy in Northern Nigeria, 1804–1906: The Sokoto Caliphate and Its Enemies* (New York: Humanities Press, 1971).

47. Hausa traders were famed regional commercial brokers and experts at arbitrage. Along with the Wangara of Songhai/Mali, they constituted the bulk of West Africa's trading diasporas.

48. The evidence for this is the debate over the adoption of the Hausa language in the Northern Nigerian colonial bureaucracy, a debate that congealed into two camps, those favoring the use of a Romanized script and those inclined to the use of an Ajami (or Hausa Arabic) script. As the archive of the debate shows, Middle Belt peoples were wary of Ajami because they considered it a subtle endorsement of Arabic and Islam, both of them understood as symbols of caliphal supremacy and overrule over the non-Muslim peoples in the region. See Philips, *Spurious Arabic*.

49. Lugard, *The Dual Mandate in British Tropical Africa*, 193–194.

50. Ibid., 196.

51. Ibid., 198.

52. For a discussion of the origins and meanings of the Hamitic Hypothesis, see Edith R. Sanders, "The Hamitic Hypothesis; Its Origin and Functions in Time Perspective," *Journal of African History* 10, no. 4 (January 1, 1969): 521–532.

53. Jean-Loup Amselle, *Mestizo Logics: Anthropology of Identity in Africa and Elsewhere*, trans. Claudia Royal (Stanford, Calif.: Stanford University Press, 1994), chap. 3.

54. Alamin A. Mazrui, *Swahili beyond the Boundaries: Literature, Language, and Identity* (Athens: Ohio University Press, 2007), 1–2.

55. See James Rhodes Wilson-Haffenden, *The Red Men of Nigeria: An Account of a Lengthy Residence among the Fulani or "Red Men," and Other Pagan Tribes of Central Nigeria, with a Description of Their Head-Hunting, Pastoral and Other Customs, Habits and Religion*, 1st ed. (London: Cass, 1967); Charles Kingsley Meek, *Tribal Studies in Northern Nigeria* (London: Kegan Paul, Trench, Trubner, 1931); A. H. M. Kirk-Greene, ed., *Gazetteers of the Northern Provinces of Nigeria*, vol. 1: *The Hausa Emirates* (London: F. Cass, 1972); Lugard, *The Dual Mandate in British Tropical Africa*, 109.

56. Lugard, *The Dual Mandate in British Tropical Africa*, 204.

57. Lugard, *The Dual Mandate in British Tropical Africa*.

58. Ibid., 210.

59. Ibid., 214.

60. Ibid., 210.

61. Ibid., 214.

62. This contention is borne out by the influential arguments advanced by Charles Temple, a pioneer British resident in Northern Nigeria. See Temple, *Native Races and Their Rulers*. Temple's ideas about caliphate superiority and the utility of caliphate ideas and personnel lack the nuance of Lugard's prescriptions.

63. Lugard, *The Dual Mandate in British Tropical Africa*, 220.

64. Quoted in ibid.

65. Ibid.

66. Charles Kingsley Meek, *A Sudanese Kingdom: An Ethnographical Study of the Jukua-Speaking Peoples of Nigeria* (London: Kegan Paul, Trench, Trubner, 1931). C. K. Meek was the anthropological officer of the Northern Nigerian Colonial Administration in the late 1920s and wrote for the British much of the ethnological notes on the ethnic groups of Northern Nigeria. By 1931, he had risen to the position of anthropological officer, Administrative Service, Nigeria. One of Meek's assistants, Bitemya Sambo Garbosa II, wrote a history of the Chamba of the Benue based on research he conducted in Donga in 1927. It was published in two volumes as *Labarun Chambawa da Al' Amurransa* and *Salsalar Sarakunen Donga*. The two were published privately in about 1960 and were microfilmed by the University of Ibadan. For more bibliographic information on this, see Fardon, *Raiders and Refugees*, 78, 345.

67. Margery Perham, *Native Administration in Nigeria* (London: Oxford University Press, 1962), 147.

68. Ibid., 145.

69. Margery Perham, *Lugard: The Years of Authority, 1898–1945: The Second Part of the Life of Frederick Dealtry Lugard, Later Lord Lugard of Abinger.* (London: Collins, 1960), 148–149.

70. Flora L. Shaw, *A Tropical Dependency; an Outline of the Ancient History of the Western Soudan with an Account of the Modern Settlement of Northern Nigeria* (London: J. Nisbet, 1905), 83–84, 454.

71. Ibid.

72. Temple, *Native Races and Their Rulers*, chap. 1.

73. Philip Serge Zachernuk, "Of Origins and Colonial Order: Southern Nigerian Historians and the 'Hamitic Hypothesis,' C. 1870–1970," *Journal of African History* 35, no. 3 (1994): 427–455, 443.

74. Ibid.

2. Zazzau and Southern Kaduna in Precolonial and Colonial Times

1. Meek, *Tribal Studies in Northern Nigeria*, 76.

2. Ibid.

3. James, *Studies in the History, Politics and Cultures of Southern Kaduna Peoples Groups*, 115.

4. See Adamu, *The Hausa Factor in West African History*.

5. Paul Staudinger, *In the Heart of the Hausa States*, trans. Johanna Moody (Athens: Ohio University Press, 1990), 78. Originally published in Berlin in 1889.

6. James, *Studies in the History, Politics, and Cultures of Southern Kaduna Peoples Groups*, 123.

7. See James C. Scott, *The Art of Not Being Governed: An Anarchist History of Upland Southeast Asia* (New Haven, Conn.: Yale University Press, 2009).

8. J. A. Ballard, "'Pagan Administration' and Political Development in Northern Nigeria," *Savanna* 1, no. 1 (1972): 1–14.

9. Chunun Logams, "The Middle Belt Movement in Nigerian Political Development: A Case Study of Political Identity, 1949–1967" (PhD dissertation, University of Keele, 1985), 82–87.

10. Michael Garfield Smith, *Government in Zazzau, 1800–1950* (Oxford: International African Institute and Oxford University Press, 1960), 3.

11. Nengel, *Precolonial African Intergroup Relations*, 92.

12. Ibid., 88.

13. Ibid., 88–90; Mailafiya Aruwa Filaba and Lawrence A. Gojeh, *Koro and Gbagyi Subgroup Relations in Central Nigeria* (Ethiopia: Self-published, 2008).

14. This is Ibrahim James's demarcation, which relies on Smith's dating of the official beginning of Zazzau's indirect control of Southern Kaduna polities. It marked the formal appointment of titular heads, *katukai* (sing. *katuka*) to supervise the affairs of some Southern Kaduna peoples.

15. Nengel, *Precolonial African Intergroup Relations*, 84–85.

16. J. C. Sciortino, *Notes on Nasarawa Province Nigeria* (London: Waterlow and Sons, 1920), in Kirk-Greene, *Gazetteers of the Northern Provinces of Nigeria*, vol. 3: *The Central Kingdoms (Kontagora, Nasarawa, Nupe, Ilorin)*, 5.

17. Lawrence A. Gojeh, *The History of Origin and Tradition of the Koro People* (Kaduna, Nigeria: Tereship Publishers, 1998), 25–26.

18. James, *Studies in the History, Politics, and Cultures of Southern Kaduna Peoples Groups*, 124.

19. Meek, *Tribal Studies in Northern Nigeria*, 78.

20. Smith, *Government in Zazzau, 1800–1950*, 174.

21. Meek, *Tribal Studies in Northern Nigeria*, 78.

22. Ibid.

23. Ballard, "'Pagan Administration' and Political Development in Northern Nigeria."

24. Interview with Magaji Galadima, Agwom Adara, on June 5, 2009, in Kachia; Logams, "The Middle Belt Movement in Nigerian Political Development," 88.

25. Filaba and Gojeh, *Koro and Gbagyi Subgroup Relations in Central Nigeria*, 43.

26. NAK/SNP10, Zaria Province Annual Report 1913. The Pitti developed an elaborate ritual of mounted warriorhood that continued to awe Zazzau and British colonialists as late as 1913.

27. Ibid.

28. For contemporary evidence of this, see Clapperton, *Hugh Clapperton into the Interior of Africa;* and Barth, *Travels and Discoveries in North and Central Africa.*

29. Staudinger, *In the Heart of the Hausa States,* 2:26.

30. Ibid., 1:181.

31. Mary Bull, "Indirect Rule in Northern Nigeria: 1906–1911," in *Essays in Imperial Government* (Oxford: Basil Blackwell, 1963), 79.

32. Logams, "The Middle Belt Movement in Nigerian Political Development," 86.

33. Interview with Magaji Galadima.

34. James, *Studies in the History, Politics, and Cultures of Southern Kaduna Peoples Groups,* 199.

35. NAK/SNP 10, Zaria Province Annual Report 1913, 20.

36. Last, "The Idea of 'Frontier' in the Nigerian Context."

37. Interview with Magaji Galadima, Agom Adara. Because of the recent nature of these contacts between captives and their relatives in the Adara-Kachia frontier, I suspect—and Chief Galadima claims—that this practice of nonviolent, intimidation-based "slave removal" continued in the early years of the British colonial administration, occurring beneath the supervisory vigilance of the few British officials stationed in Zaria Province.

38. Ibid.

39. NAK/SNP 10 95P/1919.

40. For instance, as late as 1927, the British and their Zazzau administrative allies were still having trouble persuading the Kono and Dungi hill-dwelling peoples to descend and settle their vulnerable former plain settlements and to get into administrative communication with their former Hausa-Fulani raiders. NAK/SNP File Number K6653, Zaria Province Annual Report for 1927—ACC no. 1573, 2.

41. Interview with Agom Adara, Magaji Galadima.

42. James, *Studies in the History, Politics, and Cultures of Southern Kaduna Peoples Groups,* 198.

43. Meek, *Tribal Studies in Northern Nigeria,* 79.

44. James, *Studies in the History, Politics, and Cultures of Southern Kaduna Peoples Groups,* 198.

45. Meek, *Tribal Studies in Northern Nigeria,* 80.

46. Filaba and Gojeh, *Koro and Gbagyi Subgroup Relations in Central Nigeria,* 54.

47. Meek, *Tribal Studies in Northern Nigeria,* 78.

48. Ibid., 80.

49. Interview with Agom Adara, Magaji Galadima.

50. NAK Zarprof. SNP 17 K 2554 (cited in James, *Studies in the History, Politics, and Cultures of Southern Kaduna Peoples Groups,* 243).

51. Smith, *Government in Zazzau, 1800–1950,* 177.

52. James, *Studies in the History, Politics, and Cultures of Southern Kaduna Peoples Groups,* 200.

53. Annual reports of Northern Provinces of Nigeria, blue books, vol. 1, 1901–1911 466, cited in Yusufu Turaki, *The British Colonial Legacy in Northern Nigeria: A Social Ethical Analysis of the Colonial and Post-Colonial Society and Politics in Nigeria* (Jos, Nigeria: Challenge Press and Turaki, 1993), 98.

54. Z. A. Bonat, "Colonialism and Underdevelopment in Zaria Province, 1902–1945" (MA thesis, Ahmadu Bello University, 1985), 155–156.

55. C. G. Ames, *Gazetteer of Plateau Province* (Jos Native Authority, 1920), in *Gazetteers of the Northern Provinces of Nigeria, vol. 4: The High-Land Chieftaincies (Plateau Province)*, ed. A. H. M. Kirk-Greene (London: Frank Cass, 1972), 231.

56. Ibid., 253.

57. Staudinger, *In the Heart of the Hausa States*, 153.

58. For a full list of "Hausa farming colonies" in the Southern Kaduna area, see James, *Studies in the History, Politics, and Cultures of Southern Kaduna Peoples Groups*, 114.

59. Staudinger, *In the Heart of the Hausa States*, 157.

60. Ibid., 128. Staudinger reports seeing the grisly evidence of Zazzau's military campaigns against the sporadic rebellions of Keffi as late as the 1880s.

61. For a fuller, albeit pro-British, account of the conquest of Zazzau and its areas of hegemonic influence, see E. J. Arnett, *Gazetteer of Zaria Province* (London: Waterlow & Sons), in Kirk-Greene, *Gazetteers of the Northern Provinces of Nigeria, vol. 3: The Central Kingdoms (Kontagora, Nasarawa, Nupe, Ilorin)*, 7–11.

62. Frederick Lugard, Arewa House Archive (thereafter AHA), Kaduna, Annual Reports, Northern Nigeria, 1900, 26–27.

63. Frederick Lugard, Northern Nigeria: Report for 1902–1907, London: HMSO, cited in Perham, *Lugard*, 148–149.

64. Arnett, *Gazetteer of Zaria Province*, 7–11.

65. NAK/SNP 10, Correspondence Number 144/1916. Reply to Governor General's comments on the Annual Report for Zaria Province 1915.

66. Ibid.

67. Smith, *Government in Zazzau, 1800–1950*, chap. 6.

68. NAK/Nasarawa Province Annual Report 1912, Kagoro District, quoted in Turaki, *The British Colonial Legacy in Northern Nigeria*, 98.

69. NAK/SNP File Number 18939, Zaria Province Annual Report 1932, 7.

70. Ibid.

71. NAK/SNP File Number 21304, Zaria Province Annual Report 1933, 1.

72. NAK/SNP File Number 25670, Zaria Province Annual Report 1935, 2.

73. NAK/SNP 18939, Zaria Province Annual Report for 1932, 7.

74. NAK/Zaria Province Annual Report 1937, pt. 3, 14–15.

75. James, *Studies in the History, Politics, and Cultures of Southern Kaduna Peoples Groups*, 202.

76. See ibid., 127, for a comprehensive list of Zazzau titles that made their way into the political traditions and lexicons of Southern Kaduna peoples through the administrative initiatives of Zazzau-appointed district chiefs.

77. Smith, *Government in Zazzau, 1800–1950*, 242.

78. Ibid.

79. NAK/K 4046, vol. 1: Hugh Clifford, Minutes, 1st June, 1920

80. Ibid.

81. CO 583/173/842, Colonial Office Papers, PRO: Donald Cameron to Passfield, 10th December 1931.

82. NAK/SNP9/100/1924, 5.

83. Ibid., 7.

84. NAK/ SNP10, Zaria Province Report 1913, 20.

85. NAK/SNP9/100 1924, 7.

86. NAK/ ACC no. 1573, Zaria Province Annual Report for 1927, 4.

87. Ibid., 5.

88. Ibid.

89. NAK/SNP 10/95P/1919.

90. NAK/SNP17/4, Zaria Province Annual Report 1944.

91. Ibid.

92. Ibid.

93. NAK/SNP 17, Zaria Province Annual Report 1946, 3.

94. Ibid.

95. Ibid.

96. Ibid.

97. Donald Cameron, *Principles of Native Administration and Their Application* (Lagos: Government Printer, 1931).

98. Logams, "The Middle Belt Movement in Nigerian Political Development," 116; James, *Studies in the History, Politics, and Cultures of Southern Kaduna Peoples Groups,* 207.

99. NAK/Jema'a NA 245 A, Yohanah (Kafanchan) to the Resident, Plateau Province, Jos.

100. Ibid.

101. Ibid.

102. Ibid.

103. Ibid.

104. Ibid. Talakawa Kasar Madaki to D. O. Kafanchan i/c Jema'a Division.

105. Interview with the chief of Moroa, Mallam Tagwai Sambo, in Manchok, April 21, 2009.

106. Ibid.

3. Emirate Maneuvers and "Pagan" Resistance in the Plateau-Nasarawa Basin

1. Nengel, *Precolonial African Intergroup Relations,* 100–101.

2. Ibid.

3. C. G Ames, *Gazetteer of Plateau Province* (Jos: Jos Native Authority, 1934), in Kirk-Greene, *Gazetteers of the Northern Province of Nigeria,* vol. 3: *The Central Kingdoms,* 30.

4. Ibid.

5. NAK/588P/1913 Appendix A: Ningi Group: General Remarks. For a detailed discussion of Ningi's often successful challenge to caliphate suzerainty, see Adell Patton Jr., "An Islamic Frontier Polity: The Ningi Mountain of Northern Nigeria, 1846–1902," in *The African Frontier: The Reproduction of Traditional African Societies,* ed. Igor Kopytoff (Bloomington: Indiana University Press, 1987), 195–213.

6. Ames, *Gazetteer of Plateau Province,* 33.

7. Ibid., 36.

8. NAK/ 444P/1914 Central Province Report No. 59 for June Quarter 1914.

9. NAK/SNP 10/126P/1913 Central Province Annual Report, 1912.

10. Ibid.

11. Ibid.

12. Ibid.

13. Ibid.

14. NAK/306P/1913 Central Province Report, March Quarter 1913, 5.

15. Ibid.

16. Ibid.

17. NAK/SNP 10/126P/1913 Central Province Annual Report, 1912.

18. See Bill Freund, *Capitalism and Labor in the Nigerian Tin Mines* (New York: Humanities Press, 1981).

19. NAK/SNP 10/126P/1913 Central Province Annual Report, 1912.

20. See chapter 7 of this book for a discussion of the Berom agitation for an indigenous chief of Jos and for the removal of Hausa chieftaincy from the city.

21. Adam Higazi, "Social Mobilization and Collective Violence: Vigilantes and Militias in the Lowlands of Plateau State, Central Nigeria," presented at the Mobilization for Political Violence: What Do We Know?, Center for Research on Inequality, Human Security, and Ethnicity, University of Oxford, 2009, 5.

22. Ibid., 7.

23. Joseph Aliu Ohiare, "The Kingdoms of Opanda and Igu, 1700–1939: A Study of Intergroup Relations" (PhD dissertation, Ahmadu Bello University, 1988).

24. Samuel Crowther, *Journal of an Expedition up the Niger and Tshadda Rivers, Undertaken by Maegregor Laird in Connection with the British Government in 1854.* (London: Cass, 1855), 37.

25. Richard Lander, *Records of Captain Clapperton's Last Expedition to Africa*, vol. 2 (London: Henry Colburn and Richard Bentley, 1830), 48–49.

26. Ibid., 50.

27. Ibid.

28. Ibid., 55.

29. Staudinger, *In the Heart of the Hausa States*, 108.

30. Interview with Mutuwa Gambo, chief of Angbaku, July 11, 2012, in Angbaku village.

31. Interview with Arugben Ogye in Angbako village, July 11, 2012.

32. Interview with Joel Ebuga in Ginda, Nasarawa-Eggon Local Government, July 11, 2012.

33. Interview with Moses Anduwa, in Gudi, Nasarawa State, July 11, 2012.

34. I saw well-preserved remains of the protective stone walls in Ginda during a research trip there in July 2012. Photos of the walls will be used in a spin-off project on resistance against jihadist slave raids in the Middle Belt in the nineteenth century.

35. Staudinger, *In the Heart of the Hausa States*, 146.

36. Ibid., 55.

37. William Balfour Baikie, "Inclosure 1 No. 74 (General Rules for Dealing with the Natives along the River Niger) Rule 15," in *Accounts and Papers of the House of Commons*, vol. 43: *The Slave Trade* (London: Harrison and Sons, 1863), 91.

38. See Streets-Salter, *Martial Races*.

39. Staudinger, *In the Heart of the Hausa States*, 60–61.

40. Ibid., 59.

41. Ibid., 58.

42. NAK/SNP 10/2/493p/1914: Nasarawa Emirate, Loko District Report by Mr. H. Cadman.

43. A. H. M. Kirk-Greene, ed., Gazetteers of the Northern Provinces of Nigeria, vol. 1: *The Hausa Emirates* (London: F. Cass, 1972), 19.

44. The headquarters was subsequently moved to Keffi, and in 1912 it was moved to Jema'a.

45. Sciortino, *Notes on Nasarawa Province, Nigeria*, 19–20.

46. Ibid.

47. Onah John Idoko, "The Hausa-Agatu Relations in Loko District, 1900–1960" (BA thesis, Nasarawa State University, 2007), 59.

48. Sciortino, *Notes on Nasarawa Province, Nigeria*, 21.

49. Lugard, *Political Memoranda*, 193–198.

50. Idoko, "The Hausa-Agatu Relations in Loko District," 59.

51. Ibid.

52. Jonathan Mamu Ayuba, *Economy and Society in Colonial North-Central Nigeria: The History of Akwanga Region, 1911–1960* (Zaria, Nigeria: Ahmadu Bello University Press, 2008), 80.

53. Ibid., 81.

54. NAK/SNP 9/830: Mada District, Plateau Province, Administration of, 1922. Quoted in Ayuba, *Economy and Society in Colonial North-Central Nigeria*, 81.

55. Ayuba, *Economy and Society in Colonial North-Central Nigeria*, 86.

56. Ibid., 169.

57. Rhodes House Mss. Af.s 1833, Stevenson, G. L.: "Nigerian and Other Days," 96.

58. Ibid.

59. Sciortino, *Notes on Nasarawa Province, Nigeria*, 11 (Founding of Nasarawa Emirate).

60. Ibid. (Founding of Lafia Beriberi).

61. Dickson Eyoh, "Differentiating Communities in Central Nigeria: Political and Economic Change in Colonial Lafia, Nigeria, 1900–1950," *International Journal of African Historical Studies* 29, no. 3 (1997): 499.

62. Ibid.

63. Ibid.

64. Ibid.

65. Ibid.

66. Ibid., 501.

67. Ibid.

68. Rhodes House Mss. Af.s 1833, Stevenson, G. L.: "Nigerian and Other Days," 97.

69. Ibid.

70. Ibid., 102.

71. Ibid.

72. Ibid., 103.

73. Ibid.

74. Ibid., 104.

75. Ibid.

76. Ibid., 105–106.

77. Ibid., 108.

78. For a full history of the cultural and religious profile of the NPC, see Billy J. Dudley, *Parties and Politics in Northern Nigeria* (London: Cass, 1968).

79. Rhodes House Mss. Af. s. 925: Stephenson, G.L, Nigeria Administration: Report of Tour of Keana District.

80. Ibid., 2.

81. Ibid.

82. Ibid.

83. Ibid, 3.

84. Ibid.

85. Ibid.

86. Ibid.

87. Ibid., 4.

88. Ibid.

89. Ibid., 7.

90. Ibid.

91. Ibid., 8.

92. Ibid.

93. Ibid., 10.

94. Ibid.

4. Hausa Colonial Agency in the Benue Valley

1. See Philips, *Spurious Arabic.*

2. W. R. Crocker, journal, Rhodes House Mss. Af. s. 1073, 1 (hereafter Crocker's journal), 11/19/1933.

3. Ibid.

4. Most of the Hausa interpreters were not ethnic Hausa but Hausaized Nupe, Gbagyi, and Ilorin Yoruba, but they were all Muslims and were chosen because of their understanding of, and/or prior participation in, caliphate administrative practices, and because they had lived or traded in the Benue Valley and had interacted with the Idoma.

5. The RNC was reconstituted from the National African Company in 1886 as a conglomerate uniting the major British trading firms on the Niger. The company grew through the brinkmanship of its first head, George Goldie, who oversaw the formation of the company's army, the RNC constabulary, signed most of the treaties that gave the British a foothold on the Niger, eliminated French and German trade rivals, and engaged in informal imperial practices such as expeditions and interference in African political affairs. All this was possible because the company had a royal charter. The British government withdrew the charter in 1899. This led to an inchoate British colonial authority in Northern Nigeria taking control of the territorial, material, and logistical assets of the company and the compensation of its shareholders. George Goldie was succeeded by Frederick Lugard, who presided over the company's liquidation and its transformation into a colonial administrative and quasi-military entity. Lugard also oversaw the formal annexation and routinization of the territories over which the RNC had established informal colonial administrative control.

6. Tesemchi Makar, *The History of Political Change among the Tiv in the 19th and 20th Centuries* (Enugu, Nigeria: Fourth Dimension, 1994), 99.

7. These encounters involved alleged Tiv theft of Hausa-Fulani cattle and Tiv raid of Hausa merchandise along the Abinsi trade corridor. See Ikime, *The Fall of Nigeria*, 169–177.

8. Makar, *The History of Political Change among the Tiv in the 19th and 20th Centuries*, 119.

9. Ibid., 103.

10. Adamu, *The Hausa Factor in West African History*, 43.

11. See ibid. for a discussion of the ivory trade pioneered by the Hausa in the Niger-Benue area.

12. Crocker's journal, 11/11/1933.

13. Walter R. Crocker, *Nigeria: A Critique of British Colonial Administration* (Freeport, N.Y.: Books for Libraries Press, 1971), 31.

14. *Sojan gona* literally means farm raider or farm-raiding soldier. This was a fairly common crime in colonial Northern Nigeria whereby people would dress up in colonial army or police uniforms or present themselves as interpreters and agents of the British colonial authorities to demand money, compliance, and resources from individuals and communities on the basis of their false status. The British called it "personation." See Steven Pierce, *A Moral Economy of Corruption: State Formation and Political Culture in Northern Nigeria* (Unpublished book manuscript, n.d.). Colonial sources on Idoma Division are rife with complaints about sojan gona. Most of those fingered or suspected of perpetrating the act were Hausa people, legitimate colonial agents who moonlighted as sojan gona for personal gain or nonagents whose Hausa identity and speech made them credible impersonators.

15. See NAK/OTUDIST ACC26, "Eastern District of Okwoga," by N. J. Brooke.

16. A. P. Anyebe, *Man of Courage and Character: The Ogbuloko War in Colonial Idomaland of Nigeria* (Enugu, Nigeria: Fourth Dimension, 2002), 66.

17. Ibid.

18. Ibid.

19. Ibid.

20. Kukah, *Religion, Politics and Power in Northern Nigeria*, 11.

21. Ibid., 3.

22. See Adamu, *The Hausa Factor in West African History*.

23. Anyebe, *Man of Courage and Character*, 64.

24. Ibid.; V. G. Okwu, "The Establishment of Colonial Administration in Idomaland, 1921–1930," *Savannah* 5, no. 1 (1976): 29–44.

25. Interview with Umoru Atenyi, August 7, 1987, Adoka. Interview conducted by Yakubu Ochefu, Idoma Economic History Texts, compiled by Yakubu Ochefu, Department of History, University of Calabar, Nigeria, January 1991.

26. Anyebe, *Man of Courage and Character*, 65.

27. Ibid., 63.

28. Ibid., 66.

29. Ibid.

30. Crocker's journal, 11/18/1933.

31. Ibid.

32. Ibid., 11/10/1933.

33. Ibid., 11/14/1933.

34. Interview with Onazi Egwurube, retired NA messenger, aged 90, Otukpo, August 18, 1987. Interview conducted by Yakubu Ochefu, Idoma Economic History Texts.

35. Interview with Onazi Egwurube. "Mallam" was a reverential title that the Idoma used for Hausa colonial clerks.

36. Ibid.

37. Makar, *The History of Political Change among the Tiv in the 19th and 20th Centuries*, 89.

38. Adamu, *The Hausa Factor in West African History*, 2.

39. Justin Iyorbee Tseayo, *Conflict and Incorporation in Nigeria: The Integration of the Tiv* (Zaria, Nigeria: Gaskiya, 1975), 40.

40. NAI, E. S. Pemberton, 1929, CSO 26/12874, vol. 8, quoted in ibid., 41.

41. NAI, H. H. Wilkinson, 1937, CSO 26/12874, vol. 11.

42. Makar, *The History of Political Change among the Tiv in the 19th and 20th Centuries*, 175.

43. For more detail on the day-to-day administrative activities of the Hausa auxiliaries, see the journals of Hugh Elliot (Journal of H. P. Elliot, assistant district officer, Rhodes House Mss. Afr. S. 1336), and that of W. R. Crocker (Rhodes House Mss. Afr. S. 1073, 1). In these journals the Hausa dogarai (policemen), mallams (scribes and tax collectors), and messengers feature prominently in the daily records of administrative proceedings in Idoma Division. The malleability of Hausa as a category is underscored by the fact that some of these auxiliary colonial actors were identified as Muslim Nupe, who were "Hausa" enough for the task of administering Idoma Division by virtue of their descent from the caliphate tradition.

44. Moses E. Ochonu, "A Colony in Crisis: Northern Nigeria, British Colonialism, and the Great Depression" (PhD Dissertation, University of Michigan, 2004), chap. 5.

45. Ibid.

46. Interview with Ochekwu Adama and others, Otukpo, 08/15/1987. Interview conducted by Yakubu Ochefu, Idoma Economic History Texts.

47. Ibid.

48. Ibid.

49. Interview with Ochekwu Adama and others, Idoma Economic History Texts. For a discussion of the locust invasion and how it compounded the effect of the Great Depression on

Northern Nigerian peasants, see Moses E. Ochonu, *Colonial Meltdown: Northern Nigeria in the Great Depression* (Athens: Ohio University Press, 2009), 55–70.

50. Interview with Ochekwu Adama and others, Idoma Economic History Texts.

51. Anyebe, *Man of Courage and Character*, 81.

52. Ibid.

53. Interview with Ama Ojeche, 80, male, 09/17/2011; Suleiman Elaigwu, 78, 09/18/2011; and Adanu Enegela, 76, 09/17/2011. All were interviewed in Obagaji.

54. Interview with Umoru Anteyi.

55. For a full examination of the Idoma experience as a site of Jihadist slave raids and attacks, see Yakubu A. Ochefu, *The Economic Transformation of Idoma Society, 1860–1960* (Makurdi, Nigeria: Aboki Publishers, 2000), chap. 1.

56. Interview with Alhaji Ibrahim Apochi, July 15, 1988, Obagaji, Agatu, Idoma Economic History Texts.

57. Ibid.

58. Ibid.

59. Interview with Sgt. Ada Sule (Rtd.), Oweto Agatu, July 14, 1988, Idoma Economic History Texts.

60. Interview with Alhaji Ibrahim Apochi.

61. Ibid.

62. Ibid.

63. Interview with Sgt. Ada Sule.

64. Ibid.

65. Interview with Alhaji Ibrahim Apochi.

66. Ibid.

67. Ibid.

68. Ibid.

69. Interview with Ngbede Ode, 75+, at Edikwu, August 27, 1987, Idoma Economic History Texts.

70. Interview with Anya Ujo, 70+, in Ogobia, Ugboju, September, 22, 1987, Idoma Economic History Texts.

71. Ibid.

72. Ibid.

73. Ibid.

74. Ibid.

75. Ibid.

76. Ibid.

77. Ibid.

78. Ibid.

79. Crocker, *Nigeria: A Critique of British Colonial Administration*, 31. This statement was an entry in his official diary, which was submitted to his superiors and arguably became the basis of official policies toward the Idoma and other peoples on the Lower Benue Valley.

80. Crocker's journal, 11/11/1933.

81. Ibid.

82. Ibid., 02/11/1933.

83. Ibid., 11/11/1933.

84. Journal of H. P. Elliot, September 5, 1935.

85. Charles Kingsley Meek, *The Northern Tribes of Nigeria: An Ethnographical Account of the Northern Provinces of Nigeria Together with a Report on the 1921 Decennial Census,* (New York: Negro Universities Press, 1969).

86. H. P. Elliot, *Reminiscence of Colonial Administrative Service in Nigeria*, Rhodes House Mss. Afr. S. 1836.

87. Lugard Papers, Girouard to Lugard # ff 152–237 1908–09, Rhodes House Mss Brit. Emp. S. 63.

88. Ibid.

5. Fulani Expansion and Subcolonial Rule in Early Colonial Adamawa Province

1. Hindi Livinus, "Raucous Reception Greets Yola University Name Change," *Next*, July 24, 2011, http://234next.com/csp/cms/sites/Next/Home/5735441-146/story.csp. Although this report estimates the population of non-Hausa-Fulani indigenes of the state at 80 percent, the more relevant number in the context of this controversy is the number of non-Muslims, since the greatest outrage on the renaming was felt by non-Muslim, non-Fulani Adamawa indigenes. Non-Fulani Muslims were less likely to openly resist the renaming of the university after a precolonial Islamic hero even if they thought that a non-Fulani deserved the honor. Many of them were indifferent or conflicted. The population of non-Muslim, non-Fulani indigenes is hard to estimate, but it is widely believed that they constitute slightly more than half of the state's population, a reality that is a source of friction in the state's politics since the levers and fulcrums of political and economic power reside with a Fulani Muslim elite.

2. Ibid.

3. Ibid.

4. M. Z. Njeuma, *Fulani Hegemony in Yola (Old Adamawa) 1809–1902* (Yaounde, Cameroon: Publishing and Production Center for Teaching and Research, 1978), 5; Derrick Stenning, *Savannah Nomads: A Study of the Wodaabe Pastoral Fulani of Western Borno Province, Northern Region, Nigeria* (London: International Africa Institute and Oxford University Press, 1959), 18–25; Sa'ad Abubakar, *The Lamibe of Fombina: A Political History of Adamawa 1809–1901* (Zaria, Nigeria: Ahmadu Bello University Press and Oxford University Press, 1977), 29–32. Abubakar differs from other inquirers into the history of Fulani migration into Adamawa (Fombina). Unlike other scholars, he asserts a direct migration from Hausaland, claiming that because earlier migrants to Bornu had been forced to acquiesce to the authority of the Mai of Bornu, the migrants who entered Adamawa bypassed Bornu altogether, migrating southeast from Hausaland to areas on the banks of the Benue and Gongola rivers.

5. Njeuma, *Fulani Hegemony*, 6.

6. Abubakar, *The Lamibe of Fombina*, 31.

7. Njeuma, *Fulani Hegemony*, 9.

8. Ibid., 6

9. Ibid.

10. Ibid., 8.

11. Abubakar, *The Lamibe of Fombina*, 39; Njeuma, *Fulani Hegemony*, 8.

12. Abubakar, *The Lamibe of Fombina*, 39.

13. Ibid.

14. Ibid., 37.

15. Ibid., 43–71; Njeuma, *Fulani Hegemony*, chap. 2.

16. NAK/Yolaprof/F3; "pagan" Administration, Collected Papers/ 295/1920, Tour Report for Kona District.

17. Ibid., Notes on the Treatment of Raw "pagan"s in Districts Not Yet under Control.

18. Ibid., Tour Report for Kona District.

19. Ibid.

20. Ibid.

21. Ibid.

22. Ibid.

23. Ibid., From Assistant Resident No. 2 Division to Resident, Yola Province.

24. Ibid., Fulani District Head Lala Tribe.

25. Ibid., From Assistant Resident No. 2 Division to Resident, Yola Province; From the Resident Yola Province to the Resident Touring "pagan" Emirate 12/9/12.

26. Ibid., From Assistant Resident No. 2 Division to Resident, Yola Province; From the Resident Yola Province to the District Officer I/C E.P Division. The Kilba and the Yungur and Gaada were northern Adamawa non-Muslim groups that were never part of Adamawa Emirate (or Fombina, as it was called) but that found themselves placed under the lamido of Adamawa by the early British colonial administrators of Adamawa Province. See J. H. Pongri, "The Jihad and the Establishment of Colonial Rule in Adamawa, c. 1809–1980," presented at the Postgraduate Seminar, Ahmadu Bello University, Zaria, Nigeria, 1980, 3.

27. NAK/Yolaprof/F3; "pagan" Administration, Collected Papers / Y2098 /12, "pagan" Administration and Collected Papers, Chiefs of "pagan" Districts.

28. Ibid.

29. J. H. Pongri, "The Jihad and the Establishment of Colonial Rule in Adamawa, C. 1809–1980" (presented at the Postgraduate Seminar, Ahmadu Bello University, Zaria, Nigeria, 1980), 11.

30. Ibid., 17.

31. NAK/Yolaprof/F3; "pagan" Administration, Collected Papers / Y2098 /12, Chiefs of "pagan" Districts.

32. Fardon, *Raiders and Refugees*. See also NAK/Adamawa Provincial Archives J.9, The Chamba, by C. K. Meek; see also NAK/Adamawa Provincial Archives, Chamba Area Reorganization 1933–1940, vol. 2, 1937–1940.

33. See Fardon, *Raiders and Refugees*.

34. Ibid.

35. Ibid.; for parallels in the northern Adamawa area, see Pongri, "The Jihad and the Establishment of Colonial Rule in Adamawa," 6.

36. NAK/Adamawa Provincial Archives, Chamba Area Reorganization 1933–1940, vol. 2, 1937–1940; Adamawa Province: Proposed Reorganization of the Chamba Districts of Adamawa Division.

37. NAK/Yolaprof/C.778/9/Chamba Federation, Separatist Movement, Report on the Chamba Subordinate Native Authority, 7.

38. NAK/Yolaprof/F3; "pagan" Administration, Collected Papers / Y2098 /12, Chiefs of "pagan" Districts.

39. Ibid.

40. NAK/Yolaprof/F3; "pagan" Administration, Collected Papers/ 295/1920, Notes on the Treatment of Raw "pagan"s in Districts Not Yet under Control; D.O. Numan Division, to Resident, Yola Province.

41. Ibid.

42. Ibid.

43. Ibid.

44. NAK/Yolaprof/C 778: Chamba Federation, Chamba Federation Separatist Movement.

45. NAK/Yolaprof/F3; "pagan" Administration, Collected Papers/ 295/1920, Notes on the Treatment of Raw "pagan"s in Districts Not Yet under Control; D.O. Numan Division, to Resident, Yola Province.

46. For a full accounting of the many cultural frictions between the Fulani and their non-Muslim host communities in the eighteenth and nineteenth centuries see Abubakar, *The Lamibe of Fombina*, chap. 2.

47. NAK/Yolaprof/F3; "pagan" Administration, Collected Papers /Y2098/12, No. E.P 78/1914, From D.O ii i/c E.P Div to the Resident Yola Province, Supervision of Lala "pagan" Sub-district.

48. Ibid.

49. NAK/Yolaprof/F3; "pagan" Administration, Collected Papers /Y2098/12, Resident Yola Province to Jamo Goila.

50. Ibid.

51. NAK/ACC 27/YolaProf. Marghi and Uba 1916–1918, 1927.

52. Ibid.

53. NAK/Yolaprof/F3; "pagan" Administration, Collected Papers / Y2098 /12, To the DO, EP Division, Pella.

54. NAK/ YolaProf. Provincial Reorganization 1924 and 1926, DO i/c Yola Division to Resident Yola Province.

55. NAK/ YolaProf. Provincial Reorganization 1924 and 1926, Memo No. 207/1926/45, 21st September, 1926, From Resident Adamawa Province to Secretary, Northern Provinces, Kaduna.

56. NAK/ YolaProf. Provincial Reorganization 1924 and 1926, From ADO Touring Shellem District to DO i/c Yola Division.

57. Ibid.

58. NAK/ YolaProf. Provincial Reorganization 1924 and 1926, Memo No. 207/1926/45, 21st September, 1926, From Resident Adamawa Province to Secretary, Northern Provinces, Kaduna.

59. Ibid.

60. Ibid.

61. NAK/ YolaProf. Provincial Reorganization 1924 and 1926, DO i/c of Yola Division to Resident Yola Province, 13th August, 1926.

62. NAK/ YolaProf. Provincial Reorganization 1924 and 1926, From ADO Touring Shellem District to DO i/c Yola Division, Resident's comments.

63. NAK/ YolaProf. Provincial Reorganization 1924 and 1926, Memo No. 207/1926/45, 21st September, 1926, From Resident Adamawa Province to Secretary, Northern Provinces, Kaduna.

64. NAK/Adamawa Provincial Archives, Chamba Area Reorganization 1933–1940, vol. 2, 1937–1940.

65. Ibid. ("Geographical"). The census of 1937 showed a total Chamba population in the four Chamba districts of Nassarawo, Binyeri, Gurumpawo, Yebbi, and in the village area of Tsugu to be 13,049 against a population of 44,313 for the Chamba.

66. NAK/YolaProf, File C778/2238 A, "The Chamba Tribe (Report by W. T. Hunter-Shaw)."

67. Ibid., Proposals for the Establishment of Chamba Federation: Resident's Summary and Recommendations.

68. NAK/YolaProf. Chamba Area Reorganization 1933–1940. In two volumes, Volume II 1937–1940.

69. NAK/YolaProf/"pagan" Administration 1933–1935 in Two Volumes, Volume I. Memorandum 209/ No. 13474/332,1935: From Secretary, Northern Provinces, Kaduna to The Resident Adamawa Province. "pagan" Reorganization—Notes for the guidance of officers engaged in enquiries connected with.

70. See Jean-Loup Amselle, *Mestizo Logics*, 68–69.

6. Non-Muslim Revolt against Fulani Rule in Adamawa

1. NAK/Yolaprof/C778; Chamba Federation, Separatist Movement, Confidential memo from the DO Yola Division to the Resident Adamawa Province, September 1951, "Chamba District Affairs."

2. Ibid.

3. Ibid.

4. Ibid.

5. Ibid.

6. Ibid.

7. Ibid.

8. Ibid.

9. Ibid.

10. Ibid.

11. Ibid.

12. Ibid., Secret Memo from the Provincial Official Office, Yola, to the Permanent Secretary, Ministry of Local Government, Kaduna, "Chamba Districts, Adamawa Emirate."

13. NAK/Yolaprof/C778; Chamba Federation, Separatist Movement, Confidential memo from the DO Yola Division to the Resident Adamawa Province, September, 1951, "Chamba District Affairs."

14. NAK/Yolaprof/C778; Chamba Federation, Separatist Movement, Letter from Simon of N.T.S. Numan to Chief of Yebbi; original in Hausa, translated by the office of the DO Yola Division.

15. Ibid.

16. Ibid.

17. Ibid.

18. Ibid.

19. Niels Kastfelt, *Religion and Politics in Nigeria: A Study in Middle Belt Christianity* (London: British Academic Press, 1994); Andrew E. Barnes, *Making Headway: The Introduction of Western Civilization in Colonial Northern Nigeria* (Rochester, N.Y.: University of Rochester Press, 2009).

20. See Turaki, *The British Colonial Legacy in Northern Nigeria;* Matthew Hassan Kukah, Religion, Politics, and Power in Northern Nigeria (Ibadan, Nigeria: Spectrum Books, 1993); Logams, "The Middle Belt Movement in Nigerian Political Development"; Barnes, *Making Headway;* Kastfelt, *Religion and Politics in Nigeria.*

21. See Philip Serge Zachernuk, *Colonial Subjects: An African Intelligentsia and Atlantic Ideas* (Charlottesville: University Press of Virginia, 2000).

22. For an exploration of a parallel set of political anxieties displayed and acted upon by another minority ethnic group in the vortex of Hausa-Fulani political preeminence, see Moses E. Ochonu, "Masculine Anxieties, Cultural Politics, and Debates over Independent Womanhood among Idoma Male Migrants in Late Colonial Northern Nigeria," *Interventions* 13, no. 2 (2011): 278–298.

23. NAK//Yolaprof/C778/9; Chamba Federation, Separatist Movement, Confidential memo from the Resident, Adamawa Province, Yola to the Secretary, Northern Provinces, Kaduna, 3rd March, 1951.

24. NAK//Yolaprof/C778; Chamba Federation, Separatist Movement, Confidential memo from Yola the Senior DO, Yola Division to the Resident Adamawa Province, February 22, 1951.

25. For the findings and recommendations of the commission, see *Report of the Commission Appointed to Enquire into the Fears of Minorities and the Means of Allaying Them,* presented

to Parliament by the Secretary of State for Colonies by Command of Her Majesty, July 1958 (Published by Her Majesty's Stationery Office, 1959).

26. NAK//Yolaprof/C778; Chamba Federation, Separatist Movement, Confidential memo from the Senior DO, Yola Division to the Resident Adamawa Province, February 22, 1951.

27. Ibid.

28. Ibid.

29. Ibid.

30. Kastfelt, *Religion and Politics in Nigeria,* 87–91.

31. Ibid.

32. Ibid.

33. Ibid.

34. Ibid.

35. NAK//Yolaprof/C778/9; Chamba Federation, Separatist Movement, Confidential memo from the Resident, Adamawa Province, Yola to the Secretary, Northern Provinces, Kaduna, 3rd March, 1951.

36. Ibid.

37. Ibid.

38. Ibid.

39. NAK//Yolaprof/C778/9; Chamba Federation, Separatist Movement, No. HJAC/2, From the Touring Officer, Chamba Area to the Senior District Officer, Adamawa Division, Yola.

40. Ibid.

41. Ibid.

42. Ibid.

43. Ibid.

44. Ibid.

45. Ibid.

46. Ibid.

47. Ibid.

48. Ibid.

49. Ibid., "S.U.M. Gurumpawo."

50. Kastfelt, *Religion and Politics in Nigeria,* 49.

51. NAK//Yolaprof/C778/9; Chamba Federation, Separatist Movement, No. C. 778/33, From the Resident Adamawa Province to the Permanent Secretary, Ministry of Local Government, Kaduna, 30 September 1955.

52. Ibid.

53. Ibid.

54. Rhodes House Mss. Afr. S. 1485, the Chamba Subordinate Native Authority, A Statement Prepared for the Visit of the Minorities Commission to Adamawa Province in February, 1958 by P. S. Crane, A.D.O. See also NAK//Yolaprof/C778/9; Chamba Federation, Separatist Movement, Report on the Chamba Subordinate Native Authority. Although housed in different archives, the document is exactly the same in both places. Subsequent references to it correspond to the pagination in both copies of the report.

55. Ibid., 10.

56. Ibid., 4.

57. Ibid., 8.

58. Ibid.

59. Ibid., 10.

60. Ibid.

61. Ibid. Anonymous official comment on the report's list of Chamba grievances.

62. Ibid., 10–11.

63. Ibid., 11.

64. Ibid.

65. Ibid., 13.

66. Ibid.

7. Middle Belt Self-Determination and Caliphate Political Resurgence in the Transition to National Independence

1. "Hausa" in the context of the unique ethno-religious alchemy of Jos denotes the Hausa-speaking residents from a composite group of Muslim migrants to the town. This definition is valid even in today's ethno-religious politics in Jos, where the category of "Hausa" applies to those with Caliphate or Bornuan origins and who are Muslims. Throughout the colonial period, migrants from the populous Kano Emirate came to dominate the "Hausa" population in sheer numbers and increasingly in political influence. See John N. Paden, *Ahmadu Bello, Sardauna of Sokoto: Values and Leadership in Nigeria* (London: Hodder and Stoughton, 1986), 344.

2. Ibid.

3. Ibid., 346.

4. "Don't Appoint Hausa Chief—Bitrus Warns North Premier," *Nigerian Citizen*, March 20, 1957.

5. Ibid.

6. "Hausas Oppose Jos NA Decision on Chiroma," *Nigerian Citizen*, December 18, 1957.

7. See Billy J. Dudley, *Parties and Politics in Northern Nigeria* (London: Cass, 1968); Coleman, *Nigeria*; Turaki, *The British Colonial Legacy in Northern Nigeria*, 346–347. Although the UMBC began operations as early as 1952, it was only formally ratified in Kafanchan in 1955.

8. Pastor David Lot's testimony at the Jos hearings of the Willink Commission as reported by the *Nigerian Citizen*, Saturday, February 22, 1958.

9. Ibid.

10. Ibid.

11. Ibid.

12. "Hausa Being Imposed? No, He Says," *Nigerian Citizen*, February 22, 1958.

13. See Coleman, *Nigeria*; Dudley, *Parties and Politics in Northern Nigeria*.

14. *Nigerian Citizen*, October 5, 1957.

15. "If You Want Respect, Dress Like Hausa He Says," *Nigerian Citizen*, February 19, 1958.

16. Ibid.

17. For an illuminating discussion of the development and mutation of the One-North ideology, see George A. Kwanashie, *The Making of the North in Nigeria, 1900–1965* (Kaduna, Nigeria: Arewa House, Ahmadu Bello University, 2002).

18. "If You Want Respect, Dress Like Hausa He Says."

19. Ibid.

20. Ibid.

21. Ibid.

22. See "Abuul's Party Urges Colonial Secretary: Do Not Grant Self-Government until Middle Belt Is Created," *Nigerian Citizen*, June 4, 1958.

23. The testimonies, countertestimonies and cross-examinations of Mr. Abdul-Razaq, the NPC's lead lawyer during those hearings, were particularly unsparing in their hostility to the main points of the Middle Belt struggle. See "No Genuine Fears to Necessitate the Creation of a Middle Belt State, Says NPC Counsel," *Nigerian Citizen*, February 22, 1958.

24. See "Hausa Being Imposed? No, He Says."

25. "Sardauna's Address to the Minority Commission," *Nigerian Citizen*, February 5, 1958.

26. Ibid.

27. "Any Attempt to Split the North Will Result in Bloodshed—Federal Minister Tells Kano NPC Convention," *Nigerian Citizen*, March 8, 1958.

28. "UK Northerners Decide: Middle Belt Creation Will Weaken Our Solidarity," *Nigerian Citizen*, January 26, 1957.

29. Paden, *Ahmadu Bello*, 345n75.

30. "No Genuine Fears to Necessitate the Creation of the Middle Belt State."

31. "North Is Minority in the Federal Set-up, Barrister Razak Tells Commission," *Nigerian Citizen*, January 8, 1958.

32. "Middle Belt? Only Tivs Agitate for It in Benue Says This Minister," *Nigerian Citizen*, January 8, 1958.

33. See Kwanashie, *The Making of the North in Nigeria*, for fuller discussion of how carefully cultivated patronage systems came to form the basis of Northern unity and functional cohesion.

34. Ibid., 202.

35. Paden, *Ahmadu Bello*, 568n66, quoting several editions of *Nigerian Citizen*.

36. "Islamic Conversion Campaign Hots Up," *Nigerian Citizen*, May 8, 1965.

37. The *Nigerian Citizen* was begun in 1949 as a counterpart to *Gaskiya ta fi Kwabo*, Gaskiya Corporation's flagship Hausa-language newspaper. Both newspapers were founded on and operated as pro-establishment media organs. *Gaskiya ta fi Kwabo* even operated as an anti-Germany propaganda arm of the British colonial government during World War II. The company's publications continued to play the role of defenders and propaganda tool of the NPC incumbency when the party ascended to political and governing preeminence in the 1950s. For a history of the company and its tradition of pro-establishment advocacy, see Graham Furniss, "On Engendering Liberal Values in the Nigerian Colonial State: The Idea behind Gaskiya Corporation," *Journal of Imperial and Commonwealth History* 39, no. 1 (2011): 95–119.

38. "In the Footsteps of Othman Dan Fodio: Sardauna Launches Great Islamic Conversion Campaign," *Nigerian Citizen*, April 28, 1965.

39. Paden, *Ahmadu Bello*, chap. 16; for a discussion of Ahmadu Bello's religious politics, including his active participation in, and support for, global Islamic networks, see Ousmane Kane, *Muslim Modernity in Northern Nigeria: A Study of the Society for the Removal of Innovation and the Restatement of Tradition* (Leiden: Brill, 2003), 152–158.

40. Kane, *Muslim Modernity in Northern Nigeria*, 83.

41. Joseph Nanven Garba, *Revolution in Nigeria: Another View* (London: Africa Books, 1982), 52.

42. Kwanashie, *The Making of the North in Nigeria*, 202–203.

43. Joseph Nanven Garba, *Diplomatic Soldiering: Nigerian Foreign Policy, 1975–1979* (Ibadan: Spectrum Books, 1987). Garba, a former major general in the Nigerian Army and Nigeria's ambassador to the United Nations, tells the story of how his father, a non-Muslim district chief in Langtang Division of Plateau Province, faced enormous pressure from the NPC-controlled Northern regional government to convert to Islam as a way of enjoying a higher chiefly and political status. Finding the benefits of conversion appealing, Garba's father sought advice from his son, who in turn sought counsel from his boss, Brigadier Maimalari. Maimalari, Garba recalls, advised him to stick with soldiering and stay out of a "political" matter. Garba's father subsequently converted, an action that paid immediate dividend as Garba's younger brother was appointed a government-paid Quranic teacher with a steady income and other perks.

44. "UMBC Convention in Jos: Party Calls for Nigerian Leaders to Parley on Unity Issue," *Nigerian Citizen,* April 11, 1964.
45. See Hawkins, *Writing and Colonialism in Northern Ghana,* 114.
46. Akiga Sai, *Akiga's Story; the Tiv Tribe as Seen by One of Its Members,* trans. Rupert East (London: Oxford University Press, 1939).
47. Ibid., 385.
48. Ibid., 386.
49. Ibid., 388.
50. Ibid., 390.
51. Ibid.; Paul Bohannan, "Extra-Processual Events in Tiv Political Institutions," *American Anthropologist* 60, no. 1 (February 1, 1958): 1–12.
52. Personal communication with Sevza Asongo, July 11, 2011.
53. Ibid.
54. Ibid.
55. Ibid.
56. Ibid.
57. See, for instance, the December 2 edition of the *Nigerian Citizen.* It ran two such stories. One was titled "Tivs Are behind NPC En-mass—Says Jos Secretary of Tiv NPC Branch," the other had the headline: "Idomas Pledge Support for NPC—'To Die or Live with NPC.'"
58. Ochayi Okpeh Okpeh, "Ethnic Minorities, Decolonization Politics and Political Participation: A Study of Idoma Hope Rising Union (1944–1960)," *Jos Journal of Minority Studies* 1, no. 1 (2003): 21.
59. See "Why Idoma People Should Vote for the NNA," *Nigerian Citizen,* December 2, 1964.
60. *Nigerian Citizen,* November 18, 1964.
61. NAK/PLT/27/Makprof 2/60; N.P.C—Activities in Benue Province, Complaint and General Matters.
62. See chapter 4 for a fuller discussion of the protest over dan Afoda's successor and the demand of the Tiv for a Tiv replacement for him.
63. Personal conversation with Sevza Asongo.
64. Ibid.
65. NAK/MakProf/Pol/48; Tiv Riot General Correspondence.
66. Ibid., Native Authority Police for Makurdi.
67. Ibid., Makurdi Sub N.A. Wants Its Own Trained Staff.
68. "9 Tiv Rioters to Hang, Helicopter Sent In," *Nigerian Citizen,* November 18, 1964.
69. See NAK/Markprof 2/61/ Pol/ 35/S. 1, "Riot Damage Tax Collection of Tax."
70. Ibid., "Tiv People Want More Time to Pay Riots Damage Tax."
71. "Tiv Inquiry Report: A New Era Begins in Tiv Land," *Nigerian Citizen,* April 21, 1965.
72. Ibid.
73. Particularly illustrative of the thrust of the report is its long-winded analysis of Tiv rituals, social organization, culture, history, and conflict.
74. "Bread and Butter Instead of Guns and Bullets—An Era of Prosperity Begins," *Nigerian Citizen,* January 20, 1965.
75. NAK/PLT/27/Makprof 2/60: N.P.C—Activities in Benue Province, Complaint and General Matters; 1963/N.P.C no. 1, NPC Office Gboko to the Senior District Officer i/c Tiv Division, Gboko ("Report of Riot Cases Released on Bail").
76. Interview with Malam Tagwai Sambo, Moroa, April 21, 2009.
77. Ibid.
78. Ibid.
79. Interview with Gen. Zamani Lekwot (rtd.), Kaduna, April 23, 2009.

80. Ibid.
81. Interview with Retired Air Vice Marshal Adamu Mbaka, Kaduna, April 17, 2009.
82. Ibid.
83. Ibid.

Conclusion

1. For a comprehensive discussion of the phases of African historical writing and a good analysis of the post-independence nationalist historical project, see Abdullahi Mu'azu Saulawa, "A History of Historical Writings in Nigeria since c. 1960 A.D.," *Savanna: A Journal of the Environmental and Social Sciences* 10, no. 2 (1989): 76–85; Cooper, "Conflict and Connections." The seminal works of the following scholars are examples of histories and studies written in the nationalist-instrumental mold: Yusufu Bala Usman, Adiele Afigbo, J. A Atanda; Obaro Ikime; Ben Magubane; Adu Boahen, Walter Rodney, and Claude Ake. For an unsparing critique of nationalist history, see Mbembe, "African Modes of Self-Writing." Mbembe's critique dramatizes the blind spots of this historiographical and epistemological vision, but it loses some of its sting for its tendentious caricature of that pioneering conceptualization of African history and for its failure to acknowledge the seminal validity of nationalist historiographical perspectives in the context of decolonization, independence, and internationalized racism.

2. See Jeffrey Ira Herbst, *States and Power in Africa: Comparative Lessons in Authority and Control* (Princeton, N.J.: Princeton University Press, 2000) for a critique of the notion of a ubiquitous colonial political presence. See also Henry S. Wilson, *African Decolonization* (London: Edward Arnold, 1994), chap. 1, for a discussion of the dearth of European personnel and mechanisms of control in many African colonies. Wilson calls the phenomenon the "thin white line" of colonial control.

3. Herbst, *States and Power in Africa*; Wilson, *African Decolonization*, chap. 1.

4. For a comprehensive enunciation of Tutsi subcolonial rule among the Hutu, see Mamdani, *When Victims Become Killers*, chaps. 2 and 3.

5. Gayatri Spivak, "Can the Subaltern Speak?," in *Marxism and the Interpretation of Culture*, ed. Cary Nelson and Lawrence Grossberg (Urbana-Champagne: University of Illinois Press, 1988).

6. Glassman, "Sorting Out the Tribes."

7. Frederick Cooper, *Decolonization and African Society: The Labor Question in French and British Africa* (Cambridge: Cambridge University Press, 1996), Introduction.

8. Mamdani, *When Victims Become Killers*; Catharine Newbury, "Ethnicity and the Politics of History in Rwanda," *Africa Today* 45, no. 1 (1998): 7–24; Catharine Newbury, "Background to Genocide in Rwanda," *Issue: A Journal of Opinion* 23, no. 2 (1995): 12–17.

9. Mahmood Mamdani, *Saviors and Survivors: Darfur, Politics, and the War on Terror* (New York: Pantheon Books, 2009).

10. Bishop Matthew Hassan Kukah, Interview, Kaduna, Nigeria, May 5, 2009.
11. Ibid.

12. For a comprehensive analysis of the spread of and constraints on Western education in colonial Northern Nigeria, see Albert O. Ozigi and Lawrence Ocho, *Education in Northern Nigeria* (London: Allen & Unwin, 1981).

Bibliography

Archives

Arewa House Archive for Historical Preservation, Kaduna, Nigeria (AHA)
    Annual reports
    Archived editions of *Nigerian Citizen* newspaper
    Memos
    Colonial correspondence
National Archive Kaduna (NAK)
    Annual reports
    Colonial government publications
    Colonial anthropological notes
    Colonial correspondence
    Colonial reports
    Northern regional government records (post-independence)
    Provincial records of Benue and Plateau Provinces (post-independence)
Northern Nigerian History Project Archive, Ahmadu Bello University, Zaria, Nigeria
    Dissertations and theses
    Seminar papers
    Colonial anthropological notes
    Hausa language notes
National Archive Ibadan (NAI)
    Annual reports
    Colonial correspondence
Rhodes House, Oxford Africa Collection, Oxford University, United Kingdom
    Colonial annual and quarterly reports
    Colonial correspondence
    Colonial reports
    Personal diaries of colonial officials
    Personal diaries and notes of colonial subjects
    Unpublished colonial memoirs
National Archives of Britain (formerly Public Records Office)
    Colonial office records
    Colonial office correspondence
    Her Majesty's Stationery Office (HMSO) Publications
    Memoirs of colonial service
British Library Newspaper Archive at Collindale
Next newspaper (online archive: http://234next.com/)

Interviews

    Umoru Atenyi, Adoka, Benue State, August 7, 1987. Interview conducted by
    Yakubu Ochefu, and archived in the Idoma Economic History Texts Collection

compiled by Yakubu Ochefu for the Department of History, University of Calabar, Nigeria (hereafter Idoma Economic History Texts Collection).

Ochekwu Adama and others, Otukpo, August 15,1987. Idoma Economic History Texts Collection.

Onazi Egwurube, Retired N.A. Messenger, Otukpo, August 18, 1987. Idoma Economic History Texts Collection.

Ngbede Ode, age 75+, Edikwu, August 27, 1987. Idoma Economic History Texts Collection.

Anya Ujo, age 70+ in Ogobia, Ugboju, September 22, 1987. Idoma Economic History Texts Collection.

Sergeant Ada Sule (rtd), Oweto Agatu, July 14, 1988. Idoma Economic History Texts Collection.

Alhaji Ibrahim Apochi, July 15, 1988, Obagaji, Agatu. Idoma Economic History Texts Collection.

Air Vice Marshal Adamu Mbaka (rtd), Kaduna, April 17, 2009.

Mallam Tagwai Sambo, the chief of Moroa, Manchok, Kaduna State, April 21, 2009.

General Zamani Lekwot (rtd), Kaduna, April 23, 2009.

Bishop Matthew Hassan Kukah, Kaduna, May 5, 2009.

Magaji Galadima, Agwom Adara, Kachia, Kaduna State, June 5, 2009.

Personal conversation with Sevza Asongo, Tiv community leader in Ikpa-Yongo, Gwer-East LGA, July 11, 2011.

Adanu Enegela, age 76, Obagaji, September 17, 2011.

Ama Ojeche, age 80, Obagaji, September 17, 2011.

Suleiman Elaigwu, age 78, Obagaji, September 18, 2011.

Arugben Ogye, Angbaku, July 11, 2012.

Joel Ebuga, Ginda, July 11, 2012.

Moses Anduwa, Gudi, July 11, 2012.

Mutuwa Gambo, chief of Angbaku, July 11, 2012.

Sources

Abubakar, Sa'ad. *The Lamibe of Fombina: A Political History of Adamawa, 1809–1901.* Zaria, Nigeria: Ahmadu Bello University Press and Oxford University Press, 1977.

Adamu, Mahdi. *The Hausa Factor in West African History.* Zaria, Nigeria: Ahmadu Bello University Press, 1978.

Adeleye, R. A. *Power and Diplomacy in Northern Nigeria, 1804–1906: The Sokoto Caliphate and Its Enemies.* New York: Humanities Press, 1971.

Afeadie, Philip. *Brokering Colonial Rule: Political Agents in Northern Nigeria, 1886–1914.* Saarbrücken: VDM Verlag Dr. Müller, 2008.

Afigbo, Adiele. *The Warrant Chief: Indirect Rule in Southeastern Nigeria.* London: Longman, 1972.

Allman, Jean Marie. *The Quills of the Porcupine: Asante Nationalism in an Emergent Ghana.* Madison: University of Wisconsin Press, 1993.

Ames, C. G. *Gazetteer of Plateau Province.* Jos: Jos Native Authority, 1934. Republished in *Gazetteers of the Northern Provinces of Nigeria, vol. 3: The Central Kingdoms*

(Kontagora, Nasarawa, Nupe, Ilorin), ed. A. H. M. Kirk-Greene, 30. London: Frank Cass, 1972.

Amselle, Jean-Loup. *Mestizo Logics: Anthropology of Identity in Africa and Elsewhere.* Trans. Claudia Royal. Stanford, Calif.: Stanford University Press, 1994.

Anderson, David, and David Killingray. "Consent, Coercion and Colonial Control: Policing the Empire, 1830–1940." In *Policing the Empire: Government, Authority, and Control, 1830–1940*, ed. David M. Anderson and David Killingray, 1–15. Manchester: Manchester University Press, 1991.

Anyebe, A. P. *Man of Courage and Character: The Ogbuloko War in Colonial Idomaland of Nigeria.* Enugu, Nigeria: Fourth Dimension, 2002.

Arnett, Edward John. *The Rise of the Sokoto Fulani: Being a Paraphrase and in Some Parts a Translation of the Infaku'l Maisuri of Sultan Mohammed Bello.* London: School of Oriental and African Studies, 1922.

Asiwaju, A. I. *Western Yorubaland under European Rule, 1889–1945: A Comparative Analysis of French and British Colonialism.* Atlantic Highlands, N.J.: Humanities Press, 1976.

Austen, Ralph. "Colonialism from the Middle: African Clerks as Historical Actors and Discursive Subjects." *History in Africa* 38 (2011): 21–33.

———. "Who Was Wangrin and Why Does It Matter?" *Mande Studies* 9 (1997): 149–164.

Ayuba, Jonathan Mamu. *Economy and Society in Colonial North-Central Nigeria: The History of Akwanga Region, 1911–1960.* Zaria, Nigeria: Ahmadu Bello University Press, 2008.

Ba, Amadou Hampate. *The Fortunes of Wangrin.* Bloomington: Indiana University Press, 1999.

Baikie, William Balfour. "Inclosure 1 No. 74 (General Rules for Dealing with the Natives along the River Niger) Rule 14." In *Accounts and Papers of the House of Commons.* Vol. 43. London: Harrison and Sons, 1863.

———. "Inclosure 1 No. 74 (General Rules for Dealing with the Natives along the River Niger) Rule 15." In *Accounts and Papers of the House of Commons.* Vol. 43. London: Harrison and Sons, 1863.

———. *Narrative of an Exploring Voyage up the Rivers Kwóra and Bínue (Commonly Known as the Niger and Tsádda) in 1854.* London: J. Murray, 1856.

Ballard, J. A. "'Pagan Administration' and Political Development in Northern Nigeria." *Savanna* 1, no. 1 (1972): 1–14.

Barber, Karin. "Translation, Publics and the Vernacular Press in 1920s Lagos." In *Christianity and Social Change in Africa: Essays in Honor of J.D.Y. Peel*, ed. Toyin Falola, 187–208. Durham, N.C.: Carolina Academic Press, 2005.

Barnes, Andrew E. *Making Headway: The Introduction of Western Civilization in Colonial Northern Nigeria.* Rochester, N.Y.: University of Rochester Press, 2009.

Barth, Heinrich. *Travels and Discoveries in North and Central Africa: Being a Journal of an Expedition Undertaken under the Auspices of H.B.M.'s Government in the Years 1849–1855.* London, 1857.

Barua, Pradeep. "Inventing Race: The British and India's Martial Races." *Historian: Journal of History* 58 (1995): 107–116.

Bashir Salau, Mohammed. *The West African Slave Plantation: A Case Study.* New York: Palgrave Macmillan, 2011.

Beidelman, T. O. *The Culture of Colonialism: The Cultural Subjection of the Ukaguru.* Bloomington: Indiana University Press, 2012.

Berman, Bruce. "Ethnicity, Patronage and the African State: The Politics of Uncivil Nationalism." *African Affairs* 97, no. 388 (1998): 305–341.

Bivar. "The Wathiqat Ahl Al-Sudan: A Manifesto of the Fulani Jihad." *Journal of African History* 2, no. 2 (1961): 235–243.

Bohannan, Paul. "Extra-Processual Events in Tiv Political Institutions." *American Anthropologist* 60, no. 1 (February 1, 1958): 1–12.

Bonat, Z. A. "Colonialism and Underdevelopment in Zaria Province, 1902–1945." MA thesis, Ahmadu Bello University, 1985.

Bovill, E. W. *The Niger Explored.* London: Oxford University Press, 1968.

Bull, Mary. "Indirect Rule in Northern Nigeria: 1906–1911." In *Essays in Imperial Government Presented to Margery Perham,* ed. Kenneth Robinson and Frederick Madden, 47–87. Oxford: Basil Blackwell, 1963.

Burbank, Jane, and Frederick Cooper. *Empires in World History: Power and the Politics of Difference.* Princeton, N.J.: Princeton University Press, 2010.

Cameron, Donald. *Principles of Native Administration and Their Application.* Lagos: Government Printer, 1931.

Chabal, Patrick, and Jean-Pascal Deloz. *Disorder Works: Disorder as Political Instrument.* Bloomington: Indiana University Press, 1999.

Chanock, Martin. *Law, Custom, and Social Order: The Colonial Experience in Malawi and Zambia.* Cambridge: Cambridge University Press, 1985.

Clapperton, Hugh. *Hugh Clapperton into the Interior of Africa: Records of the Second Expedition, 1825–1827.* Ed. Jamie Bruce-Lockhart and Paul E. Lovejoy. Leiden: Brill, 2005.

———. *Journal of a Second Expedition into the Interior of Africa from the Bight of Benin to Soccatoo.* Philadelphia: Carey, Lea and Carey, 1829.

Clayton, Anthony. *The Zanzibar Revolution and Its Aftermath.* Hamden, Conn.: Archon Books, 1981.

Cohen, Abner. *Custom and Politics in Urban Africa: A Study of Hausa Migrants in Yoruba Towns.* 2nd ed. London: Routledge, 2004.

Coleman, James S. *Nigeria: Background to Nationalism.* Berkeley: University of California Press, 1958.

Conklin, Alice L. *A Mission to Civilize: The Republican Idea of Empire in France and West Africa, 1895–1930.* Stanford, Calif.: Stanford University Press, 1997.

Cooper, Frederick. "Conflict and Connections: Rethinking Colonial African History." *American Historical Review* 99, no. 5 (1994): 1516–1545.

———. *Decolonization and African Society: The Labor Question in French and British Africa.* Cambridge: Cambridge University Press, 1996.

Crampton, E. P. T. *Christianity in Northern Nigeria.* London: Macmillan, 1975.

Crocker, Walter R. *Nigeria: A Critique of British Colonial Administration.* Freeport, N.Y.: Books for Libraries Press, 1971.

Crowther, Samuel. *Journal of an Expedition up the Niger and Tshadda Rivers, Undertaken by Maegregor Laird in Connection with the British Government in 1854.* London: Cass, 1855.

Daley, P. "Ethnicity and Political Violence in Africa: The Challenges to the Burundi State." *Political Geography* 25 (n.d.): 657–679.

Davis, Thomas J., and Azubike Kalu-Nwiwu. "Education, Ethnicity and National Integration in the History of Nigeria: Continuing Problems of Africa's Colonial Legacy." *Journal of Negro History* 86, no. 1 (January 1, 2001): 1–11.

Dudley, Billy J. *Parties and Politics in Northern Nigeria.* London: Cass, 1968.

Eyoh, Dickson. "Differentiating Communities in Central Nigeria: Political and Economic Change in Colonial Lafia, Nigeria, 1900–1950." *International Journal of African Historical Studies* 29, no. 3 (1997): 493–517.

Fallers, Lloyd A. *Bantu Bureaucracy: A Century of Political Evolution among the Basoga of Uganda.* Chicago: University of Chicago Press, 1965.

Falola, Toyin. *Nationalism and African Intellectuals.* Rochester, N.Y.: University of Rochester Press, 2001.

Fardon, Richard. *Raiders and Refugees: Trends in Chamba Political Development, 1750–1950.* Washington, D.C.: Smithsonian Institution Press, 1988.

Filaba, Mailafiya Aruwa, and Lawrence A. Gojeh. *Koro and Gbagyi Subgroup Relations in Central Nigeria.* Ethiopia: Self-published, 2008.

Freund, Bill. *Capitalism and Labor in the Nigerian Tin Mines.* New York: Humanities Press, 1981.

Furniss, Graham. "On Engendering Liberal Values in the Nigerian Colonial State: The Idea behind Gaskiya Corporation." *Journal of Imperial and Commonwealth History* 39, no. 1 (2011): 95–119.

Garba, Joseph Nanven. *Revolution in Nigeria: Another View.* London: Africa Books, 1982.

Gikandi, Simon. "Introduction: African Subjects and the Colonial Project." In Ham Mukasa, *Uganda's Katikiro in England,* 1–34. Manchester: Manchester University Press, 1998.

———. *Maps of Englishness: Writing Identity in the Culture of Colonialism.* New York: Columbia University Press, 1996.

Glassman, Jonathon. "Sorting out the Tribes: The Creation of Racial Identities in Colonial Zanzibar's Newspaper Wars." *Journal of African History* 41, no. 3 (January 1, 2000): 395–428.

———. *War of Words, War of Stones: Racial Thought and Violence in Zanzibar.* Bloomington: Indiana University Press, 2011.

Gojeh, Lawrence A. *The History of Origin and Tradition of the Koro People.* Kaduna, Nigeria: Tereship Publishers, 1998.

Hall, Bruce. *A History of Race in Muslim West Africa 1600–1960.* Cambridge: Cambridge University Press, 2011.

Hall, Catherine. *Civilizing Subjects: Metropole and Colony in the English Imagination, 1830–1867.* Chicago: University of Chicago Press, 2002.

Haour, Anne, and Benedetta Rossi, eds. *Being and Becoming Hausa: Interdisciplinary Perspectives.* Leiden and Boston: Brill, 2010.

Hawkins, Sean. *Writing and Colonialism in Northern Ghana: The Encounter between the LoDagaa and "the World on Paper."* Toronto: University of Toronto Press, 2002.

Herbst, Jeffrey Ira. *States and Power in Africa: Comparative Lessons in Authority and Control.* Princeton, N.J.: Princeton University Press, 2000.

Higazi, Adam. "Social Mobilization and Collective Violence: Vigilantes and Militias in the Lowlands of Plateau State, Central Nigeria." Center for Research on Inequality, Human Security, and Ethnicity, University of Oxford, 2009.

Hiskett, M. "Kitab al-farq: 'A Work on the Habe Kingdoms Attributed to Uthman dan Fodio.'" *Bulletin of the School of Oriental and African Studies* 23, no. 3 (1960): 558–579.

Hunt, Nancy Rose. *A Colonial Lexicon of Birth Ritual, Medicalization, and Mobility in the Congo.* Durham, N.C.: Duke University Press, 1999.

Idoko, Onah John. "The Hausa-Agatu Relations in Loko District, 1900–1960." BA thesis, Nasarawa State University, 2007.

Ikime, Obaro. *The Fall of Nigeria: The British Conquest.* London: Heinemann, 1977.

Irobi, Emmy Godwin. "Ethnic Conflict Management in Africa: A Comparative Case Study of Nigeria and South Africa." *Beyond Intractability,* 2005. http://www.beyondintractability.org/casestudy/irobi-ethnic.

James, Ibrahim. *Studies in the History, Politics, and Cultures of Southern Kaduna Peoples Groups.* Jos, Nigeria: Crest, 1997.

Johnson, Marion. *Salaga Papers.* Legon: Institute of African Studies, University of Ghana, 1965.

Kane, Ousmane. *Muslim Modernity in Northern Nigeria: A Study of the Society for the Removal of Innovation and the Restatement of Tradition.* Leiden: Brill, 2003.

Kastfelt, Niels. *Religion and Politics in Nigeria: A Study in Middle Belt Christianity.* London: British Academic Press, 1994.

Kaye, Tony. "Civilizing (the) Chiefs: Islam and Indirect Rule in the Northern Territories of the Gold Coast Colony." MA thesis, University of Saskatchewan, 2011.

Kukah, Matthew Hassan. *Religion, Politics, and Power in Northern Nigeria.* Ibadan, Nigeria: Spectrum Books, 1993.

Killingray, David. "Guarding the Extending Frontier: Policing the Gold Coast, 1865–1913." In *Policing the Empire: Government, Authority, and Control, 1830–1940,* ed. David M. Anderson and David Killingray, 106–125. Manchester: Manchester University Press, 1991.

———. "Imagined Martial Communities: Recruiting for the Military and Police in Colonial Ghana, 1860–1960." In *Ethnicity in Ghana: The Limits of Invention,* ed. Carola Lentz and Paul Nugent, 119—36. New York: Palgrave Macmillan, 2000.

Kirk-Greene, A. H. M., ed. *Gazetteers of the Northern Provinces of Nigeria.* Vol. 1: *The Hausa Emirates.* London: F. Cass, 1972.

———. *Gazetteers of the Northern Provinces of Nigeria.* Vol. 3: *The Central Kingdoms (Kontagora, Nasarawa, Nupe, Ilorin).* London: Frank Cass, 1972.

———. *Gazetteers of the Northern Provinces of Nigeria.* Vol. 4: *The High-Land Chieftaincies (Plateau Province).* London: Frank Cass, 1972.

Kolapo, Femi, and Kwabena Akurang-Parry, eds. *African Agency and European Colonialism: Latitudes of Negotiation.* Lanham, Md.: University Press of America, 2007.

Kukah, M. H. *Religion, Politics and Power in Northern Nigeria.* Ibadan, Nigeria: Spectrum Books, 1993.

Kwanashie, George A. *The Making of the North in Nigeria, 1900–1965.* Kaduna, Nigeria: Arewa House, Ahmadu Bello University, 2002.

Lander, Richard. *Journal of an Expedition to Explore the Course and Termination of the Niger, with a Narrative of a Voyage Down That River to Its Termination.* New York: J. & J. Harper, 1832.

———. *Records of Captain Clapperton's Last Expedition to Africa.* Vol. 2. London: Henry Colburn and Richard Bentley, 1830.

Last, Murray. "The Idea of 'Frontier' in the Nigerian Context." Paper presented at the Conference on Political Crisis on West Africa's Islamic Frontier, SAOS London, 1982.

———. *The Sokoto Caliphate.* London: Longman, 1967.

Lawrance, Benjamin Nicholas, Emily Osborne, and Richard Roberts, eds. *Intermediaries, Interpreters, and Clerks: African Employees in the Making of Colonial Africa.* Madison: University of Wisconsin Press, 2006.

Lentz, Carola. *Ethnicity and the Making of History in Northern Ghana.* Edinburgh: Edinburgh University Press, 2006.

Leonard, Karen. "Reassessing Indirect Rule in Hyderabad: Rule, Rulers, or Sons-in-Laws of the State." *Modern Asian Studies* 37, no. 2 (2003): 363–379.

Leopold, Joan. "British Applications of the Aryan Theory of Race to India, 1850–1870." *English Historical Review* 89, no. 352 (July 1, 1974): 578–603.

Liebnow, Gus. "Legitimacy or Alien Relationship: The Nyaturu of Tanganyika." *Western Political Quarterly* 14, no. 1, part 1 (1961): 74.

Livinus, Hindi. "Raucous Reception Greets Yola University Name Change." *Next,* July 24, 2011. http://234next.com/csp/cms/sites/Next/Home/5735441-146/story.csp.

Logams, Chunun. "The Middle Belt Movement in Nigerian Political Development: A Case Study of Political Identity, 1949–1967." PhD dissertation, University of Keele, 1985.

Lugard, Frederick. *The Dual Mandate in British Tropical Africa.* Hamden, Conn.: Archon Books, 1965.

———. *Political Memoranda, Revision of Instructions to Political Officers on Subjects Chiefly Political and Administrative 1913–1918.* London: Frank Cass, 1970.

Magid, Alvin. *Men in the Middle: Leadership and Role Conflict in a Nigerian Society.* New York: Africana Publishing, 1976.

Makar, Tesemchi. *The History of Political Change among the Tiv in the 19th and 20th Centuries.* Enugu, Nigeria: Fourth Dimension, 1994.

Mamdani, Mahmood. *Citizen and Subject: Contemporary Africa and the Legacy of Late Colonialism.* Princeton, N.J.: Princeton University Press, 1996.

———. *Saviors and Survivors: Darfur, Politics, and the War on Terror.* New York: Pantheon Books, 2009.

———. *When Victims Become Killers: Colonialism, Nativism, and the Genocide in Rwanda.* Princeton, N.J.: Princeton University Press, 2001.

Mazrui, A. Alamin. *Swahili beyond the Boundaries: Literature, Language, and Identity.* Athens: Ohio University Press, 2007.

Mazrui, Ali Alamin, and Ali A. Mazrui. *The Power of Babel: Language and Governance in the African Experience.* Oxford: James Currey, 1998.

M'bayo, Tamba E. "African Interpreters, Mediation, and the Production of Knowledge in Colonial Senegal: The Low Land Middle Senegal Valley, ca. 1850s to ca. 1920s." PhD dissertation, Michigan State University, 2009.

Mbembe, Achille. "African Modes of Self-Writing." *Public Culture* 14, no. 1 (2002): 239–273.

———. *On the Postcolony.* Berkeley: University of California Press, 2001.

Meek, Charles Kingsley. *The Northern Tribes of Nigeria: An Ethnographical Account of the Northern Provinces of Nigeria Together with a Report on the 1921 Decennial Census*. New York: Negro Universities Press, 1969.

———. *A Sudanese Kingdom: An Ethnographical Study of the Jukua-Speaking Peoples of Nigeria*. London: Kegan Paul, Trench, Trubner, 1931.

———. *Tribal Studies in Northern Nigeria*. London: Kegan Paul, Trench, Trubner, 1931.

Metcalf, Thomas. *Ideologies of the Raj*. Cambridge: Cambridge University Press, 1997.

Mitchell, Timothy. *Rule of Experts: Egypt, Techno-Politics, Modernity*. Berkeley: University of California Press, 2002.

Myers, Jason Conard. *Indirect Rule in South Africa: Tradition, Modernity, and the Costuming of Political Power*. Rochester, N.Y.: University of Rochester Press, 2008.

Nengel, John G. *Precolonial African Intergroup Relations in the Kauru and Pengana Polities of the Central Nigerian Highlands, 1800–1900*. Frankfurt: Peter Lang, 1999.

Newbury, Catharine. "Background to Genocide in Rwanda." *Issue: A Journal of Opinion* 23, no. 2 (1995): 12–17.

———. "Ethnicity and the Politics of History in Rwanda." *Africa Today* 45, no. 1 (1998): 7–24.

Newbury, Colin Walter. *Patrons, Clients, and Empire: Chieftaincy and Over-Rule in Asia, Africa, and the Pacific*. Oxford: Oxford University Press, 2003.

Njeuma, M. Z. *Fulani Hegemony in Yola (Old Adamawa) 1809–1902*. Yaounde, Cameroon: Publishing and Production Center for Teaching and Research, 1978.

Nnoli, Okwudiba, ed. *Ethnic Conflicts in Africa*. Dakar, Senegal: Codesria Book Series, 2000.

———. *Ethnicity and Development in Nigeria*. Aldershot, England: Avebury, 1995.

Ochefu, Yakubu A. *The Economic Transformation of Idoma Society, 1860–1960*. Makurdi, Nigeria: Aboki Publishers, 2000.

Ochonu, Moses E. *Colonial Meltdown: Northern Nigeria in the Great Depression*. Athens: Ohio University Press, 2009.

———. "A Colony in Crisis: Northern Nigeria, British Colonialism, and the Great Depression." PhD dissertation, University of Michigan, 2004.

———. "Masculine Anxieties, Cultural Politics, and Debates over Independent Womanhood among Idoma Male Migrants in Late Colonial Northern Nigeria." *Interventions* 13, no. 2 (2011): 278–298.

Ohiare, Joseph Aliu. "The Kingdoms of Opanda and Igu, 1700–1939: A Study of Intergroup Relations." PhD dissertation, Ahmadu Bello University, 1988.

Okpeh, Ochayi Okpeh. "Ethnic Minorities, Decolonization Politics and Political Participation: A Study of Idoma Hope Rising Union (1944–1960)." *Jos Journal of Minority Studies* 1, no. 1 (2003): 10–24.

Okwu, V. G. "The Establishment of Colonial Administration in Idomaland, 1921–1930." *Savannah* 5, no. 1 (1976): 29–44.

Osborn, Emily Lynn. "'Circle of Iron': African Colonial Employees and the Interpretation of Colonial Rule in French West Africa." *Journal of African History* 44, no. 1 (January 1, 2003): 29–50.

Osborn, Myles. "The Kamba and Mau Mau: Ethnicity, Development, and Chiefship, 1952–1960." *International Journal of African Historical Studies* 43, no. 1 (2010): 63–87.

Ozigi, Albert O., and Lawrence Ocho. *Education in Northern Nigeria*. London: Allen & Unwin, 1981.

Paden, John N. *Ahmadu Bello, Sardauna of Sokoto: Values and Leadership in Nigeria*. London: Hodder and Stoughton, 1986.

Patton, Adell, Jr. "An Islamic Frontier Polity: The Ningi Mountain of Northern Nigeria, 1846–1902." In *The African Frontier: The Reproduction of Traditional African Societies*, ed. Igor Kopytoff, 193–213. Bloomington: Indiana University Press, 1987.

Perham, Margery. *Lugard: The Years of Authority, 1898–1945: The Second Part of the Life of Frederick Dealtry Lugard, Later Lord Lugard of Abinger*. London: Collins, 1960.

———. *Native Administration in Nigeria*. London: Oxford University Press, 1962.

Philips, John Edward. *Spurious Arabic: Hausa and Colonial Nigeria*. Madison: University of Wisconsin Press, 2000.

Pierce, Steven. *Farmers and the State in Colonial Kano: Land Tenure and the Legal Imagination*. Bloomington: Indiana University Press, 2005.

———. "Looking for the Legal: Land, Law, and Colonialism in Kano Emirate, Nigeria." PhD dissertation, University of Michigan, 2000.

———. "A Moral Economy of Corruption: State Formation and Political Culture in Northern Nigeria." Unpublished book manuscript, n.d.

Pongri, J. H. "The Jihad and the Establishment of Colonial Rule in Adamawa, c. 1809–1980." Presented at the Postgraduate Seminar, Ahmadu Bello University, Zaria, Nigeria, 1980.

Ramusack, Barbara. *The Indian Princes and Their States*. Cambridge: Cambridge University Press, 2004.

Roberts, A. D. "The Sub-Imperialism of the Baganda." *Journal of African History* 3, no. 3 (January 1, 1962): 435–450.

Sai, Akiga. *Akiga's Story: The Tiv Tribe as Seen by One of Its Members*. Trans. Rupert East. London: Oxford University Press, 1939.

Salomone, Frank A. "Becoming Hausa: Ethnic Identity Change and Its Implications for the Study of Ethnic Pluralism and Stratification." *Africa: Journal of the International African Institute* 45, no. 4 (January 1, 1975): 410–424.

———. *The Hausa of Nigeria*. Lanham, Md.: University Press of America, 2010.

Sanders, Edith R. "The Hamitic Hypothesis: Its Origin and Functions in Time Perspective." *Journal of African History* 10, no. 4 (January 1, 1969): 521–532.

Saulawa, Abdullahi Mu'azu. "A History of Historical Writings in Nigeria since c. 1960 A.D." *Savanna: A Journal of the Environmental and Social Sciences* 10, no. 2 (1989): 76–85.

Sciortino, J. C. *Notes on Nasarawa Province, Nigeria*. London: Waterlow and Sons, 1920. Republished in *Gazetteers of the Northern Provinces of Nigeria, vol. 3: The Central Kingdoms (Kontagora, Nasarawa, Nupe, Ilorin)*, ed. A. H. M. Kirk-Greene, 19–20. London: Frank Cass, 1972.

Scott, James C. *The Art of Not Being Governed: An Anarchist History of Upland Southeast Asia*. New Haven, Conn.: Yale University Press, 2009.

Shaw, Flora L. *A Tropical Dependency: An Outline of the Ancient History of the Western Soudan with an Account of the Modern Settlement of Northern Nigeria*. London: J. Nisbet, 1905.

Shelton, Austin J. *The Igbo-Igala Borderland: Religion and Social Control in Indigenous African Colonialism*. Albany: State University of New York Press, 1971.

Sklar, Richard L. *Nigerian Political Parties: Power in an Emergent African Nation.* Princeton, N.J.: Princeton University Press, 1963.

Smith, Michael Garfield. *The Affairs of Daura.* Berkeley: University of California Press, 1978.

———. *Government in Zazzau, 1800–1950.* Oxford: International African Institute and Oxford University Press, 1960.

Spivak, Gayatri. "Can the Subaltern Speak?" In *Marxism and the Interpretation of Culture,* ed. Cary Nelson and Lawrence Grossberg, 271–313. Urbana-Champagne: University of Illinois Press, 1988.

Staudinger, Paul. *In the Heart of the Hausa States.* Trans. Johanna Moody. Athens: Ohio University Press, 1990.

Stenning, Derrick. *Savannah Nomads: A Study of the Wodaabe Pastoral Fulani of Western Borno Province, Northern Region, Nigeria.* London: International Africa Institute and Oxford University Press, 1959.

Streets-Salter, Heather. *Martial Races: The Military, Race and Masculinity in British Imperial Culture, 1857–1914.* Manchester: Manchester University Press, 2004.

Temple, Charles Lindsay. *Native Races and Their Rulers: Sketches and Studies of Official Life and Administrative Problems in Nigeria.* Cape Town: Argus, 1918.

Tibenderana, Peter K. "British Administration and the Decline of the Patronage-Clientage System in Northwestern Nigeria, 1900–1934." *African Studies Review* 32, no. 1 (April 1, 1989): 71–95.

Tseayo, Justin Iyorbee. *Conflict and Incorporation in Nigeria: The Integration of the Tiv.* Zaria, Nigeria: Gaskiya, 1975.

Turaki, Yusufu. *The British Colonial Legacy in Northern Nigeria: A Social Ethical Analysis of the Colonial and Post-Colonial Society and Politics in Nigeria.* Jos, Nigeria: Challenge Press and Turaki, 1993.

Twaddle, Michael. *Kakungulu and the Creation of Uganda, 1868–1928.* Athens: Ohio University Press, 1993.

Ukpabi, Sam C. *The Origins of the Nigerian Army: A History of the West African Frontier Force, 1897–1914.* Zaria, Nigeria: Gaskiya, 1987.

Wilson, Henry S. *African Decolonization.* London: Edward Arnold, 1994.

Wilson-Haffenden, James Rhodes. *The Red Men of Nigeria: An Account of a Lengthy Residence among the Fulani or "Red Men," and Other Pagan Tribes of Central Nigeria, with a Description of Their Head-Hunting, Pastoral and Other Customs, Habits and Religion.* 1st ed. London: Cass, 1967.

Zachernuk, Philip Serge. *Colonial Subjects: An African Intelligentsia and Atlantic Ideas.* Charlottesville: University Press of Virginia, 2000.

———. "Of Origins and Colonial Order: Southern Nigerian Historians and the 'Hamitic Hypothesis,' C. 1870–1970." *Journal of African History* 35, no. 3 (1994): 427–455, 443.

Index

Abaagu, H. O., 187
Abinsi, 108, 198, 241n7
Abisi, 52
Abubakar, 113, 123
Abuja, 49, 62, 90
Abuul, Achiga, 187
accountability, 53, 94, 143; political, 56, 96
Action Group (AG), 185, 189, 202
activists, 20, 99, 170, 173, 200, 205. *See also* Middle Belt, activists; Southern Kaduna, activists; United Middle Belt Congress, activists
Adama, Modibbo, 129
Adamawa, 28, 129–142, 144, 146, 148, 149, 150, 153, 155–156, 157, 163–164, 172, 173, 176, 178, 181, 230nn1–2, 244n1, 244n4, 245n26; Adamawa Basin, 132, 135; Adamawa Division, 145–146, 154; Adamawa Elders Forum, 129; Adamawa (Fombina) Emirate, 129, 134–135, 174, 256n26; Adamawa Province, 19–20, 130–131, 135–137, 141, 144, 155, 157, 163, 164, 166, 167, 168, 169, 175, 177, 178, 195, 212, 245n26; Adamawa State, 129–130, 230n2; hinterlands, 31, 132, 133, 139, 149; *lamido*, 20, 40, 41, 169–170, 176, 245n26
Adamu, Mahdi, 110, 116
Adara, 52, 54, 55, 56, 69, 236n37
administrators, 63, 201, 216. *See also* British, administrative practice; Fulani, administration; Hausa-Fulani, administrators
Adoka, 113, 121
Afizere, 18, 79, 81, 82, 84, 180
Afo, 90, 92
Africa, 3, 5–7, 11, 12, 13, 14, 108, 128, 215–216, 241n5, 252n1; Africans, 3–4, 6, 7, 10, 14, 15, 31, 33, 35, 36, 43, 76, 96, 125, 136–137, 140, 143, 196, 197, 207, 208–212, 213, 215, 218, 220, 227n9, 228n23; colonial, 4, 5–6, 8, 9, 11–13, 35, 77, 207, 210, 213, 228n24; North Africa, 37, 194; postcolonial, 7, 215, 220; societies, 9, 143, 207, 208; West Africa, 15–16, 24, 26, 36, 112, 233n47. *See also* agency, African; British, perception of Africans; hierarchy, of African peoples
Agatu, 86, 88, 90, 91–92, 111, 120–123; Agatuland, 120–121
Agatu Idoma, 27, 28

Agbiri, 52
agency, 11, 62, 74; African, 11, 13, 209, 211; colonial, 11, 107; subcolonial, 13, 18, 104, 146, 218. *See also* Fulani, agency; Hausa-Fulani, agency
agriculture, 27, 50, 53, 54, 60, 118, 121, 143, 145, 146, 175
Agworok, 59
Ajiya, 142
Alago, 18, 95–96, 97, 98–105, 179; Alago State Union, 100, 101
Alantika Mountains, 129–130, 132
Aliade, 198
Aloko, 122
Aluor, Gondo, 200
amana (peace agreements), 28, 51, 77, 79–82
Amanyi, 113–114, 122–123
Amap, 52
Amselle, Jean-Loup, 36
Anaguta, 79, 82, 84, 180
Angan, 52
Angass District, 84
Aninka, 59
Ankwe, 80
anthropology, 6, 23, 29, 34, 82–83, 126, 135, 144, 215, 217
Anyebe, A. P., 111–112, 119
Arden-Clarke, Charles, 93
Ari, Alhaji, 201
Arnett, E. J., 63
Assadugu, Jonah, 166–168, 170, 172–173, 187
assistant divisional officers (ADOs), 165
Atatenji, 143
Atsam, 52, 65
authority, 2, 8, 26, 45, 46, 57, 80, 86, 90, 106, 113, 133, 136, 137, 138, 146, 148, 168, 181, 202, 208, 210, 244n4; imperial, 52, 63; judicial, 99, 154; political, 24, 56, 88, 90, 95–96, 155; subcolonial, 68, 94, 98, 101, 145, 147. *See also* British, colonial authority; caliphate, authority; Chamba, authority; chiefs, chiefly authority; emirates, authority; Fulani, authority
autochthony, 1, 5, 12, 27, 37, 45, 73, 78, 90, 133, 137, 141, 146, 150, 152, 175, 180, 213, 216–217, 227n9
autonomy, 4, 11, 24, 28, 61, 64, 71, 74, 80–82, 132, 134, 150, 154, 168, 169, 179, 181, 196, 210–212, 213

132, 133, 137, 140, 143, 144, 176, 177, 187, 192, 193, 195, 210; ethno-religious communities, 3, 180, 183; religious discrimination, 185–186, 188, 191. *See also* Christianity; difference, ethno-religious, religious; identity, ethno-religious; Islam

resources, 1, 7, 10, 57, 65, 163, 192, 200, 220, 241n14; economic, 55, 117, 219; military, 55, 59; political, 75, 219

Ribadu, Muhammadu, 189

rights, 163, 177, 216–217; hereditary, 143; land, 141; political, 2. *See also* minorities, minority rights

Roberts, A. D., 8, 14

Royal Niger Company, 89, 108. *See also* Niger Company, The

Rukuba, 55, 69

rumada (slave farm), 54

Rumaya, 50

Ruruma, 50

Ruwa, Hamman, 133

Rwanda, 7, 8, 9, 210, 215

Rwang, Moses, 184, 185, 187

Sai, Akiga, 196

Salamone, Frank, 229n40

Salihu, 123

Sambo, Malam Tagwai, 203–204

Sambo, Sarki, 55

schools, 171, 176, 186; mission, 163, 167, 168; religious, 37

scribes, 2, 3, 5, 8, 11, 45, 113, 117, 118, 119, 127, 197, 242n43; district, 72, 159, 160; tax, 18, 128

self-determination, 36, 38, 39, 60, 75, 76, 99, 174, 177. *See also* Chamba, self-determination; indigeneity, indigenous self-determination; Middle Belt, self-determination; non-Muslims, self-determination

self-governance, 36, 64, 71, 74, 76, 97, 98, 99, 100, 137, 151, 152, 168, 179. *See also* Chamba, self-governance

Senegambia, 132

separatism. *See* Chamba, separatism; Middle Belt, separatism

Shaabu, 95

Shaw, Flora, 42

Shelton, Austin J., 232n27

Shendam, 80, 81, 184

Sikhs, 14

slavery, 28, 53, 54, 120, 135; slave raids, 4, 27, 28, 34, 45, 48, 50, 52, 53–56, 59–60, 80, 81, 85, 86, 94, 134, 135, 217, 236n37, 239n34; slaves, 6, 28,

48, 49–50, 52, 53–56, 59, 66, 81, 95, 120–121, 134; slavers, 120–121. *See also* *rumada* (slave farm)

Smith, M. G., 66

sociolinguistics, 13, 31, 108, 141

sociology, 13, 15, 16, 23, 29, 31, 33, 43, 141, 155, 175, 196

sojan gona (unauthorized taxation), 111, 241n14

Sokoto Caliphate, 1–2, 4, 15, 24–25, 26–27, 29–32, 33–34, 38, 54, 78, 94, 95, 155, 209, 230n2, 231n11, 232n20, 232n27, 233n41

Song, 133, 138, 139, 140, 147

Songhai empire, 24

South Asia, 9

Southern Emirate, 150

Southern Kaduna, 18, 28, 31, 45–46, 48, 51–54, 56, 57–68, 70–75, 105, 139, 204, 230n2, 235n14; activists, 75–76; elites, 70, 71; peoples, 45, 49, 50–54, 56–71, 73–76, 105, 235n14; Southern Kaduna plateau, 54, 57, 61–62, 64

Southern Trust Territory Division, 176

Spivak, Gayatri, 7, 210

Staudinger, Paul, 47, 61, 86–87, 88, 237n60

Stephenson, Lawrence, 97, 98, 101

Sudan, 216, 231n6; Central, 42; Western, 132, 231n9

Sudan Interior Mission (SIM), 163

Sudan United Mission (SUM), 163

sultans, 29–30, 33, 54, 184

Sura, 83

suzerainty, 46, 69, 71, 80, 95, 99, 152

Swahili, 12, 36

Taban Sani, 54

Tanganyika, 12

Taraba State, 129, 230n2

Taraku, 16, 198

Tarka, Joseph, 183, 191, 194, 195, 196, 203, 204

Tarok, 80, 85

tax collectors, 3, 11, 45, 118, 119, 150, 242n43

Temple, Charles L., 6, 23, 43, 227n9, 234n62

theocracy, 95

Tikar, 133

Tiv, 18–19, 27, 31–32, 95–96, 106, 108–110, 115–117, 127, 128, 190–191, 196–202, 206, 233n37, 241n7, 251n73; culture, 196–197, 251n73; Tiv Division, 18, 106, 108, 109, 114, 116, 117, 127, 128, 195–196, 199, 200, 202, 206; Tivland, 27, 108, 110, 115, 116, 117, 196–197, 198–201, 202–203, 206

Toro, 78–79, 80, 81

Toto, 86

tours, 18, 40, 55, 56, 63, 68–69, 75, 97, 99, 100–101, 118, 123, 124, 135, 159, 165, 166, 170–171, 173

MOSES E. OCHONU is Associate Professor of African History at Vanderbilt University and is author of *Colonial Meltdown: Northern Nigeria in the Great Depression* (2009).

www.ingramcontent.com/pod-product-compliance
Lightning Source LLC
Chambersburg PA
CBHW050338270326
41926CB00016B/3514